THE GREEK COMMENTARIES

ON PLATO'S PHAEDO

I OLYMPIODORUS

EDITED WITH TRANSLATION

BY

L G WESTERINK

The Prometheus Trust

The Prometheus Trust
6 Fairways
Dilton Marsh, Westbury
Wiltshire, BA13 3RU, UK

A registered charity, number 299648

The Greek Commentaries on Plato's Phaedo - Olympiodorus
A revised second edition 2009

L G Westerink

ISBN 978 1 898910 46 6
(Complete Work 978 1 898910 50 3

First edition published by
North Holland Publishing in 1976

British Library Cataloguing-in-Publication Data.
A catalogue record for this book is
available from the British Library.

Printed in the UK by 4edge Limited, Hockley

THE GREEK COMMENTARIES

ON PLATO'S PHAEDO

I OLYMPIODORUS

L G Westerink

Platonic Texts and Translations

Volume II

Contents

PREFACE

to the Second Edition

L G Westerink's fine translations of the Commentaries on Plato's Phaedo by Olympiodorus and Damascius were originally published in 1973 in two volumes and have been highly regarded ever since. The two authors, living and writing as they did at the end of the era of pagan philosophy, were able to draw on a long and uninterrupted tradition of philosophical thought which stretched back beyond Pythagoras, and which was given impetus by Plato, Aristotle, Plotinus and Proclus amongst many others. These volumes, then, give us a glimpse at least of the insights which were being transmitted from thinker to thinker in late antiquity in the schools of philosophy.

The Prometheus Trust editions of the Commentaries have additions and amendments taken from the marginal notes of Westerink's own copies of the original publications. We would like to thank Joannes Westerink for allowing us to use his father's notes, as well as for permission to publish the resulting editions. Our thanks, too, to all those who have had a hand in the production of our new edition. Most of the amendments comprise added cross-references, occasional corrections to typographical errors, some slight adjustments to the phrasing of the translations, and the very occasional adjustment to a word or two in the text itself.

The original edition had the following translator's note:

The translation of the Plato text (in vol. I) owes a good deal to earlier ones, especially Hackforth's. Usually, however, it had to be adapted to suit the Neoplatonist interpretations, as far as this is possible.

Thanks are due to the Netherlands Organization for the Advancement of Pure Research for photocopies and other materials, as well as for a travel grant; to Professor R. Klibansky for sending me the *Phaedo* section of the *Summarium Librorum Platonis*, to Mrs. Hilda Lefevre for revising the references, to Mr. R. D. Grejtak for assistance in preparing the indices, and to Mr. K. M. Dickson, who took care of the layout.

INTRODUCTION

I. The commentaries on the Phaedo

Plato's *Phaedo* must have been a classic from the moment of its appearance, since nobody ventured to write a rival account of Socrates' death. Though testimonies to confirm this are almost completely lacking,[1] which is not surprising in view of the scarcity of Hellenistic philosophical texts in general, the very absence of anything that could have taken its place justifies us in postulating for it, in the Socratic schools of Hellenistic times, the same kind of canonicity it enjoyed in the Roman period.

While the narrative part was considered common property, it was assumed as equally obvious that the doctrinal content was entirely Plato's. As such it was examined critically and partly accepted, partly rejected by the Peripatos. ARISTOTLE, in the *Eudemus* and the *De anima* (I 4, 407b27–408a29) repeats some of Plato's arguments against the belief that soul is harmony (*Ph.* 91e5–95a3), and further cites the passage on detachment from the body (66b1–67b4) as a matter of *communis opinio* in support of his own position (*an.* I 3, 407b2–5). On the other hand, he attacks the doctrine of the ideas as causes of being and process (*Ph.* 100c9–101d2) in the *Metaphysics* (A 9, 991b3–4=M 5, 1080a2–3) and in the *De generatione et corruptione* (II 9, 335b7). *De caelo* II 3, 295b10–16, he criticizes Plato's account of the central position of the earth (*Ph.* 108e4–109a7) and in the *Meteorology* (II 2, 355b32–356a14) the mythical or half-mythical description of Tartarus as the source of all rivers and streams (*Ph.* 111c4–112e3). These points are raised separately, incidentally in a sense, each in its own context.

This is no longer the case with STRATO's comprehensive criticism of the arguments for immortality, summed up and refuted by Damascius: the argument from opposites (frg. 122=Dam. II § 63); that from recollection (frg. 127=II § 65; cf. frg. 126=I § 294); that on harmony (frg. 118=I § 388); and the final argument on the essence of the soul (frg. 123=I §§ 431–443; frg. 124=II § 78; perhaps also II §§ 79–80). In other words, all the five arguments are included, with the sole exception of the third, that from similarity to the intelligible world. It is true that to this one, too, there are some anonymous objections in Dam. I §§ 336–338 =II §§ 41–43=Ol. 13 § 6, of a type not unlike those of Strato to the

---

[1] A notable exception is Callimachus' famous epigram, *Anthol. Pal.* 7,141; further the hostile criticism in Athenaeus XI 505e (Phaedo himself disavows the the conversation). Panaetius' alleged denial of the authenticity (frg. 127) is plausibly explained by Pohlenz as a misunderstanding of frg. 126: Panaetius had his doubts περὶ τῶν Φαίδωνος, i.e. the Socratic dialogues ascribed to Phaedo (*RE* art. Panaitios, 18,3, 1949, 427.45–56).

other arguments; but then Olympiodorus plainly did not know the debate against Strato, which may have figured in Proclus' commentary as a separate monograph or appendix,[2] therefore only the extremely slender chance remains that this material found its way into our commentaries by a detour. However this may be, there can be no reasonable doubt that the absence of Strato's objections against argument III is purely accidental and that his polemic methodically covered the entire argumentation of the *Phaedo*. In the list of Strato's works in Diogenes Laertius (5,59–60) there is, with the possible exception of Περὶ φύσεως ἀνθρωπίνης, no title which could fit his criticism of Plato. It may have been part of a more general work on soul, or a critical monograph on Plato's doctrine of soul (whether limited to the *Phaedo*, or wider in scope; Dam., of course, had no reason to refer to a debate on the *Phaedrus*, the *Republic* or the *Laws*); there is a parallel in the criticism of Plato's political theory by Strato's contemporaries Zeno and Persaeus.[3]

According to Philoponus (*an.* 143.1–144.19), the objection against Plato's argument from gradation (*Ph.* 93a11–94b3) discussed by Dam. I § 379 comes from EPICURUS. We have no way to verify this and can only guess at the context.

These attacks on specific works of Plato suggest the likelihood of a similar line of defense on the part of the Old Academy, though we have no record of anything of the kind. More than half a century before, however, immediately after Plato's death, if not already during his lifetime, the debate about the correct interpretation of his philosophy had started within the walls of the Academy. The most notable instance is of course the controversy on the creation of the world in the *Timaeus*. In the case of the *Phaedo*, we have the rather cryptic statement of Dam. I § 2, that according to XENOCRATES, the 'custody' of 62b4 'is of the Titanic order and culminates in Dionysus.' Already in Porphyry (who must have transmitted the information on Xenocrates), Dionysus is the World Mind, the Titans symbolize Mind scattered and imprisoned in matter; man, created from their ashes, shares their suffering and imprisonment. If the doxographical note in Dam. is completely accurate, Xenocrates must have explained that this Orphic myth was the 'esoteric tradition' referred to by Plato. It is not easy to imagine in what connection he can have done so; the real subject may have been the myth and Plato may have been mentioned just incidentally (if at all). There can be no question of a real commentary, since we have Proclus' well-known statement that Crantor was the first commentator of Plato.[4]

Crantor, as far as we know, wrote only a commentary on the *Timaeus*. As regards the *Phaedo*, an early interest in it is proved by two shreds

---

[2] See note on Dam. II §§ 63–64.
[3] *SVF* I frgs. 260 and 435.
[4] Pr., *Tim.* I 76.1–2.

of PAPYRUS assigned to the third cent. B.C. and relating to the subject-matter of *Ph.* 106b–c and 92e–93a.[5] In neither case is there sufficient evidence to show that they were part of real commentaries. Even if they should be, however, and even if other more convincing samples should turn up eventually, this would hardly change the general picture of Hellenistic philosophy as mainly concerned with polemic and doxography.

It was only several centuries later that the philosophical commentary really came into its own. The most obvious and most general cause of this is certainly the retrospective attitude which is characteristic of the beginning of our era and which in literature produced the Atticistic movement. In the field of philosophy, the reappearance of the *Corpus Aristotelicum* must have been a powerful, if not the decisive, impulse. This is proved by the very fact that the Peripatos led the Academy by more than a century. The discovery of an almost entirely new and extremely difficult Aristotle set the program to which his school devoted itself from the first century B.C. onward, at a time when platonizing Stoics and stoicizing Platonists were still searching for a common truth on the traditional lines. Among Platonists there are no commentators, at this early time, who could be compared to such men as Andronicus, Boethus and Nicolaus; the first that can be named are Eudorus (end of first cent. B.C.) and Dercylides, who is better known, except precisely as regards the time when he worked. Posidonius is of course considerably earlier, but he was a Stoic, and therefore could not be an ἐξηγητής in the strict sense, i.e. the professed representative of an accepted doctrine and the expositor of a well-defined body of writing. In spite of this, we may postulate a considerable influence of his commentary on the *Timaeus* on later Platonic studies, unless Reinhardt[6] and others were right in believing, on the grounds just mentioned, that such a commentary never existed and that Sextus' reference to 'Posidonius explaining the *Timaeus*'[7] designates a passage on Plato's theory of sensation in a work of a different nature.

Though the Platonic philosophers eventually followed the example of their colleagues in the Peripatos, progress was slow and it was not until the second half of the second century A.D. that the commentary was fully established as the principal medium for the expression of philosophical ideas. Even then, it is interesting to observe how long the mental attitudes that were typical of the doxographical period persisted. Alcinous (Albinus) still read the dialogues as material for a systematic survey of Plato's doctrines, and we shall find traces of the same approach as late as Porphyry. It could not be illustrated better than from the anonymous

---

[5] R. A. Pack, *The Greek and Roman Literary Texts from Greco-Roman Egypt*, [2]Ann Arbor 1965, 2560–2561; A. Carlini, *Studi sulla tradizione antica e medievale del Fedone*, Rome 1972, 8–10.

[6] K. Reinhardt, *RE* art. Poseidonios, 22, 1953, 569.29–61.

[7] *Adv. dogm.* 7,93 τὸν Πλάτωνος Τίμαιον ἐξηγούμενος.

SUMMARIUM LIBRORUM PLATONIS discovered by R. Klibansky.[8] If the *Phaedo* happened to be lost, the 250 word 'summary' of that dialogue would fail to give us even the remotest notion of its real content; all the epitomator has done is go through the text noting down isolated pronouncements on isolated subjects (dreams, suicide, providence, immortality, reincarnation, inadequacy of senses, nature of ideas, etc.), obviously to be rearranged later on a systematic plan. In more recent times, material of this type would have been collected in preparation of an *Index analyticus;* in the second century, it can have been destined only for an epitome of Plato's teaching such as those by Alcinous and Apuleius.

It would be rash, though, to make any general statement regarding Middle Platonic methods of interpretation without the reminder that our information is extremely fragmentary. No full-fledged commentary is extant and in the case of the *Phaedo* there are only three or four which are reasonably well attested. I list the evidence in a roughly chronological order.

PLUTARCH OF CHAERONEA[9] is the first author whose extant work contains anything resembling commentaries on Plato, though he preferred to deal more incidentally with selected passages, as in the *Quaestiones Platonicae* and the two treatises on the *Timaeus*. The extracts on recollection preserved by Damascius (I §§ 275–292 and II § 28 = frgs. 215–217) are from an unknown work plausibly identified as the *De anima;* in any case their anecdotal character points to a dialogue rather than to a regular commentary, and there is no reference to the *Phaedo*. The author of the *Consolatio ad Apollonium* promises his addressee an explanation of the arguments for immortality in the *Phaedo*, but there are, to say the least, good reasons to doubt if he was Plutarch, and we do not know if he ever realized his project.

The leading Platonist of the middle of the second century, ALBINUS, gave the *Phaedo* an important place in the curriĉulum. To him the essential dialogues were: the *Alcibiades*, the *Phaedo*, the *Republic* and the *Timaeus*, in the order named. The *Phaedo*, he says (*isag.* 5), makes it clear to us (i) who the philosopher is (through the example of Socrates),

---

[8] The lost Greek text can be assigned to the second cent. A.D. on the ground of parallels with Apuleius and Alcinous; Latin translation not later than the sixth cent. in Vat. Regin. lat. 1572. See *Proceedings of the British Academy*, Annual Report 1948–9 (London 1949) p. 8; id. 1955–6 (*ibid.* 1956) p. 11; R. Klibansky, *The Continuity of the Platonic Tradition*, London 1950, 10; Union Académique Internationale, Compte Rendu de la 44e session annuelle (Brussels 1970) p. 74; id., 45e session (*ibid.* 1971) p. 68. Prof. Klibansky was kind enough to provide me with a copy of the *Phaedo* part. Publication to be expected in the *Corpus Platonicum* in the near future.

[9] Proclus distinguishes him from his Athenian namesake by adding ὁ Χαιρωνεύς, *Tim.* I 112.26; 381.26; 415.18; 454.13; but he is Plutarch *simpliciter* I 276.31; 326.1; 384.4; II 153.29; III 212.9. Plutarch of Athens is ὁ καθηγεμὼν ἡμῶν *Rep.* II 64.5–6; ὁ ἡμέτερος προπάτωρ *Parm.* 1058.22.

(ii) what the aim of his life is (apparently, detachment from the body) and (iii) what the fundamental assumption of his teaching is (the immortality of the soul). Commentaries on the *Timaeus* and on the myth of the *Republic* are cited by Proclus, but as to the other two we have no information, which fact, in view of our fairly full documentation on these dialogues, makes it unlikely that commentaries by Albinus were available to the Neoplatonists. What we do have is a discussion, in ch. 25 of the *Didaskalikos* or *Epitome* preserved under the name of Alcinous,[10] of the arguments for immortality in the *Phaedo*, *Republic* and *Phaedrus*. Although there is no mention of any previous controversy, the peculiar way in which the arguments are arranged seems to indicate awareness of earlier criticism. The passage begins with the final argument, which the later Neoplatonists considered as the only one that was completely conclusive: soul cannot die because it is the giver of life, any more than fire, the source of heat, can become cold. Apparently to answer the criticism that Plato's substitution of 'indestructible' for 'deathless' (106b2) is unwarranted, since it has been proved only that soul cannot die so long as it exists (Strato cited by Dam. I § 442), the author then proceeds to demonstrate this point with the help of the other arguments: those from similarity to the intelligible, from opposites, from recollection. In dealing with the argument from opposites he introduces the distinction between opposites with and without intermediate terms, another trace of an earlier discussion (cf. Ol. 10 § 10; Dam. I § 192).

ATTICUS, about a generation later, wrote a commentary on the *Timaeus*, and he may have written another on the *Phaedo*. The only extant quotation (Dam. I § 100) concerns the identity of the 'genuine philosophers' at 66b2, a point more likely to be raised in a commentary than in a passing reference.

In the case of the rather mysterious ONETOR, who is cited jointly with Atticus as holding the same opinion on the same question (which may mean that Atticus' commentary was the direct source for the information

---

[10] Generally identified with Albinus since Freudenthal. Recently, objections have been raised by M. Giusta, '*Aλβίνου Ἐπιτομή ο Ἀλκινόου Διδασκαλικός*? Atti della Accad. delle Sc. di Torino 95, 1960–61, 167–194, and J. Whittaker, *Parisinus Graecus 1962 and the Writings of Albinus*, Phoenix 28, 1974, 320–354; 450–456, who have pointed out that the correspondences are neither as close nor as striking as it was thought, that the *name* Alcinous is attested at the time, and that the corruption of 'Albinus' would require at least two stages ($AABINOY > AAKINOY > AAKINOOY$), or even three, if there was also a subscription (which was by no means always the case). The alternative assumption is that there were two roughly contemporary Middle Platonists, with names closely resembling each other and doctrines indistinguishable to us, both teaching full courses on Plato while also writing manuals, and one of whom, in spite of an extant work, was never noticed by the Neoplatonists. Though I still believe that Freudenthal was very probably right, I have returned to the traditional designation in order not to prejudice the issue.

on Onetor), the other evidence does not seem to point to a commentator. Diogenes Laertius (3,9) refers to him (or a namesake?) as the author of an essay 'Will the Wise Man Go Into Business?' in which he said that Plato received eighty talents from Dionysius; the information on Stilpo's mistress (2,114) may come from the same work. Finally, a scholium on Proclus (*Rep.* II 378.23–24) cites a work *On Arithmetic Proportion*, in at least five books, if Kroll's supplement is correct.[11] He cannot be dated with any certainty; Diogenes' latest authorities are second cent. A.D. (Favorinus, Sextus).

NUMENIUS may have written on the *Phaedo*, as he is known to have written on the myth in the *Republic* (test. 21 Leemans = Pr., *Rep.* II 96.11); however, his view of immortality (Dam. I § 177) may have been expressed in any context, while a work Περὶ τῶν παρὰ Πλάτωνι ἀπορρήτων (frg. 23 Des Places) could have contained his explanation of the 'custody' (Dam. I § 2).

The unknown author of the COMMENTARY ON THE THEAETETUS published from a Berlin papyrus by Diels and Schubart, who also wrote (or lectured) on the *Timaeus* and the *Symposium*, refers to a forthcoming commentary (or course) on the *Phaedo* for a discussion of Platonic anamnesis.[12]

The only Middle Platonic author whose commentary on the *Phaedo* is quoted often enough to give us at least a very general picture of its character, is HARPOCRATIO of Argos (ca. 200 A.D.).[13] According to the *Suda*, he wrote a comprehensive commentary on Plato in 24 books, to which the known comments on the *Alcibiades*, *Phaedo*, *Phaedrus*, *Republic* and *Timaeus* must have belonged. The *Phaedo* commentary is the best attested (frgs. 2–8). Most of the fragments deal with questions of detail, the greater part of which had apparently been raised before: who is the true philosopher of 63e9–10? how can all wars be said to be fought for the sake of wealth (66c7–8)? why is the lover of the body described as a lover of money and glory, but not of pleasure (68c1–3)? what does the 'likely' at 70b7 mean? Of a wider interest is the attempt at 69a6–c3 (frg. 5) to ascertain the relationship between the various aspects or categories of virtues as described in Plato and Aristotle. Confronted with the Peripatetic objection that the virtues of the mind when detached from the body can only be those called *dianoetic* by Aristotle, Harpocratio 'yields' and admits that the virtues of the *Phaedo* are not really different from those in the *Republic*. This account of his view by Damascius (I § 149) may be due to post-Plotinian hindsight, as Dillon thinks, but it rather looks as if the 'Attic commentators' (and possibly other Middle Platonists

---

[11] ἐν τῷ πέ[μπτῳ] Kroll, ἐν τῷ πέρατι Mai, ἐν τῷ πε′, scil. κεφαλαίῳ, Norvin.

[12] *Anonymer Kommentar zu Platons Theaetet*, Berlin 1905 (Berliner Klassikertexte Heft 2). *Timaeus :* 35.10–12; *Symposium :* 70.10–12; *Phaedo :* 48.10–11.

[13] Fragments recently collected by J. M. Dillon, *Harpocration's Commentary on Plato : Fragments of a Middle Platonic Commentary*, California Studies in Classical Antiquity 4, 1971, 125–146.

as well) had already made some sort of distinction between the social virtues and virtue as purification, which was to be developed later by Plotinus.[14] The last fragment (8), which identifies Plato's 'Earth' (108c5 ff.) as the entire cosmos, through which the freed soul makes her upward way, reminds of Numenius and Cronius and can be added to frgs. 11 and 12 as another instance of Numenian ideas in Harpocratio.

The two remaining Middle Platonists, each cited only once for an opinion on the *Phaedo*, belong to the middle of the third century, so that they are already contemporaries of Plotinus. DEMOCRITUS is mentioned and characterized by Longinus *ap*. Porph., *vit. Plot*. 20.31 and 60; see further Iambl. *ap*. Stob. I 49,35; Syr., *met*. 105.36–106.2. There were commentaries by him on the *First Alcibiades* (Ol., *Alc*. 105.17–106.2) and on the *Timaeus* (Pr., *Tim*. II 33.13–28), hence the citation by Dam. I § 503 is very probably from a complete commentary on the *Phaedo*.

LONGINUS is quoted by Dam. I § 110 for an opinion on 66c7–8 (money the cause of *all* wars). The most likely source is a lecture (through Porphyry).

A minor puzzle remains, the ATTIC COMMENTATORS [15] of Dam. I § 110 and § 164. When later authors, of the school of Ammonius, use the term, they refer to the fifth century Athenian Neoplatonists: Philoponus (*an*. 21.21–32; 46.10–22; 51.15–29; 411.1–5) probably to Plutarch; Olympiodorus (*cat*. 120.33–121.3) possibly to Proclus; Elias (*cat*. 133.14–17) apparently to Proclus' introduction to Aristotle (the Συνανάγνωσις of 107.24–26). In Dam., however, they represent a pre-Neoplatonic explanation of the passage on virtues (69a6–c3), and their opinions are contrasted, once, with those of Harpocratio and Longinus, once, with Harpocratio's only; the phrase must therefore stem from Dam.'s ultimate source (Porphyry?) and it may, for instance, denote the Athenian professors Theodotus and Eubulus, mentioned by Longinus *ap*. Porph., *vit. Plot*. 20.39–40.

The list of the Middle Platonists who, according to Porphyry (*vit. Plot*. 14.11–12), were read and discussed in PLOTINUS' classes, Severus, Cronius, Numenius, Gaius, Atticus (along with the Peripatetics Aspasius, Alexander and Adrastus) is certainly not exhaustive; Porphyry makes it clear that he is choosing his examples more or less at random and that any author was welcome who could offer food for reflection. The results of some discussions bearing upon the *Phaedo* were written down by Plotinus and had a lasting influence on the later interpretation of the dialogue. This is especially true of the disquisitions on virtue as purification (*Ph*. 69a6–c3), which inspired *Enneads* I 2, *On Virtues*. As shown above, the exact relationship between virtues of the *Phaedo* and those of the *Republic* seems already to have been the subject of a dispute among Middle

---

[14] See note on Dam. I §§ 148–149.

[15] Cf. O. Immisch, Ἀττικοὶ ἐξηγηταί, Philologus 63, 1904, 31–40; H. Dörrie, *Kontroversen um die Seelenwanderung im kaiserzeitlichen Platonismus*, Hermes 85, 1957, 414–435 (422).

Platonists, and so had the concept of becoming like God through virtue
(Alcin., *did.* 28). Plotinus made the distinction between civic and
purificatory virtue definitive, adding also a state of perfect purity, to
which Porphyry (*sent.* 32) was to assign a rank of its own, that of
contemplative virtue. Later Neoplatonists, in particular Iamblichus and
Proclus, extended the scale at both ends (Ol. 8 §§ 2-3; Dam. I §§ 138-144).
In *Enneads* IV 7 Plotinus restated the case for the soul's immortality,
incorporating and adapting most of the arguments of the *Phaedo* (ch. 8 [4]
harmony, ch. 11 soul as the source of life, ch. 12 the arguments from
opposites and recollection); it is not quite clear whether the argument
attributed to Plotinus by Dam. I § 311 (and parallel texts) is a remodeled
version of *Enneads* IV 7 (by Iamblichus?) or a fragment of some non-
Enneadic tradition. The attempt made in *Enn.* III 4 to rationalize the
guiding spirit of *Ph.* 107d5-6 by making it into a faculty of the soul,
next in degree to the level of our actual life (a refinement of *Tim.* 90a2-7)
was not acceptable to the later Platonists: in a universe populated with
Gods, angels, demons, heroes and blessed or damned souls there was room
also for a personal guardian spirit.

With PORPHYRY, Neoplatonism abandons the method of Plotinus and
retruns to the Middle Platonic medium of the commentary. Beutler [16]
lists commentaries on the *Cratylus, Parmenides, Phaedo, Philebus, Republic,
Sophist* and *Timaeus;* further on Aristotle's *Categories, Interpretation,
Physics, Metaphysics Λ, Ethics.* Direct references to Porphyry in our
commentaries are rare: apart from Dam. I § 172 and § 177, which have
nothing to do with the *Phaedo* in particular, there is only the note on
the 'custody' already discussed above (p. 8) and another on the sense
in which soul can be said to be harmony (Dam. II § 59). In other cases
his influence can be inferred with more or less probability: see the notes
on Ol. 4 §§ 2-3 (parallel between the three aspects of detachment,
Ph. 64d2-66a10, and Porphyry's three degrees of virtue); 6 § 2.5-10
(Calypso symbolizing imagination); Dam. I §§ 120-123 (exhortation to
asceticism, with emphasis on vegetarianism); I §§ 148-149 (Porphyrian
scale of virtues); I § 471 (the three 'descents into Hades'). His most
signal contribution, however, is all (or most of) the information on his
predecessors; the working hypothesis that the Middle Platonic material
in the Athenian Neoplatonists comes from Porphyry must be substantially
sound. There are further traces of Porphyry in Macrobius, *somn. Scip.* I
13,5-8, where *Ph.* 64a4-c9 is paraphrased in terms closely resembling
Sent. 8-9; and in the analysis of the argument on harmony presented
by Nemesius and Philoponus (cf. note on Dam. I §§ 361-370), where
only joint borrowing from Porphyry can explain the close correspondence
between the two texts. The last case is perhaps the most interesting,
inasmuch as it shows Porphyry, the 'last of the Middle Platonists', still

---

[16] *RE* art. Porphyrios (21), 22, 1953, 273-313 (280-284).

adhering to the methods of the old school. Without too much concern for Plato's (rather puzzling) argumentation, the passage is divided into five independent 'proofs'; what matters is not so much the discussion as separate tenets and arguments, ready for convenient presentation and memorization.

The new method of interpretation, developed by IAMBLICHUS and described in a wellknown article of Praechter,[17] does not aim at correcting this. Iamblichus' purpose is to make Plotinus' belief of the superiority of intuition to reason the guiding principle of a new systematic approach to Plato. Intuition, which is a superior form of sight, does not proceed from point to point, but has a unified vision of the structure of all reality. Since this structure is fundamentally the same, or analogous, at every level (metaphysical reality, physical reality, the progress of the human mind, human reason and human speech), the inspired thinker will, from his high point of vantage, be able to discern the same essential patterns everywhere. He will find in all perfect literature (whether Plato, the Chaldean Oracles, Orpheus or Homer) the faultless reflection of the entire transcendental, physical and moral world. Thus each of Plato's dialogues can be interpreted on a theological, a physical and a moral plane; the ideal course on Plato, assigning to each work its natural place in the whole, will proceed on a plan corresponding to the progress of the mind, i.e. the scale of virtues. This is the curriculum described *Proleg.* 26: after the (introductory) *Alcibiades*, the *Gorgias* deals with the civic virtues, then the *Phaedo* with the purificatory virtues, followed by seven others which contain, in systematic arrangement, the subject-matter for speculation (contemplative virtues): *Cratylus* and *Theaetetus* (epistemology), *Sophist* and *Statesman* (physical world), *Phaedrus* and *Symposium* (theology), with the *Philebus* (on the Good) as the end of the series; the essential doctrines receive their final shape in the second cycle, the 'perfect' dialogues: *Timaeus* (physics) and *Parmenides* (metaphysics). Each of the dialogues, in order to be firmly embedded in the series, must have its one and only 'target' ($\sigma\varkappa o\pi\delta\varsigma$, a term deliberately adopted to replace the old notion of $\dot{v}\pi\delta\vartheta\varepsilon\sigma\iota\varsigma$); there is no room, in this rigorous system, for loose ends, open questions, partial or provisional solutions. In the *Phaedo*, Iamblichus insisted on finding five absolute proofs of immortality and he tried to defend this position, which his predecessors had taken for granted, by a fresh interpretation. The later Neoplatonists saw that it was untenable. Damascius (I § 207) speaks of the great Iamblichus overshooting the mark, and Olympiodorus (10 § 1), probably repeating a remark of Syrianus', says that the inspired thinker Iamblichus from his high point of vantage overlooked the details of the text. Olympiodorus also provides some particulars about his handling of the arguments from

---

[17] *Richtungen und Schulen im Neuplatonismus*, Genethliakon Carl Robert, Berlin 1910, 108 ff.

opposites (11 § 2), recollection (*ibid.*) and similarity to things intelligible (13 § 4), adding that all the other commentators (i.e., presumably, Proclus, Ammonius and Damascius, to whom his field of vision was limited) regarded only the final argument as full proof. It is difficult to decide how much of the report on the argument from similarity at 13 § 4 is really Iamblichus, how much Olympiodorus; it looks as if Iamblichus is already defending his reading of the argument against a narrower view, but he may be dealing merely with the intrinsic limitation of the argument: compared with the visible and the invisible world, soul *more* strongly resembles the invisible. Apart from (and no doubt because of) this fundamental difference of opinion, Iamblichus' comments receive little attention, the sole exception being Ol. 10 § 7; all other references to him relate to general points of doctrine without any particular connection with the *Phaedo*.

A somewhat younger contemporary, and on many issues an adversary, of Iamblichus was Porphyry's pupil THEODORUS of Asine. There are numerous citations from his commentary (or lectures) on the *Timaeus* in Proclus; the single reference to his explanation of the Earth at *Ph.* 108c5–8 (Dam. I § 503 = test. 42/42A Deuse) does not make it possible to decide whether there was an entire commentary by him.

There was certainly a commentary on the *Phaedo* by PATERIUS, and probably another one on the myth of the *Republic*. He is cited for an opinion on the 'custody' (62b4) by Dam. I § 2, on the 'true philosophers' of 66b2 at I § 100, on the omission of the pleasure-seeker (68c1–3) at I § 137. His name is coupled with that of Plutarch (of Athens?) at I § 100 and appears instead of it in the scholium on I § 177. Though there are no characteristic doctrines or terms, the formula used by Proclus (τοὺς ἀμφὶ Πατέριον ἐξηγητάς, ἄνδρας ἡμῖν αἰδοίους [18]) seems to point to a contemporary or near-contemporary rather than to a little-known Middle Platonist.

The case of PLUTARCH OF ATHENS shows how incomplete and haphazard our tradition is, in spite of the survival of considerable parts of three commentaries. Marinus, *vit. Pr.* 12, says that Plutarch, then a very old man, read the *De anima* and the *Phaedo* with young Proclus in the two years following the latter's arrival at Athens, encouraging him to take notes, so that eventually there should be a '*Proclus in Phaedonem*'. There is no doubt that the notes were taken; Marinus does not say if and how the rest of the suggestion was realized. So much is certain that Plutarch's influence on the interpretation of the *De anima* is very much in evidence, both in Philoponus' part of the commentary (books I–II) and in Stephanus' (book III), while in the commentaries on the *Phaedo*, all three of which derive from Proclus, only two or three quotations remain: Dam. I § 100

---

[18]   Cf. Pl., *Theaet.* 183e5 (Parmenides); Pr., *Rep.* II 110.17–18 (Theodorus of Asine); *theol.* I 8, p. 33.19–20 S.-W. (Neoplatonists from Porphyry to Plutarch). On Paterius see R. Beutler, *RE* 18,2, 1949, 2562–2563.

on the 'true philosophers' of 66b2, and I § 503 on the Earth of 108c5 ff.; the doxographical note at I § 177 can come from any other work as well. The other two deal with points of detail that give us little or no possibility of forming an opinion on the content or method of his interpretation.

The new trend, as far as it is possible to tell on this flimsy evidence, was initiated by SYRIANUS, to whom Proclus owes (and acknowledges) so heavy a debt of gratitude that it is not easy to see what will be left when all is paid. Its main features are these. While, on the one hand, continuing Iamblichus' method of intuitive interpretation, searching for structure, patterns and analogies, the Athenian school at the same time makes a point of reading the discussion as a discussion. The argument from opposites is now no longer a weapon with which the Platonist equips himself to defeat an adversary, it is only what Socrates needs for the moment to answer Cebes' doubts on the basis of Cebes' own assumptions. It becomes relevant now what Cebes has in mind when comparing the soul to 'air or smoke' (70a5): is he using a metaphor or is he thinking of something kindred to those two substances? Syrianus believes the latter (Dam. I § 222); Damascius draws attention to the Homeric idiom, in which the soul is sometimes described as resembling smoke, sometimes as being like 'a dream or a shadow,' in other words, things obviously incorporeal (ibid.). An enlightening example is the comment on Socrates' 'likely' (εἰκός, 77b7) in Dam. I § 182: while the Middle Platonists' only concern is to show that it does not indicate any scepticism or probabilism on Plato's part, the Athenians had the additional responsibility of avoiding to construe the argument as a categorical proof (cf. Dam. I § 207.12–13; § 208.4; § 216). The interpretation of Plato's reasoning becomes increasingly careful as a result: the painstaking analyses of the argument on harmony by Proclus and Damascius (Dam. I §§ 361–370; §§ 405–406; II §§ 45–53) are a far cry from the simplifying treatment Porphyry gave it (above pp. 14–15). As far as Syrianus himself is concerned, we have the express testimony of Damascius (I §§ 207–208) and Olympiodorus (9 § 2) that he wrote a monograph on the argument from opposites, which Proclus incorporated in his commentary. A fairly extensive and fairly accurate survey of it is found in Dam. I §§ 183–206. Outside this limited area Syrianus is mentioned only once (Dam. II § 147), for his view on eternal punishment. He explained away the 'nevermore' of 113e6 as meaning 'not during a whole period'. It is not necessary to assume an entire commentary on the strength of this one note; Proclus may have referred to his recollection, or to his personal notes, of Syrianus' lectures on the Gorgias, the Republic or the Phaedo, in all of which the point was raised. There is, for that matter, no hard and fast line between such personal notes and a 'commentary'. In Marinus (vit. Pr. 13) we are told that that Syrianus went through practically the whole Corpus Aristotelicum with Proclus in two years' time, then proceeded to deal with Plato, 'in due order and without omissions', which probably refers to the canon of Iamblichus, since in ch. 14 Marinus mentions a separate course in the *Laws* and the *Republic*. Some of the lectures must have been generally available (we happen to know that Hermias attended the course on the *Phaedrus* together with Proclus and published it under his own name, hardly without authorization), but it is not impossible that a considerable part of the material listed by Praechter [19] was accessible to Proclus only (or, as Praechter suggests, belonged to the school, which may have come to the same thing), and through Proclus to Ammonius, Damascius and Simplicius. The treatise on the argument from opposites, in any case, was distinctly marked off as such (much as Dam.'s treatise, I §§ 207–252, in our commentaries). Pr.'s commentary may have included other similar monographs by Syrianus, which we are unable to isolate. However this may be, there can be no doubt that Syrianus had an important share in the remainder of the commentary as well, as in almost all of Proclus' work, a fact of which Proclus never made a secret.

The two commentaries on the *Phaedo* in vol. II are essentially a summing-up of the commentary of PROCLUS with abundant critical footnotes by Damascius. Besides, as it will be pointed out in detail in my notes, Olympiodorus used Proclus as his principal and almost only source, partly directly, partly through Ammonius and Damascius. Finally, there is a certain amount of indirect tradition, mainly from Proclus citing himself: *Rep.* I 12.25–13.6 ('elsewhere'; see Ol. 8 § 3.8–10; Dam. I § 152.1–3); *ibid.* II 178.15–28; 179.9–24; 183.16–25 ('on the myth of the *Phaedo*'; [20] cf. Dam. I § 547.4–8 and §§ 537–541); but also a fairly long report in Elias, *isag.* 2.10–25, on which see Ol. 11 § 4.16–18, note. An Arabic translation by Ibn Zur^ca (from the Syriac) is apparently lost.[21] We have some extracts, in Priscianus, *solut.* 47–49, and in Miskawayh's *Fawz al-aṣghar*, of an independent *monobiblon* discussing Plato's three arguments for immortality, in the *Phaedo*, the *Republic* and the *Phaedrus*.[22]

Proclus is the first author on the *Phaedo* of whose work we can form a coherent and reasonably complete picture. Its composition is not clear: it may have been a conglomerate of various materials, including Syrianus' essay on the argument from opposites and Proclus' work on the myth, comparable to the 'commentary' on the *Republic*, but different from it insofar as it covered the entire dialogue; or it may have been a continuous commentary, interrupted only by Syrianus' monograph. With its full doxographical material, the work bore a closer resemblance to the early commentary on the *Timaeus* (finished ca. 440, though it may have been

---

[19] *RE* art. Syrianos (1), 4A, 1932, 1728–1775 (1731.18–58).

[20] I.e. (probably) in that part of the commentary, rather than in a monograph on the myth. Similar forms of quotation *Rep.* II 309.20–21; 371.14–16; but cf. also *Tim.* I 308. 19–20 and Ol., *Alc.* 2.4–5.

[21] *Fihrist* 252.22–23=transl. 608.

[22] L. G. Westerink, *Proclus on Plato's Three Proofs of Immortality*, Zetesis, aangeboden aan Prof. Dr. Emile de Strycker, Antwerpen-Utrecht 1973, 296–306.

revised later) than to those on the *Parmenides* and *Alcibiades*, where Proclus, perhaps for stylistic, perhaps for philosophical reasons, makes a point of referring to his sources or opponents by a tantalizing 'somebody' or 'some'. An obvious possibility is that it might be essentially the '*Proclus in Phaedonem*' called for by Plutarch and based on his interpretation, then revised in the following years in the light of Syrianus' lectures; but this cannot be more than a hypothesis.

The structure of the commentary will be discussed later, in the context of Olympiodorus' work (pp. 28–29). A general characteristic of the exegetical practice of the Athenian school has already been given above; it remains to draw attention to a few salient points typical of Proclus. One of them is his partiality for triads, sometimes paralleled with other triads, sometimes multiplied by other triads, sometimes multiplied by themselves. It is seen in the first place in the supposed framework of the dialogue, but there are plenty of examples throughout (e.g. Ol. 4 §§ 2–3 = Dam. I § 74; Ol. 5 § 3; Ol. 8 § 3 = Dam. I § 152; Dam. I § 41; § 397; II § 131). More interesting is his assumption that Plato will imperceptibly shift the meaning of certain terms within the same passage. Thus, in *theol.* V 23 (cf. Dam., *Phil.* § 130) he explains that *Phil.* 30c2–d4 deals with the immanent world mind as far as 30c11, whereas the Zeus of 31d1–4 must be the transcendent Creator of the *Timaeus;* similarly, the Good of *Republic* VI is split into (1) the immanent good, (2) the idea of the Good, (3) the Absolute Good (note on Dam. I § 417.3–4). This technique is carried to its farthest extreme at *Ph.* 68d2–69d2, where instead of Socrates' straightforward contrast between sham virtue and true virtue, which is purification, no less than six different kinds emerge: spurious virtue, natural, moral, civic, purificatory and contemplative virtue (Ol. 8 § 4.5–6.17 = Dam. I §§ 145–148). Such distortions were of course prompted by the necessity to adapt the text of Plato to the complicated structures of late Neoplatonism. They need not cause the more valuable aspects of Athenian exegesis, already pointed out above, to be forgotten.

AMMONIUS came to Athens, with his mother Aedesia and his brother Heliodorus, as *designatus* to the chair of Alexandria after the death of his father Hermias, to study with Proclus; this must have been before 470. He seems to have held the chair from his return some years later until his death about 520. Besides the commentary on the *De interpretatione* (perhaps a sort of dissertation) Ammonius is not known to have written any larger books, but his lectures circulated, partly under his own name, partly under those of Asclepius and Philoponus, and some *monobibla* of his own hand are cited, one of them dealing with *Phaedo* 69d5–6 and showing (against the claim of the Middle Academy) that Plato was not a sceptic (Ol. 8 § 17). Olympiodorus has also preserved some notes from his lectures on the *Phaedo*, on the passages 68c1–2 (Ol. 7 § 5) and 70d7–e2 (10 § 7); 'our own professor' at 6 § 3 may be either Ammonius or Olympiodorus. A much farther reaching influence may be assumed; it is

more especially probable where Olympiodorus does not repeat Proclus/
Damascius, or shows striking agreement with Philoponus (see notes on
4 § 7; 6 § 2; 11 § 4.16–18; 13 § 2).

The lectures of DAMASCIUS will be dealt with separately in the
introduction to vol. II. I have already briefly characterized them as a
critical discussion of Proclus' commentary. They have survived in two
versions, one (Dam. I) complete except for the beginning (57a1–62b2)
and including a separate essay on the argument from opposites (§§ 207–252);
the other (Dam. II) beginning at 69e6. The version to which Olympiodorus
refers twice (4 § 10 and 8 § 9) was different from both.

SIMPLICIUS once cites a commentary on the *Phaedo* which may be
either his own or the one by Damascius. The reference occurs *cael.* 369.3–5
(book II), in the words 'as we have seen in Plato's *Phaedo*.' It cannot
be to Plato, who does not mention the point reported by Simplicius:
immortality means continuity of life, permanency continuity of being.
In the commentaries, however, it is discussed in connection with memory
as continuity of knowledge (Ol. 11 § 3, Dam. I § 256). Whether a
commentary on the *Phaedo* should be added to the list of Simplicius'
(lost) writings depends on Damascius' share in the *De caelo*, which, at
least as regards book I, seems to have been considerable.[23]

II. OLYMPIODORUS

What little external evidence we have on Olympiodorus rests on
demonstrable errors. Anastasius Sinaita seems to confuse him with a
namesake; at least he gives the title of 'the Great Philosopher' to the
deacon Olympiodorus,[24] author of a series of commentaries on the Bible,
the remains of which are collected in *PG* 93. He was a deacon as early
as the year 510 (the canonical age being 25), at a time when the philosopher
Olympiodorus must still have been a minor. In the alchemical texts to
be discussed later, Olympiodorus is called *oikoumenikos didaskalos*, a title
bestowed for the first time on Stephanus when he was appointed to the
chair at Constantinople, about half a century after Olympiodorus' death.
We depend therefore on indications in Olympiodorus' own work. I have
discussed them in the introduction to the *Prolegomena philosophiae
Platonicae* (XIII–XIV), arriving at 495/505 as his approximate birthdate;
the death year is some time, probably not long, after 565.

His extant work[25] consists entirely of lecture notes by students:

---

[23] Simpl., *cael.*, praef. VIII–IX; app. crit. at 1.1.

[24] *PG* 89, 936C9–11; 1189A12–14. On the exegete cf. O. Bardenhewer, *Geschichte
der altkirchlichen Literatur* V, Freiburg i. B. 1932 (Darmstadt 1962); Ehrhard in
Krumbacher, *Geschichte der byzantinischen Literatur*, ² München 1897, 127–128;
H. G. Beck, *Kirche und theologische Literatur im byzantinischen Reich*, München
1959, 416.

[25] Listed by Beutler, *RE* art. Olympiodoros (13), 18,2, 1949, 207–228;
C. B. Schmitt in *Catalogus translationum et commentariorum*, ed. P. O. Kristeller,
vol. II, Washington 1971, 199–204.

COMMENTARIES on Plato's GORGIAS, ALCIBIADES and PHAEDO (all preserved in Marc. gr. 196, ff. 1–241); on Aristotle's CATEGORIES (including the usual prolegomena to Aristotelian philosophy) and METEOROLOGY; and probably, as J. Warnon has plausibly argued, one on PAULUS OF ALEXANDRIA (the so-called Heliodorus).[26] The *Gorgias* commentary can be dated tentatively around 525 (*Proleg.*, introd. XV), the one on the *Alcibiades* hardly before 560, that on the *Meteorology* after March/April 565,[27] the lectures on Paulus were given May-July 564.

The commentaries on Aristotle and Plato were part of a more comprehensive course: there is evidence of a lost commentary on Porphyry's *Isagoge*,[28] and among the scholia in Vatic. Urb. gr. 35 there are some extracts from a commentary on the DE INTERPRETATIONE. The unpublished commentary on this work in Paris. gr. 2064, ff. 1–35, which Busse claimed for Olympiodorus,[29] does not include these extracts, nor does it show any of the usual characteristics of Olympiodorus' commentaries. It must therefore belong to another, unidentifiable, lecturer between Ammonius and Stephanus.[30] Scepticism is justified with regard to the commentary on the PRIOR ANALYTICS in Jerusalem MS. Taphos 150, attributed to Olympiodorus by a 17th or 18th cent. reader on the ground of the *theoria-lexis* division, to be dealt with below (p. 25). Commentaries on the *Analytics* of this type are found in a great many MSS.,[31] but they have never been examined methodically. As things stand, at least three known commentators (in the first place Stephanus) and a number of unknown ones have as much right to be considered as Olympiodorus. Commentaries on the DE GENERATIONE ET CORRUPTIONE and the DE ANIMA are cited from Arabic sources.[32] The attribution to Olympiodorus of *CAG* XIX 2 on the *Nicomachean Ethics* in a group of MSS. is certainly

---

[26] *In Paulum Alexandrium commentarium*, ed. Ae. Boer, Leipzig 1962. – J. Warnon, *Le commentaire attribué à Héliodore sur les ΕΙΣΑΓΩΓΙΚΑ de Paul d'Alexandrie*, Recherches de Philologie et de Linguistique, Travaux de la Faculté de Philosophie et Lettres de l'Université Catholique de Louvain II, section de philologie classique I, Louvain 1967, 197–217; L. G. Westerink, *Ein astrologisches Kolleg aus dem Jahre 564*, Byz. Zeitschr. 64, 1971, 6–21.

[27] Prof. O. Neugebauer points out to me that this is the correct date, by the Egyptian calendar, for the comet mentioned *CAG* XII 2, 52.31 (Aug.-Sept. is Alexandrian calendar). – On the *Alc.* commentary see A. Cameron, *The Last Days of the Academy at Athens*, Proc. of the Cambridge Philol. Society No. 195 (N.S. No. 15) 1969, 7–29 (12).

[28] *CAG* IV 1, Praef. XLII–XLIV.

[29] *CAG* IV 5, Praef. XXIII–XXVI.

[30] Edition of the anonymous commentary (with the fragments of Olympiodorus) in preparation by L. Tarán.

[31] Extracts in C. A. Brandis, *Scholia in Aristotelem*, Berlin 1836, 139 ff.

[32] *Fihrist* 251.5=transl. 604: (*De gener. et corr.*) 'Olympiodorus wrote an exposition of Eustathius' translation' (?); 251.13–14=transl. 604: (*De anima*) 'Olympiodorus wrote a commentary, which I read written in Syriac in the hand-writing of Yaḥyā ibn ʿAdī.'

false. As for the course on Plato, Olympiodorus himself announces lectures on the Sophist (*Alc.* 110.8–9); a commentary by him is mentioned also in Arabic bibliography,[33] but the hope of its being rediscovered is dwindling, now that most of the oriental libraries have been searched more thoroughly. Finally, the *Prolegomena philosophiae Platonicae* has been claimed repeatedly and confidently for Olympiodorus; the evidence, however, is at best inconclusive and on important points negative (see introd. XLI–L).

Another text raises a more complicated problem. In Berthelot's corpus of the Greek alchemists,[34] Olympiodorus 'the Alexandrian philosopher' appears as the author of a COMMENTARY ON THE KAT' ENERGEIAN OF ZOSIMUS (III 69–104, French translation II 75–113); there are also a few incidental references to him.[35] While students of the alchemical texts seem to be inclined to take the authenticity of the treatises by Olympiodorus and Stephanus for granted, those dealing primarily with the philosophical work are almost unanimous in not considering them seriously; Beutler does not even mention alchemy.

A priori, one cannot deny that in the sixth century a philosopher (pagan or Christian) could have adopted the curious amalgam that is now called alchemy. In the case of Olympiodorus, who was accustomed to deal with two incompletely coordinated philosophies and with two completely uncoordinated religions, it is not inconceivable that he may have had another separate compartment in his mind for the nebulous philosophy of the alchemists and for their Jewish-Christian jargon. However, though I cannot go into the alchemical content of the treatise for lack of special knowledge, the other evidence is mainly against the authenticity. In the first place, since the corpus includes (or cites) writings attributed to Plato, Aristotle, Democritus, Theophrastus, Xenocrates, Porphyry, Iamblichus, Synesius, the burden of proof rests with the believer. Chronologically, Olympiodorus and Stephanus are borderline cases between these bogus attributions and genuine famous names such as Psellus; the dividing line might even be between them, for it looks as if Olympiodorus came into the corpus in the wake of Stephanus. It

---

[33]   *Ibid.* 246.11–12=transl. 593: 'I read what was written in the handwriting of Yaḥyā ibn ᶜAdī, Isḥāq [ibn Ḥunayn] translated the *Sophistes*, with the commentary of Olympiodorus.'

[34]   M. Berthelot, Ch. M. Ruelle, *Collection des anciens alchimistes grecs*, 3 vols., Paris 1887–88 (repr. London 1963). See also P. Tannery, *Un fragment d'Anaximène dans Olympiodore le chimiste*, Archiv für Geschichte der Philos. 1, 1888, 314–321.

[35]   III 26.3–4 οὗτοί εἰσιν οἱ πανεύφημοι καὶ οἰκουμενικοὶ διδάσκαλοι καὶ νέοι ἐξηγηταὶ τοῦ Πλάτωνος καὶ Ἀριστοτέλους, which must be a displaced note to 25.8–9 ὁ μέγας Ὀλυμπιόδωρος, Στέφανος ὁ φιλόσοφος. Similarly 425.4–9 οὗτοι οἰκουμενικοὶ πανεύφημοι φιλόσοφοι καὶ ἐξηγηταὶ τοῦ Πλάτωνος καὶ Ἀριστοτέλους, διὰ διαλεκτικῶν δὲ θεωρημάτων Ὀλυμπιόδωρος καὶ Στέφανος, οἵτινες ἔτι σκεψάμενοι τὰ περὶ χρυσοποιΐας μεγάλα ὑπομνήματα μετὰ μεγίστων ἐγκωμίων συνεγράψαντο, πιστωσάμενοι τοῦ μυστηρίου τὴν ποίησιν, where the words οὗτοι - Ἀριστοτέλους must be again a gloss referring to Olympiodorus and Stephanus, not to the preceding names (Hermes, John, Democritus, Zosimus).

was Stephanus,[36] not Olympiodorus, who bore the title of *oikoumenikos didaskalos*, bestowed on him by Heraclius upon his appointment to the chair at Constantinople; Stephanus and not Olympiodorus was designated as 'the new commentator'.[37] Further, it is hard to see how Olympiodorus, who understood classical prosody, could have taken seriously the doggerel of the 'oracles' at 95.2–15. Generally, there is no trace of Olympiodorus' vocabulary, style or method, even in those passages where this could be expected. The most difficult question to answer is how a man who had a lifelong routine in explaining texts could, for this special purpose, have written a commentary that explains nothing at all. Of the two passages dealing directly with philosophy, neither could have been written by Olympiodorus as it stands. The first (70.4–16) says that the philosophers, no less than the alchemists, used to hide their meaning by means of an enigmatic terminology: thus Aristotle said that substance is not in a substratum, accident is in a substratum, Plato on the contrary said that what is not in a substratum is substance and what is in a substratum belongs to accident (one manuscript corrects: substance is in a substratum and accident is not); the origin of this is Ar., *cat.* 5, 2a11–19, and it echoes the debate as to which is the primary substance, the individual or the universal. The second sample, the doxography of the Presocratics at 80.19–83.14, is based on Ar., *phys.* I 2, 184b15–22 and *met.* A 3, 983b20–984a8, but the classification of opinions on the first principle(s) is completely distorted. If all this comes ultimately from Olympiodorus, it must have been corrupted beyond recognition; a more likely author is some muddle-headed charlatan, who, as appears from the above, tried to pass for the philosopher. In spite of the comparative frequency of the name, there was certainly no real Olympiodorus the Alchemist different from the philosopher.

If the ascription to a well-known philosopher of so eccentric a piece of writing as this can be a point of consideration at all, this is due to the great pliability of Olympiodorus' doctrine, a pliability so extreme indeed that it might be more correct to speak of a teaching routine than of a philosophy. The compromise character of the Alexandrian school as opposed to the diehard orthodoxy of Athens is the dominating fact in the history of fifth and sixth century philosophy. It is true, as Lloyd points out,[38] that there was a constant exchange of students and professors between the two cities: most of the great men of the Athenian school (Syrianus, Proclus, Isidorus, Damascius) came to it from, or by way of, Alexandria; most of the Alexandrian professors were at Athens during

---

[36] On Stephanus see H. Usener, *De Stephano Alexandrino*, Bonn 1879; *Anon. Proleg.*, introd. XXIV–XXV.

[37] Steph., *progn.* 118 et al. (assuming the medical writer to be identical with the philosopher, which is doubtful, though).

[38] *The Cambridge History of Later Greek and Early Medieval Philosophy*, Cambridge 1967, 316.

the decisive stage of their education (Hierocles, Hermias, Ammonius);
however, doctrines were shaped, not by the speculations of the individual,
but by the tradition of the school and of the society surrounding it.
At Athens this meant a rigid anti-Christian Platonism, with Aristotelian
logic as its handmaiden; at Alexandria, harmonization of Platonism and
Aristotelianism as the foundation for a monotheistic philosophy,
independent of pagan cults.

The Alexandrian tradition was strong enough to survive the interregnum
after the death of Hermias; the city authorities had enough confidence
in it to continue the payment of Hermias' salary to his widow (an unheard-of
measure), while her two sons went to Athens with her, not only, as
everybody must have understood, to complete their training, but also
for a period of intensive indoctrination.

The teaching of Ammonius, which had so far-reaching an influence
in Byzantium, the West and the Muslim world, has never been studied
in detail. His commentary on the *De interpretatione* was written under
the direct influence of Proclus, while on the other hand in the reports
of his lectures there are interpolations by Christian students and copyists;
there were also clashes and changes of policy. It is also true that we
are very incompletely informed about his metaphysics. Yet one essential
point is clear: [39] from the testimonies of Simplicius (*cael.* 271.13–21;
phys. 1363.8–12), Asclepius (*met.* 103.3–4; 151.15–32) and Stephanus
(*an.* 571.1–5) we learn that to Ammonius the Aristotelian Intelligence
is both the final and the efficient cause; [40] as this Intelligence is identified
with the Creative Mind of the *Timaeus*, it follows that the Creator is
also the Supreme God. Accordingly, the Alexandrian school has the
characteristic habit of referring to God as 'the Demiurge', a practice
continued later by the Christian Olympiodoreans. The reason for the
identification was no doubt partly to bring Plato into harmony with
Aristotle, but the ultimate motive (as already in Hierocles) was to adapt
both to Christian monotheism. As a result, the complicated metaphysical
superstructure of Athenian Platonism had to be discarded, or at least
had lost its interest, so that Olympiodorus (*Gorg.* 244.12–15) could leave
it to his students to explain the divine 'orders' as hypostases or as
attributes (as Hierocles did), according to preference. So radical a change
affected the Plato curriculum, too; though Olympiodorus continued to
follow (entirely or partly) the course prescribed by Iamblichus, it no
longer made sense when the theological interpretation of the *Parmenides*
was abandoned. Ammonius still follows the Athenian interpretation
int. 133.18–20, but substitutes his own theology for it *isag.* 45.10–12.
The Olympiodoreans hardly seem to know the dialogue at all: Ol., *cat.*
14.22–27 cites *Parm.* 135d as '*Phaedo*', Elias, *cat.* 119.4–8 (in the same

---

[39]   *Ibid.* 317.
[40]   The 'Platonic' doctrine in *Proleg.* 9.24–34; cf. Dam., *Phil.* § 114.

context) as *'Sophist'*, Elias, *anal. pr.* 136.5–10 correctly as *'Parmenides'*, but in all the three cases, as well as in Philop., *anal. pr.* 9.18–19, and Anon., *CAG* XII 1, p. X, the assumption is that Plato is dealing with formal logic. In the last, Christian, commentary [41] all metaphysical relevance is denied to the hypotheses section.

The compromise philosophy of Alexandria was developed under the stress of constant pressure and occasional persecution. Damascius (*vit. Isid.* 83.5–11) describes Hierocles' bloody clash with the authorities at Constantinople and his subsequent banishment, and later (pp. 250–255) the persecution of Isidorus and his group by a certain Nicomedes, during which Ammonius came to terms with the patriarch (Athanasius II?). The comparative freedom which Olympiodorus enjoyed may be due to the persistent monophysite schism and the consequent weakening of central authority; still, as he himself confesses (*Alc.* 22.14–23.1), with the warning example of Socrates' fate before him, he sometimes preferred a non-committal interpretation of the text to one that might give offense.

Whatever the exact details, he succeeded in keeping his position and even in acquiring the honorific title 'the Great'. Though his doctrines underwent further modification under his Christian successors, his teaching routine and the note-taking technique he prescribed remained the same for several generations: each lecture *(praxis)* is marked as such, and subdivided into a *theoria* (survey of the pericope under discussion) and a *lexis* part (separate observations on the text). The entire proceeding and the various standard formulas used have been described more than once,[42] so that there is no need to go into details again. There is, however, some point in an attempt at reconstructing the curriculum as a whole.

The starting-point must be the length of the commentaries. In the case of Olympiodorus himself, the number of lectures is: *Alcibiades* 28, *Gorgias* 50, *Phaedo* ca. 50 (13 extant, covering slightly more than a quarter of the text); *Categories* 34; *Meteorology* 51; in Elias: *Isagoge* 40; *Categories* 35/40; David: *Isagoge* 39 or 40; Ps.-Elias: *Isagoge* 51; Stephanus: *Interpretation* 21; *De anima*, book III, 20, making ca. 60 for the whole work. In other words, with few exceptions, the normal number of sessions for any work, irrespective of its length, is between 40 and 50. Assuming daily classes (as we are warranted to do by the frequent references to 'yesterday's meeting') and making ample allowance for holy-days and other special occasions,[43] we thus arrive at about five texts finished per year per course, which means two or three years for a course in Platonic

---

[41] Pr., *Parm.* 1257–1314. Cf. M. Roueché, *Notes on a Commentary on Plato's Parmenides*, Greek, Roman and Byzantine Studies, 12, 1971, 553–556.

[42] Beutler, *RE* art. Olympiodoros 221–227; M. Richard, *'Απὸ φωνῆς*, Byzantion 20, 1950, 191–222; A. J. Festugière, *Modes de Composition des Commentaires de Proclus*, Museum Helveticum 20, 1963, 77–100 (77–80); Westerink, *Ein astrologisches Kolleg*, 7–8.

[43] *Ibid.* 16–17.

philosophy on the twelve dialogue plan of Iamblichus, and roughly the same time for a course in Aristotle including the *Organon, Physics, De caelo, De generatione et corruptione, Meteorology, De anima, Metaphysics*, i.e. logic, physics and theology. Going by the extant commentaries, these must have formed the main substance of the actual teaching in the school of Ammonius; ideally, the order was logic, ethics, physics, mathematics, theology,[44] but in practice the Aristotelian ethics received less attention than the rest, an alternative possibility being to replace the course in theoretical ethics by the reading of a small practical guide (the Pythagorean *Golden Verse*, or Epictetus' *Manual*) at the beginning of the curriculum, as a form of mental preparation; the mathematics, in this context, must be pure Platonic theorizing, since the *Corpus Aristotelicum* contains no mathematical work to speak of. As regards the duration of the course, Marinus (*vit. Pr.* 13) mentions that Syrianus took Proclus through the whole of Aristotelian philosophy (logic, ethics, politics, physics, metaphysics) in not quite two years, though this was clearly exceptional. With the ethics and politics left out, two years may eventually have become normal.

From Marinus (*vit. Pr.* 23) we learn also that Proclus taught as many as five classes a day, not counting evening sessions. This is again said to show Proclus' excessive zeal and cannot be considered usual, but it is still likely that Olympiodorus taught more than the advanced courses in Aristotle and Plato alone. There are several possibilities to be considered: (1) mathematics, i.e. the quadrivium, (2) medicine, (3) rhetoric, (4) the somewhat mysterious *enkyklioi exegeseis*, which he mentions twice himself (1 § 11; 4 § 8). The tangible evidence for most of these is of the slightest.

Mathematics was certainly still a part of the program in the Alexandrian school. Ps.-Elias (19,30), half a century or more after Olympiodorus, lists the standard authors read in the quadrivium course: Nicomachus and Diophantus in arithmetic; Euclid (conjectural, but virtually certain; called ὁ στοιχειωτής by Elias, *cat.* 251.18) and Hero in geometry; Aristoxenus in musicology, Paulus and Theodosius in astronomy. But David (64.32–65.3) quotes Olympiodorus as saying that music had become a legend in his day, while there were 'remnants' only of the other branches; he adds himself that books on music were still available, but Olympiodorus evidently refers to the teaching program. It may by this time have been customary for the professor of philosophy to take care of the course in mathematics: in any case, Ammonius lectured on Nicomachus' *Isagoge* (reports by Asclepius and Philoponus are extant [45]) and, as mentioned before, it looks as if we have Olympiodorus' own lectures on the astrological work of Paulus of Alexandria, astrology being, already to the great Ptolemy, the practical part of astronomy.

---

[44] Amm., *cat.* 5.31–6.20; Philop., *cat.* 5.15–6.16; Ol., *cat.* 8.29–10.2; El., *cat.* 117.15–121.19.

[45] See bibliography.

Medicine took an ever larger place, according as the importance of philosophy decreased.[46] Elias (*isag.* 6.7–9) refers to his own course on Galen *De sectis*, and his lectures are usually faithful copies of his master's; though Olympiodorus himself makes no such statement, he was certainly familiar enough with Hippocrates for teaching on an elementary level; this is, in fact, the most obvious explanation for his frequent quotations.[47]

As for rhetoric, we have little more to go by than Olympiodorus' general familiarity with the classics (Homer, Euripides, Demosthenes) and an occasional reference to a rule for literary composition.[48] Of course, Syrianus and Damascius had also been professors of rhetoric at some time in their career; and we find rhetoric, too, adopting some of the didactic practices of the Alexandrian school.[49]

The question remains whether some of these rather divergent subjects may have been taught by Olympiodorus in the so-called *enkyklioi exegeseis*, if I have explained the expression correctly (1 § 11.6, note) as denoting a general education course addressing itself to a larger audience. When Philoponus, *anal. post.* 157.2–6, defining the *enkyklia mathemata*, describes them as open to all and contrasts them with specialisms such as medicine and rhetoric, this does not necessarily mean that these subjects were not included at an elementary level. All we know for certain, however, is that there was an introduction to philosophy. In the first occurrence of the term, 1 § 11.6, Olympiodorus sounds as if he is referring to a course of his own; this is less likely at 4 § 8, and practically out of the question in the case of Elias, *isag.* 27.1–8.

Most of the Neoplatonists wrote poetry on occasion. Porphyry (*vit. Plot.* 15) mentions a poem on the 'Sacred Marriage', which he recited on Plato Day. Iamblichus composed hymns (Dam., *Phil.* § 19.5), and so did Proclus, Asclepiodotus (Dam., *vit. Isid.* 179.6–7), Isidorus (*ibid.* 90.1-3), Heraiscus (*ibid.* 138.27-139.1) and Syrianus (*Hymn to Achilles*, Zosimus IV, 18,4). We have epigrams by Syrianus (*Anthol. Pal.* 9, 358), Proclus (ed. Vogt p. 34), Damascius (*Anthol. Pal.* 7, 553) and Simplicius (Pr., *Tim.* I 468.14-16); Damascius, as a young man, also wrote a panegyric in hexameters which he recited at Aedesia's funeral (*vit. Isid.* 107.20-22). Olympiodorus continued the tradition. Two samples have been preserved, both hexameter couplets. One is a reflection inspired by Callimachus' epigram on Cleombrotus (Dav. 31.34-32.2; cf. El., *isag.* 14.8-10), the other defends the authenticity of the *Categories* (El., *cat.* 133.24-26), imitating Syrianus' lines on the *Phaedo*. If they have no other merit, they at least show that Olympiodorus could still write a correct hexameter.

---

[46] Cf. my paper *Philosophy and Medicine in Late Antiquity*, Janus 51, 1964, 169–177.

[47] See *indices locorum* Ol., *Gorg.*, *Alc.* (add 55.3–4=*aphor.* II 38), *Ph.*, *cat.*, *mete.*; cf. also *infra* 2 § 15.2–3 (and note) and 4 § 7.7–8.

[48] *Alc.* 104.3–6; *Ph.* 2 § 7.7.

[49] *Prolegomenon sylloge*, ed. H. Rabe, Leipzig 1931, Nos. 1, 2, 5.

III. Olympiodorus on the Phaedo

The Venice MS. has preserved little more than a quarter of Olympiodorus' commentary on the *Phaedo*: thirteen lectures out of about fifty, covering sixteen of the sixty-two Stephanus pages of the dialogue. At the beginning, the general introduction and the commentary on 57a1–61c9 are missing. This would normally be the equivalent of four or five lectures, or 10–12 leaves; if the marginal note in the MS. is correct, only 6 leaves, or 2–3 lectures, are lost, but then the format of the exemplar may have been larger. Two more lectures (5 leaves according to another marginal note) are missing between 12 and 13, dealing with 75c7?–78b4; after lecture 13 the rest of the exemplar was lost (80a10–118a17).

Since Olympiodorus and Damascius both follow the same division of the dialogue (Proclus's), it is easy to reconstruct the plan.

In the introductory lectures to the *Gorgias* and the *Alcibiades*, Olympiodorus does not discuss all of the eight points that were more or less compulsory in the course on Aristotle: *skopos*, or central theme, usefulness, order of treatment, title, authenticity, division, form of presentation, branch of philosophy to which the work belongs. In the *Phaedo*, too, he was probably content to discuss a selection of the more important ones.

Since Iamblichus, the establishing of the *skopos* was the essential part of the introduction. According tot he *Prolegomena philosophiae Platonicae* (27), since the *skopos* must be one, it is wrong to admit a threefold theme for the *Phaedo*, viz. immortality, the death of the wise, and the philosophical life. The actual formula arrived at is not known, but it must have been something like the life of purification (περὶ καθαρτικοῦ βίου). This also marks its place in the curriculum (τάξις): the *Phaedo* should follow the *Alcibiades* (introductory) and the *Gorgias* (on life in society), and precede the rest of the ten dialogues, which are all 'contemplative' (*Proleg.* 26.25–27). The disposition of the dialogue, as well as the question of its main divisions, called 'sections' (τμήματα) by Olympiodorus (8 § 7; 9 title), 'parts' (μέρη) by Damascius (I § 466; II § 81), should be related to the central theme: the first part deals with death, i.e. the separation of the soul from the body, the second with the immortality of the soul, the third with the condition of the disembodied soul.

They are preceded by the 'proem' of the dialogue, in which the stage is set and the characters are presented. The theory of its interpretation is outlined by Proclus, *Alc.* 18.13–19.10 (and *Proleg.* 16), again, of course, in relation to the *skopos*. The characters are given a metaphysical or epistemological explanation, each according to the degree of his perfection. This portion is lost, as is all the rest of the introductory matter, both in Olympiodorus and Damascius; a sample is extant in the scene of the interruption by the jailer (Ol. 2 § 8; Dam. I §§ 46–47).

The general title of part I ('on death') is not extant. It is subdivided into two 'problems': 'on suicide' and 'on the will to die' (Ol. 1 § 23; Dam. I § 165.4–5). The second problem, in its turn, contains the three *καθαρτικοὶ λόγοι*, or 'reasons for detachment': (1) soul and body; (2) soul by itself; (3) soul and form (Dam. I § 66).

Part II, which forms the nucleus of the dialogue, consists of the five arguments for immortality (Ol. 2 § 7; 8 § 7; *mete.* 144.14–15): (I) the argument from opposites (Ol. 10 § 5; § 16; Dam. I § 66; § 107; II § 1 title); (II) the argument from recollection (Ol. 11 § 1 title; 13 § 4; Dam. I § 66; § 242); (III) the argument from similarity to things intelligible (Ol. 13 § 1; § 4; Dam. I § 66; § 215; § 220; Pr., *theol.* I 26, p. 113.18–19 S.-W.); (IV) the argument on harmony (Dam. I § 183; § 361 title); (V) the final argument on the essence of the soul (Ol. 11 § 2; 13 § 4; Dam. I § 183; II § 66 title).

Part III is the myth, or *νέκυια* (Dam. I § 466; II § 81). It is again subdivided into three parts: (1) transition; (2) description of the Earth; (3) destinations of souls (Dam. II § 84). The epilogue, the death of Socrates, is not marked or mentioned separately.

A general table of contents would look as follows:

	Ol.	Dam. I	Dam. II
Introduction	–	–	–
Proem (57a1–61c9)	–	–	–
Part One: On Death:			
First Problem: Suicide (61c9–62c8)	1	1–25	–
Second Problem: The Will to Die			
(62c9–69e5)	2–8	26–175	–
Part Two: On Immortality:			
I. Opposites (69e6–72e2)	9–10	176–252	1–3
II. Recollection (72e3–78b3)	11–12**	253–310	4–28
III. Similarity (78b4–85b9)	13**	311–360	29–44
IV. Harmony (85b10–95e6)	–	361–406	45–65
V. Essence of Soul (95e7–107b10)	–	407–465	66–80
Part Three: The Myth:			
i. Transition (107c1–108c5)	–	466–502	81–113
ii. The Earth (108c5–113c8)	–	503–542	114–145
iii. Destinations (113d1–114c8)	–	543–551	146–148
Epilogue (114d1–118a17)	–	552–562	149–157

IV. THE TEXT

The volume containing Olympiodorus' three (or more?) commentaries on Plato shared the fate of the majority of Neoplatonic writings: it survived long enough to be saved thanks to the renewed interest in Platonism during the first Byzantine Renaissance, but in a mutilated and neglected condition.[50] It is impossible to say whether it is substantially the holdings of one library that have come down to us in this way, or rather various smaller collections and stray items. If the former is the case, the collection must have reached Constantinople by way of Alexandria (presumably with Stephanus, under Heraclius), since the Athenians would hardly have bothered to provide themselves with copies of Olympiodorus' lectures.

However this may be, about 900 A.D. an unknown scholar with a strong interest in Platonism possessed a number of fine vellum codices, of which at least nine have been preserved (entirely or partially):[51] (1) Paris. gr. 1807, Plato A; (2) Marc. gr. 246, Dam., princ. and Parm.; (3) Paris. gr. 1962, Maximus Tyrius and Alcinous; (4) Paris. suppl. gr. 921, Pr., Tim. palimpsest fragment; (5) Laur. 80,9 + Vat., gr. 2197, Pr., Rep.; (6) Palat. Heid. gr. 398, Paradoxographi; (7) Marc. gr. 196, Ol., Gorg., Alc., Ph. + Dam., Ph., Phil.; (8) Marc. gr. 258, Alexander Aphr.; (9) Marc. gr. 226, Simpl., phys. V–VIII.

A possible connection with this group may be considered for three more texts of which no copies belonging to this early period are extant, namely (1) Plotinus; (2) Ammonius on the De interpretatione (same type of marginalia in both);[52] (3) Hermias on the Phaedrus (schol. at 13.3–4 cites Ol., Alc. 2.64–65, but cf. schol. Pl. TW Phaedr. 227a; further some lines of iambic verse, on which see below).

It has been suggested that the owner may have been Leo the Philosopher, i.e. Leo Choerosphactes,[53] who is, besides Arethas, the only one in this period known to have engaged seriously in Platonic studies. A small point of interest in this connection is that the scholiast occasionally uses iambic verse of the type written also by Choerosphactes (Byzantine trimeters, with here and there some freedom in the use of dichrona). Though I have found no especially striking correspondences, and the fact by itself is hardly evidence (especially as long as the relationship between the owner, the scholiast and the revisor has not been firmly established), I list the occurrences here.

Ol., Gorg. 1.1 Ὀλύμπιον δώρημα πεμφθεὶς τῷ βίῳ / χρυσῆν Ἀλεξάνδρειαν ἔσχες πατρίδα. – Alc. 94.12 Βίαντος υἱοῦ Τευτάμου Πριηνέως. – Ibid. 160.9 Εἰ καὶ μάλιστα δριμὺς εὐνοῦχος τύχοι / Ἡφαιστόπους τε μιξοβάρβαρος γένος. (Another outburst against eunuchs, but in prose, schol. Pr., Tim. I 460.20–21.) – Vatopedi MS. 655 f. 2ʳ (a copy of Palat. gr. 398, of which this part is lost) Ὁ τῶν γραφέντων ὧδε βιβλίων πίναξ. – Paris, gr. 1962

---

[50] Details in Pr., theol. I, introd. CLV; add Pr., Crat. (end missing) and Hermias, Phaedr. (large lacuna at 108.3).

[51] T. W. Allen, A Group of Ninth-century Greek Manuscripts, Journ. of Philol. 21, 1893, 48–55. J. Whittaker, cited above, n. 10.

[52] H. Arts, De scholiën op vijf Griekse filosofen, Plato, Plotinus, Olympiodorus, Ammonius en Proclus (diss. lic. Louvain 1962; not publ.).

[53] Cf. Beck, op. cit. 594–595. But Westerink later noted that he considered this suggestion to be wrong.

f. 146ᵛ ʿΗ βίβλος ἥδε ταῦτ' ἔχει γεγραμμένα. – End of schol. Dam., princ. 51.22
... αὕτη δὲ τούτων οὐδὲν ὡς ἀνείδεος (probably accidental; proparoxytone).
– Hermias 108.3 (lacuna in the text) Τί δὴ τὸν εἰρμὸν ἐξέκοψας τοῦ λόγου /
ἄφνω στερήσας ἡδονῆς ἀθανάτου; – Ibid. 266 (end of text; cf. 94.21 and
168.24) ʿΟ πρῶτος ʿΕρμῆς μνημονεύσας ἐν βίῳ / τρίτον γενέσθαι καὶ σοφὸν
τοσαυτάκις / ἐπωνομάσθη τρισμέγιστος εἰκότως· / ὁ δεύτερος δὲ πανσόφως
σαφηνίσας / τὸν τοῦ Πλάτωνος Φαῖδρον ἐν τρισὶν βίβλοις / τρισόλβιος καλοῖτ'
ἂν οὐκ ἀπὸ τρόπου.⁵⁴

Some time, this may help to identify the poet; for the moment, the
lines on Olympiodorus and Hermias, in both cases puns on their names,
suggest that the writer may have been the same. (Cf. Leo the philosopher
on Porphyry, A.P. 9, 214).

The revisor of Marc. gr. 196, whoever he was, added the marginalia
and collated the copy with the two originals (Olympiodorus and Damascius),
supplying omissions (e.g. Ol. 2 § 16.2; 8 § 6.1; 9 § 4.4; 11 § 6.8–9; 13 § 3.2–3)
and filling blanks where the copyist had been unable to decipher the
original (Ol. 13 § 8.6; § 15.8; Dam. I § 23.3; § 232.9; § 505.2–3). Some
of these supplements are conjectural, others are certainly not, such as
Ol. 13 § 3.2–3; § 15.8; Dam. I § 232.9. He further corrected the spelling
carefully, and collated the lemmata with a codex of Plato, which had
the readings of BW at 65b3 (Ol. 4 § 13.1) and 73c6 (11 § 15.1), of BTW
at 65e1–2 (5 § 8.1), of BTY at 71a12 (10 § 10.1), of BT²Y at 9 § 9.1,
of TY at 10 § 6.1 and § 11.1, of W at 66b4 (5 § 14.1), of Y at 62d6
(2 § 9.1). The rareness of readings peculiar to TY is noteworthy in view
of the current theory⁵⁴ᵃ that T is a descendant of the lost first volume
of A (i.e. Paris. gr. 1807, which to all appearances was once owned by
the possessor of the Marcianus). The variant τε Mᶜ Pl. Y instead of γε
at 62d6 is hardly significant enough to affect the evaluation of Y.⁵⁵

Shortly after their production, two of the precious volumes owned by
the unknown Platonist disappeared completely from view for over five
hundred years: throughout the Middle Ages there is no trace of the
commentaries of Olympiodorus and Damascius on Plato, or of Damascius
De principiis and In Parmenidem. No transcripts are known and, what
is perhaps even more telling, Michael Psellus, who bought every Platonist
volume he could lay his hands on, was obviously unaware of their
existence. There are two conceivable explanations: either the codices
went to the West at an early date, a possibility suggested to me by H.-
D. Saffrey, on the ground of some marginal notes in Latin⁵⁵ᵃ (little more
than the name Aristoteles wherever it occurs in the text); or else they
must have been stored in the palace, the patriarchate or one of the larger
monasteries, an institution, in any case, that lasted throughout those
five centuries. A possible assumption would then be that they were first

---

⁵⁴ Schol. Strab. A (86ᵛ) on III, 161c. Καῖσαρ θεός σός, νῷ διά<σ>προφε Στράβων
(Diller p. 35). A is a transcript of a lost MS. of the group, according to Diller. The same line
is in the Strabo Chrestomathy of Palat. 398 (F. 75²).
⁵⁴ᵃ Carlini, op. cit. 160. Diller, The Scholia on Strabo, Traditio 10, 1954. 31.
⁵⁵ Ibid. 161–163. ⁵⁵ᵃ Maybe Bessarion, cf. Marc. 24b, f IIᵛ

deliberately withdrawn from circulation and after that lay forgotten in a closet or chest.

During the Middle Ages, Olympiodorus was known only for his work on Aristotle, and more especially for the commentary on the *Meteorology*. After his commentaries on Plato had turned up in Bessarion's library, there was a modest but regular demand for written copies during the fifteenth and sixteenth centuries;[56] the two commentaries of Damascius, which followed in the archetype without their author's name, were as a matter of course added to Olympiodorus' literary property. None of the five appeared in print before the nineteenth century.

---

[56]   Listed Ol., *Ph.* (ed. Norvin), praef. VII–X; Dam., *Phil.*, introd. XII–XIV.

ABBREVIATIONS

LITERATURE

Beierwaltes: W. Beierwaltes, *Proklos, Grundzüge seiner Metaphysik*, Frankfurt am Main [1965].
Beutler, art. Ol.: R. Beutler, *RE* art. Olympiodoros (13), vol. 18,1, 1939, 207–228.
Beutler, art. Pr.: id., *RE* art. Proklos (4), vol. 23, 1957, 186–247.
Courcelle: P. Courcelle, *Les lettres grecques en occident*, Paris 1943.
Des Places: see Chald. Or.
Dodds: see Pr., *elem.*
Finckh: see Ol., *Ph.*
Kroll: see *Chald. Or.*
Lewy: H. Lewy, *Chaldaean Oracles and Theurgy*, Cairo 1956.
LSJ : Liddell-Scott-Jones, *A Greek-English Lexicon*.
Norvin: see Ol., *Ph.*
Norvin, 1915: W. Norvin, *Olympiodoros fra Alexandria og hans commentar til Platons Phaidon*. Copenhagen 1915.
Pépin: J. Pépin, *Mythe et allégorie*, Paris [1958].
RE: Pauly-Wissowa-Kroll, *Realencyclopädie der classischen Altertumswissenschaft.*
Rosán: L. J. Rosán, *The Philosophy of Proclus*, New York 1949.
Theiler: W. Theiler, *Forschungen zum Neuplatonismus*, Berlin 1966.

TEXTS

Alb., *isag.*: Albinus, *Isagoge*, ed. C. F. Hermann, *Platonis Dialogi* VI, Leipzig 1853, 147–151.
Alcin., *did.*: Alcinous, *Didascalicus, ibid.* 152–187=Albinos, *Epitomé*, ed. P. Louis, Paris 1945.
Alex., *met.*: Alexander, *In metaphysica, CAG* I.
Alex., *top.*: Alexander, *In topica, CAG* II 2.
Amm., *anal. pr.*: Ammonius, *In analytica priora, CAG* IV 6.
Amm., *cat.*: Ammonius, *In categorias, CAG* IV 4.
Amm., *int.*: Ammonius, *De interpretatione, CAG* IV 5.
Amm., *isag.*: Ammonius, *In Porphyrii Quinque voces, CAG* IV 3.
Ar.: Aristotle.
Ascl., *met.*: Asclepius, *In metaphysica, CAG* VI 2.
Ascl., *Nicom.*: Asclepius, *Commentary to Nicomachus' Introduction to Arithmetic*, ed. L. Tarán, Philadelphia 1969.
Atticus: *Fragments*, ed. E. des Places (to appear Paris 1976).
CAG : *Commentaria in Aristotelem Graeca*, ed. Acad. litt. reg. Boruss., Berlin 1882–1909.
Chald. Or.: *Oracles chaldaïques*, ed. E. des Places, Paris 1971.
Chald. Or.: W. Kroll, *De oraculis Chaldaicis*, Breslau 1894 (repr. Hildesheim 1962).
CPG : *Corpus Paroemiographorum Graecorum*, edd. Leutsch-Schneidewin, 2 vols., Göttingen 1839–51 (repr. Hildesheim 1958).
Dam., *Parm.*: Damascius, *In Parmenidem*, ed. C. A. Ruelle, *Damascii Dubitationes et solutiones*, Paris 1889 (repr. Amsterdam 1966), II 5–322.
Dam., *Ph.*: Damascius, *On the Phaedo* (vol. II of this ed.).
Dam., *Phil.*: Damascius, *On the Philebus*, ed. Westerink, Amsterdam 1959.
Dam., *princ.*: Damascius, *De principiis*, ed. C. A. Ruelle, *Damascii Dubitationes et solutiones*, I; II 1–4.

Dam., *vit. Isid.*: Damascius, *Vitae Isidori reliquiae*, ed. C. Zintzen, Hildesheim 1967.
Dav.: David, *In isagogen*, *CAG* XVIII 2.
El., *anal. pr.*: Elias, *On the Prior Analytics*, ed. L. G. Westerink, Mnemosyne, S. IV, 14, 1961, 126–139.
El., *cat.*: Elias, *In categorias*, *CAG* XVIII 1, 105–255.
El., *isag.*: Elias, *In isagogen*, *CAG* XVIII 1, 1–104.
Eunap., *vit. soph.*: Eunapius, *Vitae sophistarum*, ed. G. Giangrande, Rome 1956.
FHG: *Fragmenta Historicorum Graecorum*, ed. C. Müller, Paris 1841–70.
Fihrist: *Kitâb-al-Fihrist*, hrsg. von G. Flügel, Leipzig 1871–72 (repr. Beirut 1964).
Fihrist: *The Fihrist of al-Nadim*, transl. Bayard Dodge, vol. II, New York and London 1970.
Gnomol. Vat.: *Gnomologium Vaticanum*, ed. L. Sternbach, Wiener Studien 9–11, 1887–1889; repr. Berlin 1963.
Harpocratio: Fragments, ed. J. M. Dillon, California Studies in Class. Ant. 4, 1971, 125–146.
Heliodorus: *Heliodori ut dicitur in Paulum Alexandrinum commentarium*, ed. Ae. Boer, Leipzig 1962.
Hermias: *Hermiae Alexandrini in Platonis Phaedrum scholia*, ed. P. Couvreur, Paris 1901.
Hierocl., *carm. aur.*: Hierocles, *In aureum carmen*, ed. F. W. A. Mullach, *Fragm. philos. Gr.* I, Paris 1857, 416–484.
Iambl., *comm. math.*: Iamblichus, *De communi mathematica scientia*, ed. N. Festa, Leipzig 1891.
Iambl., *myst.*: Iamblichus, *Les mystères d'Egypte*, ed. E. des Places, Paris 1966.
Iambl., *protr.*: Iamblichus, *Protrepticus*, ed. H. Pistelli, Leipzig 1888.
Iambl., *vit. Pyth.*: Iamblichus, *De vita Pythagorica*, ed. L. Deubner, Leipzig 1927.
Iambl., *frgs.*: Iamblichus, *In Platonicos dialogos commentariorum fragmenta*, ed. J. M. Dillon, Leiden 1973.
Marin., *vit. Pr.*: Marinus, *Vita Procli*, ed. J. F. Boissonade, Leipzig 1814.
Numenius: *Fragments*, ed. E. des Places, Paris 1973.
 E. A. Leemans, *Studie over den wijsgeer Numenius van Apamea met uitgave der fragmenten*, Brussels 1937.
Ol., *Alc.*: Olympiodorus, *On the Alcibiades*, ed. Westerink, Amsterdam 1956.
Ol., *cat.*: Olympiodorus, *In categorias*, *CAG* XII 1.
Ol., *Gorg.*: Olympiodorus, *In Gorgiam*, ed. Westerink, Leipzig 1970.
Ol., *mete.*: Olympiodorus, *In meteora*, CAG XII 2.
Ol., *Ph.*: Olympiodorus, *In Phaedonem*, ed. Norvin, Leipzig 1913. Ed. C. E. Finckh, Heilbronn 1847. Ed. A. Mustoxydes – D. Schinas, Venice 1816.
Orphica: O. Kern, *Orphicorum fragmenta*, Berlin 1922 (repr. 1963).
Panaetius: *Panaetii Rhodii fragmenta*, ed. M. van Straaten, [3] Leiden 1962.
PG: J. P. Migne, *Patrologiae cursus completus*, Series Graeca.
Philop., *aet.*: Philoponus, *De aeternitate mundi*, ed. H. Rabe, Leipzig 1899.
Philop., *an.*: Philoponus, *De anima*, *CAG* XV.
Philop., *anal. pr.*: Philoponus. *In analytica priora*, *CAG* XIII 2.
Philop., *anal. post.*: Philoponus, *In analytica posteriora*, *CAG* XIII 3.
Philop., *cat.*: Philoponus, *In categorias*, *CAG* XIII 1.
Philop., *mete.*: Philoponus, *In meteora*, *CAG* XIV 1.
Philop., *Nicom.*: Philoponus, *In Nicomachi arithmeticam introductionem*, ed. R. Hoche, Wesel 1864–67.
Philop., *phys.*: Philoponus, *In physica*, *CAG* XVI–XVII.
Porph., *abst.*: Porphyrius, *De abstinentia*, ed. Nauck (*Porphyrii opuscula selecta*, [2] Leipzig 1886).
Porph., *de antro*: Porphyrius, *The Cave of the Nymphs*, ed. Seminar Cl. 609, Buffalo 1969.
Porph., *isag.*: Porphyrius, *Isagoge*, *CAG* IV 1.

Porph., *sent.*: Porphyrius, *Sententiae ad intelligibilia ducentes*, ed. E. Lamberz, Leipzig 1975.

Porph., *vit. Plot.*: Porphyrius, *Vita Plotini* (*Plotini opera*, edd. Henry-Schwyzer, I, Paris-Brussels 1951).

Porph., *vit. Pyth.*: Porphyrius, *Vita Pythagorae*, ed. Nauck (see above).

Priscian., *solut.*: Priscianus, *Solutiones ad Chosroem*, ed. Bywater, Suppl. Ar. I 2, Berlin 1886.

Pr., *Alc.*: Proclus, *On the Alcibiades*, ed. Westerink, Amsterdam 1954.

Pr., *Crat.*: Proclus, *In Cratylum*, ed. G. Pasquali, Leipzig 1908.

Pr., *de arte hier.*: Proclus, *De arte hieratica*, ed. J. Bidez (*Catalogue des manuscrits alchimiques grecs* VI, Brussels 1928, 148–151).

Pr., *decem dub.*: Proclus, *De decem dubitationibus*, ed. H. Boese (*Procli Tria opuscula*, Berlin 1960, 3–108).

Pr., *elem.*: Proclus, *The Elements of Theology*, ed. E. R. Dodds, ² Oxford 1963.

Pr., *Hes.*: Proclus, in: *Scholia vetera in Hesiodi opera et dies*, ed. A. Pertusi, Milan 1955.

Pr., *hymns*: Proclus, *Hymni*, ed. E. Vogt, Wiesbaden 1957.

Pr., *inst. phys.*: Proclus, *Institutio physica*, ed. A. Ritzenfeld, Leipzig 1912.

Pr., *Parm.*: Proclus, *In Parmenidem*, ed. V. Cousin, *Procli opera*, Paris 1864 (repr. Hildesheim 1961).

Pr., *prov.*: Proclus, *De providentia et fato*, ed. Boese, *op. cit.* 109–171.

Pr., *Rep.*: Proclus, *In Rempublicam*, ed. W. Kroll, 2 vols., Leipzig 1899–1901 (repr. Amsterdam 1965).

Pr., *theol.*: Proclus, *Théologie platonicienne*, Livres I/II, edd. Saffrey-Westerink, Paris 1968/74.

In theologiam Platonis, ed. Portus, Hamburg 1618 (repr. Frankfurt am Main 1960).

Pr., *Tim.*: Proclus, *In Timaeum*, ed. E. Diehl, 3 vols., Leipzig 1903–06 (repr. Amsterdam 1965).

Proleg.: *Anonymous Prolegomena to Platonic Philosophy*, ed. Westerink, Amsterdam 1962.

Ps.-El.: Pseudo-Elias (Pseudo-David), *On Porphyry's Isagoge*, ed. Westerink, Amsterdam 1967.

Psell., *de aurea catena*: ed. C. Sathas, *Sur les commentaires byzantins relatifs aux comédies de Ménandre, aux poèmes d'Homère, etc.*, Annuaire de l'Association 9, 1875, 1–36 (29–33).

Psell., *omnif. doctr.*: *De omnifaria doctrina*, ed. Westerink, Nijmegen-Utrecht 1948.

Psell., *orac. Chald.*: *Commentaire des Oracles chaldaïques*, in *Chald. Or.*, ed. Des Places, 163–186.

Salustius, *de diis*: ed. G. Rochefort, Paris 1960.

Schol. Pl.: *Scholia Platonica*, ed. W. C. Greene, Haverford 1938.

Simpl., *an.*: Simplicius, *De anima*, *CAG* XI.

Simpl., *cael.*: Simplicius, *De caelo*, *CAG* VII.

Simpl., *cat.*: Simplicius, *In categorias*, *CAG* VIII.

Simpl., *Epict.*: Simplicius, *In Epicteti enchiridion*, ed. F. Dübner (in: *Theophrasti characteres*, etc., Paris 1840).

Simpl., *phys.*: Simplicius, *In physica*, *CAG* IX–X.

Steph., *an.*: Stephanus, *De anima*=Philop., *an.*, lib. III, pp. 406–607.

Steph., *aphor.*: Stephanus, *In aphorismos* I–II: MS. Paris. gr. 2222. III–IV: MS. Escor. Σ.II.10.

Steph., *progn.*: Stephanus, *In prognosticon*, ed. F. R. Dietz in *Scholia in Hippocratem et Galenum*, Königsberg 1834 (repr. Amsterdam 1966) I 51–232.

SVF: *Stoicorum veterum fragmenta*, ed. H. von Arnim, 4 vols., Leipzig 1905–24 (repr. Stuttgart 1964).

Theodorus of Asine: W. Deuse, *Theodoros von Asine, Sammlung der Testimonien und Kommentar*, Wiesbaden 1973.

SIGLA

M Marcianus graecus 196 Z., ca. a. 900

M¹ scriba in scribendo aut corrigendo

Mᶜ corrector, qui et titulos et marginalia adscripsit

Mˣ utrum M¹ an Mᶜ incertum

Mʳ manus Bessarionis in margine

Mˢ alia manus recens

μ apographa

Fh Finckh

Nv Norvin

Wk Westerink

Fischer Joh. Fr. Fischer, *Platonis Euthyphro*, etc., Leipzig 1783.

Wyttenbach D. Wyttenbach, *Platonis Phaedo*, Leiden 1810.

⟨ ⟩ addenda

[[ ]] delenda

* * lacuna

OLYMPIODORUS

1

Lecture **

1. Yet he will not, I suppose, do violence to himself, for they say it is unlawful [61c9–62c9].

Socrates has remarked that Euenus, if a philosopher, will be willing to die; then, to avoid the impression that these words are meant as a recommendation of voluntary death, he adds: 'Yet he will not, I suppose, do violence to himself, for suicide is an impious deed to commit'. In the text this is proved by two arguments, one mythical and Orphic, the other dialectical and philosophical.

2. Before turning to the text, however, let us show by arguments of our own this very point, that suicide is not permissible.

(1) If God has two kinds of powers, elevative and providential, and if those by which he extends his providential care to secondary beings do not impede his powers of elevation and conversion upon himself, but he exercises both simultaneously, then there is no reason why the

---

Lect. 1. On suicide: the mythical and the philosophical argument. Socrates states two reasons why we are not free to dispose of our own lives: (i) according to a sacred tradition, we are in a sort of 'custody', from which we must not set ourselves free (the mythical argument); (ii) the Gods are our masters and take care of us (the philosophical argument). Ol., after mentioning these two arguments (§ 1), first discusses three additional ones against suicide (§ 2), then deals with the mythical (§§ 3–6) and the philosophical argument (§ 7); next he states the case for suicide, based on the authority of Pl., Plotinus and the Stoa (§ 8), and ends with a conclusion of his own, in which suicide is not unconditionally rejected (§ 9). Most of this material bears the stamp of Pr., but as Dam. I is incomplete, starting in the middle of the discussion of the mythical argument, we have no means to verify in how far Ol. was directly indebted to Pr. or Dam. In Ol.'s successors (El., *isag.* 12.3–16.8; Dav. 29.12–34.12; Ps.-El. 12–13) the subject-matter of §§ 1–2 and 8 belongs to the standard content of the introductions to philosophy which precede the commentaries on Porphyry's *Isag.*, the context being the third definition of philosophy as 'preparation for death'. There is little of this in Amm. (*isag.* 4.15–5.27), so that it was apparently introduced (i.e. transferred from the *Ph.* commentaries) by Ol., whose own commentary on the *Isag.* is lost. See Westerink, *Elias und Plotin*, Byz. Zeitschr. 57, 1964, 26–32.

§ 1. 5–7. Cf. schol. Pl. 10.9–13.

§ 2. The principles underlying arguments (1) and (2) are formulated by Pr.,

1

$\langle Π ρ \tilde{α} ξ ι ς \ σ ὺ ν \ θ ε \tilde{ῷ} \rangle$ (1)

Οὐ μέντοι ἴσως βιάσεται αὐτόν· οὐ γάρ φασι θεμιτὸν εἶναι 1
[61c9–62c9].

Εἰπὼν ὁ Σωκράτης ὅτι εἰ φιλοσοφεῖ ὁ Εὔηνος ἐθελήσει ἀποθνήσκειν, ἵνα μὴ δόξῃ διὰ τούτων παρεγγυᾶν ἡμῖν τὸν ἑκούσιον θάνατον, φησὶν ὅτι 'οὐ μέντοι ἴσως βιάσεται ἑαυτόν· καὶ γὰρ ἀνόσιον τὸ ἐξαγαγεῖν ἑαυτόν'. καὶ τοῦτο ἡ μὲν λέξις 5 δείκνυσι διὰ δύο ἐπιχειρημάτων, ἑνὸς μὲν μυθικοῦ καὶ Ὀρφικοῦ, ἑτέρου δὲ διαλεκτικοῦ καὶ φιλοσόφου.

Ἡμεῖς δὲ πρὸ τῆς λέξεως φέρε οἰκείοις ἐπιχειρήμασι τοῦτο αὐτὸ δείξωμεν, 2 ὅτι οὐ δεῖ ἐξαγαγεῖν ἑαυτούς.

α΄ Εἰ τοῦ θεοῦ διττὰς ἔχοντος δυνάμεις, ἀναγωγούς τε καὶ προνοητικάς, μὴ ἐμποδίζονται αἱ προνοητικαὶ τῶν δευτέρων δυνάμεις ὑπὸ τῶν ἀναγωγῶν καὶ αὐτεπιστρόφων, ἀλλ᾽ ἅμα κατὰ ἄμφω ἐνεργεῖ, οὕτως οὖν καὶ τὸν φιλόσοφον 5

---

§ 1. 1 μέντοι] μέντοι γε Pl. B²W | βιάσεται M¹: βιάζεται Mᶜ | αὐτὸν] ἑαυτὸν Pl. W — 3 φιλοσοφεῖ ὁ Mˣ: φιλόσοφο≡ M¹ | Εὔηνος M¹ (hic et infra 7 § 1.7): Εὐηνός Mᶜ — 4 fort. τὸν ἑκούσιον θάνατον
§ 2. 1 δείξωμεν μ: -ομεν M — 4 ἐμποδίζονται M¹: -ωνται Mᶜ — 5 αὐτεπιστρόφων Wk (cf. Ol., Alc. 209.2): αὐταῖς ἐπιστρόφων M

---

elem. 122 Πᾶν τὸ θεῖον καὶ προνοεῖ τῶν δευτέρων καὶ ἐξῄρηται τῶν προνοουμένων, μήτε τῆς προνοίας χαλώσης τὴν ἄμικτον αὐτοῦ καὶ ἑνιαίαν ὑπεροχὴν μήτε τῆς χωριστῆς ἑνώσεως τὴν πρόνοιαν ἀφανιζούσης. μένοντες γὰρ ἐν τῷ ἑνιαίῳ τῷ ἑαυτῶν καὶ ἐν τῇ ὑπάρξει τὰ πάντα πεπληρώκασι τῆς ἑαυτῶν δυνάμεως· καὶ πᾶν τὸ δυνάμενον αὐτῶν μεταλαγχάνειν ἀπολαύει τῶν ἀγαθῶν ὧν δέχεσθαι δύναται κατὰ τὰ μέτρα τῆς οἰκείας ὑποστάσεως, ἐκείνων αὐτῷ τῷ εἶναι, μᾶλλον δὲ προεῖναι, τἀγαθὰ τοῖς οὖσιν ἐπιλαμπόντων. In other words: (1) divine providence does not exclude transcendence; (2) the measure in which its gifts are received depends on the fitness of the recipient. Ol.'s terminology (esp. in lines 3–5 and 7–8) is distinctly Procline, and there can be little doubt that Ol. took this passage from the commentary of Pr., adapting it, however, to the Alexandrian theology, in which the attributes of the different divine orders become functions of the one supreme God (cf. Pr., elem. 151–159 and Dodds' note p. 278; Ol., Gorg. 243.16–244.15). There is already a certain measure of confusion in our text of Ol., for the reference to the Theaet. (lines 14–16) must relate to the first instead of to the second argument; in El. (isag. 15.23), Dav. (30.8–21) and Ps.-El. (12,10–12) only the second argument remains, but it is erroneously presented as a quotation from Plotinus I 9. Argument (3) goes beyond the Ph. only in that it adds the terminological distinction between 'natural' and 'voluntary' death, which occurs already in Amm. (isag. 5.7–27; cf. El. 12.22–13.12; Dav. 31.7–19; Ps.-El. 12,21–29) and also in Macrob. (somn. Scip. I 13,5–8); the common source is obviously Porphyry (cf. sent. 8–9).

philosopher as God's imitator (philosophy being assimilation to God) should not be active creatively and providentially, while at the same time leading a life of purification. For when one is separated from the body after death, detachment is not difficult to achieve, but as long as we are imprisoned in the body, to pursue purification is a noble thing.

(2) In the same way as the Deity is always present to all, and the degree in which each participates in it depends on its own fitness or unfitness, so the soul should be present to the body and not withdraw herself from it, and it will depend on the fitness or unfitness of the body whether it shares in the soul's life or not. Thus Plato in the *Theaetetus* [173c6–174a2] represents the perfect philosopher as not even knowing what kind of man he is himself, and moreover as ignorant of the fact that he does not know this, though he lives in the body.

(3) The voluntary shackle should be unfastened voluntarily, the involuntary shackle involuntarily, and not conversely. That is to say, from natural life, which is involuntary, we should be released in the involuntary way by natural death, while from affective life, which we have chosen of our own free will, we should release ourselves in the voluntary way by purification.

3. So much in addition to the text of Plato. To come to the text itself: as we said already, it establishes by two arguments that suicide is not allowed.

The mythical argument is as follows: in the Orphic tradition [frg. 220] we hear of four reigns. The first is that of Uranus, to which Kronos succeeds after emasculating his father; after Kronos Zeus becomes king having hurled down his father into Tartarus; then Zeus is succeeded by Dionysus, whom, they say, his retainers the Titans tear to pieces through Hera's plotting, and they eat his flesh. Zeus, incensed, strikes them with his thunderbolts, and the soot of the vapors that rise from them becomes the matter from which men are created. Therefore suicide is forbidden,

---

6. ὁμοίωσις γὰρ θεῷ ἡ φιλοσοφία : another of the six standard definitions of philosophy (Amm., *isag.* 3.8–9; El. 16.10; Dav. 34.16; Ps.-El. 10,11), derived from Pl., *Theaet.* 176b1–2.

§§ 3–6. The mythical (Orphic) argument: the four generations of divine kings, and the myth of Dionysus and the Titans (§ 3); ethical interpretation of the divine succession: the four realms are levels of virtue (§ 4–§ 5.9); theological interpretation of the myth of Dionysus: D. as the patron of genesis and of life and death (§ 5.9–§ 6). From the corresponding passage in Dam. I §§ 1–13 (which is essentially Pr., as summed up by Ol. § 3.10–14, with a few points of detail corrected by Dam.), the introductory passage on the Orphic kings is missing, but since Ol. expressly refers to 'the commentators' (§ 4) and for the next sentence there is a very close parallel in Pr., he is probably the source for this paragraph. Some of the illustrating commonplaces in § 6 may have been added by Ol. from his own memory.

§ 3. Of course, there were six, not four, generations of divine monarchs, already

μιμητὴν ὄντα θεοῦ (ὁμοίωσις γὰρ θεῷ ἡ φιλοσοφία) οὐδὲν κωλύει [[ἐνεργεῖν]] ἅμα
καὶ | γενεσιουργῶς ἐνεργεῖν καὶ προνοητικῶς τῶν δευτέρων, οὐ μὴν ἀλλὰ καὶ (2)
καθαρτικῶς. χωρισθέντα μὲν γὰρ τοῦ σώματος μετὰ τὸν θάνατον οὐδὲν μέγα
καθαρτικῶς ζῆν, ἐν δὲ τῷ σώματι κατεχόμενον γενναῖόν ἐστιν ἀντέχεσθαι τῆς
καθάρσεως.   10

β'   Δεύτερον ἐπιχείρημα· ὥσπερ τὸ θεῖον ἀεὶ πᾶσι πάρεστι, καὶ τὰ μὲν αὐτοῦ
δι' οἰκείαν ἐπιτηδειότητα ἢ ἀνεπιτηδειότητα μᾶλλον ἢ ἧττον μετέχει, οὕτως
καὶ τὴν ψυχὴν δεῖ παρεῖναι τῷ σώματι καὶ μὴ χωρίζειν ἑαυτήν, τοῦτο δὲ δι'
οἰκείαν ἐπιτηδειότητα ἢ ἀνεπιτηδειότητα μεθέξει αὐτῆς ἢ οὐ μεθέξει. οὕτω γὰρ
καὶ ἐν τῷ Θεαιτήτῳ [173c6–174a2] ὑποτίθεται τὸν κορυφαῖον φιλόσοφον μηδὲ   15
ὁποῖός ἐστιν εἰδότα, ἀλλὰ καὶ ἀγνοοῦντα ὅτι ἀγνοεῖ, καίτοι ἐν τῷ σώματι ὄντα.

γ'   Τρίτον ἐπιχείρημα· τὸν μὲν ἑκούσιον δεσμὸν ἑκουσίως δεῖ λύειν, τὸν δὲ ἀκούσιον
ἀκουσίῳ λύσει λυτέον καὶ μὴ ἀναμίξ· τὴν μὲν οὖν φυσικὴν ζωὴν ἀκούσιον οὖσαν
ἀκουσίῳ λύσει λυτέον τῷ φυσικῷ θανάτῳ, τὴν δὲ μετ' ἐμπαθείας ζωήν, ἣν
ἡμεῖς κατὰ προαίρεσιν ᾑρησάμεθα, ἑκουσίῳ λύσει λυτέον τῇ καθάρσει.   20

Καὶ ταῦτα μὲν ἔξωθεν· ἡ δὲ λέξις ὡς εἴρηται διὰ δύο ἐπιχειρημάτων κατασκευ-   3
άζει ὅτι οὐ δεῖ ἐξάγειν ἑαυτούς.

α'   Καὶ ἔστι τὸ μυθικὸν ἐπιχείρημα τοιοῦτον· παρὰ τῷ Ὀρφεῖ [frg. 220] τέσσαρες
α' β' βασιλεῖαι παραδίδονται. πρώτη μὲν ἡ τοῦ Οὐρανοῦ, ἣν ὁ Κρόνος διεδέξατο
γ'   ἐκτεμὼν τὰ αἰδοῖα τοῦ πατρός· μετὰ δὲ τὸν Κρόνον ὁ Ζεὺς ἐβασίλευσεν καταταρ- 5
δ'   ταρώσας τὸν πατέρα· εἶτα τὸν Δία διεδέξατο ὁ Διόνυσος, ὅν φασι κατ' ἐπιβουλὴν
τῆς Ἥρας τοὺς περὶ αὐτὸν Τιτᾶνας σπαράττειν καὶ τῶν σαρκῶν αὐτοῦ ἀπο-
γενέσθαι. καὶ τούτους ὀργισθεὶς ὁ Ζεὺς ἐκεραύνωσε, καὶ ἐκ τῆς αἰθάλης τῶν
ἀτμῶν τῶν ἀναδοθέντων ἐξ αὐτῶν ὕλης γενομένης γενέσθαι τοὺς ἀνθρώπους.
οὐ δεῖ οὖν ἐξάγειν ἡμᾶς ἑαυτούς, οὐχ ὅτι, ὡς δοκεῖ λέγειν ἡ λέξις, διότι ἔν τινι 10

---

17 δεῖ λύειν] λ- in ras. 2 litt. Mᶜ (δεῖν λύειν M¹?) — 18 ἀκουσίῳ λύσει] -ι λ- in ras.
2 litt. Mᶜ (ἀκουσίως λύσει M¹?)

---

in Pl.'s version of the myth (*Phil.* 66c8–9): Phanes, Night, Uranus, Kronos, Zeus,
Dionysus; see *Orphica* frg. 107 (esp. Pr., *Tim.* III 168.15–169.9); cf. also Pr.,
Crat. 54.12–55.22. I have no satisfactory explanation for the omission of the first
two, Phanes and Night, who could have been made to correspond to the exemplary
and the hieratic virtues respectively (Dam. I §§ 143–144). There is very little
likelihood that the passage can have come directly from Porphyry (who did use
the *Orphica*), thus representing the pre-Iamblichean form of the scale of virtues
(Porph., *sent.* 32); Ol. seems to have had no direct knowledge of Porphyry's
commentary, there is a clear connection with Pr. (see note on § 4) and we have no
evidence that Porphyry ever added the ethical virtues at the bottom of his list.
It is conceivable that Amm. may have eliminated the two, in order to get rid of
the association both with Orphism and with theurgy; in the extant texts his scale does
not go beyond the contemplative virtues (*int.* 135.19–32; Philop., *cat.* 141.25–142.3).
    6–14. Cf. Dam. I §§ 2–12.

not because, as the text appears to say, we wear the body as a kind of
shackle, for that is manifest, and Socrates would not call it an esoteric
doctrine; but it is forbidden because our bodies belong to Dionysus;
we are, in fact, a part of him, being made of the soot of the Titans who
ate his flesh.

4. Socrates, demonstrating by his very reserve the esoteric character
of the myth, adds nothing but 'that we are in a sort of custody' [62b3–4];
the commentators, however, add the myth from other sources. Its allegorical
meaning is this: just as Empedocles [fr. B 17] said that the intelligible
and the sensible world come into existence alternately, not because the
sensible world begins at this moment, the intelligible world at another
(both, indeed, exist always), but because our soul sometimes lives in
accordance with intelligible reality, and it is then said that the intelligible
world begins, and sometimes in accordance with sensible things, when
the sensible world is said to begin, so, too, these four reigns of Orpheus
[frg. 107] are not sometimes existent, sometimes non-existent, but they
are always there and they represent in mystical language the several
degrees of virtues that our soul can practice, having in herself the tokens of
all the virtues, contemplative, purificatory, civic and ethical. **5.** For either
she practices the contemplative virtues, of which the reign of Uranus
(to begin at the top) is the prototype; hence the name Uranus, which
is derived from 'seeing things above'. Or else she lives the life of purification,

---

11–12. Cf. Dam. I § 1.3–5.

§ 4. 2. οἱ δὲ ἐξηγηταί: the plural sometimes denotes Ol. himself (*Alc.* 9.22–23
and perhaps *Gorg.* 252.14; sim. Steph., *aphor.* IV 28, f. 88ᵛ; IV 61, f. 120ᵛ), sometimes
his predecessors in general: 8 § 4 ('some'), 8 § 9 (where Pr. and Dam. are mentioned)
and 13 § 4 ('all the others' as opposed to Iamblichus). Here, Syrianus and Pr.
seem to be meant in particular, cf. the reference to Empedocles (lines 3–7) with
Pr., *Tim.* II 69.23–27 τὰ δὲ αὐτὰ καὶ 'Εμπεδοκλῆς· διττὸν γὰρ ποιεῖ τὸν Σφαῖρον καὶ
ἐκεῖνος, τὸν μὲν αἰσθητόν, ἐν ᾧ τὸ νεῖκος δυναστεύει, τὸν δὲ νοητόν, ὑπὸ τῆς 'Αφροδίτης
συνεχόμενον, καὶ θατέρου τὸν ἕτερον εἰκόνα καλεῖ, δῆλον δὲ ποτέρου πότερον.

3–11. Pr., *Hes.* 50.7–17: the 'reigns' of Kronos and Zeus do not represent changes
on the divine level, but different dispositions of the human soul. – The notion
that it is characteristic of myth to express in terms of time what exists eternally
and simultaneously, is current since Plot. III 5,9.24–26 (δεῖ δὲ τοὺς μύθους, εἴπερ
τοῦτο ἔσονται, καὶ μερίζειν χρόνοις ἃ λέγουσι, καὶ διαιρεῖν ἀπ' ἀλλήλων πολλὰ τῶν ὄντων
ὁμοῦ μὲν ὄντα, τάξει δὲ ἢ δυνάμεσι διεστῶτα), cf. Salustius, *de diis* 4,9 (ταῦτα δὲ ἐγένετο
μὲν οὐδέποτε, ἔστι δὲ ἀεί· καὶ ὁ μὲν νοῦς ἅμα πάντα ὁρᾷ, ὁ δὲ λόγος τὰ μὲν πρῶτα τὰ
δὲ δεύτερα λέγει). Julian, *or.* 8 (5), 171C–D (καὶ οὐδέποτε γέγονεν ὅτε μὴ ταῦτα τοῦτον
ἔχει τὸν τρόπον ὅνπερ νῦν ἔχει, ἀλλ' ἀεὶ μὲν ῎Αττις ἐστὶν ὑπουργὸς τῇ Μητρὶ καὶ ἠνίοχος,
ἀεὶ δὲ ὀργᾷ εἰς τὴν γένεσιν, ἀεὶ δὲ ἀποτέμνεται τὴν ἀπειρίαν διὰ τῆς ὡρισμένης τῶν
εἰδῶν αἰτίας). Pr., *Rep.* I 135.8–13; 17–30; Ol., *Gorg.* 227.22–228.7; 229.3–13. J. Pépin,
Le temps et le mythe, Les Etudes Philosophiques 1962, 55–68.

10. σύμβολα ἔχουσα πασῶν τῶν ἀρετῶν: on 'symbols' in the Chaldean Oracles
and in the later Neoplatonists see Kroll p. 50; Dodds pp. 222–223; O. Geudtner,
Die Seelenlehre der chaldäischen Orakel, Meisenheim 1971, 48–50; Rosán 104–105,
n. 22; Lewy 190–192 (in the magical and sacramental sense, cf. Iambl., *myst.* 96.19;
184.11; Pr., *de arte hier.* 150.17; 151.1; 21); Beierwaltes 328, n. 70; Theiler 296;

δεσμῷ ἐσμεν τῷ σώ|ματι (τοῦτο γὰρ δῆλόν ἐστι, καὶ οὐκ ἂν τοῦτο ἀπόρρητον (3)
ἔλεγεν), ἀλλ᾽ ὅτι οὐ δεῖ ἐξάγειν ἡμᾶς ἑαυτοὺς ὡς τοῦ σώματος ἡμῶν Διονυσια-
κοῦ ὄντος· μέρος γὰρ αὐτοῦ ἐσμεν, εἴ γε ἐκ τῆς αἰθάλης τῶν Τιτάνων συγκείμεθα
γευσαμένων τῶν σαρκῶν τούτου.

Ὁ μὲν οὖν Σωκράτης ἔργῳ τὸ ἀπόρρητον δεικνὺς τοῦ μύθου οὐδὲν πλέον 4
προστίθησιν τοῦ ʽὡς ἔν τινι φρουρᾷ ἐσμεν᾽ [62b3–4]· οἱ δὲ ἐξηγηταὶ τὸν μῦθον
προστιθέασιν ἔξωθεν, καὶ ἔστιν ἡ τοῦ μύθου ἀλληγορία τοιαύτη. ὥσπερ ὁ Ἐμπεδοκλῆς [frg. Β 17] ἔλεγε τὸν νοητὸν καὶ τὸν αἰσθητὸν παρὰ μέρος γίνεσθαι τόπους,
οὐχ ὅτι ποτὲ μὲν οὗτος γίνεται, ποτὲ δὲ ὁ νοητός (ἀεὶ γάρ εἰσιν), ἀλλ᾽ ὅτι ἡ 5
ἡμετέρα ψυχὴ ποτὲ μὲν κατὰ νοητὸν ζῇ καὶ λέγεται τότε γίνεσθαι ὁ νοητὸς κόσμος,
ποτὲ δὲ κατὰ αἰσθητὸν καὶ λέγεται ὁ αἰσθητὸς γίνεσθαι κόσμος, οὕτως καὶ
παρὰ τῷ Ὀρφεῖ [frg. 107] αἱ τέσσαρες βασιλεῖαι αὗται οὐ ποτὲ μέν εἰσι, ποτὲ
δὲ οὔ, ἀλλ᾽ ἀεὶ μέν εἰσι, αἰνίττονται δὲ τοὺς διαφόρους βαθμοὺς τῶν ἀρετῶν
καθ᾽ ἃς ἡ ἡμετέρα ψυχὴ ⟨ἐνεργεῖ⟩ σύμβολα ἔχουσα πασῶν τῶν ἀρετῶν, τῶν 10
α᾽ τε θεωρητικῶν καὶ καθαρτικῶν καὶ πολιτικῶν καὶ ἠθικῶν. ἢ γὰρ κατὰ τὰς 5
θεωρητικὰς ἐνεργεῖ, ὧν παράδειγμα ἡ τοῦ Οὐρανοῦ βασιλεία, ἵνα ἄνωθεν
β᾽ ἀρξώμεθα· διὸ καὶ Οὐρανὸς εἴρηται παρὰ τὸ τὰ ἄνω ὁρᾶν. ἢ καθαρτικῶς ζῇ,

§ 4. 4 τόπους Wk (κόσμους Nv): τούτους Μ — 10 ἐνεργεῖ Nv (cf. 1 § 5.2;
8 § 2.17; 18): om. Μ

Des Places p. 178, n. 3; Pr., theol. II p. 56, n. 5 S.-W. They represent the divine
in soul and nature, as λόγοι represent the intelligible. Pr., theol. II 8, 56.16–25
πᾶσι γὰρ ἐνέσπειρεν ὁ τῶν ὅλων αἴτιος τῆς ἑαυτοῦ παντελοῦς ὑπεροχῆς συνθήματα, καὶ
διὰ τούτων περὶ ἑαυτὸν ἵδρυσε τὰ πάντα, καὶ πάρεστιν ἀρρήτως πᾶσιν ἀφ᾽ ὅλων ἐξῃρημένος.
ἕκαστον οὖν εἰς τὸ τῆς ἑαυτοῦ φύσεως ἄρρητον εἰσδυόμενον, εὑρίσκει τὸ σύμβολον τοῦ
πάντων πατρός· καὶ σέβεται πάντα κατὰ φύσιν ἐκεῖνον, καὶ διὰ τοῦ προσήκοντος αὐτῷ
μυστικοῦ συνθήματος ἐνίζεται τὴν οἰκείαν φύσιν ἀποδυόμενα, καὶ μόνον εἶναι τὸ ἐκείνου
σύνθημα σπεύδοντα. Tim. I 4.31–33 καὶ ἡ ψυχὴ παράγεταί τε ἀπὸ τοῦ δημιουργοῦ καὶ
πληροῦται λόγων ἁρμονικῶν καὶ συμβόλων θείων καὶ δημιουργικῶν. I 144.12–18 αἱ δὲ
Ἀθηναϊκαὶ ψυχαὶ μάλιστα κατὰ ταύτην τοῦ Ἡφαίστου τὴν ἐνέργειαν δέχονται τὰ ὀχήματα
παρ᾽ αὐτοῦ καὶ εἰσοικίζονται ἐν σώμασιν ἐκ τῶν Ἡφαίστου λόγων καὶ τῆς γῆς ὑποστᾶσιν,
τῶν λόγων Ἀθηναϊκὰ συνθήματα λαβόντων· οὗτος γάρ ἐστιν ὁ πρὸ τῆς φύσεως τελεστὴς τῶν
σωμάτων ἄλλοις ἄλλα σύμβολα τῶν θείων ἐπιτιθείς. I 161.5–9 ἡ τοῦ παντὸς ψυχὴ λόγους
ἔχουσα τῶν θείων ἀπάντων καὶ ἐξηρτημένη τῶν πρὸ αὐτῆς ἄλλοις τοῦ διαστήματος μορίοις
πρὸς ἄλλας δυνάμεις ἐντίθησιν οἰκειότητα καὶ σύμβολα ἄττα τῶν διαφόρων ἐν θεοῖς τάξεων.
I 211.1–2 (prayer contributes to reversion) συμβόλοις ἀρρήτοις τῶν θεῶν, ἃ τῶν ψυχῶν
ὁ πατὴρ ἐνέσπειρεν αὐταῖς. The basic text for all these passages is Chaldean Oracles,
frg. 108 σύμβολα γὰρ πατρικὸς νόος ἔσπειρεν κατὰ κόσμον, †ὃς τὰ νοητὰ νοεῖ καὶ ἄφραστα
κάλλη . .ειταί† (attempts at correction Kroll p. 50, Lewy 191, n. 55; E. R. Dodds,
New Light on the Chaldaean Oracles, Harvard Theol. Rev. 54, 1961, 273, n. 34);
cf. Psellus, orac. Chald. 1141a12–b9.
§ 5. 1–9. Cf. infra 8 §§ 2–3; Dam. I § 119; §§ 138–144.
2–5. The etymologies of Uranus and Kronos are those of Pl., Crat. 396b3–c1.

of which the prototype is the reign of Kronos, who is therefore called Kronos, i.e. 'sated intelligence', because he sees himself; this is the reason why he is said to devour his own offspring, in the sense that intelligence converts upon itself. Or again she practices the civic virtues, symbolized by the reign of Zeus; accordingly Zeus is the Creator, whose activity is directed on secondary existents. Or, finally, she lives by the ethical and physical virtues, symbolized by the reign of Dionysus; hence he is torn to pieces, because these virtues do not imply each other; and the Titans chew his flesh, mastication standing for extreme division, because Dionysus is the patron of this world, where extreme division prevails because of 'mine' and 'thine'. In the Titans who tear him to pieces, the *ti* ('something') denotes the particular, for the universal form is broken up in genesis, and Dionysus is the monad of the Titans. When it is said that he is torn by genesis, 'genesis' stands for its causes, just as we call Demeter wheat and Dionysus wine; for, as Proclus [*Hymns*, frg. I] says: 'What they saw in the children, they expressed in the parents' names'. And the plot is Hera's, because she is the patron deity of motion and procession; hence it is she who, in the *Iliad*, is continually stirring up Zeus and stimulating him to providential care of secondary existents.

5–6. Cf. Dam., *Parm.* 134.17–19 καὶ γὰρ ὁ παρ' 'Ορφεῖ Κρόνος ... καταπίνει τὰ οἰκεῖα γεννήματα (*Orphica* frg. 146).

9. ἀντακολουθοῦσιν ἀλλήλαις αἱ ἀρεταί: a Socratic concept, based on the thesis that virtue is insight; hence it does not hold true of natural virtues (Ar., *eth. Nic.* VI 13, 1144b32–1145a2). The Neoplatonists use the Stoic term (*SVF* III frgs. 275; 295; 299): Plot. I 2,7.1=Porph., *sent.* 32 (p. 28.4–5); Pr., *Alc.* 319.9; Ol., *Alc.* 214.10 (wrongly listed as a Stoic fragment, *SVF* III frg. 302); Dam. I § 140.

11. διὰ τὸ ἐμὸν καὶ σόν: cf. *infra* 8 § 7.7; Pl., *Rep.* V 462c4–8.

12–13. Dam. I § 4; § 9.

12. τοῦ 'τὶ' μερικὸν δηλοῦντος: Pr., *Crat.* 56.13–19 καὶ τάχ' ἂν ὁ Πλάτων ἐν τούτοις (396b5) τοῦ τῶν Τιτάνων ὀνόματος διττὰς ἐξηγήσεις ἡμῖν ἀρχοειδεῖς παραδίδωσιν, ἃς 'Ιάμβλιχός τε καὶ 'Αμέλιος ἀναγέγραφεν· Τιτᾶνας γὰρ ὁ μὲν παρὰ τὸ διατείνειν ἐπὶ πάντα τὰς ἑαυτῶν δυνάμεις, ὁ δὲ παρὰ τό τι ἄτομον κεκλῆσθαί φησιν, ὡς τοῦ μεριστοῦ (μερισμοῦ Kroll) καὶ τῆς διακρίσεως τῶν ὅλων εἰς τὰ μέρη τὴν ἀρχὴν ἐκ τούτων λαμβανούσης (ὁ δὲ is the last mentioned, cf. *Rep.* I 90.9–13). Dam., *princ.* 57.20–23 ὁ Πλάτων ἐν 'Επιστολαῖς (II 313a3–4) ... τοῦτο τῶν κακῶν αἰτιᾶται πάντων, τὸν τοῦ ἰδίου μερισμὸν κατὰ τὸ ποιὸν καὶ τὸ τί· τῷ γὰρ ὄντι τοῦτο Τιτανικὸν πάσχομεν.

13. Dam. I §§ 2–3. Ol. follows Pr. (§ 3), not Dam. (§ 4).

13–17. Dam. I § 8.4–7.

14. ⟨γενέσεως⟩ τῶν αἰτίων ταύτης ἀκουόντων: what Ol. meant to say can only be that the Titans, as the lowest ranking creative deities and closest to the world of process, symbolize their own creation; the intramundane intelligence is dispersed in genesis. Pr., *Tim.* I 390.27–391.4 ἄξιον δὲ μηδὲ ἐκεῖνο παραλιπεῖν, ὅτι μιμεῖται τοὺς θεολόγους πρὸ τῆς κοσμοποιίας τὸ πλημμελὲς καὶ ἄτακτον ὑφιστάς· ὡς γὰρ ἐκεῖνοι πολέμους καὶ στάσεις εἰσάγουσι τῶν Τιτάνων πρὸς τοὺς 'Ολυμπίους, οὕτω δὴ καὶ ὁ Πλάτων δύο ταῦτα προϋποτίθεται, τό τε ἄκοσμον καὶ τὸ κοσμοποιόν, ἵνα θάτερον κοσμηθῇ καὶ μετάσχῃ τῆς τάξεως. ἀλλ' ἐκεῖνοι μὲν θεολογικῶς· αὐτοὺς γὰρ τοὺς προστάτας τῶν σωμάτων ἀντιτάττουσι τοῖς 'Ολυμπίοις· ὁ δὲ Πλάτων φιλοσόφως ἀπὸ τῶν θεῶν ἐπὶ τὰ διοικούμενα τὴν τάξιν μετήγαγε. The doubling of γενέσεως, which seems to be the

ἧς παράδειγμα ἡ Κρονία βασιλεία· διὸ καὶ Κρόνος εἴρηται, οἷον [ὁ] κορόνους
τις ὢν διὰ τὸ ἑαυτὸν ὁρᾶν· διὸ καὶ καταπίνειν τὰ οἰκεῖα γεννήματα λέγεται   5
γ′   ὡς αὐτὸς πρὸς ἑαυτὸν ἐπιστρέφων. ἢ κατὰ τὰς πολιτικάς, ὧν σύμβολον ἡ τοῦ
δ′   Διὸς βασιλεία· διὸ καὶ δημιουργὸς ὁ Ζεύς, ὡς περὶ τὰ δεύτερα ἐνεργῶν. ἢ κατὰ
τὰς ἠθικὰς καὶ φυσικὰς ἀρετάς, ὧν σύμβολον | ἡ τοῦ Διονύσου βασιλεία· διὸ   (4)
καὶ σπαράττεται, διότι οὐκ ἀντακολουθοῦσιν ἀλλήλαις αἱ ἀρεταί. καὶ τὰς σάρκας
μασῶνται οἱ Τιτᾶνες, τῆς μασήσεως δηλούσης τὸν πολὺν μερισμόν, διότι τῶν   10
τῇδε ἔφορός ἐστιν, ἔνθα ὁ πολὺς μερισμὸς διὰ τὸ ἐμὸν καὶ σόν. καὶ ὑπὸ τῶν
Τιτάνων σπαράττεται, τοῦ ʽτίʼ μερικὸν δηλοῦντος, σπαράττεται δὲ τὸ καθόλου
εἶδος ἐν τῇ γενέσει· μονὰς δὲ Τιτάνων ὁ Διόνυσος. λέγεται δὲ σπαράττεσθαι
ὑπὸ τῆς γενέσεως, ⟨γενέσεως⟩ τῶν αἰτίων ταύτης ἀκουόντων· οὕτω γὰρ καὶ
τὴν Δήμητραν πυροὺς καλοῦμεν καὶ τὸν Διόνυσον οἶνον· φησὶ γὰρ ὁ Πρόκλος   15
[hymn. frg. I]

ʽὅσσʼ ἴδον ἐν τεκέεσσιν ἐφημίξαντο τοκεῦσινʼ.

κατʼ ἐπιβουλὴν δὲ τῆς ῞Ηρας, διότι κινήσεως ἔφορος ἡ θεὸς καὶ προόδου· διὸ
καὶ συνεχῶς ἐν τῇ Ἰλιάδι ἐξανίστησιν αὕτη καὶ διεγείρει τὸν Δία εἰς πρόνοιαν

---

§ 5. 4 ὁ M: del. μ — 14 γενέσεως Wk: om. M — 15 δημήτραν M — 17 ἴδον ἐν]
εἶδον Ol., Alc. 2.62

---

obvious correction, is based on this explanation. Ol. is in that case referring to
the usual kind of metonymy: 'itaque tum illud quod erat a deo natum nomine
ipsius dei nuncupabant, ut cum fruges Cererem appellamus, vinum autem Liberum'
(Cic., nat. deor. II 23,60). What follows must then be a slip for οὕτω γὰρ καὶ τοὺς
πυροὺς Δήμητραν καλοῦμεν καὶ τὸν οἶνον Διόνυσον, cf. Ol., Alc. 2.59–62 εἰώθεισαν δὲ
οἱ ἀρχαῖοι τὰ αἰτιατὰ ὀνομάζειν τοῖς τῶν αἰτίων ὀνόμασι, καθάπερ καὶ τὸν οἶνον Διόνυσον
καλοῦσιν (also Pr., Crat. 41.14–15 τὰ δὲ [scil. λέγεται] ἀπὸ τῶν εὑρόντων, ὡς ὁ οἶνος
Διόνυσος). Apparently Ol. confuses this usage with its opposite, the calling of the
God by the name of his gift, cf. Pr., Crat. 108.13–20 (=Orphica frg. 216a–c) τὸν
δεσπότην ἡμῶν Διόνυσον οἱ θεολόγοι πολλάκις καὶ ἀπὸ τῶν τελευταίων αὐτοῦ δώρων
Οἶνον καλοῦσιν, οἷον Ὀρφεύς etc. (cf. ibid. 41.15–16 τὰ δὲ ἀπὸ τῶν εὑρημάτων, ὡς ὁ
῞Ηφαιστος πῦρ); however, while the relation Dionysus–wine is convertible, this
can hardly be true of the relation Demeter–wheat. The verse of Pr., which Ol.
cites both here and Alc. 2.60–62 (with εἶδον instead of ἴδον ἐν) probably describes
the latter proceeding, since the unusual dative with ἐφημίξαντο is best explained
by supposing that φημίζομαι stands for ἐπιφημίζω (v. LSJ s.v. ἐπιφημίζω II 2 and
III 3), so that the line could be paraphrased: (οἱ ἀρχαῖοι) ὅσα εἶδον ἐν τοῖς γεννήμασιν
ἐπεφήμισαν τοῖς αἰτίοις. (The correction τοκῆες adopted by Ludwich and Vogt gives
a meaning that has no visible connection with the context).

15. Δήμητραν: Pr. uses this accusative Tim. I 153.11; III 140.9; 11 (quoting
Plot. IV 4,27.16); 15; Crat. 90.28 v.l. (ibid. 80.11; 90.11; 91.5; 94.17; 103.26 -τρα);
theol. 267.31–32. His preference for the form may well mean that he read it himself
in Pl., Crat. 404b5 (with our MSS.).

18–19. On Hera cf. Pr., Crat. 79.9–15; 20–22; Tim. III 191.10–19; 194.8–9.
Her policy, in Homer, is of course precisely to prevent Zeus from intervening in
the war, and the only passage that could be cited in support of Ol. is Il. 5.748–763,
so that the word συνεχῶς is certainly out of place; but the reference is really to
the love scene on Mount Ida (Il. 14.292–353) as interpreted by Pr., Rep. I

6. In a different way, Dionysus is the patron of genesis, because he is also the patron of life and death; of life, as the patron of genesis; of death, inasmuch as wine brings about ecstasy, while, on the other hand, we also become more susceptible to ecstasy when death is drawing near, as it is seen in the case of Patroclus in Homer [*Il.* 16.851–854], who in his last moments receives the gift of prophecy. Tragedy and comedy, too, are said to be consecrated to Dionysus, comedy because it is a burlesque of life, tragedy because of passion and death. Therefore comedy writers are wrong when they criticize the tragic poets as not Dionysiac, in the phrase 'this is not the way of Dionysus'. In the story of Zeus striking them with his thunderbolts, the thunderbolt means reversion, for it is fire, which has an upward motion; the sense is, therefore, that Zeus converts them upon himself.

7. This is the mythical argument. The dialectical and philosophical is as follows: if it is the Gods who are our guardians and whose possessions we are, we should not put an end to our own lives, but leave it to them. If only one of the two were true, and either we were possessions of the Gods, but they did not take care of us, or conversely, there would be at least a reasonable ground for suicide; as it is, both reasons together forbid us to cast off the shackle.

8. Why should we not also make a case for the contrary view and show that suicide is permissible?

132.13–136.14: . . . (134.12–15) τοῦ μὲν Διὸς τὴν πατρικὴν ἀξίαν λαχόντος, τῆς δὲ Ἥρας μητρὸς οὔσης τῶν πάντων ὧν ὁ Ζεὺς πατήρ, καὶ τοῦ μὲν ἐν μονάδος τάξει τὰ ὅλα παράγοντος, τῆς δὲ κατὰ τὴν γόνιμον δυάδα τῷ Διὶ τὰ δεύτερα συνυφιστάσης . . . (135.6–13) καὶ γὰρ ὁ Ζεὺς ἐπὶ ταύτην ἀνάγει τὴν κοινωνίαν (i.e. τὴν ἐπιστρεπτικήν), τῆς Ἥρας αὐτῷ προτεινούσης τὴν καταδεεστέραν καὶ ἐγκόσμιον, ἀεὶ μὲν καθ' ἑκατέραν τῶν θεῶν ἡνωμένων, τοῦ δὲ μύθου μερίζοντος καὶ τὰ ἀιδίως ἀλλήλοις συνυφεστηκότα χωρίζοντος, καὶ τὴν μὲν χωριστὴν τοῦ παντὸς μῖξιν εἰς τὴν τοῦ Διὸς βούλησιν ἀναπέμποντος, τὴν δὲ εἰς τὸν κόσμον προϊοῦσαν αὐτῶν κοινὴν συνεργίαν ἐπὶ τὴν τῆς Ἥρας πρόνοιαν.

§ 6. Dionysus, the immanent world-mind governing all individual creation (§ 5; Pr., *Crat.* 109.5–21; *Tim.* II 145.11–146.18) is also the patron of παλιγγενεσία (Dam. I § 11; II § 8; Ol. 6 § 13; 7 § 10.14–15; Pr., *Tim.* II 241.5–18), i.e. of the cycle of birth and death, and of coming-to-be and passing-away generally. The way in which Ol. establishes this is rather incoherent: the first lines, as they stand, make a circular argument (genesis → life → genesis), and the prophecies of the dying seem to form a purely associative link between Dionysus and death. The latter point becomes clearer when set in its original context, Ar.'s account of the double origin of religion (frg. 10 R.[3]) . . . ἀπὸ μὲν τῶν περὶ τὴν ψυχὴν συμβαινόντων διὰ τοὺς ἐν τοῖς ὕπνοις γινομένους ταύτης ἐνθουσιασμοὺς καὶ τὰς μαντείας. ὅταν γάρ, φησίν, ἐν τῷ ὑπνοῦν καθ' ἑαυτὴν γένηται ἡ ψυχή, τότε τὴν ἴδιον ἀπολαβοῦσα φύσιν προμαντεύεταί τε καὶ προαγορεύει τὰ μέλλοντα. τοιαύτη δέ ἐστι καὶ ἐν τῷ κατὰ τὸν θάνατον χωρίζεσθαι τῶν σωμάτων. ἀποδέχεται γοῦν καὶ τὸν ποιητὴν Ὅμηρον ὡς τοῦτο παρατηρήσαντα· πεποίηκε γὰρ τὸν μὲν Πάτροκλον ἐν τῷ ἀναιρεῖσθαι προαγορεύοντα περὶ τῆς Ἕκτορος ἀναιρέσεως, τὸν δ' Ἕκτορα περὶ τῆς Ἀχιλλέως τελευτῆς. In other words, Dionysiac rapture, prophetic inspiration, and death are only different ways in

τῶν δευτέρων. καὶ γενέσεως ἄλλως ἔφορός ἐστιν ὁ Διόνυσος, διότι καὶ ζωῆς   6
καὶ τελευτῆς· ζωῆς μὲν γὰρ ἔφορος, ἐπειδὴ καὶ τῆς γενέσεως, τελευτῆς δέ, διότι
ἐνθουσιᾶν ὁ οἶνος ποιεῖ καὶ περὶ τὴν τελευτὴν δὲ ἐνθουσιαστικώτεροι γινόμεθα,
ὡς δηλοῖ ὁ παρ᾽ Ὁμήρῳ [Π 851–854] Πάτροκλος μαντικὸς γεγονὼς περὶ τὴν
τελευτήν. καὶ τὴν τραγῳδίαν δὲ καὶ τὴν κωμῳδίαν ἀνεῖσθαί φασι τῷ Διονύσῳ,   5
τὴν μὲν κωμῳδίαν παίγνιον οὖσαν τοῦ βίου, τὴν δὲ τραγῳδίαν διὰ τὰ πάθη
καὶ τὴν τελευτήν. οὐκ ἄρα καλῶς οἱ κωμικοὶ τοῖς τραγικοῖς ἐγκαλοῦσιν ὡς
μὴ Διονυσιακοῖς οὖσιν λέγοντες ὅτι ᾽οὐδὲν ταῦτα πρὸς τὸν Διόνυσον᾽. κεραυνοῖ
δὲ τούτους ὁ Ζεύς, τοῦ κεραυνοῦ δηλοῦντος τὴν ἐπιστροφήν, πῦρ γὰρ ἐπὶ τὰ
ἄνω κινούμενον· ἐπιστρέφει οὖν αὐτοὺς πρὸς ἑαυτόν.   10

β′   Καὶ τοῦτο μὲν τὸ μυθικὸν ἐπιχείρημα. τὸ δὲ διαλεκτικὸν καὶ φιλόσοφον   7
τοιοῦτόν ἐστιν, ὅτι εἰ θεοὶ ἡμῶν εἰσιν ἐπιμεληταὶ καὶ κτήματα ἐκείνων ἐσμέν,
οὐ δεῖ ἐξάγειν ἑαυτούς, ἀλλ᾽ ἐπιτρέπειν ἐκείνοις. εἰ μὲν γὰρ θάτερον | ἦν τούτων, (5)
καὶ ἢ κτήματα ἦμεν τῶν θεῶν οὐ μὴν ἐπεμελοῦντο ἡμῶν, ἢ ἀνάπαλιν, χώραν
ὅπως οὖν εἶχεν εὔλογον τὸ ἐξάγειν ἡμᾶς ἑαυτούς· νῦν δὲ δι᾽ ἄμφω οὐ δεῖ λύειν   5
τὸν δεσμόν.

Τί οὖν οὐ δεῖ συνηγορῆσαι καὶ τῷ ἀντικειμένῳ καὶ δεῖξαι ὅτι δεῖ ἐξάγειν   8
ἑαυτούς;

---

§ 7. 4 ᾗ¹ Fh: εἰ M

---

which the soul is separated from the visible world, and thus they all are under
the sway of Dionysus Lyseus. – The observation that both tragedy and comedy
are legitimate forms of the cult of Dionysus must be somehow connected with
Pl.'s reflections on the subject (*Symp.* 223d2–6; *Rep.* III 395a3–7; discussed by
Pr., *Rep.* I 51.26–54.2, but from an entirely different angle).
3–5. See the material collected by A. S. Pease on Cic., *divin.* I 30,63 (repr.
Darmstadt 1963, p. 206); Pr., *Rep.* II 186.19–20.
8. *CPG* I 137 (Zenob. 5,40 and note).
8–10. Cf. Dam. I § 7.5–6. Lightning as an elevating force: Jul., *or.* 7, 220A
εἶτ᾽ ἐπανήγαγε διὰ τοῦ κεραυνίου πυρὸς πρὸς ἑαυτόν, ὑπὸ τῷ θείῳ συνθήματι τῆς αἰθερίας
αὐγῆς ἥκειν παρ᾽ ἑαυτὸν τῷ παιδὶ κελεύσας. Dam., *Phil.* § 61. Lewy 218, n. 167.
§ 7. 3–6. Dam. I § 18: the same statement, also without further explanation.
§§ 8–9. On suicide generally see Th. Thalheim, *RE* art. Selbstmord, 2A, 1921,
1134–35; J. M. Rist, *Stoic Philosophy*, Cambridge 1969, 233–255. The attitude of
Platonism was determined throughout by the 'It is unlawful' of the *Ph.* (e.g. Hierocl.,
carm. aur. 462b10–15); in theory, however, the question remained an open one,
partly no doubt on account of Pl.'s own utterances cited in § 8, partly under Stoic
influence. Cf. Plot. I 4,7.31–32; 43; Porph., *vit. Plot.* 11; *abst.* 4,18; Macrob.,
somn. Scip. I 13. That Ol. still maintains this open-minded attitude is an interesting
example of the survival of pagan ethics in the Alexandrian school as late as the
middle of the 6th cent. The Christian Olympiodoreans Elias (*isag.* 14.15–16.8),
David (32.11–34.12) and Ps.-Elias (13) all reject suicide unconditionally. – The
case in defense of suicide is entirely based on authority: (i) of Pl. himself in the *Ph.*;
(ii) of Pl. elsewhere; (iii) of Plot.; (iv) of the Stoa.

(i) In the very passage under discussion, in which Plato argues that we should not dispose of our own lives, he hints at the contrary possibility too, first by saying 'He will not, I suppose, do violence to himself' [61c9], the 'I suppose' suggesting that there are circumstances in which one should; next by adding that one should not take one's own life, 'unless God brings a strong necessity upon us, such as has now come upon me' [62c7-8].

(ii) Plato himself in so many words permits suicide to the wise man, to a middle group, and to the common, worthless man. To the wise man, as in the present passage; to the middle group, as in the *Republic* [III 407d4–e2], where he says that a man who suffers from a long and incurable disease ought to end his life because he is of no use to the state, for Plato wants his citizens to live for the good of the community and not for their own; in the *Laws* [IX 854a5–c5] to the masses, where he says that a man in the grip of incurable passions, for instance an inclination to incest or sacrilege or a similar thing, if he is unable to restrain himself, should commit suicide.

(iii) Plotinus [I 9] has written about 'justified suicide'; consequently it is sometimes right to take one's own life.

(iv) According to the Stoics [*SVF* III 768] there are five cases in which suicide is justified. They compared life to a party and said that all the reasons for breaking up a party hold good also for ending one's life. A party, then, may be broken up (1) because of a weighty obligation that suddenly presents itself, e.g. the unexpected arrival of a friend, or (2) because of intruders who use foul language, or (3) because of beginning drunkenness; or again it may be broken up (4) because the food is spoiled,

---

§ 8. 9–16. Argument (ii) is complicated by the Stoic classification of the kinds of people involved: σπουδαῖος, μέσος, φαῦλος (*SVF* III frg. 519), which made Norvin (1915, p. 48) think that it is Platonic doctrine restated by a later Stoic (Posidonius ?). To the evidence should be added a passage in Dav. and Ps.-El., which may, or may not, be identical in origin with the present one. It follows argument (iv), dealing with the five Stoic τρόποι, and runs in Dav. 33.27–33: Ἰστέον δὲ ὅτι ἕτεροί τινες τρεῖς μόνους τρόπους παραδιδόασι, καθ' οὓς εὐλόγως τις ἀναιρεῖ ἑαυτόν· φασὶ γὰρ ὅτι φύσει ἡ ζωὴ τριττή ἐστιν· ἢ γὰρ ἀρίστη ἐστὶν ἢ μέση ἢ χειρίστη. ἡνίκα οὖν ἐστί τις ἐν τῇ ἀρίστῃ ζωῇ ἢ ἐν τῇ μέσῃ καὶ ὁρᾷ ἑαυτὸν μᾶλλον ἐπὶ τὸ χεῖρον ἐκκλίνοντα, εὐλόγως ἀναιρεῖ ἑαυτόν. πάλιν ἡνίκα τις ἐν τῇ χειρίστῃ ζωῇ ἐστι καὶ ὁρᾷ ἑαυτὸν ἀεὶ ἐν τοῖς αὐτοῖς ὄντα καὶ μηδέποτε ἐπὶ τὴν ἀρίστην μετερχόμενον, εὐλόγως ἀναιρεῖ ἑαυτόν. In Ps.-El. 13,18–19: ἕτεροι δὲ ἄλλους φασὶ τρόπους ἐξάγοντας εὐλόγως· λέγουσι γὰρ τρία εἴδη εἶναι τῆς ζωῆς, καλὴν ζωήν, κακὴν ζωήν, καὶ μέσην. ἐὰν οὖν, φασίν, ἐν τῇ καλῇ ζωῇ ὤν τις ἐπὶ τῇ χείρονι προκόπτῃ, δεῖ ἐξάγειν ἑαυτόν· πάλιν ἐὰν ἐν τῇ κακῇ ζωῇ ὤν τις μὴ προκόπτει πρὸς τὴν κρείττω ἀλλὰ μένει ἐν τῇ αὐτῇ, δεῖ οὕτως ἐξάγειν ἑαυτόν· πάλιν ἐάν τις ὢν ἐν τῇ μέσῃ ζωῇ ἐπὶ τὴν χείρω προκόπτῃ, δεῖ δή, φασίν, ἐξάγειν καὶ τοῦτον ἑαυτόν. In spite of the rather wide divergence in actual content (the texts in Dav. and Ps.-El. deal with moral development in general, while Ol. discusses certain special situations), the common element can scarcely be explained by coincidence. Accepting this, two possibilities remain: either the passages where Pl. deals with suicide or could appear

α′　Πρῶτον μὲν ὅτι ἐν αὐτῇ τῇ νῦν προκειμένῃ λέξει, ἐν ᾗ κατασκευάζει ὁ Πλάτων
ὅτι οὐ δεῖ ἐξάγειν ἑαυτούς, ἔμφασιν δίδωσι καὶ τοῦ ἀντικειμένου, πρῶτον μὲν
λέγων 'οὐ μέντοι ἴσως βιάσεται ἑαυτόν' [61c9], τὸ γὰρ 'ἴσως' ὑπόνοιαν δίδωσιν　5
ὅτι ποτὲ καὶ δεῖ ἐξάγειν ἑαυτούς· καὶ πάλιν ἐφεξῆς φησιν ὅτι οὐ δεῖ ἐξάγειν
ἑαυτούς, 'εἰ μὴ μεγάλην ὁ θεὸς ἀνάγκην ἐπιπέμψοι, οἵαν τὴν νῦν παροῦσαν'
[62c7-8].

β′　Δεύτερον ἐπιχείρημα. εἰ αὐτὸς ὁ Πλάτων φησὶν ὅτι ἐξάγειν ἑαυτὸν ἐπιτρέπει
καὶ τῷ σπουδαίῳ καὶ τῷ μέσῳ καὶ τῷ πολλῷ καὶ φαύλῳ ἀνθρώπῳ. τῷ σπουδαίῳ,　10
ὡς ἐνταῦθα· τῷ μέσῳ, ὡς ἐν Πολιτείᾳ [III 407d4–e2] λέγων ὅτι δεῖ τὸν νόσῳ
ἀνιάτῳ καὶ μακρᾷ κατεχόμενον ἐξάγειν ἑαυτὸν ὡς ἄχρηστον ὄντα τῇ πόλει,
διότι βούλεται ὁ Πλάτων τοὺς ἑαυτοῦ πολίτας τῇ πόλει χρησίμους εἶναι καὶ
οὐχ ἑαυτοῖς· ἐν δὲ τοῖς Νόμοις [IX 854a5–c5] τῷ πολλῷ ἀνθρώπῳ λέγων
ὅτι δεῖ τὸν ἀνιάτοις πάθεσι κατεχόμενον, οἷον ἔρωτι μητρὸς ἢ ἱεροσυλίας ἢ　15
τῶν τοιούτων τινί, καὶ μὴ δυνάμενον κρατεῖν ἑαυτοῦ ἐξάγειν ἑαυτόν.

γ′　Τρίτον ἐπιχείρημα. εἰ Πλωτίνῳ [I 9] γέγραπται 'περὶ εὐλόγου ἐξαγωγῆς'·
δεῖ ἄρα ποτὲ ἐξάγειν ἑαυτόν.

δ′　Τέταρτον. εἰ οἱ Στωικοὶ [SVF III 768] πέντε τρόπους ἔλεγον εὐλόγου
ἐξ|αγωγῆς. ἀπείκαζον γὰρ τὸν βίον συμποσίῳ καὶ ἔλεγον ὅτι δι' ὅσας αἰτίας 20(6)
α′　λύεται τὸ συμπόσιον, διὰ τὰς αὐτὰς δεῖ καὶ τὸν βίον λύειν. λύεται τοίνυν τὸ
συμπόσιον ἢ διὰ χρείαν ἄφνω μεγάλην ἐπιστᾶσαν, οἷον διὰ παρουσίαν φίλου
β′ γ′　ἄφνω ἐλθόντος, ἢ διὰ τοὺς ἐπεισκωμάζοντας αἰσχρορρημονοῦντας, ἢ διὰ
δ′　καταλαβοῦσαν μέθην· λύεται τὸ συμπόσιον καὶ διὰ τὰ παρατιθέμενα νοσερὰ
ε′　ὄντα, ἔτι μὴν καὶ διὰ πέμπτον τρόπον, δι' ἔνδειαν τῶν παρατιθεμένων. καὶ　25
α′　τὸν βίον δὲ λυτέον διὰ ε′ τρόπους. οἷον διὰ χρείαν λύεται τὸ συμπόσιον· δεῖ

§ 8.　23; 28 αἰσχρορρημ. M —

to do so (the Rep. passage really addresses itself to the physician, not to the patient)
were collected, and then grouped according to the convenient Stoic classes, which
were common property from the first cent. A.D. onward; or else Dav. and Ps.-El.
represent a later Stoic view, which Ol. shows to be essentially that of Pl. himself.
To the old Stoa, suicide is a moral decision, which can be taken correctly by the
wise man only because he alone possesses the right standard, and for the wise
man, of course, the ground can never be his own failure, but only external
circumstances. On the other hand, the Stoic advisor of Tullius Marcellinus in Seneca,
ep. 77,5-10, takes a line that tallies exactly with the theory stated by Dav. and
Ps.-El. Despite this, I now rather incline to the first solution, because Ol. is almost
always closer to the original material than his successors (El. has only the reference
to Pl., Rep., embodied in the following paragraph).

17–18. The appeal to Plot. I 9 proves that Ol. remembered only the title and
had no clear notion of the content of the treatise, which is entirely concerned with
arguments against suicide and shows no trace of the more lenient attitude taken
in the later Περὶ εὐδαιμονίας (I 4,7).

19–39. El., isag. 14.15–15.22; Dav. 32.11–33.26; Ps.-El. 13,1–17. – The Stoic
comparison between life and a party has all the characteristics of Chrysippean
casuistry and of his typical picturesque illustrations. This must have been von Arnim's
reason to give it a place among the fragments of the Old Stoa (III frg. 768=El.,
isag. 14.15–15.22, then still anonymous, followed by a reference to Ol. h.l.).

or finally (5) because provisions have run out. So life, too, may be cut short in five cases: (1) as a party may be broken up because of an obligation, so may life, as in the example of Menoeceus, when he sacrificed himself for his country; (2) because of foul language: thus we should end our life, if a tyrant tries to force us to betray secrets, as a Pythagorean woman did when pressed to reveal why she did not eat beans: she said 'I would sooner eat them than tell', then, when they tried to make her eat them, she said 'I would rather tell than eat them', and she ended by biting off her tongue, as the organ both of speech and of taste; (3) a party may be broken up also because of drunkenness, and by analogy one may end one's life because of the senility that results from the condition of the body; senility, in fact, is a kind of drunkenness induced by nature; (4) another reason is spoiling of the food, and thus a man may end his life because his body is troubled by incurable diseases and unfit to minister to the soul; (5) lastly, a party is broken up because supplies have run out, and so suicide is permissible in case of poverty, when there is no chance of support from the side of the good; for we should not accept it from the wicked, since the gifts of the unclean are themselves unclean, and we must not soil our hands with them.

9. What is our own opinion, then, now that the argument has ended in contradictory conclusions? Of course, suicide can hardly be unlawful and justified at the same time. What we say is this: suicide is forbidden with a view to the body, which it harms, but it may be justified because of a greater good gained by the soul, for instance when the soul is hampered

---

Norvin 1915, p. 47, disputes this on the ground that Chrysippus did not consider poverty a valid reason for suicide, according to III frg. 167, where he refers precisely to the lines of Theognis (175–176) quoted in all the three parallel versions of the present text (El., Dav., Ps.-El.), which are missing from our redaction of Ol. only by pure accident. Rather than $X\varrho\grave{\eta}$ $\pi\varepsilon\nu\acute{\iota}\eta\nu$ $\varphi\varepsilon\acute{\upsilon}\gamma o\nu\tau\alpha$ . . ., Chrysippus said, we should read $X\varrho\grave{\eta}$ $\varkappa\alpha\varkappa\acute{\iota}\alpha\nu$ $\varphi\varepsilon\acute{\upsilon}\gamma o\nu\tau\alpha$ $\varkappa\alpha\grave{\iota}$ $\dot{\varepsilon}\varsigma$ $\beta\alpha\theta\upsilon\varkappa\acute{\eta}\tau\varepsilon\alpha$ $\pi\acute{o}\nu\tau o\nu$ $\dot{\varrho}\iota\pi\tau\varepsilon\~{\iota}\nu$ $\varkappa\alpha\grave{\iota}$ $\pi\varepsilon\tau\varrho\~{\omega}\nu$, $K\acute{\upsilon}\varrho\nu\varepsilon$, $\varkappa\alpha\tau$' $\dot{\eta}\lambda\iota\beta\acute{\alpha}\tau\omega\nu$. Plutarch points out inconsistencies on two sides: on the one hand, Chrysippus contradicts his own doctrine that moral achievement or failure cannot be decisive for life or death (*Stoic. repugn.* 14); on the other hand, the Stoics' lofty contempt of poverty is difficult to reconcile with the importance they attach to such external circumstances as sickness and pain, which they do consider adequate grounds for suicide (*comm. not.* 22). In the second passage there is some support for Norvin's opinion, since, at that moment at least, Plutarch (or his source) could not think of a passage where poverty figured as a ground for voluntary death. However, in view of the enormous bulk of the *corpus Chrysippeum* this is not quite decisive. In the testimonies that relate beyond any doubt to the Old Stoa, a great number of $\tau\varrho\acute{o}\pi o\iota$ is attested by Stobaeus (*SVF* III frg. 758); Diog. Laert. (*SVF* III frg. 757) mentions death for one's country or friends, violent pain, mutilation or incurable sickness, so that the only really problematic case is poverty. With the reservations added by Ol. (lines 38–39), there is little reason why Chrysippus could not have held this view and could not have quoted Theognis in support of it, while using the same

λύειν τὸν βίον καὶ διὰ μεγάλην χρείαν, ὡς Μενοικεὺς ἀποσφάξας ἑαυτὸν ὑπὲρ
β′ τῆς πατρίδος. ἀλλὰ καὶ δι' αἰσχρορρημοσύνην· οὕτω δεῖ λύειν καὶ τὸν βίον
διὰ τύραννον ἀναγκάζοντα εἰπεῖν τὰ ἀπόρρητα. ὃ καὶ Πυθαγορεία τις γυνὴ
πεποίηκεν ἀναγκαζομένη εἰπεῖν διὰ τί οὐκ ἐσθίει κυάμους· ἔφη γὰρ 'φάγοιμι   30
ἂν ἢ εἴποιμι ἄν', εἶτα ἀναγκαζομένη φαγεῖν ἔφη 'εἴποιμι ἂν ἢ φάγοιμι ἄν',
καὶ τέλος ἀπέτεμεν τὴν γλῶτταν ὡς καὶ διαλεκτικὸν καὶ γευστικὸν ὄργανον.
γ′ ἀλλὰ καὶ διὰ μέθην λύεται τὸ συμπόσιον· οὕτω καὶ τὸν βίον λύειν δεῖ διὰ τὸν
δ′ παρεπόμενον τῷ σώματι λῆρον, φυσικὴ γάρ ἐστι μέθη ὁ λῆρος. ἀλλὰ καὶ διὰ
τὰ παρατιθέμενα νοσερὰ ὄντα· καὶ τὸν βίον λυτέον διὰ [[τὸ]] τὸ σῶμα νόσοις   35
ε′ ἀνιάτοις κατεχόμενον καὶ ἀνεπιτήδειον πρὸς τὸ ὑπουργεῖν τῇ ψυχῇ. ἀλλὰ καὶ
δι' ἔνδειαν τῶν προσαγομένων λύεται τὸ συμπόσιον· οὕτω καὶ διὰ πενίαν δεῖ
ἐξάγειν ἑαυτούς, ἐὰν μὴ πάρεστιν ἀπὸ ἀγαθῶν λαμβάνειν· οὐ γὰρ ληπτέον ἀπὸ
φαύλων, μιαρὰ γὰρ ἀπὸ μιαρῶν δῶρα, καὶ οὐ δεῖ [[οὐδὲ]] τούτοις μολύνειν ἑαυτόν.

Τί οὖν ἡμεῖς φαμεν; εἰς ἀντίφασιν γὰρ περιέστη ὁ λόγος· πῶς γὰρ καὶ ἀθέμιτον 9 (7)
τὸ ἐξάγειν ἑαυτὸν καὶ εὔλογον; ἢ οὐ δεῖ μὲν ἐξάγειν ἑαυτὸν ὅσον ἐπὶ τῷ σώματι,
πρὸς κακοῦ γάρ ἐστι τοῦτο τῷ σώματι· ἀλλὰ καὶ εὔλογον ἐξάγειν ἑαυτοὺς διὰ
μεῖζον ἀγαθὸν συντελοῦν τῇ ψυχῇ, οἷον ὡς ἡνίκα βλάπτεται ὑπὸ τοῦ σώματος.
ὥσπερ γὰρ ὁ βουλευόμενος ἐκεῖνα αἱρεῖται οἷς ἐλάσσονα μὲν κακὰ ἕπεται,   5

---

29 πυθαγορία (et sim. semper) M° — 35 τό¹ M: del. μ — 39 οὐδὲ M: del. Wk
§ 9. 3 κακοῦ Wk: -ῶι M

---

lines for a totally different purpose on a different occasion. – In our group of texts,
El. is almost identical with Ol., except that case (3) is listed last. Dav. and Ps.-El.
have a rather confused version, which in Dav. includes six items instead of five:
(1) lack of food=poverty; (2) spoiled food=sickness; (3) διὰ περίστασίν τινα ἰδικήν
(illness of host, or bad news)=περίστασις ἰδική in life (the Pythagorean woman);
(4) drunkenness=senility (in Ps.-El. drunkenness of the guests, and the use of
foul language); (5) διὰ κοινὴν περίστασιν (fire or invasion)=enemy invasion and the
enforcement of immoral laws (in Dav.: (5) fighting and misbehavior=immoral laws
enforced by enemy, and (6) διὰ κοινὴν περίστασιν, e.g. fire or invasion=enemy
occupation). As usual, it is doubtful if the later version has preserved any elements
of authentic tradition; the ἰδικὴ and κοινὴ περίστασις sound genuine, but they are
difficult to fit into the scheme of Ol. and El., though the κοινὴ περίστασις would
fit case (2) in Ol. (the gatecrashers).
    27–28. Eurip., Phoen. 1009–1014.
    29–32. The story of the Pythagorean woman: Iambl., vit. Pyth. 31, 193–194,
with Deubner's parallel texts.
    34. φυσικὴ γάρ ἐστι μέθη ὁ λῆρος : cf. SVF III frgs. 643–644; 712 (p. 179.14–20);
Plot. I 9.11.
    39. μιαρὰ γὰρ ἀπὸ μιαρῶν δῶρα : cf. SVF III 660 (τοὺς φαύλους ἀνοσίους εἶναι
καὶ ἀκαθάρους (sic Stobaeus, ed. Wachsmuth, and SVF : surely a misprint?) καὶ
ἀνάγνους καὶ μιαροὺς καὶ ἀνεορτάστους. Pl., Laws IV 716e3–717a1 παρὰ δὲ μιαροῦ δῶρα
οὔτε ἄνδρ' ἀγαθὸν οὔτε θεὸν ἔστιν ποτὲ τό γε ὀρθὸν δέχεσθαι.

by the body. Anyone who has to make a decision chooses that which involves the lesser evil and the greater good: now just as it is perfidy not to help a friend when he is beaten, but if the one who beats him should happen to be one's own father, intervention is not justified, so here too suicide is forbidden for the sake of the body and justified in certain cases for the sake of the soul, because it may sometimes be beneficial to the soul. Thus far the survey.

10. **While saying this he lowered his legs [61c10–d1]**: Socrates takes a more active and more dignified posture, because he is going to discuss a more serious subject.

11. **Cebes asked him: 'What do you mean by that, Socrates?' [61d3–4]**: To Cebes it was a problem, how suicide can be unlawful, when the philosopher is ready to die: if death is beneficial to him, he will not wait for somebody else, but render himself this service. To Socrates it was no problem, because he was referring to death in different senses; as we know already from the general course, the one thesis (that suicide is forbidden) relates to corporeal death, the other (that the philosopher is willing to die) to 'voluntary' death.

12. **What do you mean by that, Socrates, that it is unlawful to do violence to oneself, but that the philosopher would be willing to follow a man who dies? [61d3–5]**: There are two points under discussion, that suicide is not allowed, and that the philosopher is willing to die; of these,

---

§ 10. Schol. Pl. 8.20–22. – Similar comments on Socrates' posture Hermias 17.22–25 (on *Ph.* 60b1–2) and 33.7–9 (on *Ph.* 61d1) ὡς καὶ ἐν Φαίδων 'ὁ δὲ Σωκράτης ἀνακαθιζόμενος ἐκ τῆς κλίνης,' ὅτε ἔμελλε τοὺς περὶ τοῦ φιλοσόφου λόγους διατιθέναι. This indicates that the introductory conversation was supposed to end, and the dialogue proper (the 'First Problem') to begin, at this point.

§ 11. Cf. *supra* § 2.17–20.

6. ἐκ τῶν ἐγκυκλίων ἐξηγήσεων : the term occurs again *infra* 4 § 8: οὐ πεισόμεθα τῷ Περιπάτῳ λέγοντι ἀρχὴν ἐπιστήμης τὴν αἴσθησιν … εἰ δὲ δεῖ καὶ ταῖς ἐγκυκλίοις ἐξηγήσεσι πείθεσθαι καὶ ἀρχὴν εἰπεῖν τὴν αἴσθησιν τῆς ἐπιστήμης, λέξομεν αὐτὴν ἀρχὴν οὐχ ὡς ποιητικήν, ἀλλ' ὡς ἐρεθίζουσαν τὴν ἡμετέραν ψυχὴν εἰς ἀνάμνησιν τῶν καθόλου. Also El., *isag.* 27. 1–8 εἰς δύο δὲ διαιρεῖται ἡ φιλοσοφία, οὐχ ὥς φασιν αἱ ἐγκύκλιοι ἐξηγήσεις, ὅτι ἐπειδὴ ἡ φιλοσοφία γνῶσις θείων καὶ ἀνθρωπίνων ἐστί, διὰ μὲν τὰ θεῖα τὸ θεωρητικὸν προεβάλλετο …, διὰ δὲ τὰ ἀνθρώπινα προεβάλλετο τὸ πρακτικόν· παραλογίζονται γὰρ ἐκ τῆς ὁμωνυμίας τοῦ ἀνθρωπείου … φέρε οὖν εἴπωμεν ἡμεῖς … Dav. 1.13–15 δοκεῖ δέ μοι μικρὸν ἀναβάλλεσθαι τὴν ἐγκύκλιον ἐξήγησιν Ἀριστοτελικοῖς πειθομένῳ θεσμοῖς, ὡς δεῖ ἐν ἑκάστῳ σχεδὸν πράγματι τὰ τέσσαρα ταῦτα ζητεῖν κεφάλαια· εἰ ἔστι, τί ἐστι, ὁποῖόν τί ἐστι καὶ διὰ τί ἐστι. To begin with the last: to Dav., the phrase refers to the running commentary on Porph., as opposed to the introductory material, which he arranges according to Ar.'s four points. In the remaining instances, the reference is precisely to the subject-matter of the routine introductions to philosophy (in the commentaries on the *Isagoge*): the principles of knowledge (Ol. 4 § 8, cf. Dav. 5.1–6.21), philosophy defined as knowledge of things divine and human (El.), philosophy defined as preparation for death (Ol. *h.l.*). However, whereas in the present case Ol. appears to be citing a course of his own, both Ol. 4 § 8 and El.

μείζω δὲ ἀγαθά, καὶ ὥσπερ ἀνόσιον μὲν φίλῳ τυπτομένῳ μὴ ἀμύνειν, εἰ δὲ
τύπτοιτο ὑπὸ πατρός, οὐκ εὔλογον ἀμύνειν, οὕτω καὶ ἐνταῦθα καὶ ἀθέμιτον
ἐξάγειν ἑαυτὸν διὰ τὸ σῶμα καὶ εὔλογόν ποτε διὰ τὴν ψυχήν, λυσιτελοῦντος
αὐτῇ ποτε τούτου. ταῦτα ἔχει ἡ θεωρία.

Καὶ ἅμα λέγων ταῦτα καθῆκε τὰ σκέλη [61c10–d1]: συντονώτερον 10
σχῆμα ἀνέλαβε καὶ σεμνότερον ὡς περὶ προβλήματος σεμνοτέρου μέλλων
διαλέγεσθαι.

Ἤρετο οὖν αὐτὸν ὁ Κέβης· πῶς τοῦτο λέγεις, ὦ Σώκρατες 11
[61d3–4]: παρὰ Κέβητι μὲν ἄπορον ἦν, πῶς ἀθέμιτον τὸ ἐξάγειν ἑαυτόν, δεῖ
δὲ τὸν φιλόσοφον ἐθέλειν ἀποθνήσκειν· εἰ γὰρ συμβάλλεται αὐτῷ ὁ θάνατος,
οὐ περιμενεῖ ἄλλον, ἀλλ᾽ αὐτὸς ἑαυτὸν εὐεργετήσει. παρὰ δὲ Σωκράτει οὐκ ἦν
τοῦτο ἄπορον, περὶ ἄλλου γὰρ καὶ ἄλλου θανάτου ἔλεγεν· πρόδηλον δὲ τοῦτο 5
ἐκ τῶν ἐγκυκλίων ἐξηγήσεων, ὅτι τὸ μὲν περὶ τοῦ φυσικοῦ θανάτου λέγεται,
ὅτι οὐ δεῖ ἐξάγειν ἑαυτόν, τὸ δὲ περὶ τοῦ προαιρετικοῦ, τὸ ἐθέλειν ἀποθνήσκειν.

Πῶς τοῦτο λέγεις, ὦ Σώκρατες, τὸ μὴ θεμιτὸν εἶναι ἑαυτὸν 12
βιάζεσθαι, ἐθέλειν δὲ ἂν τῷ ἀποθνήσκοντι τὸν φιλόσοφον ἔπεσθαι;
[61d3–5]: δύο ὄντων προβλημάτων, τοῦ τε μὴ δεῖν ἐξάγειν ἑαυτὸν | καὶ τοῦ (8)

---

§ 10. 2 σχῆμα ἀνέλαβε] ἀνέλαβε σχῆμα schol. Pl.
§ 11. 4 περιμενεῖ Fh: -μένει M

---

contradict opinions expressed in the ἐγκύκλιοι ἐξηγήσεις, and the latter is actually
teaching the *Isagoge* course himself. Norvin (1915) p. 62 therefore explains 'the
commentators in general', and at p. 280 more especially the older commentators
in contrast with the Neoplatonists. This, however, does not agree with the way
in which the contemporary texts explain Ar.'s use of ἐγκύκλιος: Simpl., *cael.*
288.31–289.2 (on I 9, 279a30) ἐγκύκλια δὲ καλεῖ φιλοσοφήματα τὰ κατὰ τάξιν ἐξ ἀρχῆς
τοῖς πολλοῖς προτιθέμενα, ἅπερ καὶ ἐξωτερικὰ καλεῖν εἰώθαμεν, ὥσπερ καὶ ἀκροαματικὰ
καὶ συνταγματικὰ τὰ σπουδαιότερα· λέγει δὲ περὶ τούτου ἐν τοῖς Περὶ φιλοσοφίας. Philop.,
anal. post. 157.2–6 (on III 12, 77b33 κύκλος) ἢ κύκλον λέγει τὰ ἐγκύκλια λεγόμενα
μαθήματα, οὕτω καλούμενα ἢ ὡς πᾶσαν ἱστορίαν περιέχοντά πως ἢ ὡς πάντων περὶ αὐτὰ
εἰλουμένων (περὶ μὲν γὰρ τὰ ἄλλα τῶν μαθημάτων οὐ πάντες στρέφονται, οἷον περὶ ἰατρικὴν
ἢ ῥητορικὴν ἢ ἄλλην τινα· περὶ ταῦτα μέντοι σχεδὸν πάντες καὶ οἱ περὶ τὰς ἄλλας λογικὰς
ἐπιστήμας ἔχοντες). This text is the more important one, because Philop. (i.e.,
presumably, Amm.) here defines what he himself understood by ἐγκύκλια μαθήματα:
a comprehensive general education course addressing itself to a large audience;
very possibly the curriculum outlined by Courcelle p. 325, on the basis of Amm.,
isag. 1.10–17 δεῖ τοίνυν ὁρισμὸν τῆς φιλοσοφίας εἰπεῖν, ὥσπερ καὶ τῆς γραμματικῆς
ἀρχόμενοι τὸν ὁρισμὸν ἐμανθάνομεν... ὁμοίως καὶ ῥητορικῆς ἀρχόμενοι τὸν ὁρισμὸν
ἐμάθομεν. There can hardly be a difference between ἐγκύκλια μαθήματα and ἐγκύκλιοι
ἐξηγήσεις, since by this time all courses took the form of commentaries on standard
textbooks. The objections raised by both Ol. and El. against certain opinions
expressed in these courses may mean that they were (sometimes) taught by others;
or perhaps it was felt that a critical discussion of the Aristotelian position ought
to be reserved for students specializing in philosophy.

Socrates places the willingness to die before the ban on suicide [61c8–10], Cebes on the contrary mentions the unlawfulness of suicide first and then continues about the willingness to die. Socrates, in defending his point of view against him, does not follow his own arrangement, but that of Cebes, and answers Cebes's first question first [62a1–c8]. We must try to account for this. Socrates mentioned the willingness to die before the law against suicide for the good reason that this, the willingness to die, was the main point to him, and then he remarked in passing that one should not take one's own life; Cebes, on the other hand, knew thanks to his philosophical training that suicide is to be rejected, but he did not see how the philosopher can be willing to die, so he kept his difficulty for the last. Then Socrates begins with the injunction against suicide as more universal and of more general application; this precept, indeed, holds good for all of us, not only for philosophers, but for every human being, that no one should kill himself, whereas seeking death is the philosopher's mission only, and therefore he mentions this last as the less comprehensive.

13. **Have you not heard, you and Simmias, when you studied with Philolaus? [61d6–7]**: Socrates asks if they had heard nothing of the kind from Philolaus. He was a Pythagorean, and the Pythagoreans were accustomed to express themselves in riddles; typical of them was the silence by which they indicated the mystery of God, whose imitator the philosopher is. Philolaus had put the precept against suicide in an enigmatic form; he said: 'On your way to a temple do not turn about' and 'Do not chop wood on a journey'. The meaning of the latter maxim was not to cut off one's own life, for life is a journey; preparation for death was taught in the precept not to turn about on one's way to a temple, the temple being life in the beyond, where 'our Father and our fatherland are' [Plot. I 6, 8.21]. The sense is therefore that while leading a life of purification one should not turn about, in other words, not interrupt

---

§ 12. 4–5. Schol. Pl. 10.1–4.
7. Schol. Pl. 9.1–2.
§ 13. Schol. Pl. 9.3–10.
4. Cf. Strabo X 3,9 (C. 467); Porph., *de antro* 27; Iambl., *myst.* 263.4–6; Pr., *theol.* II 9, p. 58.21–24 (note 4 S.-W.); II 11, p. 65.13.
5–13. The connection of the Pythagorean symbols with Philolaus and the attempt to explain them as warnings against suicide is an expedient aimed at finding support in the Pythagorean tradition for Pl.'s testimony on Philolaus forbidding suicide. It is interesting in so far as it shows that in late antiquity no texts to this effect were extant; the originator is hardly Ol., possibly Pr. The first symbol is found in Simpl., *Epict.* 134.49–54 in the form εἰς τὸ ἱερὸν ἀπερχόμενος μὴ ἐπιστρέφου (explained ὅτι τὸν εἰς θεὸν ὁρμηθέντα οὐ χρὴ δίγνωμόν τι ἔχειν καὶ τῶν ἀνθρωπίνων ἀντεχόμενον). It is a conflation from two different maxims, viz. (1) Iambl., *protr.* 21, p. 107.14–15 ἀποδημῶν τῆς οἰκίας μὴ ἐπιστρέφου, Ἐρινύες γὰρ μετέρχονται (cf. Hippol., *refut.* 6,25,1–2, Porph., *vit. Pyth.* 42 and Diog. Laert. 8,17) and (2) Iambl.,

ἐθέλειν ἀποθνήσκειν, ὁ μὲν Σωκράτης προτάττει τὸ θέλειν ἀποθνήσκειν τοῦ
μὴ ἐξάγειν ἑαυτόν [61c8–10], ὁ δὲ Κέβης τὸ ἀνάπαλιν τὸ μὴ θεμιτὸν εἶναι 5
ἀποθνήσκειν καὶ οὕτως ἐπάγει τὸ ἐθέλειν ἀποθνήσκειν· καὶ ὁ Σωκράτης ἐν τῇ
πρὸς τοῦτον ἀπολογίᾳ οὐχ ἑαυτῷ κατακολουθεῖ, ἀλλὰ τῇ τάξει τοῦ Κέβητος,
καὶ ὁ Κέβης πρῶτον ἠρώτησε, πρὸς ἐκεῖνο καὶ αὐτὸς ἀποκρίνεται [62a1–c8].
τούτων οὖν τὴν αἰτίαν δεῖ εἰπεῖν. ὁ μὲν οὖν Σωκράτης προέταξεν τὸ ἐθέλειν
ἀποθνήσκειν τοῦ μὴ ἐξάγειν ἑαυτὸν εἰκότως, ἐπειδὴ τοῦτο προηγούμενον ἦν 10
αὐτῷ, λέγω δὴ τὸ περὶ τοῦ ἐθέλειν ἀποθνήσκειν, καὶ κατὰ παρέκβασιν λοιπὸν εἶπεν
καὶ ὅτι οὐ δεῖ ἐξάγειν ἑαυτόν· ὁ δὲ Κέβης ᾔδει μὲν ἐκ τῶν φιλοσόφων συνουσιῶν
ὅτι οὐ δεῖ ἐξάγειν ἑαυτόν, ἠπόρει δὲ πῶς ἐθελήσει ἀποθνήσκειν ὁ φιλόσοφος,
διὸ ὃ ἠπόρει ἔσχατον εἶπεν. ὁ δὲ Σωκράτης ἄρχεται ἀπὸ τοῦ μὴ ἐξάγειν ἑαυτὸν
ὡς καθολικωτέρου καὶ κοινοτέρου· τοῦτο γὰρ πᾶσιν ἐπιτρέπεται, οὐ μόνον 15
φιλοσόφοις, ἀλλὰ καὶ παντὶ ἀνθρώπῳ, τὸ μὴ ἐξάγειν ἑαυτόν, τὸ δὲ ἐθέλειν
ἀποθνήσκειν μόνοις φιλοσόφοις ἐπιτρέπεται, διὸ τὸ μερικώτερον ὕστερον ἔταξεν.

Οὐκ ἀκηκόατε σύ τε καὶ Σιμμίας Φιλολάῳ συγγεγονότες; 13
[61d6–7]: ἐρωτᾷ εἰ οὐδὲν τοιοῦτον ἤκουσαν παρὰ τοῦ Φιλολάου. ὁ δὲ Φιλόλαος
Πυθαγόρειος ἦν, ἔθος δὲ ἦν τοῖς Πυθαγορείοις δι᾽ αἰνιγμάτων λέγειν· τούτων
γὰρ καὶ ἡ σιωπὴ ἐνδεικνυμένων διὰ τῆς σιωπῆς τὸ ἀπόρρητον τοῦ θεοῦ, ὃν
μιμεῖσθαι δεῖ τὸν φιλόσοφον. ἦν δὲ ὁ Φιλόλαος εἰπὼν ὅτι οὐ δεῖ ἐξάγειν ἑαυτὸν
δι᾽ αἰνιγμάτων· ἔλεγεν γὰρ ᾽ἀπιόντι εἰς ἱερὸν οὐ δεῖ | ἐπιστρέφεσθαι᾽ καὶ ᾽ἐν (9)
α' ὁδῷ μὴ σχίζειν ξύλα᾽. ἐδήλου δὲ τοῦτο, τουτέστι ᾽μὴ σχίζε καὶ τέμνε τὸν βίον᾽,
β' ὁδὸς γὰρ ὁ βίος· τὸ δὲ μελετᾶν θάνατον ἐδήλου διὰ τοῦ ᾽ἀπιόντα εἰς ἱερὸν μὴ
ἐπιστρέφεσθαι᾽, ἱερὸν γὰρ ὁ ἐκεῖσε βίος, ᾽πατὴρ γὰρ ἡμῶν καὶ πατρὶς ἐκεῖ᾽
[Plot. I 6,8.21]. ἔλεγεν οὖν ὅτι ᾽καθαρτικῶς ζῶν μὴ ἐπιστρέφων᾽, τουτέστι 10
γ' ᾽μὴ διάκοπτε τὴν καθαρτικὴν ζωήν᾽. ἔλεγε δὲ καὶ ἄλλως μὴ ἐξάγειν ἑαυτόν, διότι

---

§ 12. 15 καθολικοτέρου M
§ 13. 1 post Σιμμίας] περὶ τῶν τοιούτων add. Mᶜ (Pl.) — 8 τοῦ Fh: τὸ M

---

protr. 21, p. 106.19–20 εἰς ἱερὸν ἀπιὼν προσκυνῆσαι μηδὲν ἄλλο μεταξὺ βιωτικὸν μήτε
λέγε μήτε πρᾶττε (cf. Plut., Numa 14). The former is explained as an exhortation
to μελέτη θανάτου by Iambl., p. 114.29–115.18, whereas Hippolytus, Porphyry and
Diogenes make it apply to physical death. The second, ἐν ὁδῷ μὴ σχίζειν ξύλα, is
cited as ἐν ὁδῷ μὴ σχίζε by Iambl. (p. 107.22 and 118.4), who must have found
this text already in his source, though the ξύλα (also in CPG II 401, Apostolius 7,24a)
has to be either understood or supplied to provide the concrete meaning characteristic
of the symbola. Iambl.'s interpretation (p. 118.4–119.3) is 'do not swerve from
indivisible truth and the unity of the incorporeal', Apostolius paraphrases προχώρει
καὶ μὴ αἰτίαν δὸς πρὸ καιροῦ τελευτῆσαι, simply referring to an uncompleted task.
The third, φορτίον μὴ συγκαθαιρεῖν, συνεπιτιθέναι δέ (Diog. Laert. 8,17; Plut.,
quaest. conv. 8,7,4, 728C–D; Iambl., p. 107.8–9; 113.19–114.5) is given the obvious
meaning of μηδενὶ πρὸς ῥᾳστώνην, ἀλλὰ πρὸς ἀρετὴν συμπράττειν.
10. Plot. I 6,8.21 πατρὶς δὴ ἡμῖν, ὅθεν παρήλθομεν, καὶ πατὴρ ἐκεῖ. Same quotation
infra § 16; 7 § 2; Alc. 94.21–22.

it. Another way in which he expressed the law against suicide was the Pythagorean precept of not removing burdens but adding to them, that is to say, working with life, not against it. Cebes had studied with Philolaus in Boeotia, at Thebes. How, then, did Philolaus come to leave the *homakoïon*, which was the Pythagorean school in Italy? It happened like this: their practice was to lead a communal life, in which all the property was shared. Now if a man was found unfit for philosophy, they expelled him with his possessions, built a cenotaph for him and mourned him as one deceased. So one Gylon, who had been a member and to whom this had happened, set fire to the school, and all perished in it, except two, Philolaus and Hipparchus. Philolaus then came to Thebes because he owed funeral libations to his master Lysis, who was dead and was buried there, the one after whom Plato has named his dialogue *Lysis or on Friendship*. Thus far the survey.

14.   **Well, I speak about these things from hearsay myself [61d9]:** The phrase 'from hearsay' means that there was no affinity of disposition; the 'hearsay' is as it were a sack in which the information was contained.

15.   **What I happen to have heard, I shall not begrudge you [61d9–10]:** Envy is the lowest of passions; it is appropriate to matter, which can only receive, not give. That is what envy means, to receive only and not to share with others.

16.   **Perhaps it is even especially appropriate now that I am setting out on my journey to the other world [61d10–e1]:** 'Perhaps' because of the mythical, 'especially' because of the philosophical argument. One wonders if the word 'setting out' is correctly chosen: rather he ought to speak of 'going home', for 'our Father and our fatherland are yonder' [Plot. I 6, 8.21]. We must conclude that either Socrates wilfully scorns current usage, or else that the speaks of 'setting out' from the point of view

---

13–23.   The principal texts on the cenotaphs, Cylon and the Pythagorean diaspora are Diod. Sic. 10,11; Plut., *gen. Socr.* 13–15; Origen, *c. Cels.* 2,12 (p. 141.16–17); Diog. Laert. 2,46; 8,39; 49; Porph., *vit. Pyth.* 55; Iambl., *vit. Pyth.* 17,73–74; 35,248–250; Themist., *or.* 23, 285b; Ol., *Alc.* 132.11–14; El. 126.5–9. Ol.'s account differs on five points from the standard version: (1) the name Gylon instead of Cylon (also in Them., though unfortunately corrected away in Downey-Norman); (2) Philolaus as a survivor instead of Lysis (also in Plutarch); (3) Hipparchus instead of Archippus as the other (there is, however, a Pythagorean Hipparchus, the addressee of the letter of Lysis, *Pythagoreorum ep.* 3=Iambl., *vit. Pyth.* 17,75–78, and the alleged author of a treatise Περὶ εὐθυμίας, Stob. IV 44,81); (4) Philolaus as a disciple of Lysis, who comes to Thebes to visit his master's grave; (5) Lysis identified with the boy in Pl.'s dialogue. Since Ol. is certainly not responsible for variants (1) and (2) and possibly not for (3), the fourth also may come from an earlier source; it looks like a combination of Theanor, the mysterious visitor of Lysis' grave in Plutarch, with Pl.'s implication (not confirmed by other sources) that Philolaus spent some time at Thebes towards the end of the fifth cent. Point (5), a signal

Πυθαγόρειον παράγγελμα 'μὴ ἀποτιθέναι, ἀλλὰ συνεπιτιθέναι βάρη', τουτέστι συμπράττειν τῇ ζωῇ, οὐκ ἀντιπράττειν. συνεγένετο δὲ ὁ Κέβης Φιλολάῳ ἐν Βοιωτίᾳ, ἐν ταῖς Θήβαις γάρ. πῶς δὲ ἄρα καταλέλοιπε τὸ ὁμακόϊον, ὅπερ ἦν ἐν Ἰταλίᾳ Πυθαγορικὸν διδασκαλεῖον; ἰστέον δὲ ὅτι ἔθος ἦν παρ' αὐτοῖς ὥστε   15
ἐν κοινῷ βίῳ ζῆν τὴν οὐσίαν πᾶσαν κοινὴν ποιουμένους. εἴ τις οὖν ἀνεπιτήδειος ηὑρέθη πρὸς φιλοσοφίαν, ἐξῆγον αὐτὸν μετὰ τῆς οὐσίας καὶ κενοτάφιον ἐποίουν καὶ ὡς περὶ ἀποιχομένου ἀπωδύροντο. Γύλων δέ τις εἰσελθὼν καὶ πεπονθὼς τοῦτο ὑφῆψε πῦρ τῷ διδασκαλείῳ καὶ πάντες ἐκαύθησαν πλὴν δύο, Φιλολάου καὶ Ἱππάρχου. ἦλθεν οὖν ὁ Φιλόλαος εἰς Θήβας ὀφείλων χοὰς τῷ οἰκείῳ   20
διδασκάλῳ τεθνεῶτι καὶ ἐκεῖ τεθαμμένῳ ποιήσασθαι, τῷ Λύσιδι, οὗ καὶ κατὰ ὁμωνυμίαν γέγραπται τῷ Πλάτωνι διάλογος 'Λύσις ἢ περὶ φιλίας'. ταῦτα ἔχει ἡ θεωρία.

Ἀλλὰ μὴν καὶ ἐγὼ ἐξ ἀκοῆς περὶ αὐτῶν λέγω [61d9]· 'ἐξ ἀκοῆς',   14
τουτέστιν οὐκ ἀπὸ διαθέσεως τοιαύτης, ἀλλὰ ἐξ ἀκοῆς δίκην θυλάκου ἐν ᾧ ἦσαν οἱ λόγοι.

Ἃ μὲν οὖν τυγχάνω ἀκηκοὼς φθόνος οὐδεὶς λέγειν [61d9–10]:   15
τὸ γὰρ φθονεῖν ἔσχατον πάθος ἐστὶ τῇ ὕλῃ ἀνῆκον τῇ μετα|λαμβανούσῃ μόνον.   (10)
⟦οὐκ⟧ ἔστι δὲ φθονεῖν τὸ μεταλαμβάνειν μόνον, ἀλλὰ ⟦καὶ τὸ⟧ μὴ μεταδιδόναι.

Καὶ γὰρ ἴσως καὶ μάλιστα πρέπει μέλλοντα ἐκεῖσε ἀποδημεῖν   16
[61d10–e1]: τὸ μὲν 'ἴσως' εἴρηται διὰ τὸ μυθικὸν ἐπιχείρημα, τὸ δὲ 'μάλιστα' διὰ τὸ φιλόσοφον. μήποτε οὐ καλῶς εἶπεν 'ἀποδημεῖν', ἔδει γὰρ εἰπεῖν 'ἐπιδημεῖν', διότι 'πατὴρ ἡμῶν καὶ πατρὶς ἐκεῖ' [Plot. I 6, 8.21]. ἢ οὖν κατεφρόνησεν τῆς συνηθείας ἢ ἀποδημίαν αὐτὴν εἶπεν ὡς πρὸς τὸ σῶμα· τῷ γὰρ δεδημευμένῳ   5
ἀποδημία ἐστὶν ἡ ἀναχώρησις τῆς ψυχῆς ἀπὸ τοῦ σώματος.

---

§ 15. 3 οὐκ M: del. Wk | καὶ τὸ M: del. Wk

---

blunder, must be Ol.'s, or the reportator's.
   16. ἐν κοινῷ βίῳ : Iambl., vit. Pyth. 6,29 τὸ λεγόμενον κοινοβίους . . . γενομένους.
   22–23.   ταῦτα ἔχει ἡ θεωρία : the formula usually separates the general part of a lecture (θεωρία) from the λέξις, but it can also serve to end an entire lecture (Ol., Gorg. 8.12). Finckh and Beutler (art. Ol. 225.53–226.4) deleted it here, because it has neither of these two functions and because it occurs already at § 9.9. However, the lecture is an unusually long one, and it is easier to explain the disappearance of a πρᾶξις heading than the gratuitous insertion of the present formula. It is possible, therefore, that there were really two lectures, 1 §§ 1–12 and §§ 13–23: after the lengthy discussion of suicide, Ol. may have dismissed his class, reserving most of the λέξις for the next session. The reportator would then have regarded the historical digression on the Pythagorean school, though it really deals with the lemma 61d6–7, as an adequate substitute for the usual θεωρία.
   § 14. 2–3. Cf. Pl., Theaet. 161a8.
   § 15.   On φθόνος cf. Pr., Tim. I 362.31–365.3.
   § 16. 2–3.   Schol. Pl. 9.11–13.
   3–4.   Cf. infra 7 § 2.1–4.
   4.   Cf. supra § 13.9.

of the body; for to the part that this world has made its own, the departure
of the soul from the body is a setting out.

17.   **During the time till sunset [61e3–4]:** It was the custom at Athens
to have no executions by day, a custom comparable to that of the
Pythagoreans not to sleep at noon, when the sun is at the height of
its strength.

18.   **For you may hear something still. Perhaps ... [61a1–2]:** The
'perhaps' is rightly added in view of the mythical argument, which conceals
the matter rather than reveals it. In a myth indeed, there is no question of
'expressing' things 'well' [62b6–7] or badly, since it *expresses* nothing at all.

19.   **If, unlike all other things, this is uncomplicated [62a2–3]:** It seems
strange to you, Socrates says, that while all other things are ambivalent
and may be either good or bad (e.g. riches, a sword), death should be
only good.

20.   **And Cebes, laughing softly, said 'Yes by Zeus', in his own dialect
[62a8–9]:** Cebes laughs because Socrates called the suicide his own
benefactor. *Ittô* is dialectal, the Boeotian form for *istô*; there is a reason
why he uses the local dialect: it shows his natural and native admiration
for Socrates. There is also a reason why he swears by Zeus: the subject
of the discussion is life, and Zeus is 'the one through whom' (*di' hou*)
life (*zên*) is bestowed; for, as it is argued in the *Cratylus* [396a2–b3],
there is nothing against making up one etymology from more than
one word.

21.   **To be illogical this way [62b1–2]:** i.e. unexplained, for *logos* means
reason, as we have seen in the *Gorgias* [Ol., *Gorg.* 70.16–21].

22.   **And not easy to see its meaning [62b5–6]:** That is to say, it is
not easy to see so long as one is active on the level of sense perception;
this is why Socrates speaks of 'sight', which is the first activity of the
senses. One must therefore close one's eyes to contemplate it.

23.   **That it is the Gods who are our guardians [62b7]:** the second
argument. End of the first problem, that of suicide; follows the second,
concerning the philosopher's will to die.

---

§ 17.   Schol. Pl. 9.14–17.

1–2.   The legal time at Athens was *before* sunset (*Ph.* 116e1–6). Norvin cites
Herod. IV 146,2, who says that in Sparta executions took place by night, the reason
for which might be the one stated by Ol.

2–3.   μηδένα καθεύδειν ἐν μεσημβρίᾳ : the alleged Pythagorean custom may have
been inferred by a combination of Aristophon, frg. 10.6–7 Kock (from his play
The Pythagorean: πνῖγος ὑπομεῖναι καὶ μεσημβρίας λαλεῖν τέττιξ) with Pl., *Phaedr.*
259a1–6, in which case it may come from a commentary on the *Phaedrus* (not in
Hermias, however; cf. 213.11–14). Cf. Proclus, *On the Golden Verses*, 106b "They used not
to countenance sleeping at sunrise, so that the giver of light and life should not rise while they
were asleep." (Linley, p.75).

Ἐν τῷ μέχρι ἡλίου δυσμῶν χρόνῳ [61e3–4]: νόμος γὰρ ἦν παρὰ   17
τοῖς Ἀθηναίοις τὸ μηδένα φονεύειν ἐν ἡμέρᾳ, ὡς καὶ παρὰ Πυθαγορείοις μηδένα
καθεύδειν ἐν μεσημβρίᾳ, ἡνίκα ὁ ἥλιος τὴν ἰσχυροτάτην αὐτοῦ ἐνέργειαν
ἐνδείκνυται.

Τάχα γὰρ ἂν καὶ ἀκούσαις. ἴσως [62a1–2]: καλῶς τὸ 'ἴσως' διὰ   18
τὸ μυθικὸν ἐπιχείρημα, διότι μᾶλλον σιωπᾷ ἢ λέγει. οὐ γὰρ διαφορὰ μύθου
τὸ 'εὖ λέγειν' [62b6–7] τὰ πράγματα ἢ κακῶς, ὅπου γε οὐδὲν λέγει ὅλως.

Εἰ τοῦτο μόνον τῶν ἄλλων ἁπλοῦν ἐστιν [62a2–3]: 'θαυμαστόν   19
σοι φαίνεται', φησίν, 'ὅτι τῶν ἄλλων πάντων ἐπαμφοτεριζόντων καὶ ἀγαθῶν
καὶ κακῶν δυναμένων εἶναι, οἷον πλούτου, ξίφους, ὁ θάνατος μόνως ἀγαθός ἐστιν'.

Καὶ ὁ Κέβης ἠρέμα ἐπιγελάσας, ἴττω Ζεύς, ἔφη, τῇ ἑαυτοῦ 20(11)
φωνῇ [62a8–9]: ἐγέλασε διότι ἐκάλεσε τὸν φονεύοντα ἑαυτὸν εὐεργέτην. τὸ
δὲ 'ἴττω' ἐπιχωριάζοντός ἐστιν ἀντὶ τοῦ 'ἴστω' τῇ Βοιωτίδι διαλέκτῳ· καὶ
εἰκότως ἐγχωρίᾳ γλώττῃ ἐχρήσατο ἐνδεικνύμενος τὸ φυσικὸν καὶ ἐγχώριον
θαῦμα ὃ εἶχε πρὸς τὸν Σωκράτην. καὶ εἰκότως περὶ ζωῆς ὄντος τοῦ λόγου εἰς   5
τὸν Δία ὤμοσε, Ζεὺς γὰρ εἴρηται δι' οὗ τὸ ζῆν· ὡς γὰρ ἐν τῷ Κρατύλῳ λέγεται
[396a2–b3], οὐκ ἄτοπον ἐκ πλειόνων ὀνομάτων μίαν ἐτυμολογίαν ποιεῖν.

Οὕτω γὰρ εἶναι ἄλογον [62b1–2]: ἀναιτιολόγητον· λόγος γὰρ ἡ αἰτία,   21
ὡς ἐν Γοργίᾳ εἴρηται [Ol., Gorg. 70.16–21].

Καὶ οὐ ῥᾳδίως διιδεῖν [62b5–6]: τουτέστιν οὐ δυνατὸν αἰσθητικῶς   22
ἐνεργοῦντα διιδεῖν τοῦτον· διὸ καὶ ὄψεως ἐμνημόνευσεν, πρώτη γὰρ αὕτη ἐνέργεια
τῶν αἰσθήσεων. ἀνάγκη οὖν μῦσαι τὸν μέλλοντα θεάσασθαι αὐτόν.

Τὸ θεοὺς εἶναι ἡμῶν τοὺς ἐπιμελουμένους [62b7]: τὸ δεύτερον   23
ἐπιχείρημα. ἐν οἷς τὸ πρῶτον πρόβλημα τὸ περὶ ἐξαγωγῆς· διαδέχεται καὶ τὸ
δεύτερον τὸ τὸν φιλόσοφον ἐθέλειν ἀποθνήσκειν.

---

§ 17. 1 μέχρι M¹ (Pl.): μέχρις Mᶜ.
§ 18. 1 ἀκούσαις] -σαιο Pl. TY
§ 19. 1 post ἄλλων] ἁπάντων add. Mᶜ (Pl.)
§ 20. 1 ἴττω M¹, Pl. W²: ἴττ' ὦ Mˢ (ἴττι ὦ Pl. B, ἰττίω B²TY, εἰττίω W¹) | ζεύς M¹,
Pl. B¹T: ζεῦ Mˢ, Pl. B²WY | post τῇ] αὐτός add. Mᶜ (om. M¹, Pl.) | ἑαυτοῦ M, Pl. W:
αὐτοῦ Pl. B, αὐτοῦ Pl. TY — 2 εὐεργέτην mg. Mᶜ: om. M¹ — 3 ἴστω μ: ἴττω M, schol. Pl. |
Βοιωτίδι schol. Pl. h.l.: βοιωτίαι M, schol. Pl. Ep. 345a
§ 21. 1 γὰρ¹] γ' Pl.
§ 22. 1 ῥᾳδίως M¹: ῥάιδιον Mᶜ (ῥᾴδιος Pl.)

---

§ 18. The note relates both to the τάχα here and to the ἴσως at 62b6, since
Ol. goes on to discuss εὖ λέγεσθαι at b6–7.
§ 19. Schol. Pl. 9.18–20. – On the interpretation of Ol. and Simpl. (Epict.
28.33–40) see L. Tarán, Plato, Phaedo 62A, Am. Journ. Philol. 87, 1966, 326–336
(328 n. 1).
§ 20. 2–5. Schol. Pl. 10.5–8; 394.4–7.
5–6. Similar remarks on the appropriateness of oaths: Pr., Alc. 233.4–234.5
(=Ol., Alc. 87.3–10); 241.3–9; infra 5 § 6.
§ 23. Cf. schol. Pl. 10.9–16.

2

Lecture **

**1. As regards what you said already, that philosophers will easily ...
[62c9–63e8].**

Socrates has shown that it is unlawful to commit suicide, though it
is sometimes justifiable (it is unlawful in so far as the soul does violence
to the body), and he is further going to show that the philosopher is
willing to die. Cebes was not convinced as to the first point, and so he
naturally raised objections; taking the second for granted, since he knew
as a disciple of Philolaus that the philosopher is willing to die – taking
this for granted he reduces Socrates's view to absurdity by the following
reasoning: 'The philosopher is willing to die, one who is willing to die
runs away from good masters, he who runs away from good masters is
foolish, therefore the philosopher is foolish'. What contradiction could
be more flagrant than this, that the one who claims to know all things
that are, and who must consequently be the wisest of men, should be
proved a fool? Next he argues the point in a different way in the second
figure, on the lines of Aristotle's so-called parasyllogism from contradictory
premises [*Anal. pr.* II 15], as follows: 'The philosopher shuns the good;
no philosopher shuns the good, for neither does anybody else, since all
beings aspire after the good; therefore the philosopher is not a philosopher'.
This is the strongest contradiction possible, for a thing not to be what it is.

2. Simmias applies the same objection to Socrates personally; he says:
'So Socrates is willing to die, leaving his friends and his masters'. We see
from this that Cebes has made further progress than Simmias, since Cebes
takes his cues from Socrates, Simmias from Cebes. Both arguments are
stated well: Cebes, reasoning in general terms, criticizes philosophy only,
while Simmias, who brings Socrates into the discussion, does not mention
the major premise ('Such a man is a fool') to avoid criticizing Socrates.
3. Each of the two arguments has an advantage and a disadvantage
as compared with the other: that of Cebes is more scientific, because it

---

Lect. 2.   Questions raised by Cebes and Simmias, and Socrates' answer. Interruption
by the jailer. The objections of Cebes (62c9–e7) and Simmias (63a4–9) with Socrates'
answer (63b4–c7) are dealt with in much the same way by Dam. The allegorical
interpretation of the conversation with the jailer (§ 8) also has its counterpart
in Dam. I §§ 46–47, the source for the entire lecture being apparently Pr.

§ 1. 3–4. Cf. *supra* 1 § 9.

11.   Cf. *SVF* III frg. 548, and the definition of philosophy as γνῶσις τῶν ὄντων
ᾗ ὄντα ἐστί (from Ar., *met.* Γ 3, 1005b8–11) in Amm., *isag.* 2.23–3.1; El. 10.11–11.16;
Dav. 27.1–28.21; Ps.-El. 11,1–19. Dav. (27.8–10) and Ps.-El. (11,8–14) specify that
τῶν ὄντων=πάντων τῶν ὄντων.

2

Πρᾶξις σὺν θεῷ (12)

Ὁ μὲν τοίνυν ἤδη ἔλεγες, τὸ τοὺς φιλοσόφους ῥᾳδίως [62c9– 1
63e8].

Τοῦ Σωκράτους δείξαντος ὅτι ἀθέμιτον τὸ ἐξάγειν ἑαυτόν, εἰ καί ποτε εὔλογον
(ἀθέμιτον γὰρ ὅσον ἐπὶ τῇ ψυχῇ βιαζομένῃ τὸ σῶμα), μέλλοντος δὲ δείξειν
ὅτι ὁ φιλόσοφος ἐθελήσει ἀποθνῄσκειν, ὁ Κέβης τῷ μὲν πρώτῳ μὴ πεπεισμένος 5
εἰκότως ἠπόρει πρὸς αὐτό· τὸ δὲ δεύτερον λαβὼν ὁμολογούμενον — ᾔδει γὰρ
ἅτε Φιλολάῳ συγγεγονώς, ὅτι ὁ φιλόσοφος ἐθελήσει ἀποθνῄσκειν — τοῦτο οὖν
λαβὼν ὁμολογούμενον συνάγει ἄτοπον τῷ Σωκράτει τοιοῦτον· 'ὁ φιλόσοφος
ἐθελήσει ἀποθνῄσκειν, ὁ ἀποθνῄσκειν θέλων τοὺς ἀγαθοὺς φεύγει δεσπότας,
ὁ ἀγαθοὺς φεύγων δεσπότας ἀνόητός ἐστιν, ὁ φιλόσοφος ἄρα ἀνόητος'. οὗ 10
μείζων τίς ἂν εἴη ἀντίφασις, τὸν ἐπαγγελλόμενον πάντα τὰ ὄντα εἰδέναι καὶ διὰ
τοῦτο φρονιμώτατον ἀνόητον δειχθῆναι; πλέκει δὲ αὐτὸ καὶ ἄλλως ἐν δευτέρῳ
σχήματι κατὰ τὸν λεγόμενον παρὰ Ἀριστοτέλει [Anal. pr. II 15] ἐξ ἀντικειμένων
παρασυλλογισμὸν οὕτως· 'ὁ φιλόσοφος φεύγει τὸ ἀγαθόν· οὐδεὶς φιλόσοφος
φεύγει τὸ ἀγαθόν, ὅπου γε οὐδὲ ἄλλος ἄνθρωπος (πάντα γὰρ τοῦ ἀγαθοῦ ἐφίεται)· 15
ὁ φιλόσοφος ἄρα οὐ φιλόσοφος'. καὶ ἔστιν αὕτη μεγίστη ἀντίφασις, ὅ ἐστί τι,
μὴ εἶναι.

Ὁ δὲ Σιμμίας τὸ αὐτὸ ἄτοπον συνάγει ἐπὶ τοῦ Σωκράτους, λέγων ὅτι Σωκράτης 2
ἄρα ἐθελήσει ἀποθνῄσκειν καταλιπὼν φίλους καὶ δεσπότας. καὶ ἀναφαίνεται
ἐντεῦθεν ὅτι τελειότερος Κέβης Σιμμίου, εἴ γε ὁ μὲν τὰς ἀφορμὰς τῶν λόγων
ἐκ τοῦ Σωκράτους λαμβάνει, ὁ δὲ Σιμμίας ἐκ τῶν Κέβητος λόγων. καὶ ἑκάτερος
λόγος δεόντως προήχθη· ὁ μὲν γὰρ τοῦ Κέβητος ἐπὶ τοῦ καθόλου προελθὼν 5
φιλοσοφίας μόνης καθήψατο, ὁ δὲ | τοῦ Σιμμίου ἐπὶ τοῦ Σωκράτους τῆς μείζονος (13)
προτάσεως οὐκ ἐμνημόνευσε τῆς λεγούσης ὅτι ὁ τοιοῦτος ἀνόητος, ἵνα μὴ τοῦ
Σωκράτους καθάψηται. ἑκάτερος δὲ τῶν λόγων καὶ νικᾷ καὶ νικᾶται, ὁ μὲν 3
τοῦ Κέβητος ὡς ἐπιστημονικώτερος, διότι ἐπὶ τοῦ καθόλου προῆλθεν, οἰκεῖον
δὲ τῇ ἐπιστήμῃ τὸ καθόλου, ὁ δὲ τοῦ Σιμμίου τῇ συμπαθείᾳ καὶ εὐγνωμοσύνῃ

---

§ 1. 1 μὲν τοίνυν ἤδη] μέντοι νῦν δὴ Pl. (μὲν τοίνυν δὴ Pl. W) | τὸ τοὺς φιλοσόφους
ῥᾳδίως M¹, Pl.: τὸ ῥᾳδίως τοὺς φιλοσόφους Mᶜ

12–17. Dam. I § 26. The term παρασυλλογισμός is not in LSJ; Ar. says in this
context (anal. pr. II 15, 63b13–15) δῆλον δὲ καὶ ὅτι ἐν τοῖς παραλογισμοῖς
οὐδὲν κωλύει γίνεσθαι τῆς ὑποθέσεως ἀντίφασιν, οἷον εἰ ἐστι περιττόν, μὴ εἶναι περιττόν.
So also Ol., cat. 121.26–28. Dam. I § 26 calls it τὸν ἐξ ἀντικειμένων συλλογισμόν,
and so does Philop., anal. pr. 444.27–28 (but 445.22 ἵνα μὴ παραλογιζώμεθα). Though
παρασυλλογισμός can easily be accounted for as resulting from a lectio duplex (cf. also
παρασυλλογιστικός as v.l. Etym. magn. 35.28 and schol. Aristoph., Nub. 317), it is
supported by § 10.2 and is in itself a meaningful formation.
§ 2. 4–8. Dam. I § 35.
§ 3. 2–3. Ar., met. K 1, 1059b26 πᾶσα ἐπιστήμη τῶν καθόλου.

proceeds on general lines, which is proper to science, that of Simmias has the qualities of sympathy and cordiality towards the master; he says: 'Do not leave us, Socrates, think over what Cebes says'. This is the reason why Simmias refers to friends also; and whereas Socrates in his remarks has mentioned 'God' and 'Gods', these two divide the master's words between them and both refer to 'God' as well as to 'Gods'.

4. Socrates has a common answer to the two questions, the one that starts from friends and Gods, and the one that starts from God and Gods. He presents it in two ways, both of them hypothetical, in the first and in the second mood of the hypothetical syllogism. He begins with the second mood, as follows: 'If I did not believe that I am going to better masters and friends, I should be wrong to die without regret; but I believe I am; therefore I am not wrong not to grieve'. The better masters to whom he is going are the supra-mundane Gods, who are superior to the intra-mundane Gods. But how do we account for his applying conversion by negation to the antecedent ('but I think I am'), when he ought to negative the consequent? The explanation is that when the terms are coextensive one can take either indifferently, and such is the case here. Next he expresses his solution in a hypothetical syllogism of the first mood: 'If I am going to better friends and masters, it is right that I should die without regret; the former is true; therefore so is the latter', in accordance with the rule for the first mood of the hypothetical syllogism, that if the antecedent is affirmed, the consequent becomes true too. Observe that in the first argument he says 'I should be wrong to die without regret', here, however, 'it is right that I should die without regret'.

5. Why does Socrates, in the first of these two arguments, place the masters before the friends, and in the second the friends before the masters? Because both are reasonings *a fortiori*: in the first he mentions the masters before the friends to show that, if there are no good Gods, there are even more certainly no good men; in the second he makes it clear that, if there are good friends, it is even more true that there are good Gods also, for whatever is good comes from God, as all light comes from the sun, God being the monad of goodness.

5-7. **Dam. I § 28; § 38.** – Socrates has spoken of Gods (62b7-8) and God (62c7), and so has Cebes (62d2 and 6), while Simmias refers to friends (ἡμᾶς 63a8) and Gods in the plural; cf. *infra* § 4.1-2, and Dam.

§§ 4-5. **Dam. I § 43.**

§ 4. 3-4. The theory of the hypothetical syllogism is outlined by Philop., *anal. pr.* 242.14-246.14; cf. Norvin 1915, 269. The first mood is 'If A is true, B is true; A is true; therefore so is B'; the second 'If A is true, B is true; B is not true; therefore neither is A' ('If it is day, there is light; there is no light; therefore it is not day'). When the terms are coextensive, the form '. . . A is not true; therefore neither is B' is legitimate, according to lines 9-10 ('If it is day, there is sunlight; it is not day; therefore there is no sunlight'). The same logical objection is raised

τῇ περὶ τὸν διδάσκαλον. φησὶ γὰρ ὅτι 'μὴ καταλείψῃς ἡμᾶς, ὦ Σώκρατες, ὅρα
γὰρ τί φησιν ὁ Κέβης'. διὸ καὶ φίλων μέμνηται ὁ Σιμμίας· καὶ τοῦ Σωκράτους 5
ἐν τοῖς οἰκείοις λόγοις θεοῦ καὶ θεῶν μνημονεύσαντος ἐμερίσαντο οὗτοι τοὺς
λόγους τοῦ οἰκείου διδασκάλου καὶ μέμνηνται ἄμφω καὶ θεοῦ καὶ θεῶν.

ὁ δὲ Σωκράτης πρὸς ἄμφω τὰς ἀπορίας, τήν τε ἀπὸ τῶν φίλων καὶ θεῶν 4
προελθοῦσαν καὶ τὴν ἀπὸ θεοῦ καὶ θεῶν, κοινὴν λύσιν ἐπάγει. διχῶς δὲ ταύτην
προάγει καὶ ὑποθετικῶς, κατά τε τὸν πρῶτον τρόπον τῶν ὑποθετικῶν καὶ τὸν
α′ δεύτερον. καὶ τέως κατὰ τὸν δεύτερον· φησὶ γὰρ ὅτι 'εἰ μὴ ᾤμην παρὰ κρείττους
δεσπότας καὶ φίλους ἀπιέναι, ἠδίκουν ἂν μὴ ἀγανακτῶν ἐπὶ τῷ θανάτῳ· ἀλλὰ 5
μὴν οἶμαι· οὐκ ἀδικῶ ἄρα μὴ ἀγανακτῶν'. παρὰ κρείττους γὰρ δεσπότας
ἄπεισιν ὑπερκοσμίους τῶν ἐγκοσμίων. ἀλλὰ πῶς τῇ σὺν ἀντιθέσει ἀντιστροφῇ
ἐκ τοῦ ἡγουμένου ἐχρήσατο εἰπὼν 'ἀλλὰ μὴν οἶμαι', δέον ἐκ τοῦ ἑπομένου;
ἢ ἐπὶ τῶν ἐξισαζόντων ὅρων ἀδιάφορον ὅθεν βούλεταί τις χρῆσθαι, ὥσπερ
β′ ἐνταῦθα. προάγει δὲ αὐτὴν καὶ κατὰ τὸν πρῶτον τρόπον τῶν ὑποθετικῶν λέγων 10
'εἰ παρὰ κρείττοσι φίλοις καὶ δεσπόταις ἄπειμι, δικαίως ἄρα οὐκ ἀγανακτῶ
ἐπὶ τῷ θανάτῳ· ἀλλὰ μὴν τὸ πρῶτον· καὶ τὸ δεύτερον ⟨ἄρα⟩'· νόμῳ τοῦ πρώτου
τρόπου τῶν ὑποθετικῶν τῇ θέσει τοῦ ἡγουμένου εἰσάγων καὶ τὸ ἑπόμενον. καὶ
ὅρα ὅτι ἐν μὲν τῷ πρώτῳ λόγῳ εἶπεν ὅτι 'ἠδίκουν ἂν μὴ ἀγανακτῶν', ἐνταῦθα
δὲ ὅτι 'καὶ δίκαια ποιῶ μὴ ἀγανακτῶν'. 15

Δύο δὲ ὄντων λόγων τί δή ποτε ἐν μὲν τῷ πρώτῳ προέταξεν ὁ Σωκράτης 5
τοὺς δεσπότας τῶν φίλων, ἐν δὲ τῷ δευτέρῳ τοὺς φίλους | τῶν δεσποτῶν; ⟨ἢ⟩ (14)
ἑκάτερα τῶν ἐπιχειρήσεων ἀπὸ τοῦ μᾶλλον προῆλθεν· ἐν μὲν γὰρ τῇ πρώτῃ
προέταξεν τοὺς δεσπότας τῶν φίλων, ἐνδεικνύμενος ὅτι, εἰ μή εἰσι θεοὶ ἀγαθοί,
πολλῷ μᾶλλον οὐδὲ ἄνθρωποι ἀγαθοί, ἐν δὲ τῇ δευτέρᾳ δηλῶν ὅτι, εἰ εἰσὶν φίλοι
ἀγαθοί, πολλῷ μᾶλλον καὶ θεοί· πᾶν γὰρ ἀγαθὸν ἐκ θεοῦ, ὥσπερ καὶ πᾶν φῶς 5
ἀφ' ἡλίου, διότι μονὰς ἀγαθότητος ὁ θεός.

---

§ 4. 11 ἄρα del.? (cf. lin. 12) — 12 ἄρα Wk: om. M — 13 εἰσάγων Fh: -ον M
§ 5. 2 ἢ Fh: om. M

---

and answered at Ar., an. I 1, 403a10 by Philop., an. 46.10–18. Dam. I § 474. –
It is difficult to discover in the text anything but one hypothetical syllogism in
the second mood (major b5–9, minor b9–c4, conclusion c4–5). But Dam. I § 43
shows that Pr. (the common source of Dam. and Ol.) constructed a second
hypothetical syllogism out of b9–c5.

12. ἀλλὰ μὴν τὸ πρῶτον· καὶ τὸ δεύτερον ἄρα : on this formula SVF III Crinis
frg. 5, p. 269.18–19. Cf. Baltes Weltenstehung I, p. 157, n. 279.

§ 5. 7. μονὰς ἀγαθότητος ὁ θεός : an Alexandrian formula, as also is 4 § 3.10–11
μονὰς ἀπλήθυντος. Cf. Ol., Alc. 44.9 τὸ θεῖον δὲ ἑνάς ἐστιν ὑπερούσιος, 51.16–17 ἑνάς
γὰρ ὁ θεὸς καὶ ἑνοειδής, 18–19 πολλὰ γὰρ τὰ μετὰ τὸ θεῖον καὶ τὴν μονάδα τὰ ἐξ αὐτῆς
παραγόμενα. Pr. avoids calling the One a monad, cf. elem. 100 πᾶσαι δὲ αὖ αἱ ἀμέθεκτοι
μονάδες εἰς τὸ ἓν ἀνάγονται. Also theol. II 5, p. 38.3–7.

6. One may wonder why Socrates is so positive with regard to the Gods: 'that I am going to better Gods, I do not doubt; whether to better men also, is a point of which I am less sure'. What is the reason of his hesitation in the case of men? According to some, the obvious explanation is this: Socrates speaks of 'men', not of 'people'; now since it is uncertain if some of the righteous souls we meet in the other world are not those of women rather than of men, therefore he expresses himself less positively: why, indeed, should there not be souls of good women in that world? This answer, however, is trivial, and unworthy of Plato's greatness of conception. Rather, it is modesty that makes Socrates say that he is not so sure, for it would have been in bad taste to say these things about himself, which would have made him blush if another were to say them; in the same way he says further on [69d5–6]: 'When I arrive in that other land, I shall know for certain', not as if there were any doubt about it, but because it is boastful to praise oneself.

7. There are two assumptions from which Socrates' answers proceed: one that the soul is immortal (which is necessary, if she is to have a destination at all), the other that there is a providence that gives to each according to his merit; of these, the existence of a providence that gives to each according to his merit is admitted by Cebes and his friend, but they question the immortality of the soul, which is the necessary condition of her having such or such a destination. The five arguments for immortality therefore follow logically now, but the transition is 'noiseless like a stream of oil', for in good prose there is no division into points one, two, etc.

8. Crito then says to Socrates: 'You had better not talk too much; that is a message from the man who prepares the poison, otherwise you would get hot by the exertion and digest the hemlock, in which case you may have to drink it twice or even three times'. Socrates answers: 'Do not mind him; let him just do his own job, so that I can have it a second and a third time, if necessary'. And Crito says he knew that this would be the answer. Here Socrates represents the intellective and purificatory way of life, Crito the secondary life that depends on it, the man who prepares the poison the destructive cause which has the immediate control of matter and is also in charge of privation. This is why the man who makes the poison does not address Socrates directly, to intimate that there is no immediate contact between the lowest and

---

§ 6. 7–11. Dam. I § 45. Against the claims of the Middle Academy, which explained Plato's frequent use of 'perhaps, probably', etc. as expressing suspension of judgment, the Neoplatonic commentators try to find a satisfactory way of accounting for such particles wherever they occur. Cf. El. 110.12–16; *Proleg.* 10.6–9 and note (to which add Ol., *Gorg.* 188.15–16); *infra* 6 § 14; Dam. I § 182.1.

9. Demosth., *or.* 18,128 οὐδ' ἂν εἷς εἶπεν περὶ αὑτοῦ τοιοῦτον οὐδέν, ἀλλὰ κἂν ἑτέρου λέγοντος ἠρυθρίασεν.

Ἄξιον δὲ ζητῆσαι, τί δή ποτε ἐπὶ τῶν θεῶν διαβεβαιοῦται ὁ Σωκράτης λέγων 6
'ὅτι μὲν παρὰ θεοὺς κρείττους, εὖ οἶδα, εἰ δὲ παρὰ ἄνδρας ἀγαθούς, οὐ πάνυ
διισχυρισαίμην'. τί οὖν τὸ αἴτιον αὐτῷ τῆς ἀμφιβολίας ἐπὶ τῶν ἀνδρῶν; πρὸς
τοῦτό τινές φασιν ὅτι 'εἰκότως· ἐπειδὴ γὰρ ἀνδρῶν ἐμνημόνευσε καὶ οὐκ ἀνθρώπων,
ἄδηλον δὲ μήποτε οὐκ ἀνδρῶν ψυχαὶ ἀλλὰ θηλειῶν ἀγαθαὶ εὑρεθῶσιν ἐκεῖ, 5
διὰ τοῦτο οὐ πάνυ διισχυρίζεται· τί γὰρ κωλύει θηλείας ἀγαθὰς ψυχὰς εἶναι
ἐκεῖ·' τοῦτο δὲ σμικροπρεπὲς καὶ τῆς μεγαλονοίας Πλάτωνος ἀλλότριον. λεκτέον
οὖν ὅτι μετριάζων λέγει μὴ πάνυ τοῦτο διισχυρίζεσθαι· φορτικὸν γὰρ ἦν τὸ
περὶ αὐτοῦ ταῦτα λέγειν, 'κἂν ἑτέρου' γὰρ 'λέγοντος ἐρυθριάσειεν'· ὥσπερ
ἐφεξῆς φησιν ὅτι 'ἐκεῖσε ἀπιόντες τἀκριβὲς μαθησόμεθα' [69d5–6], οὐχ ὅτι 10
ἀμφίβολον, ἀλλ' ὅτι φορτικὸν τὸ ἑαυτὸν ἐπαινεῖν.

Δύο δὲ ὄντων λημμάτων ἐξ ὧν αἱ λύσεις αἱ Σωκρατικαὶ προῆλθον, ἑνὸς μὲν 7
τοῦ ἀθάνατον εἶναι τὴν ψυχήν, ἵνα καὶ λήξεώς τινος τύχῃ, ἑτέρου δὲ τοῦ εἶναι
πρόνοιαν τὸ κατ' ἀξίαν ἀπονέμουσαν ἑκάστῳ, τὸ μὲν εἶναι πρόνοιαν τὸ κατ'
ἀξίαν ἀπονέμουσαν ἑκάστῳ συγχωροῦσιν οἱ περὶ τὸν Κέβητα, ζητοῦσι δὲ εἰ
ἀθάνατος ἡ ψυχή, ἵνα καὶ λήξεων τοίων ἢ τοίων τύχῃ. διὸ εἰκότως διαδέχονται 5
οἱ περὶ ἀθανασίας πέντε λόγοι, ἀποφητὶ τῆς μεταβάσεως γενομένης δίκην ἐλαίου
ῥέοντος· οὐ γὰρ λογογραφικὸν τὸ διαιρεῖν εἰς α' καὶ β' κεφάλαιον.

Ὁ δὲ Κρίτων φησὶ πρὸς τὸν Σωκράτην· 'μὴ διαλέγου πολλά· ἐπιτρέπει γὰρ 8 (15)
τοῦτο ὁ τὸ φάρμακον τρίβων, ἵνα μὴ ἐκ τῆς κινήσεως θερμανθῇς καὶ πέψῃς τὸ
κώνειον καὶ δεήσῃ σε δὶς ἢ καὶ τρὶς πίνειν'. ὁ δὲ Σωκράτης φησίν· 'ἔα τοῦτον
χαίρειν· μόνον τὸ ἑαυτοῦ ποιείτω ὡς ἐμοῦ καὶ δὶς καὶ τρὶς ληψομένου, ἐὰν δεήσῃ'.
καὶ ὁ Κρίτων φησὶν ὅτι ᾔδει ὅτι τοῦτο μέλλει λέγειν. καὶ ἀναλογεῖ ὁ μὲν Σωκράτης 5
τῇ νοερᾷ καὶ καθαρτικῇ ζωῇ, ὁ δὲ Κρίτων τῇ δευτερουργῷ καὶ ἐξημμένῃ ταύτης
ζωῇ, ὁ δὲ τὸ φάρμακον τρίβων τῇ φθοροποιῷ καὶ πρὸς τῇ ὕλῃ ἐφεστώσῃ αἰτίᾳ
τῇ καὶ στερήσεως ἐφόρῳ. διὸ οὐδὲ ἀμέσως τῷ Σωκράτει διαλέγεται ὁ τὸ φάρμακον
τρίβων, ἐνδεικνυμένου τοῦ λόγου ὅτι τὰ ἔσχατα τοῖς πρώτοις οὐ συνάπτεται
ἀμέσως. φησὶ δὲ ὁ Κρίτων εἰδέναι ὅτι τοῦτο μέλλει λέγειν ὁ Σωκράτης, διότι 10
πεῖραν αὐτοῦ εἶχεν ἐν τῷ ὁμωνύμῳ διαλόγῳ ὡς καταφρονητικῶς ἔχοντος περὶ
τὸν θάνατον· χρήματα γὰρ αὐτῷ προτείναντος ἐφ' ᾧ ἐξελθεῖν ἐκ τοῦ δεσμω-
τηρίου, οὐχ εἵλετο, φάσκων μὴ ἀρνεῖσθαι τοὺς νόμους οἷς ἐξ ἀρχῆς ἐμμενεῖν
ὡμολόγησεν. ταῦτα ἔχει ἡ θεωρία.

---

§ 6. 5 θηλείων M — 6 post κωλύει] ras. 1 litt. M — 8 οὖν Mᶜ: om. M¹ — 9 αὐτοῦ
Mustoxydes: αὐτοῦ M
§ 7. 5 τοιῶν (bis) M
§ 8. 3 κώνιον M | δεήσῃ μ: -σει M — 5 ᾔδει M¹: ᾔδειν Mᶜ — 11 εἶχεν] εἰ- in
ras. Mᶜ — 13 ἐμμενεῖν Nv: ἐμμένειν M

---

§ 7. The two assumptions are discussed as a preliminary to the myth by
Dam. I § 469. Cf. Ol. 9 § 1.
6. οἱ περὶ ἀθανασίας πέντε λόγοι: cf. Introduction p. 29.
6–7. Cf. Pl., Theaet. 144b5 οἷον ἐλαίου ῥεῦμα ἀψοφητὶ ῥέοντος.
§ 8. 5–10. Dam. I §§ 46–47. The theory of the interpretation of characters in
the dialogues: Proleg. 16.7–34 (and ibid. Introduction p. XXXV); applications of it:
Pr., Rep. I 6.7–12; Tim. I 9.13–22; Parm. 628–630; 659–665; Crat. 5.11–22; Dam.,
Phil. § 8; Ol., Gorg. 6.21–7.21.

the highest orders of existence. Crito can say that he knew this would be Socrates's answer, because, in the dialogue that bears his own name, he had come to know Socrates as a man who despises death; for when he offered him money to enable him to escape from prison, Socrates refused on the ground that he would not disavow the laws, having once undertaken to abide by them. Thus far the survey.

9. **For surely he does not think that he will take better care of himself when he has become free [62d6–7]**: It is better to be taken care of by God than by oneself, and in this case being moved from without is superior to self-motion. All this makes up the first syllogism.

10. **That nobody runs away from a good master [62e1–2]**: The second syllogism, which takes the form of the parasyllogism from opposite premises.

11. **It seemed to me that he was pleased by Cebes' statement of the facts [62e8–63a1]**: Plato here uses the words 'statement of the facts' for a factual objection; above, when Simmias was asking his question, he called it simply an 'objection'.

12. **And looking at us [63a1]**: Not at Cebes, but at us, as if to say: 'You should follow the example of Cebes, who goes to the bottom of things'.

13. **'You are right', he said [63b1]**: 'You are right', because it is correct to raise the question how a false conclusion could be drawn from true premises. In a debate a 'wrong' is done when untrue inferences are made from true data.

14. **As in a court of justice [63b2]**: The comparison with a court is suitable, inasmuch as the subject of the dialogue is purification, and justice consists in each part of the soul exercising its own function.

15. **'Well', he said, 'let me try' [63b4]**: Socrates does not say 'I shall certainly defend myself', but 'Let me try', for accidental circumstances, too, have to be favorable. It is, indeed, a remark often repeated that many an oncoming crisis has been checked by a sudden spell of frost.

---

§ 9. Dam. I § 23. The same idea phrased in the same way: Ol., *Alc.* 123.3–5 καὶ κρεῖττον τὸ τοιοῦτον ἑτεροκίνητον τοῦ αὐτοκινήτου· κρεῖττον γὰρ τὸ θεόθεν ἄγεσθαι ἢ ὑφ' ἑαυτῶν. *Ibid.* 231.14–15. Dam. I § 169 (on the ἐν θεῷ κεῖται of Chald. Or., frg. 130.2) ἢ τοῦτο μεῖζον καὶ παντὸς αὐτοκινήτου τελειότερον, οἷον ὑπερφυὲς αὐτοκίνητον.
4. Cf. *supra* § 1.7–12.
§ 10. Cf. *supra* § 1.12–17.
1. The reading of M¹, οὐδείς γε . . . φεύγει, might be a real variant, cf. § 1.14–15.
§ 11. 2. πραγματειώδη ἀπορίαν: cf. Dam. I § 34.1–2; Simpl., *cat.* 1.22; *phys.* 1299.4.
2–3. There is no objection by Simmias, nor does the word ἀπορία occur. The confusion may be due to a reference in Ol.'s source (Pr. or Amm.) to 85b10–c1 (Καλῶς, ἔφη, λέγεις, ὁ Σιμμίας· καὶ ἐγώ τέ σοι ἐρῶ ὃ ἀπορῶ, καὶ αὖ ὅδε, ἧ οὐκ ἀποδέχεται τὰ λεγόμενα), which could have served to illustrate the superiority of

Οὐ γάρ που αὐτός γε αὐτοῦ οἴεται ἄμεινον ἐπιμελήσεσθαι 9
ἐλεύθερος γενόμενος [62d6-7]: κρεῖττον τὸ ὑπὸ θεοῦ ἡμᾶς ἐπιμελεῖσθαι ἢ
ὑφ᾽ ἑαυτῶν, | καὶ τὸ τοιοῦτον ἑτεροκίνητον ἄμεινόν ἐστι τοῦ αὐτοκινήτου. διὰ (16)
τούτων δὲ πάντων ὁ πρῶτος συλλογισμὸς παραδίδοται.

Ὅτι οὐδείς γε τοῦ ἀγαθοῦ φεύγει [62e1-2]: ὁ δεύτερος συλλογισμός, 10
ὁ κατὰ τὸν ἐξ ἀντικειμένων παρασυλλογισμόν.

Ἡσθῆναί τέ μοι ἔδοξε τῇ τοῦ Κέβητος πραγματείᾳ [62e8-63a1]: 11
τὴν πραγματειώδη ἀπορίαν πραγματείαν ἐκάλεσεν ὁ Πλάτων· ἀνωτέρω δέ,
ἡνίκα ὁ Σιμμίας ἠρώτα, ἀπορίαν μόνην ἐκάλεσε τὴν ἐρώτησιν αὐτοῦ.

Καὶ ἐπιβλέψας εἰς ἡμᾶς [63a1]: οὐ 'πρὸς τὸν Κέβητα' ἀλλὰ 'πρὸς 12
ἡμᾶς', ἐνδεικνύμενος ὡς 'δεῖ τοῦ Κέβητος ὑμᾶς ἀντέχεσθαι ὡς ζητητικοῦ ὄντος'.

Δίκαια, ἔφη, λέγετε [63b1]: 'δίκαια λέγετε· πῶς γὰρ ἐξ ἀληθῶν προτά- 13
σεων ψευδὲς συμπέρασμα συνήχθη, ἄξιον ζητῆσαι'. ἀδικία γάρ ἐστιν ἐν λόγοις
τὸ ἐξ ἀληθῶν μὴ ἀληθὲς συνάγεσθαι.

Ὥσπερ ἐν δικαστηρίῳ [63b2]: εἰκότως ὡς ἐν δικαστηρίῳ, διότι περὶ 14
καθάρσεως ὁ σκοπός, καὶ ἡ δικαιοσύνη ἐν ἰδιοπραγίᾳ θεωρεῖται τῶν μορίων
τῆς ψυχῆς.

Φέρε δ᾽, ἦ δ᾽ ὅς, πειραθῶ [63b4]: οὐκ εἶπεν ὅτι 'πάντως ἀπολογήσομαι' 15
ἀλλὰ 'πειραθῶ'· δεῖ γὰρ καὶ τῆς συλλήψεως τῆς ἀπὸ τῆς τύχης. ὡς γὰρ πολλάκις
ἐλέχθη, κρίσιν μελετωμένην κρύος ἄφνω ἐπιστὰν ἀνέκοψεν.

---

§ 9. 1 που] πω Pl. TY | αὐτός γε αὐτοῦ] αὐτός τε ἑαυτοῦ, accent. in -ό- ex corr.,
τε ἑ- ex corr., γαρ sscr. et punctis del., Mᶜ (i.e. αὐτὸς γὰρ αὐτοῦ M¹): αὐτός γε (τε Y)
αὐτοῦ (ἑαυτοῦ TW) Pl. | ἐπιμελήσεσθαι] -εῖσθαι Pl. TY
§ 10. 1 οὐδείς γε... φεύγει M¹: οὐ δεῖ ἀπό γε... φεύγειν Mᶜ, Pl.
§ 11. 1 τέ μοι Mᶜ (Pl.): μοί τε M¹
§ 15. 1 δ᾽ι] δή Pl.

Cebes to Simmias.
§ 14. Dam. I § 36.
2-3. Pl.'s term is οἰκειοπραγία (of the classes in the city, *Rep.* IV 434c7-10;
of individual citizens, 443c9-444a2); cf. Plot. I 2,1.19-21 = Porph., *sent.* 32 (p. 23.11);
ἰδιοπραγία ibid. 40 (p. 52.3).
§ 15. 2-3. Parallel passages in Stephanus of Athens prove that the κρίσις is
to be understood in the medical sense: *aphor.* I 20-21, f. 25ᵛ (on bad tidings)
πολλάκις γὰρ οὗτοι παρεμπεσόντες γινομένην κρίσιν ἀνέκοψαν. *Ibid.* II 13, f. 34ʳ κρίσεώς
τινος μελετωμένης. *Ibid.* I 1, f. 5ʳ: external circumstances also have to be favorable;
thus a crisis may fail to take place as predicted owing to cold weather. The fact
that Ol. refers to this observation as 'often made' and that he does not feel that it
needs any further comment, seems to support the suggestion that he may have
lectured on the subject himself; cf. Introduction, p. 27. See also Palladius, *De
Sectis* 74.25-26 Baffioni: πολλάκις μέλλει ⟨κρίσις⟩ γίγνεονται διὰ ἱδρῶτος καὶ ἄφνω
ψυχρὸς ἀὴρ πυκνοῖ τοὺς πόρους καὶ οὐ γίνεται ἡ κρίσις.

16. **To be more plausible in my defense before you than before the judges [63b4–5]:** Of course he will be more plausible to them than to the judges, because in dealing with a mob one has to convince, not by instruction, but by persuasion, while disciples are open to instruction. Or else because in the other case, before the judges, the point under discussion was an individual life, and particular points can be proved only by inquiry; here, on the contrary, it is life in general. It is 'more plausible', then, either because of mass mentality or because of the subject-matter, depending on whether it is general or particular.

3

Lecture **

1. **But to you, my judges, I will now [63e8–65a8].**

There are two points at issue: one, that the philosopher does not take his own life, the other that the philosopher is ready to die. The first, that the philosopher does not take his own life, has been proved by Socrates by means of two arguments, one mythical and Orphic and esoteric, the other demonstrative and philosophical; he now proves the second, that the philosopher will also face death without fear and will prepare for it. For these are two different things, pursuit of death and readiness to die: where 'voluntary' death, i.e. detachment from affects, is concerned, the philosopher both pursues death and is ready for it, but where bodily death is concerned, there is only readiness, not pursuit.

2. His willingness to die is shown in the text by a hypothetical syllogism, as follows: 'If the philosopher trains himself for death, it follows that when death comes, he is not afraid, is not indignant, does not cringe; the former is true; therefore so is the latter'. The major premise he proves in a few words, saying that it is foolish, if one has spent all one's life preparing for a thing and pursuing it (namely, to die and be dead), then to be afraid when it comes. Nor is there ground for this objection: 'If every activity that is complete in itself has its end in this very completion and does not need an additional end (for example,

---

§ 16.   Cf. Ol. 8 § 18.
1–4.   Dam. I § 37.
2–4.   Pl., *Gorg.* 454e3–455a7.
4–6.   Cf. Ol., *Gorg.* 47.8–19; *Alc.* 165.1–8.

Lect. 3.   **Socrates on the philosopher's will to die. The first reason for detachment.** The *theoria* reduces Socrates' discourse on the philosopher's will to die to a hypothetical syllogism: 'If the philosopher trains himself for death, he will not be afraid to face it' (§ 2–§ 3.6). The minor, 'Philosophy is training for death,' is proved by a categorical syllogism with the definition of death as its major:

Πιθανώτερον πρὸς ὑμᾶς ἀπολογήσασθαι ἢ πρὸς τοὺς δικαστάς **16** (17)
[63b4–5]: *εἰκότως πιθανώτερον πρὸς τούτους ἢ πρὸς τοὺς δικαστάς, διότι ἐν*
πλήθει οὐ διδασκαλικῇ πειθοῖ, ἀλλὰ πιστευτικῇ ἀνάγκῃ χρῆσθαι, πρὸς δὲ τοὺς
μαθητὰς διδασκαλικῇ· ἢ καὶ ὅτι ἐκεῖ μὲν πρὸς τοὺς δικαστὰς περὶ μερικῆς ζωῆς
ἦν ὁ λόγος, τὰ δὲ μερικὰ ἐκ μόνης ἱστορίας πιστοῦται, ἐνταῦθα δὲ περὶ ὁλικῆς 5
ζωῆς. πιθανώτερον οὖν ἢ διὰ τὸ πλῆθος ἢ διὰ τὸ ὑποκείμενον καθόλου ὂν ἢ μερικόν.

3

Πρᾶξις σὺν θεῷ

Ἀλλ᾽ ὑμῖν δὴ τοῖς δικασταῖς βούλομαι ἤδη [63e8–65a8]. **1**

Δύο ὄντων προβλημάτων, ἑνὸς μὲν τοῦ τὸν φιλόσοφον μὴ ἐξάγειν ἑαυτόν,
ἑτέρου δὲ τοῦ τὸν φιλόσοφον ἐθέλειν ἀποθνήσκειν, τὸ μὲν πρῶτον, ὅτι οὐκ ἐξάγει
ἑαυτὸν ὁ φιλόσοφος, ἔδειξεν ὁ Σωκράτης ἤδη διὰ δύο λόγων, ἑνὸς μὲν μυθικοῦ
καὶ Ὀρφικοῦ καὶ ἀπορρήτου, ἑτέρου δὲ ἀποδεικτικοῦ καὶ φιλοσόφου· ὅτι δὲ 5
καὶ ἀδεῶς ἕξει περὶ τὸν θάνατον καὶ μελετήσει, νῦν δείκνυσιν. δύο γὰρ ὄντων,
τοῦ τε ἐπιτηδεύειν ἀποθνήσκειν καὶ τοῦ ἐθέλειν ἀποθνήσκειν, τὸν μὲν προαιρετικὸν
θάνατον καὶ τὸν χωρισμὸν τῶν παθῶν καὶ ἐπιτηδεύει καὶ ἐθέλει, τὸν δὲ σωματικὸν
ἐθέλει μέν, οὐ μὴν ἐπιτηδεύει.

Ὅτι | δὲ ἐθέλει ἀποθνήσκειν δείκνυσιν ἡ λέξις δι᾽ ὑποθετικοῦ συλλογισμοῦ **2** (18)
τοῦτον τὸν τρόπον· ᾽εἰ ὁ φιλόσοφος θάνατον μελετᾷ, ἥκοντος ἄρα αὐτοῦ οὐ
δέδιεν, οὐ δυσχεραίνει, οὐκ ἀνίλλεται· ἀλλὰ μὴν τὸ α᾽· καὶ τὸ δεύτερον ἄρα᾽.
καὶ τὸ μὲν συνημμένον διὰ βραχέων δείκνυσι, λέγων ὅτι ἄτοπόν ἐστιν, οὗ παρ᾽
ὅλον τὸν βίον μελέτην καὶ ἐπιτήδευσιν ποιεῖται, λέγω δὴ ἀποθνήσκειν τε καὶ 5
τεθνάναι, τούτου ἥκοντος δεδιέναι. καὶ μή τις ἀπορείτω ὅτι ᾽εἰ πᾶσα ἐνέργεια

---

§ 16. 1 *πιθανώτερον πρὸς ὑμᾶς* M, Pl. B: *πρὸς ὑμᾶς πιθανώτερον* Pl. TWY — 2 *εἰκότως*
- *δικαστάς* mg. M^c: om. M¹ — 3 *ἀνάγκη* μ: -ηι M

§ 1. 1 *ἤδη*] om. Pl. TY
§ 2. 3 *δέδειεν* (et sim. semper) M

'Separation of the soul from the body is death; philosophy is striving for separation
of the soul from the body; philosophy is striving for death' (§ 3,7–§ 4). The minor
is demonstrated by Socrates in three *καθαρτικοὶ λόγοι* as described by Dam. I § 65:
(i) the philosopher is indifferent to physical pleasure (64c10–65a8); (ii) the body
interferes with the acquisition of knowledge (65a9–d3); (iii) the objects of true
knowledge, the forms, can be apprehended only by the soul by itself (65d4–66a10).
The first of these is discussed in § 5, the other two are reserved for lectures 4 and 5.

§ 1. 2–5. Schol. Pl. 10.9–16. Cf. Ol. 1 § 1.
§ 2. 1–6. Dam. I § 49.
6–§ 3.6. Dam. I § 51.

when we want to pray it is for the sake of prayer itself), and if, further, the pursuit of death is an activity complete in itself, the philosopher will not need another end (death itself), but his whole existence will be a continuous pursuit of death'. **3.** The answer to this should be: "Preparation for death is not an end in itself, and this example of prayer is different: the real end is being dead. For the same reason 'dying' is distinct from 'being dead'; one in search of purification, who is training himself for death, is 'dying', that is to say, purifying himself of affects, while the contemplative is already 'dead', because he is free from affects, and therefore he will not make dying his object."

The minor premise he proves by demonstration, in the form of a categorical syllogism. And since all demonstration proceeds by definition, either of the subject or of the predicate (thus in the *Phaedrus* [245c5–246a2] Socrates proves that soul is immortal by defining the predicated term, which is the middle term, self-moving; in the *Philebus* [20d1–11], on the other hand, he shows that pleasure is a good by defining the good: if the good is that after which all things aspire, pleasure too is a good since every animal seeks pleasure), therefore Socrates now defines death as the separation of the body from the soul and the soul from the body. **4.** It is not for nothing that he mentions both, because in the case of souls that cling to the body the body is severed from the soul, not the soul from the body, with which it is still linked emotionally by what is termed a 'half-relation'. From them come the shadowy apparitions that hover about graves [81d1], as the poet [*Iliad* 16.857] says about the soul of Patroclus:

'Bewailing its fate, that it must leave manhood and youth'.

Death is separation not for all soul without exception; not, in fact, for irrational soul, which is extinguished with the body, but for rational soul;

---

7. ἐν τέλει οὖσα : cf. Ar., mete. I 2, 339a24–26 πρὸς δὲ τούτοις ἡ μὲν ἀίδιος καὶ τέλος οὐκ ἔχουσα τῷ τόπῳ τῆς κινήσεως, ἀλλ' ἀεὶ ἐν τέλει (Philop., mete. 12.7 τουτέστι τὸ τέλειον ἔχει τῆς κινήσεως).

§ 3. 7–15. Dam. I §§ 57–58. Corrections to this confused paragraph are found in Dam.: in the *Phaedrus* (245c5) Pl. proves that the soul is immortal by defining the subject (soul is the self-moved), in the *Philebus* he proves that pleasure is *not* the Good by defining the predicate (the Good). There is no formal definition of the Good in the *Phil.*, and the etymology given at line 12 is slightly different from Pl.'s (*Crat.* 412c1–5: . . . τοῦ θοοῦ . . . τῷ ἀγαστῷ); cf. Ol., *Alc.* 122.12 ὡς ἄγαν θεῖν ἐπὶ αὐτὸ ποιοῦν πάντας and *Etym. magn.* παρὰ τὸ ἄγαν θέειν ἡμᾶς ἐπ' αὐτό. Apparently Ol. found in his source only a vague reference to the *Phil.* and improvised a reconstruction of his own.

§ 4. 3. κατὰ τὴν ἡμίσχετον σχέσιν : a term coined by Theodorus of Asine, cf. Pr., *Tim.* II 142.24–27 (=Theod., test. 20) καὶ εἰ βούλει τὰ τοῦ γενναίου Θεοδώρου παραλαμβάνειν ἐν τούτοις, ὁ μὲν νοῦς ἄσχετός ἐστιν, ἡ δὲ περὶ τὸ σῶμα ζωὴ ἐν σχέσει, μέση δὲ ἡ ψυχή, ἡμίσχετός τις οὖσα. III 276.30–277.1 (=id., test. 34) καὶ πλεονάζει μὲν τῆς ὑπερκοσμίου ζωῆς ἡ τοῦ ὀχήματος συνάρτησις τῆς ψυχῆς [[τῆς]] πρὸς τὸ πᾶν καὶ

ἐν τέλει οὖσα δι' αὐτὸ τὸ τέλος ἐστὶν καὶ οὐ δεῖται ἄλλου τέλους, οἷον τὸ εὔχεσθαι δι' αὐτὸ τὸ εὔχεσθαι αἱρούμεθα· — εἰ οὖν καὶ ἡ ἐπιτήδευσις τοῦ θανάτου ἐνέργειά ἐστιν ἐν τέλει οὖσα, οὐ δεήσεται ἄλλου τέλους, οἷον αὐτοῦ τοῦ θανάτου, ἀλλὰ ἀεὶ θελήσει ὁ φιλόσοφος ἐν τῷ εἶναι θάνατον ἐπιτηδεύειν'. πρὸς γὰρ τοῦτο   3 ῥητέον· 'ἀλλ' οὐ τοῦτο τέλος ἐστὶν ἁπλῶς, τὸ θάνατον μελετῆσαι, καὶ οὐχ ὅμοιον τὸ παράδειγμα τοῦτο τὸ τῆς εὐχῆς, ἀλλὰ τὸ τεθνάναι τέλος ἐστί. διὸ καὶ διαφέρει τὸ ἀποθνήσκειν τοῦ τεθνάναι· ἀποθνήσκει μὲν γὰρ θάνατον μελετῶν ὁ καθαρτικός, καθαίρων ἑαυτὸν τῶν παθῶν, τέθνηκεν δὲ ἤδη ὁ θεωρητικός, κεχώρισται γὰρ   5 τῶν παθῶν· διὸ οὐ προσποιήσεται οὗτος τὸ ἀποθνήσκειν'.

Τὴν δὲ πρόσληψιν κατασκευάζει διὰ ἀποδείξεως κατηγορικοῦ συλλογισμοῦ. καὶ ἐπειδὴ πᾶσα ἀπόδειξις δι' ὁρισμοῦ πρόεισιν, καὶ ἡ τοῦ ὑποκειμένου ἢ τοῦ κατηγορουμένου· — οὕτω γὰρ ἐν μὲν τῷ Φαίδρῳ [245c5–246a2] ἔδειξε τὴν ψυχὴν ἀθάνατον ὁρισάμενος τὸν κατηγορούμενον ὅρον μέσον ὄντα τὸ αὐτοκίνητον,   10 ἐν δέ γε τῷ Φιλήβῳ [20d1–11] τὴν ἡδονὴν ἔδειξεν ἀγαθὸν εἰπὼν τὸν ὁρισμὸν τοῦ ἀγαθοῦ, ὅτι, εἰ ἀγαθόν ἐστιν ἐφ' ὃ πάντα θεῖ, καὶ ἡ ἡδονὴ ἀγαθόν, πᾶν γὰρ ζῷον τῆς ἡδονῆς ἐφίεται· — ὁρίζεται οὖν διὰ τοῦτο τὸν θάνατον λέγων ὅτι θάνατός ἐστι χωρισμὸς τοῦ τε σώματος ἀπὸ τῆς ψυχῆς καὶ τῆς ψυχῆς ἀπὸ | τοῦ (19) σώματος. καλῶς δὲ ἑκάτερον εἶπεν, διότι ἐπὶ τῶν φιλοσωμάτων ψυχῶν χωρίζεται   4 μὲν τὸ σῶμα τῆς ψυχῆς, οὐ μὴν ἡ ψυχὴ τοῦ σώματος, ἀλλὰ σχετικῶς ἔτι συνῆπται αὐτῷ κατὰ τὴν ἡμίσχετον σχέσιν. ἐξ ὧν καὶ τὰ σκιοειδῆ φαντάσματα περὶ τοὺς τάφους ἐνειλεῖται [81d1], ὡς καὶ ὁ ποιητὴς [Π 857] λέγει περὶ τῆς τοῦ Πατρόκλου ψυχῆς, ὅτι   5

     'ὃν πότμον γοόωσα, λιποῦσ' ἀνδροτῆτα καὶ ἥβην'.

χωρισμὸς δέ ἐστιν ὁ θάνατος οὐχ ἁπλῶς πάσης ψυχῆς, οὐ γὰρ δὴ καὶ τῆς ἀλόγου (αὕτη γὰρ συναποσβέννυται τῷ σώματι), ἀλλὰ τῆς λογικῆς· ὁ γὰρ χωρισμὸς

---

§ 3.   8 post ὑποκειμένου] ras. 3 litt. M
§ 4.   5 ὅτι Mᶜ: om. M¹

ἐστιν οἷόν φασί τινες ἡμίσχετος. Dam. *Parm.* 9.25 ἔστι μὲν ἀρχαιοπρεπεστέρα τῶν ἀπολύτων θεῶν ἡ ἰδιότης, ἀφοριζομένη τῷ ἅπτεσθαι καὶ μὴ ἅπτεσθαι καὶ τῷ ἡμισχέτῳ τῆς προνοίας.

3–4.   *Ph.* 81c11–d2 περὶ τὰ μνήματά τε καὶ τοὺς τάφους κυλινδουμένη, περὶ ἃ δὴ καὶ ὤφθη ἄττα ψυχῶν σκιοειδῆ φαντάσματα.

4–6.   Same quotation in same context: Amm., *isag.* 5.19–23; El. 13.28–31; Ps.-El. 12,28–29.

8.   αὕτη γὰρ συναποσβέννυται τῷ σώματι : the doctrine of Pr., that irrational soul is the life of the pneumatic body and can survive a number of lives in the earthly body, whereas vegetative soul animates the earthly body and dies with it (*Tim.* III 236.18–238.26; further references in Beutler, art. Pr. 236.1–9) was held also by Amm. (Philop., *an.* 12.17–21 δείξομεν ... ὅτι ἡ μὲν ἄλογος τοῦ μὲν παχέος τούτου χωριστή, ἀχώριστος δὲ τοῦ πνεύματος ... καὶ ὅτι ἡ φυτικὴ ἐν τῷ παχεῖ τούτῳ [[τῷ]] σώματι τὸ εἶναι ἔχει καὶ συμφθείρεται αὐτῷ), by Dam. (I § 217; § 239) and by Ol. (10 § 1.19–20; 13 § 3.10–12). In the present case, ἄλογος must be used loosely for φυτική, unless the redactor tampered with the text for reasons of his own, as he seems to have done at 9 § 6.

we speak of separation solely with regard to things that can not only be separated, but also exist separately.

5. Having prepared the way by this assumption he proves his point as follows: 'The philosopher, apart from the absolutely necessary, disdains the care of the body'; and he establishes this premise, the minor, in this way. There are three kinds of activities, (1) those natural and necessary, such as feeding and sleeping, (2) those natural but not necessary, such as copulation, (3) those neither natural nor necessary, as the concern for elegance and colorful clothing etc. (that these are neither natural nor necessary is seen from the fact that other animals do not have them); of these three kinds of activities the philosopher will do entirely without those that are natural but not necessary and those that are neither natural nor necessary, he will even resist them forcibly (for secretion of semen the natural emission during sleep will suffice), while with the first kind he will deal briefly and perfunctorily, not to the point of repletion. 'If this is true, the philosopher, apart from the absolutely necessary, disdains the body; he who does this will be ready to die; therefore the philosopher prepares himself for death'. Thus far the survey.

6. **There is good reason for the true philosopher [63e9–10]**: Socrates speaks of the 'true philosopher', not in contradistinction to the sophist who pretends to be a philosopher, as Harpocratio [frg. 2] chose to understand the text (such an interpretation being far beneath Plato's greatness of conception), but in contradistinction to the statesman. For the subject of the dialogue is purification; the statesman, however, is not a philosopher in the strict sense, because under circumstances he will make use of the affects, too, anger and desire: anger to defend his country against its enemies, desire, because he is interested also in the body and in the temporal world; for we do not live for our own sake, but for that of the universe as well.

7. **Who practice philosophy in the right way [64a4–5]**: This too is said in view of the statesman.

8. **Are not understood by the others [64a5]**: It is only natural that philosophers should not be understood by the majority of people, since

---

9–10. οὐ μόνον – εἶναι: careless wording for κατὰ τῶν οὐ μόνον χωρίζεσθαι δυναμένων, ἀλλὰ καὶ χωρὶς εἶναι.

§ 5. 3–11. **Dam.** I § 69. Plot. paraphrases the *Ph.* passage at I 2,5.7–9 ... καὶ τὰς ἀναγκαίας τῶν ἡδονῶν αἰσθήσεις μόνον ποιουμένην καὶ ἰατρεύσεις καὶ ἀπαλλαγὰς πόνων, ἵνα μὴ ἐνοχλοῖτο, ... (17–21) ἐπιθυμίαν δέ; ὅτι μὲν μηδενὸς φαύλου, δῆλον· σιτίων δὲ καὶ ποτῶν πρὸς ἄνεσιν οὐκ αὐτὴ ἕξει· οὐδὲ τῶν ἀφροδισίων δέ· εἰ δ' ἄρα, φυσικῶν, οἶμαι, καὶ οὐδὲ τὸ ἀπροαίρετον ἐχουσῶν· εἰ δ' ἄρα, ὅσον μετὰ φαντασίας προτυπούς καὶ ταύτης. Porph., sent. 32 (pp. 33.1–34.10) in turn paraphrases Plot.: εἰ καὶ τὰς ἀναγκαίας τῶν ἡδονῶν καὶ τὰς αἰσθήσεις ἰατρείας ἕνεκα μόνον τις παραλαμβάνοι ἢ ἀπαλλαγῆς πόνων, ἵνα μὴ ἐμποδίζοιτο ... ἐπιθυμίαν δὲ παντὸς φαύλου ἐξοριστέον, σίτων δὲ καὶ ποτῶν οὐκ αὐτὸς

φέρεται οὐ μόνον κατὰ τῶν χωρίζεσθαι δυναμένων, ἀλλὰ καὶ κατὰ τῶν χωρὶς
εἶναι.   10
Τούτου προληφθέντος δείκνυσι τὸ προκείμενον οὕτως· 'ὁ φιλόσοφος, ὅ τι 5
μὴ πᾶσα ἀνάγκη, καταφρονεῖ τῆς περὶ τὸ σῶμα θεραπείας'· καὶ κατασκευάζει
α' ταύτην τὴν πρότασιν ἐλάττονα οὖσαν οὕτως. τριῶν οὐσῶν ἐνεργειῶν, ἢ φυσικῶν
β' καὶ ἀναγκαίων, ὡς τὸ τρέφεσθαι καὶ καθεύδειν, ἢ φυσικῶν μέν, οὐκ ἀναγκαίων
γ' δέ, ὡς τὸ ἀφροδισιάζειν, ἢ οὔτε φυσικῶν οὔτε ἀναγκαίων, ὡς καλλωπισμὸς 5
καὶ ὅσα τὰ τῆς ποικίλης ἐσθῆτος· — αὗται γὰρ οὔτε φυσικαὶ οὔτε ἀναγκαῖαι,
ὡς δηλοῦσι τὰ ἄλλα ζῷα ταύταις μὴ χρώμενα — τριῶν οὖν οὐσῶν ἐνεργειῶν
ταῖς μὲν φυσικαῖς καὶ οὐκ ἀναγκαίαις καὶ ταῖς οὔτε φυσικαῖς οὔτε ἀναγκαίαις
οὐ χρήσεται ὅλως ὁ φιλόσοφος, ἀλλὰ ἀπώσεται αὐτάς (ἀρκέσει γὰρ αὐτῷ πρὸς
ἔκκρισιν τοῦ σπέρματος τὸ ὀνειρώττειν), ταῖς δὲ πρώταις ἐπ' ὀλίγον χρήσεται 10
ἀφοσιωτικῶς, ὡς μὴ ἐμφορεῖσθαι αὐτῶν. 'εἰ οὖν ταῦτα οὕτως ἔχει, ὁ φιλόσοφος,
ὅ τι μὴ πᾶσα ἀνάγκη, καταφρονεῖ | τοῦ σώματος· ὁ τοιοῦτος ἐθελήσει ἀποθνῄσ- (20)
κειν· ὁ φιλόσοφος ἄρα μελετᾷ θάνατον'. ταῦτα ἔχει ἡ θεωρία.

Εἰκότως ἀνὴρ τῷ ὄντι ἐν φιλοσοφίᾳ [63e9-10]: 'τῷ ὄντι φιλόσοφον' 6
λέγει οὐ πρὸς ἀντιδιαστολὴν τοῦ σοφιστοῦ ὑποδυομένου τὸν φιλόσοφον, ὡς
οἱ περὶ Ἀρποκρατίωνα [frg. 2] ἠξίωσαν ἀκούειν (τοῦτο γὰρ πόρρω τῆς Πλάτωνος
μεγαλονοίας), ἀλλὰ πρὸς ἀντιδιαστολὴν τοῦ πολιτικοῦ. καθαρτικὸς γὰρ ὁ
διάλογος· οὐ κυρίως δὲ φιλόσοφος οὗτος, ὃς καὶ τοῖς πάθεσιν ἐν καιρῷ χρῆται 5
καὶ θυμῷ καὶ ἐπιθυμίᾳ, θυμῷ μὲν ἀμυνόμενος τοὺς κατὰ τῆς πατρίδος πολεμίους,
ἐπιθυμίᾳ δὲ διότι καὶ τοῦ σώματος καὶ τῆς γενέσεως φροντίδα ποιεῖται· οὐ
γὰρ ἑαυτοῖς γεγόναμεν, ἀλλὰ καὶ τῷ παντί.
Ὀρθῶς ἁπτόμενοι φιλοσοφίας [64a4-5]: πάλιν τοῦτο διὰ τὸν πολιτικὸν 7
εἴρηται.
Λεληθέναι τοὺς ἄλλους [64a5]: εἰκότως τοὺς πολλοὺς λανθάνουσιν 8
ὡς κατὰ τὸ ἀφανὲς ζῶντες οἱ φιλόσοφοι, τῶν πολλῶν τὰ φανερὰ εἰδότων.

ἕξει, ᾗπερ αὐτός, ἀφροδισίων δὲ τῶν φυσικῶν οὐδὲ τὸ ἀπροαίρετον. εἰ δ'ἄρα, ὅσον μέχρι
φαντασίας προπετοῦς τῆς κατὰ τοὺς ὕπνους. Cf. Marin., vit. Pr. 19. The notion of
necessary pleasures is Platonic: it occurs Phil. 62e9; Rep. VIII 561a3–4; 6–7
(cf. also 558d8–559c7, where ἐπιθυμίαι ἀναγκαῖαι are defined); Ar., eth. Nic. VII 6,
1147b23–31; VII 8, 1150a16. It is therefore not necessary to conclude that it was
Porphyry who discovered the striking analogy between the Ph. and Epicurus'
classification of pleasures (rat. sent. 29 = Diog. Laert. 10,149). Ol.'s immediate source
is Pr. (Dam. I § 69.6–9), who adds a fourth class (necessary, but not natural,
e.g. indispensable clothing and housing) to adapt the schema to the Ph. passage.
   11. ἀφοσιωτικῶς = κατὰ ἀφοσίωσιν, an addendum lexicis.
   § 6. 2. Ar., Met. Γ 2, 1004b17-18 (de S.)
   § 6. 3. οἱ περὶ Ἀρποκρατίωνα: see Introduction pp. 12–13.

they live on the level of the invisible, while most people know only the manifest.

9. Upon my word, Socrates, though I do not feel like laughing just now [64a10–b1]: Simmias did not laugh, either because he was not inclined to laughter by nature, or because of his grief for his master.

10. And my countrymen would agree [64b3–4]: Of course they would, for Simmias came from Thebes, characterized by the phrases 'a Boeotian pig' and 'Let us leave the flute to the Thebans, who cannot talk'. The poet [*Iliad* 10.13], too, gives the flute to the Trojans, nowhere to the Greeks, because it is a hindrance, not only to speech, but also to hearing and to all rational activity in general; therefore Athena, the patroness of the Athenians, who distinguished themselves by their talent for discussion, threw away the flute.

11. For they are not aware if they long for death and deserve death, nor what kind of death [64b8–9]: Contradictory conclusions have been reached. Simmias says that people are aware that philosophers long for death, Socrates says they are not, and the rejoinder is that they are; the cause of this is homonymy. People are not aware that philosophers train themselves for voluntary death (this is what Socrates means by saying that they 'long for death', in other words, detach themselves from the body, and that they 'deserve death', i.e. voluntary death); on the other hand, they are well aware that philosophers train themselves for bodily death, which the philosopher will choose also, inasmuch as it is an image of voluntary death.

12. What do we believe death is? [64c2]: Socrates does not ask if death exists, for this point is granted, but 'What do we believe death is?'

13. That the body, parted from the soul, has come to be by itself [64c5–6]: As we said [§ 3], Socrates defines death as a separation not only of the soul from the body, but also of the body from the soul. Referring to the soul he speaks of 'being', because it is ungenerated, in the case of the body of 'having come to be', because it is generated.

14. For from this I think we shall get a clearer idea of that which

---

§ 9. The first interpretation (γελασείω as a permanent characteristic, cf. Eunap., *vit. soph.* V 1,9) can be forced upon the text only by assuming a rather awkward hyperbaton: οὐ πάνυ γέ με γελασείοντα νῦν δὴ ἐποίησας γελάσαι. It is difficult to see why it is suggested at all.

§ 10. 2–7. Ol., *Alc.* 66.4–67.5; cf. *Gorg.* 169.23–170.5.

2. *CPG*, Diogenian. 3,46 and note (from Pindar, *Ol.* 6.152).

2–3. Plut., *Alc.* 2.

3–4. Cf. schol. Hom., *Il.* 10.13 (III 6.4–9 Erbse); *Il.* 18.495 (IV 193.11–13 Dindorf).

4–5. Ar., *eth. Nic.* IX 5, 1175b1–6.

5–7. Ar., *pol.* VIII 6, 1341b3–8.

§ 11. Dam. I § 53. Either Ol. or the redactor mixed up the speakers; the correct reading would be: ὁ μὲν γὰρ Σωκράτης φησὶν ὅτι λέληθε τοὺς πολλοὺς ὅτι θανατῶσιν (a5), ὁ δὲ Σιμμίας φησὶν ὅτι οὐ λέληθεν (b5), ὁ δὲ ἐπάγει ὅτι λέληθεν (b8).

Νὴ τὸν Δία, ἔφη, ὦ Σώκρατες, οὐ πάνυ γέ με νῦν δὴ γελα-   9
σείοντα [64a10–b1]: οὐκ ἐγέλα ὁ Σιμμίας ἢ ὅτι φύσει οὐκ ἦν ἐπιτήδειος
πρὸς τὸ γελᾶν ἢ διὰ τὴν περὶ τὸν διδάσκαλον λύπην.

Καὶ ξυμφάναι ἂν τοὺς μὲν παρ' ἡμῖν ἀνθρώπους [64b3–4]: εἰκότως·   10
Θηβαῖος γὰρ ἦν ὁ Σιμμίας, παρ' οἷς καὶ ἡ 'Βοιωτία ὗς' καὶ 'αὐλούντων Θηβαίων
παῖδες, διαλέγεσθαι γὰρ οὐ | μεμαθήκασιν'. καὶ ὁ ποιητὴς δὲ [Κ 13] τὸν αὐλὸν   (21)
δέδωκε τοῖς Τρωσίν, οὐδαμοῦ δὲ τοῖς "Ελλησιν· ἐμπόδιον γὰρ γίνεται οὐ μόνον
τῷ διαλέγεσθαι, ἀλλὰ καὶ τῷ ἀκούειν καὶ ἁπλῶς πάσῃ λογικῇ ἐνεργείᾳ· διὸ   5
καὶ ἡ Ἀθηνᾶ, ἡ τῶν Ἀθηναίων πολιοῦχος τῶν διαλέγεσθαι μόνων ἐπισταμένων,
ἀπέρριψε τοὺς αὐλούς.

Λέληθε γὰρ αὐτοὺς εἴτε θανατῶσιν καὶ ἄξιοί εἰσι θανάτου καὶ   11
οἵου θανάτου [64b8–9]: ἀντίφασις συνάγεται διὰ τούτων. ὁ μὲν γὰρ Σιμμίας
φησὶν ὅτι οὐ λέληθε τοὺς πολλοὺς ὅτι θανατῶσιν, ὁ δὲ Σωκράτης φησὶν ὅτι
λέληθεν, ὁ δὲ ἐπάγει ὅτι οὐ λέληθεν· καὶ τοῦτο γέγονε διὰ τὴν ὁμωνυμίαν. λέληθε
γὰρ αὐτοὺς ὅτι τὸν προαιρετικὸν θάνατον μελετῶσι (διό φησιν ὅτι 'θανατῶσιν',   5
τουτέστι χωρίζουσιν ἑαυτοὺς τοῦ σώματος, καὶ 'ἄξιοί εἰσι θανάτου' τοῦ προαιρετικοῦ)· οὐ λέληθε δὲ αὐτοὺς ὅτι τὸν φυσικὸν θάνατον μελετῶσιν, αἱρήσονται γὰρ
καὶ τοῦτον οἱ φιλόσοφοι, εἴ γε εἴδωλόν ἐστι τοῦ προαιρετικοῦ θανάτου.

Ἡγούμεθα τί τὸν θάνατον εἶναι; [64c2]: οὐ τοῦτο λέγει, εἰ ἔστιν   12
ὁ θάνατος (ὡμολόγηται γὰρ τοῦτο), ἀλλὰ 'τί ἡγούμεθα τὸν θάνατον εἶναι;'

Χωρὶς μὲν ἀπὸ τῆς ψυχῆς ἀπαλλαγὲν αὐτὸ καθ' αὑτὸ γεγονέναι   13
τὸ σῶμα [64c5–6]: ἰδοὺ τὸν θάνατον ὡρίσατο οὐ μόνον τὸ χωρισθῆναι τὴν
ψυχὴν ἀπὸ τοῦ σώματος, ἀλλὰ καὶ τὸ χωρισθῆναι τὸ σῶμα ἀπὸ τῆς ψυχῆς· καὶ
ἐπὶ μὲν τῆς ψυχῆς τὸ 'εἶναι' εἶπεν, διότι ἀγένητος αὕτη, ἐπὶ δὲ τοῦ σώματος
τὸ 'γεγονέναι', γενητὸν γὰρ τοῦτο.   5

Ἐκ γὰρ τούτων μᾶλλον οἶμαι ἡμᾶς εἴσεσθαι περὶ ὧν σκοποῦ- 14 (22)
μεν [64d1–2]: 'ἐκ τούτων'· τῶν προτάσεων. 'περὶ ὧν'· προβλημάτων.

---

§ 9.   1–2 γελασείοντα μ, Pl.: -σιῶντα Μ
§ 10.   2 ὗς] ὕ- in ras. 2 litt. Mᶜ | αὐλούντων] αὐ- in ras. Mˣ — 6 μόνων Wk (M¹?):
μόνον Μ, -ο- in ras. Mˣ
§ 11.   1 εἴτε Μ¹: ἢ sscr. Mᶜ (ἤ τε Pl.) | post καὶ¹] ἤ ins. Mᶜ (ἤ Pl.) — 1–2 καὶ οἵου
θανάτου] om. Pl. ΤΥ
§ 12.   1 τί Nv: τι Μ (Pl.).
§ 13.   1 χωρὶς μὲν Fh (Pl.): χωρισμὸν Μ | ἀπὸ] om. Pl. Τ — 1–2 γεγονέναι τὸ σῶμα Μ¹:
τὸ σῶμα γεγονέναι Mᶜ, Pl.
§ 14.   1 οἶμαι ἡμᾶς Μ¹, Pl.: ὑμᾶς οἶμαι Mᶜ

7–8.   Cf. supra 1 § 9.
§ 12.   Dam. I § 55. Though it is just barely possible to read the text in this
way, if Simmias' Πάνυ γε is taken to express assent to Socrates' proposal ('Let us
do so by all means,' cf. Meno 82b3, often after βούλει and dubitative subjunctives),
the note in Ol. more probably results from a misunderstanding of what Dam. (I § 55)
says: the point is not εἰ ἔστιν, but εἴ τί ἐστιν (whether it is something with a specific
character), a misunderstanding caused by the familiar sequence of problems: εἰ ἔστι,
τί ἐστι, ὁποῖόν τί ἐστι, διὰ τί ἐστι (Ar., anal. post. II 1).
§ 13.   2–3.   Dam. I § 59.5–6.
3–5.   Dam. I § 59.6–7.

occupies us [64d1–2]: 'From this': the premises; 'of that which': the questions.

15. More than other men [65a2]: Do other men, then, also detach the soul from the body? Yes: since they are free agents and their impulses are ruled by innate notions, they are able, in a sense, to detach the soul from the body.

4

Lecture **

1. Then, as regards the attainment of insight itself [65a9–d3].

Socrates has first proved the philosopher's willingness to die from his way of life, by pointing out that the philosopher, apart from the absolutely necessary, does not concern himself about his body; he now goes on to establish this same thesis from the point of view of knowledge, as follows: 'The philosopher despises the senses; if so, he despises also the body, in which the senses reside; one who despises the body avoids it; one who does so detaches himself from the body; one who detaches himself from the body is willing to die, since, as we saw, death is nothing but the separation of the soul from the body'.

2. Let us take a more general view of this. The soul has three kinds of activity: either it turns towards the lower, when it apprehends things sensible; or towards itself, when through itself it sees all that exists, for soul is a 'sacred image uniting all forms', that is, possessing the principles of all things that are; or again it lifts itself up to the intelligible

---

§ 15. Dam. I § 73.

Lect. 4. **The second reason for detachment.** Analysis of the second καθαρτικὸς λόγος (§ 1). It would be false to distinguish the πολιτικός, the καθαρτικός and the θεωρητικός according to their several objects of knowledge, viz. the sensa, the reason-principles (λόγοι) and the ideas respectively; rather each is concerned with all three, but in his own way, and the difference is that to the πολιτικός the body is an instrument, to the others an encumbrance (§§ 2–3). Another distinction is that the πολιτικός deals with particulars, the others with universals, which in the case of the καθαρτικός are distinct forms in soul, in the case of the θεωρητικός undifferentiated intelligible forms (§ 4). What follows, though presenting itself as an analysis of Pl.'s argument, really reflects Pr.'s speculations on degrees of knowledge, cf. Dam. I § 78 (§ 5). With regard to the inadequacy of sense-perception three objections are raised and answered: (i) How can anything be permanently corrupted? (ii) If all knowledge participates in absolute knowledge, how can Pl. say that sense-perception 'fails to attain being and truth'? (iii) How can Ar. and Pl. describe perception as the beginning of knowledge? Answers: (i) Pl. recognizes different levels of truth, and at its own level sense-perception is dependable; (ii) sense-perception not only apprehends affections (this is a Peripatetic error), but being as well; (iii) sense-perception is not the cause of knowledge, it only acts

Διαφερόντως τῶν ἄλλων ἀνθρώπων [65a2]: ἆρα γὰρ καὶ οἱ ἄλλοι ἄν-   15
θρωποι χωρίζουσι τὴν ψυχὴν ἀπὸ τοῦ σώματος; ἢ ἐπειδὴ αὐτοκίνητοί εἰσι καὶ
κατὰ τὰς κοινὰς ἐννοίας ὁρμῶνται, τρόπον τινὰ ἴσασι χωρίζειν ἀπὸ τοῦ σώματος
τὴν ψυχήν.

4

Πρᾶξις σὺν θεῷ

Τί δὲ δὴ περὶ αὐτὴν τὴν τῆς φρονήσεως κτῆσιν [65a9–d3].   1

Δείξας ὁ Σωκράτης ὅτι ὁ φιλόσοφος ἐθελήσει ἀποθνήσκειν ἐκ τῆς ζωῆς
(ἔλεγε γὰρ ὅτι ὁ φιλόσοφος, ὅ τι μὴ πᾶσα ἀνάγκη, οὐ κήδεται τοῦ σώματος),
ἐντεῦθεν τοῦτο αὐτὸ κατασκευάζει ἀπὸ τῆς γνώσεως οὕτως· 'ὁ φιλόσοφος
καταφρονεῖ τῶν αἰσθήσεων· ὁ τοιοῦτος καὶ τοῦ σώματος, ἐν ᾧ αἱ αἰσθήσεις,   5
καταφρονεῖ· ὁ καταφρονῶν τοῦ σώματος φεύγει· ὁ τοιοῦτος χωρίζει ἑαυτὸν
τοῦ σώματος· ὁ χωρίζων ἑαυτὸν ἀποθνήσκειν ἐθέλει, οὐδὲν γὰρ ἦν ὁ θάνατος
ἢ χωρισμὸς τῆς ψυχῆς ἀπὸ τοῦ σώματος'.

Φέρε δὴ ἀναδράμωμεν ἐπί τινα θεωρίαν. τριῶν οὐσῶν | ἐνεργειῶν τῆς ψυχῆς·   2 (23)
ἢ γὰρ πρὸς τὰ δεύτερα ἐπιστρέφει τὰ αἰσθητὰ γινώσκουσα, ἢ πρὸς ἑαυτὴν δι'
ἑαυτῆς πάντα τὰ ὄντα ὁρῶσα, διότι 'πάμμορφον ἄγαλμά' ἐστι πάντων τῶν
ὄντων ἔχουσα λόγους, ἢ πρὸς τὸ νοητὸν ἀνατείνεται τὰς ἰδέας ὁρῶσα· — τριῶν
οὖν οὐσῶν ἐνεργειῶν τῆς ψυχῆς οὐ ταύτῃ οἰητέον διαφέρειν ἀλλήλων πολιτικὸν   5
καὶ καθαρτικὸν καὶ θεωρητικόν, τῷ τὸν μὲν πολιτικὸν τὰ αἰσθητὰ γινώσκειν,

---

§ 15. 1 διαφερόντως÷, -ς÷ in ras. 4 litt., Mᶜ

§ 1. 1 δέ] δαὶ Pl. BW² — 3 ὅ τι Mᶜ: om. M¹
§ 2. 2 δεύτερα] in ras. 3 litt. Mᶜ

---

as a stimulant (§§ 6–8). As an appendix the much-discussed question of the senses
of the Star-gods is dealt with (§§ 9–10).
  § 1. 2–4. On ζωή (ζωτικός) and γνῶσις (γνωστικός) as a pair of opposites see
note on Dam., Phil. § 84.2–3. Here, the complete triad of being, life and intelligence
(Pr., elem. 39; 197; Tim. II 286.24–25; infra 13 § 3 and Dam. I § 325), must be
intended, corresponding to the three καθαρτικοὶ λόγοι, but in 5 § 1 the reference
to being is missing, because Ol. adopts a different scheme there (reversion upon
the lower, upon itself, upon the higher, =Dam. I § 65; also Ol. 6 § 1).
  §§ 2–3. Dam. I §§ 65–67; 74. Cf. infra 5 § 1. The older view rejected by Ol.,
according to which the relation soul-body characterizes the πολιτικός, the relation
of soul with itself the καθαρτικός, the relation soul-forms the θεωρητικός, seems to
be Porphyry's (cf. sent. 32, pp. 29.10–30.1). The system of three triads, which Ol.
substitutes for it and which appears also in Dam. § 74, is very typical of Pr.
  § 2. 3. πάμμορφον ἄγαλμα occurs three times in Ol. (infra 11 § 7.2; Alc.
198.23–24), always with reference to the soul as containing the λόγοι of all reality.
The notion is found in Plot. IV 3,10.10–13; V 7,1.7–8; VI 2,5.11–14; Pr., elem. 195.
The expression is either a combination of reminiscences from the Chaldean Oracles,
frg. 37.2 παμμόρφους ἰδέας and frg. 101 φύσεως... αὐτόπτον ἄγαλμα, or, more
probably, a direct quotation of another line. As such it now appears in Des Places,
frg. 186bis.

by contemplating the ideas. This being so, we must not think that the
difference between those who devote themselves to statesmanship, to
purification, and to contemplation consists in this, that in civic life one
knows only things sensible, in the stage of purification only the principles
in the soul, and in contemplation only the ideas; in this case no one would
be a true philosopher, since no one would possess 'the knowledge of all
things that are', but each will have a partial knowledge only, and even
this part of reality he will not discern clearly, if he does not know its
relation to the rest. 3. Rather, each of them must know all three.
The statesman refers to the principles present in himself to organize
the visible world, his eye directed upon the soul: upon reason to guide
the leaders, upon spirit, for the soldiers, upon desire, for the laborers;
but also, by their education, he shows the leaders the upward way to
the Good, so that he must have knowledge of all three. So, too, the man
whose concern is purification: because of the center position of his activity
he knows also what is on either side, for from the intermediate we can
acquire knowledge of the extremes. Finally, the contemplative philosopher
knows sensible things in so far as he reduces them from their own plurality
to the unity of the intelligible; but since in the intelligible there is not
only unity but also plurality, he reduces the unity in the intelligible
to the unity that is in God, which is unity proper without multiplicity,
for God is nothing but a monad without multiplicity. So the difference
between those committed to civic life, to purification, or to contemplation,
does not lie there; rather it is that the statesman is concerned also with
pleasure and pain, for he pays attention to the body, too, as an instrument,
and his aim is not freedom from affects, but moderation in them; those,
on the contrary, whose pursuit is purification and contemplation pay
attention to the body as a talkative neighbor, to prevent it from intruding
upon their activities with its pointless interference, and their aim is
freedom from affects.

4. There is another difference between the statesman and the others: he
draws his conclusions from a universal major premise based on reflexion and
from a particular minor, because he uses the body as an instrument
and is therefore concerned with actions, and actions are particular, and
the particular is individual, so that the statesman depends on one

---

9. See note on 2 § 1.11.

§ 3. 3–4. Pl., *Rep.* IV 427c6–444a3. Pl. does not use the word θῆτες for his
third class, but Ar. uses it in a similar sense *pol.* III 5, 1278a12,18,22. Pr. applies
it to the Platonic state, *Rep.* II 3.14; 7.17 (φύλακες ... ἐπίκουροι ... θῆτες);
Tim. I 31.31.

6–7. ἐκ γὰρ τῶν μέσων καὶ τὰ ἄκρα γινώσκεται : the principle is usually cited
in the opposite form, e.g. Ol., *Gorg.* 258.21–22; 260.3–4; Dam., *Phil.* § 56.4–5.

14. Porph., *sent.* 32 (p. 25.6–9).

τὸν δὲ καθαρτικὸν τοὺς ἐν τῇ ψυχῇ λόγους, τὸν δὲ θεωρητικὸν τὰς ἰδέας, ἐπεὶ
οὐδεὶς κατὰ ἀλήθειαν φιλόσοφος ἔσται μὴ 'πάντων τῶν ὄντων γνῶσιν' ἔχων,
ἀλλὰ μόνον μερικήν, καὶ οὐδὲ τοῦ μέρους ἀκριβὴς θεωρὸς ἔσται, εἴ γε μὴ οἶδε
τὴν σχέσιν αὐτοῦ τὴν πρὸς τὰ ἄλλα. ἀνάγκη γὰρ ἕκαστον τὰ τρία εἰδέναι. ὁ μὲν   3
γὰρ πολιτικὸς κατὰ τοὺς ἐν ἑαυτῷ λόγους τάττει τὰ αἰσθητὰ ἀποβλέπων πρὸς
τὴν ψυχήν· καὶ πρὸς μὲν τὸν λόγον ἀφορῶν τάττει τοὺς φύλακας, πρὸς δὲ τὸν
θυμὸν τοὺς στρατιώτας, κατὰ δὲ τὴν ἐπιθυμίαν τοὺς θῆτας· ἀλλὰ καὶ ἀνάγει
τοὺς φύλακας διὰ τῆς παιδείας ἐπὶ τὸ ἀγαθόν, ὥστε τῶν τριῶν ἐπιστήμων   5
ἐστίν. ἀλλὰ καὶ ὁ καθαρτικὸς περὶ τὰ μέσα εἰλούμενος καὶ τὰ πέριξ οἶδεν· ἐκ
γὰρ τῶν μέσων καὶ τὰ ἄκρα γινώσκεται. ἀλλὰ καὶ ὁ θεωρητικὸς τὰ μὲν αἰσθητά,
ἀνάγων αὐτὰ ἀπὸ τοῦ πλήθους ἐπὶ τὸ ἓν τὸ ἐν τῷ νοητῷ· ἀλλ' ἐπειδή, εἰ καὶ
ἕν ἐστιν ἐν τῷ νοητῷ, ἀλλὰ καὶ πλῆθος, ἀνάγει τὸ ἓν τὸ ἐν τῷ νοητῷ ἐπὶ τὸ
ἓν τὸ ἐν τῷ θεῷ· τοῦτο γὰρ κυρίως ἓν ἀπλήθυντόν ἐστιν, οὐδὲν γὰρ ἄλλο ἐστὶ   10
θεὸς ἢ μονὰς ἀπλήθυντος. οὐ ταύτῃ οὖν διαφέρουσιν ἀλλή|λων πολιτικός, (24)
καθαρτικός, θεωρητικός, ἀλλ' ὅτι ὁ μὲν πολιτικὸς καὶ περὶ ἡδονὰς καὶ λύπας
καταγίνεται· καὶ γὰρ καὶ τοῦ σώματος φροντίδα ποιεῖται ὡς ὀργάνου, καὶ
τέλος αὐτοῦ οὐχ ἡ ἀπάθεια ἀλλ' ἡ μετριοπάθεια· καθαρτικὸς δὲ καὶ θεωρητικὸς
τοῦ σώματος φροντίζουσιν ὡς φλυάρου γείτονος, ἵνα μὴ ἐμποδὼν γένηται ταῖς   15
ἐνεργείαις φλυαροῦν, καὶ τέλος αὐτῶν ἡ ἀπάθεια.

Καὶ ἄλλως δὲ διαφέρει ὁ πολιτικὸς τούτων, ὅτι ὁ μὲν ἐκ μείζονος προτάσεως   4
εἰλημμένης ἐκ τῆς διανοίας καθόλου καὶ ἐξ ἐλάττονος μερικῆς τὸ συμπέρασμα
συνάγει· τῷ γὰρ σώματι ὡς ὀργάνῳ χρῆται, οὐκοῦν περὶ τὰ πρακτὰ καταγίνεται,
τὰ δὲ πρακτὰ μερικά, τὰ δὲ τοιαῦτα καθ' ἕκαστα, ὥστε ἐκ τῆς μιᾶς μερικῆς
συλλογίζεται ὁ πολιτικός. καθαρτικὸς δὲ καὶ θεωρητικὸς οὐχ οὕτως· περὶ γὰρ   5
τὰ καθόλου εἴδη καταγίνονται. ἀλλὰ τίνι διαφέρουσιν ἀλλήλων καθαρτικὸς
καὶ θεωρητικός, εἰ ἑκάτερος περὶ τὰ εἴδη καταγίνεται; ἢ ὁ μὲν καθαρτικὸς

---

§ 3. 1 τρία] in ras. 2 litt. M^c | εἰδέναι Fh: εἶναι M
§ 4. 6 εἴδη Fh: ἤδη M

14-16. The same phrase infra 6 § 3.11-12. Cf. Plot. I 2,5.25-26 (a wise neighbor);
Pr., prov. 20.7 συζῶσα μετ' αὐτῶν ὥσπερ τινῶν μὴ νηφόντων γειτόνων. The φλύαρος
may come from Ph. 66c3.
§ 4. 1-5. Ar. eth. Nic. VI 8, 1141b14-16 οὐδ' ἐστὶν ἡ φρόνησις τῶν καθόλου μόνον,
ἀλλὰ δεῖ καὶ τὰ καθ' ἕκαστα γνωρίζειν· πρακτικὴ γάρ, ἡ δὲ πρᾶξις περὶ τὰ καθ' ἕκαστα.
Further VI 12, 1143a32-b3; VI 13, 1144a31-33.
7-11. The usual formula is that forms are undifferentiated in the intelligible,
fully differentiated in the intelligence (Dam., Phil. § 105, note). On the relation
between forms in intelligence and soul cf. Pr., elem. 194 (Dodds pp. 299-300).

particular premise for his conclusions. With those engaged in purification
and contemplation it is different: they are concerned with universal
forms. But what is the difference between those in the stage of purification
and of contemplation, if both have forms as their object? To the man in the
stage of purification the forms are differentiated, for such is the character of
forms in the soul, which cannot apprehend simultaneously horse and
man or in general more than one form; the other's object, however, are
undifferentiated forms, those in the intelligible world, which are
inseparable because they interpenetrate. Hence the intelligible world has
been compared to an egg [*Orphica* frg. 60]: as in the egg all the parts
are undifferentiated and head and foot have no place of their own, so
too on the intelligible plane all the forms are united inseparably.

5. In the text the proof that the philosopher will be ready to die is
presented in the following manner: 'If the body by itself is unable to
know itself, but can do so only by participation in soul, it is even more
certain that for the soul sensory perception is a hindrance to the knowledge
of reality; therefore the philosopher will be ready to detach himself
from the body'.

6. There are three questions to be asked: Why does the text appear
to say that sight and hearing do not apprehend anything accurately?
If the senses deceive always and never tell the truth, there will be something
that is *always* in an abnormal condition.

A variant of this: If primary knowledge is pure truth, it necessarily
follows that other kinds of knowledge, lest they be cut off from their
source, cannot be entirely false. How can Socrates say, then, that sense-

---

11–12.   *Orphica* frg. 60=Dam., *princ.* 316.18–317.14; cf. Pr., *Tim.* I 427.25–428.12.
    13.   Cf. Plot. VI 4,8.7–8 πῶς αὐτοῦ τὸ μὲν ὡδὶ φήσεις, τὸ δὲ ὡδί; *Ibid.* 35–36.
Ol., *infra* 13 § 2.30–31 διὰ δὲ τὴν ὕλην ὡδὶ μὲν κεφαλή, ὡδὶ δὲ ῥίς. *Alc.* 82.3–4.
    §§ 6–8.   The three questions are (i) § 6.1–3, answered § 7.5–16; (ii) § 6.4–6,
answered 6–13; (iii) § 7.1–4, answered § 8.
    § 6. 1–3 and § 7.5–16. **Dam.** I §§ 78–81. Objection (i): nothing can be
permanently in an abnormal condition (Ar., *cael.* II 3, 286a17–18; Pr., *Alc.*
256.7–258.9; Ol., *Gorg.* 132.1–3; 263.19–22), therefore sense-perception cannot be
usually wrong. The answer: sense-perception is not knowledge properly so called,
since it (a) depends on a passive process, cf. Dam. I § 81 and *Proleg.* 10.31–35,
cited below at § 6.4–13, (b) is at a distance from its object, (c) is incapable of
perception in its pure or strongest form; but it is true and accurate in comparison
to a lower level of knowledge, εἰκασία (Pl., *Rep.* VI 509e1–511e2; cf. Pr., *Tim.* III
244.23–24; 286.2–7; *elem.* 19).
    § 6. 4–13.   Objection (ii): if primary knowledge is true, all knowledge must
contain some kind of truth; how, then, can Pl. say that sense-perception 'fails
to attain reality and being' (*Theaet.* 186c7–9, where Pr. read ἀτυχής or ἀτυχής,
ἤ instead of ἀτυχήσει, see *Class. Philol.* 65, 1970, 48–49)? Ol.'s answer, that sense-
perception is not aware of passive processes only but apprehends being as well,
contradicts Pr., *Tim.* I 249. 12–17 τὴν δὲ αἴσθησιν πάντως ἄλογον θετέον. ὅλως γὰρ
ἑκάστης τῶν αἰσθήσεων τὸ ἀπὸ τοῦ αἰσθητοῦ γενόμενον περὶ τὸ ζῷον πάθος γινωσκούσης,

περὶ εἴδη διακεκριμένα· τὰ γὰρ ἐν τῇ ψυχῇ διακεκριμένα ἐστὶν ἀπ' ἀλλήλων, οὐ γὰρ ἅμα ἵππον καὶ ἄνθρωπον καὶ πλείω εἴδη δύναται εἰδέναι ἡ ψυχή. ὁ δὲ περὶ εἴδη καταγίνεται οὐ διακεκριμένα, περὶ γὰρ τὰ ἐν τῷ νοητῷ, ἀδιάκριτα   10 δὲ ταῦτα ἀπ' ἀλλήλων ὡς δι' ἀλλήλων διιόντα. ὅθεν καί τις τὸ νοητὸν ᾠῷ ἀπείκασεν [Orphica frg. 60]· ὡς γὰρ ἐν τούτῳ ἀδιάκριτά ἐστι πάντα τὰ μέρη καὶ οὐχ ὡδὶ μὲν κεφαλή, ὡδὶ δὲ πούς, οὕτω καὶ ἐν τῷ νοητῷ ἀδιάκριτά ἐστι πάντα τὰ εἴδη ἡνωμένα ἀλλήλοις.

Κατασκευάζει οὖν ἡ λέξις ὅτι ὁ φιλόσοφος ἐθελήσει ἀποθνῄσκειν, τὸν τρόπον   5 (25) τοῦτον· 'εἰ τὸ σῶμα αὐτὸ καθ' αὐτὸ οὐχ οἷόν τε γινώσκειν ἑαυτό, ἀλλὰ διὰ τὸ μετέχειν ψυχῆς, πολλῷ μᾶλλον ἐμπόδιον γίνεται ἡ αἰσθητικὴ γνῶσις τῇ ψυχῇ πρὸς τὸ γινώσκειν τὰ ὄντα· ὥστε ἐθελήσει ὁ φιλόσοφος χωρίζειν ἑαυτὸν τοῦ σώματος'.   5

Ἄξιον δὲ ζητῆσαι τρία ταῦτα. πῶς φαίνεται ἡ λέξις λέγουσα ὅτι ὄψις καὶ   6 ἀκοὴ οὐδὲν ἀκριβὲς γινώσκουσιν; εἰ γὰρ ἀεὶ ψεύδονται καὶ μηδέποτε ἀληθεύουσιν αἱ αἰσθήσεις, ἔσται τι ἀεὶ ἐν τῷ παρὰ φύσιν.

Καὶ ἄλλως· εἰ ἡ πρώτη γνῶσις μόνως ἀληθής ἐστιν, ἀνάγκη καὶ τὰς ἄλλας γνώσεις, ἵνα μὴ τῆς οἰκείας πηγῆς ἐκπέσωσιν, μὴ πάντῃ ψευδεῖς εἶναι. πῶς   5

οἷον μήλου προσενεχθέντος ὄψεως μὲν ὅτι ἐρυθρὸν γνούσης ἐκ τοῦ περὶ τὸ ὄμμα πάθους, ὀσφρήσεως δὲ ὅτι εὐῶδες ἐκ τοῦ περὶ τὰς ῥῖνας, γεύσεως δὲ ὅτι γλυκὺ καὶ ἁφῆς ὅτι λεῖον, τί τὸ λέγον ὅτι μῆλόν ἐστι τοῦτο τὸ προσενεχθέν; οὔτε γὰρ τῶν μερικῶν τις αἰσθήσεων—τούτων γὰρ ἑκάστη ἕν τι τῶν περὶ αὐτὸ γινώσκει καὶ οὐχ ὅλον—οὔτε ἡ κοινὴ αἴσθησις—αὕτη γὰρ διακρίνει μόνον τὰς διαφορὰς τῶν παθῶν, ὅτι δὲ τοιόνδε ἔχον ἐστὶν οὐσίαν τὸ ὅλον, οὐκ οἶδε—. δῆλον οὖν, ὅτι ἔστι τις κρείττων τῶν αἰσθήσεων δύναμις, ἡ τὸ ὅλον γινώσκουσα πρὸ τῶν οἱονεὶ μερῶν καὶ τὸ εἶδος αὐτοῦ θεωροῦσα ἀμερῶς, τὸ τῶν πολλῶν τούτων δυνάμεων συνεκτικόν. ταύτην δὴ οὖν τὴν δύναμιν δόξαν ὁ Πλάτων κέκληκε καὶ τὸ αἰσθητὸν διὰ τοῦτο δοξαστόν. ἔτι τοίνυν τῶν αἰσθήσεων πολλάκις ἀλλοῖα παθήματα ἀπαγγελλουσῶν καὶ οὐχ οἷα τὰ ποιοῦντα βούλεται, τί τὸ κρῖνον ἐν ἡμῖν καὶ λέγον τὴν μὲν ὄψιν λέγουσαν ποδιαῖον τὸν ἥλιον ἠπατῆσθαι, τὴν δὲ τῶν νοσούντων γεῦσιν τὸ μέλι πικρὸν ἀποφαινομένην; πάντως γάρ που φανερόν, ὡς ἐν τούτοις ἅπασι καὶ τοῖς τοιούτοις αἱ μὲν αἰσθήσεις τὸ ἑαυτῶν ἀπαγγέλλουσι πάθος, καὶ οὐ πάντῃ ψεύδονται· τὸ γὰρ περὶ τὰ αἰσθητήρια πάθος λέγουσιν, ἐκεῖνο δὲ τὸ τοιοῦτόν ἐστι· τὸ δὲ λέγον τὴν αἰτίαν τοῦ πάθους καὶ ἐπικρῖνον ἕτερον (viz. δόξα, the view here opposed by Ol.). Pr., prov. 51.14–16 ἡ μὲν (i.e. αἴσθησις) οὐδ' ὅλως εἰδυῖα τὴν ἀλήθειαν, ὅτι μηδὲ αὐτὴν τῶν αἰσθητῶν ὦν ἐστι γνῶσις τὴν οὐσίαν οἶδεν. Cf. Proleg. 10.31–35 πρὸς οὓς ἐροῦμεν ὅτι, ὅταν εἴπῃ ὡς αἱ αἰσθήσεις οὐκ ἀντιλαμβάνονται τῶν αἰσθητῶν, τοῦτο λέγει ὅτι τὴν οὐσίαν τῶν αἰσθητῶν οὐ γινώσκουσιν· ἐπεὶ τοῦ πάθους τοῦ εἰς αὐτὰς ἐξ αὐτῶν τῶν αἰσθητῶν γινομένου ἀντιλαμβάνονται, οὐκ ἴσασι δὲ τὴν οὐσίαν αὐτὴν καθ' αὐτὰς οὖσαι. Pr. himself sometimes moderates this extreme position, that sensation is nothing but a passive process: Tim. II 83.27–29 and 85.2–5 he says that it is a mixture of being affected and

perception 'fails to attain being and truth' [*Theaet.* 186c7–9]? We shall answer this at once: sense-perception does not apprehend affections only, as the Peripatos thinks [Ar., *an.* II 5, 416b32–417a21], but essences as well: by this specific effect of redness it recognizes the rose and by his claws the lion. To the possible objection that this is the function of opinion, to apprehend essence, we reply: 'How, then, do you explain that brute animals mate only with those of their own kind and do not attack them, though they lack the faculty of opinion?' From this it follows that the senses apprehend universals also, and when it is said that sense-perception 'fails to apprehend being', real-existence should be understood.

7. Another problem is how the Peripatos [Ar., *anal. post.* II 19, 100a3–9] can call sense-perception the beginning of knowledge, if it deceives always, and how Plato can say in the *Timaeus* [47b1] that through sight and hearing 'we have received the gift of philosophy'.

Our answer to the first question [§ 6] must be that Plato says that sense-perception deceives us always, inasmuch as it is not knowledge properly so called. For since it apprehends by being affected, the affection is mixed up with the knowledge; further it knows things at a distance only (it does not for instance see the head of the probe when *in* the eye, and even touch needs air as a medium), which is a cause of inaccurate knowledge. The reason, indeed, why we say that intelligence possesses exact knowledge, is that it is itself the intelligible and apprehends itself; identity of thinker and object of thought results in exact knowledge, and consequently otherness results in knowledge that is necessarily falsified; in fact, the senses are not proof against sensory phenomena in

---

knowledge, at III 286.7 the phrase is μετὰ πάθους ἃ γιγνώσκει γιγνώσκουσαν (=Dam. I § 81), and at *Rep.* II 164.17–18 the perception as action and judgment is contrasted with the passive condition of the organ; so that he is not far from the view expressed by Dam., *Phil.* § 157.10–11 οὐκ ἄρα ἡ αἴσθησις ⟨κίνησις⟩ διὰ σώματος εἰς ψυχὴν τελευτῶσα (=Ar., *somn.* 1, 454a9–10; *phys.* VII 2, 244b11–12), ἀλλ' ἡ ἐπὶ τῇ τοιᾷδε κινήσει κρίσις ἐγειρομένη (cf. Ar., *anal. post.* II 19, 99b35; *an.* III 9, 432a16). Consequently, what Ol. rejects as Peripatetic heresy is not so much the passive element in sense-perception, as its external, mechanical character, the true Platonic doctrine being that the λόγος is one, so that it can be identified from any of its parts, and that the soul, containing all the λόγοι, knows all reality from *within*. Cf. Ol., *Alc.* 79.14–18 ἐν δὲ τῷ μέρει ἐστίν (scil. τὸ ὅλον), ὡς ὅταν τις ἀπὸ μέρους γνῷ τὸ ὅλον, ὥσπερ οἱ Πελοπίδαι ἀπὸ τοῦ ὤμου ἐλεφαντίνου ὄντος, καὶ τὸ ἐν τῇ παροιμίᾳ λεγόμενον 'ἐξ ὄνυχος τὸν λέοντα,' ὡς τοῦ μέρους ἑκάστου τοὺς καθολικοὺς λόγους ἔχοντος. There is no parallel to this in Pr.'s commentary on the *Alc.*; Ol.'s source, both in the *Alc.* and in the *Ph.* passage, must have been Dam., part of whose program was to eliminate Peripatetic influences from Platonism.

6–8. Cf. Dam. I § 81.

8. ὁ Περίπατος : the assumption, at Alexandria, is usually that there is agreement between Pl. and Ar., so that by implication any case of disagreement in Ar. is due to Peripatetic misinterpretation. For practical purposes this means that Ar.

δὴ 'ἀτυχῆ οὐσίας' τὴν αἴσθησιν 'καὶ ἀληθείας' φησίν [*Theaet.* 186c7-9]; ἢ
τοῦτο μὲν εὐθὺς ἐπιλυσόμεθα· ἡ γὰρ αἴσθησις οὐ μόνον τὰ πάθη γινώσκει, ὡς
ὁ Περίπατος οἴεται [Ar., an. II 5, 416b32-417a21], ἀλλὰ καὶ οὐσίας· ἀπὸ
γὰρ τῆς τοιᾶσδε ἰδιοπραγίας τοῦ ἐρυθροῦ οἶδε τὸ ῥόδον καὶ ἐξ ὀνύχων τὸν
λέοντα. εἰ δὲ λέγοιέν τινες ὅτι δόξης ἐστὶ τοῦτο, τὸ τὴν οὐσίαν εἰδέναι, φαμὲν 10
ὅτι 'καὶ πῶς τὰ ἄλογα μόνοις τοῖς ὁμοειδέσι συνδυάζεται κἀκείνοις οὐκ ἐπέρχεται
δόξης ἀμοιροῦντα;' ἐξ οὗ καὶ συνάγεται ὅτι καὶ τὰ καθόλου οἶδεν, λέγεται
δὲ 'ἀτυχὴς οὐσίας' ἡ αἴσθησις τῆς τῷ ὄντι οὐσίας.

Κἀκεῖνο δὲ ἄξιον ἀπορῆσαι, πῶς ὁ Περίπατος [Ar., *anal. post.* II 19, 100a3-9] 7
ἀρχὴν ἐπιστήμης λέγει τὴν αἴσθησιν, εἴ γε ἀεὶ ψεύδεται, πῶς δὲ αὐτὸς ὁ Πλάτων
ἐν τῷ Τιμαίῳ [47b1] δι' ὄψεως καὶ ἀκοῆς φησιν ὅτι τὸ 'φιλοσοφίας ἐπορισάμεθα
γένος'.

Πρὸς μὲν οὖν τὸ πρῶτον [§ 6] ῥητέον ὅτι ἀεὶ ψεύδεσθαι λέγει τὴν αἴσθησιν 5
ὁ Πλάτων διότι οὐ κυρίως γινώσκει. συμπεφυρμένον γὰρ ἔχει τὸ πάθος τῇ
γνώσει διὰ πάθους γινώσκουσα· καὶ τὰ πόρρω οἶδεν (ἐπεὶ τὸν πυρῆνα τῆς
μήλης τὸν ἐν τῷ ὀφθαλμῷ οὐχ ὁρᾷ, καὶ ἡ | ἁφὴ δὲ διὰ μέσου ἀέρος ἀντιλαμβά- (26)
νεται), ὅπερ αἴτιον μὴ ἀκριβοῦς γνώσεως. διὰ γὰρ τοῦτο τὸν νοῦν φαμεν ἀκριβῶς
γινώσκειν, διότι αὐτός ἐστι τὸ νοητὸν καὶ αὐτὸς ἑαυτὸν γινώσκει· τῇ οὖν ταυτότητι 10
τοῦ νοοῦντος καὶ νοητοῦ ἡ ἀκρίβεια τῆς γνώσεως παρακολουθεῖ, ὥστε καὶ
ἑτερότητι τὸ ἀεὶ ψεύδεσθαι· ὅπου γε οὐδὲ τῆς ἀκριβείας τῶν αἰσθητῶν ἀνέχεται,
οἷον τοῦ ἄγαν λευκοῦ, αἱ γὰρ ὑπερβολαὶ τῶν αἰσθητῶν φθείρουσι τὰς αἰσθήσεις.
καὶ διὰ τοῦτο ἡ αἴσθησις λέγεται ἀεὶ ψεύδεσθαι· ἐπεὶ εἴποις ἂν αὐτὴν καὶ ἀεὶ
ἀληθεύειν καὶ ἀκριβῆ, παραβάλλων αὐτὴν ὡς πρὸς τὴν εἰκασίαν, οἷον τὴν 15
γνῶσιν τῶν ἐν τοῖς ἐνόπτροις εἰδώλων.

---

§ 6. 6 δὴ Nv: δὲ M — 11 συνδοιάζεται M

---

is called the Peripatos when he is wrong.
　9. *CPG*, Diogenian. 5,15.
　§ 7. 1–4 and § 8. **Dam.** I § 82; cf. § 335. Objection (iii): if sense-perception
is all false, how can Pl. (*Tim.* 47b1), the Peripatos, and the ἐγκύκλιοι ἐξηγήσεις
make it the starting-point of knowledge? Answer: the lower cannot produce the
higher; sensation can be the starting-point of knowledge only in so far as it stirs
recollection. In the ἐγκύκλιοι ἐξηγήσεις (about which see note at 1 § 11) the subject
appears to have been treated in the debate against scepticism, cf. Dav. 5.1–6.21,
where the premise (knowledge derives from the senses) is taken for granted. – This
third point may come from Amm., whose commentary on the *Ph.* is cited as dealing
with it by Philop., *anal. post.* 215.3–5: ὅτι γὰρ οὐκ ἐκ τῶν αἰσθητῶν λαμβάνει τὴν
τῶν πραγμάτων γνῶσιν ἡ ψυχή, δέδεικται ἱκανῶς ἐν τοῖς εἰς τὸν Φαίδωνα (as far as we
know, Philop. himself neither wrote nor lectured on the *Ph.*).
　§ 7. 1–2. Ar. *anal. post.* II 19, 100a3–9 ἐκ μὲν οὖν αἰσθήσεως γίνεται μνήμη,
... ἐκ δὲ μνήμης ... ἐμπειρία· ... ἐκ δ' ἐμπειρίας ...τέχνης ἀρχὴ καὶ ἐπιστήμης ...
Cf. *an.* III 8, 432a3–8.
　7–8. τὸν πυρῆνα τῆς μήλης : on the operation, Paul. Aegin. VI 21 (*CMG* IX 2);
the term, Galen, *nat. fac.* III 3, 150.8 K. Cf. Plot. IV 6, 1.32–35; Philop. *de an.*
292.19-20; 350.3-4; 351.10-12, 14-17, 25-28, 37-38; 415.38-416.5
　12–13. Ar., *an.* II 11, 424a12–15; 12, 424a28–30 (φανερὸν δ' ἐκ τούτων καὶ διὰ
τί ποτε τῶν αἰσθητῶν αἱ ὑπερβολαὶ φθείρουσι τὰ αἰσθητήρια); III 13, 435b15.
　14–16. **Dam.** I § 80.4–5.

their purest form, e.g. extreme whiteness, for excessive qualities in the objects destroy the senses. For this reason, then, sense-perception is said to be always deceptive; you could equally well maintain that it is always reliable and accurate, if compared to the apprehension of images, for example those in a mirror.

8. As regards the second question [§ 7], we shall not agree with the Peripatos, which considers sense-perception the beginning of knowledge, for never can inferior and secondary things be the principles or causes of superior things. If we must adhere to what was said in the general course, that sense-perception is the beginning of knowledge, we will say that it is the beginning not in the sense of an efficient cause, but in so far as it awakes in the mind the recollection of universals and plays the part of a messenger or herald, provoking the development of latent knowledge in the soul. This is also the purport of the phrase in the *Timaeus* [47b1], that through sight and hearing 'we have received the gift of philosophy': through the objects of sense-perception we arrive at recollection.

9. According to Proclus, the heavenly bodies have no senses but sight and hearing, and this is also Aristotle's opinion; the reason is that they have only those senses that contribute to a superior mode of existence, not to existence simply, whereas the other senses serve the purpose of existence only. Homer too confirms this when he says [*Iliad* 3.277]:
'Sun, thou who seest all things and hearest all things!'
which implies that they have sight and hearing only. Another reason is that these senses are active rather than passive in perceiving, and further that they are more appropriate to the immutability of the heavenly bodies. 10. Damascius, on the contrary, holds that they have the other senses as well, arguing that they must have either all or none, otherwise animals here below will be more perfect than the stars are, if they do not have them all; so they, too, must have all the senses, in order to be perfect animate beings. Besides, if they do not have all the senses, they will not need those others either: not sight, since they would be in no danger of falling down cliffs, if devoid of sight; nor do they need hearing to communicate their thoughts to each other. Some believe that they also

---

§ 8. 6.   τὰ ἀγγέλου καὶ κήρυκος ποιοῦσαν : Plot. V 3,3.44 αἴσθησις δὲ ἡμῖν ἄγγελος, quoted by Pr., *Tim.* I 251.18–19. Dam. I § 90.3–4.

§§ 9–10.   On the senses of the visible Gods see Plut., *mus.* 25, 1140A–B; Alex. Aphrod. *ap.* Simpl., *an.* 320.20–23; Hermias 68.7–26; Pr., *Crat.* 37.6–14; *Rep.* I 232.20–21; *Tim.* II 82.3–11; 84.5–8; *Hes.* 9.2–8; Dam. I § 531; *Phil.* § 209 (and note); Philop., *an.* 228.21–27; Steph., *an.* 595.33–598.7. – Beutler, *RE* art. Plutarchos (3) 967.8–38.

§ 9. 1–5.   Ar. *an.* III 12, 434b22–25 αὗται μὲν οὖν (taste and touch) ἀναγκαῖαι τῷ ζῴῳ..., αἱ δὲ ἄλλαι τοῦ τε εὖ ἕνεκα καὶ γένει ζῴων ἤδη οὐ τῷ τυχόντι. Cf. 13, 435b19–25. G. Rodier, *Aristote, Traité de l'âme*, II, Paris 1900, 568, Beutler (above) and

Πρὸς δὲ τὸ δεύτερόν [§ 7] *φαμεν ὅτι οὐ πεισόμεθα τῷ Περιπάτῳ λέγοντι* 8
ἀρχὴν ἐπιστήμης τὴν αἴσθησιν· οὐδέποτε γὰρ τὰ χείρω καὶ δεύτερα ἀρχαὶ ἢ
αἰτιά εἰσι τῶν κρειττόνων. εἰ δὲ δεῖ καὶ ταῖς ἐγκυκλίοις ἐξηγήσεσι πείθεσθαι
καὶ ἀρχὴν εἰπεῖν τὴν αἴσθησιν τῆς ἐπιστήμης, λέξομεν αὐτὴν ἀρχὴν οὐχ ὡς
ποιητικήν, ἀλλ᾽ ὡς ἐρεθίζουσαν τὴν ἡμετέραν ψυχὴν εἰς ἀνάμνησιν τῶν καθόλου 5
καὶ τὰ ἀγγέλου καὶ κήρυκος ποιοῦσαν, κινοῦσαν τὴν ἡμετέραν ψυχὴν εἰς προβολὴν
τῶν ἐπιστημῶν, κατὰ ταύτην δὲ τὴν ἔννοιαν εἴρηται καὶ τὸ ἐν Τιμαίῳ [47b1],
ὅτι δι᾽ ὄψεως καὶ ἀκοῆς ‘τὸ τῆς φιλοσοφίας ἐπορισάμεθα γένος’, διότι ἐκ τῶν
αἰσθητῶν εἰς ἀνάμνησιν ἀφικνούμεθα.

Καὶ ὁ μὲν Πρόκλος βούλεται τὰ οὐράνια ὄψιν μόνην καὶ ἀκοὴν ἔχειν, καθάπερ 9
καὶ ᾽Αριστοτέλης· μόνας γὰρ τῶν αἰσθήσεων ἐκείνας ἔχει τὰς πρὸς τὸ εὖ εἶναι
συμβαλλομένας, οὐ μὴν τὰς πρὸς τὸ εἶναι, αἱ δὲ ἄλλαι αἰσθήσεις πρὸς τὸ εἶναι
συμβάλλονται. καὶ ὁ ποιητὴς δὲ μαρτυρεῖ τούτοις λέγων [Γ 277]
　　‘ ᾽Ηέλιος, ὃς πάντ᾽ ἐφορᾷς καὶ πάντ᾽ ἐπακούεις’, 5
ὡς ἂν ὄψιν μόνην καὶ ἀκοὴν αὐτῶν ἐχόντων. καὶ ὅτι αὗται | μάλιστα αἱ αἰσθήσεις (27)
ἐν τῷ ἐνεργεῖν μᾶλλον γινώσκουσιν ἥπερ ἐν τῷ πάσχειν, καὶ οἰκειότεραι αὗται
αὐτοῖς ὡς ἀναλλοιώτοις. ὁ δέ γε Δαμάσκιος καὶ τὰς ἄλλας αἰσθήσεις βούλεται 10
αὐτὰ ἔχειν· ἢ γὰρ πάσας ἕξουσι, φησίν, ἢ οὐδεμίαν· εἰ γὰρ μή, μέλλει τὰ τῇδε
ζῷα τελειότερα αὐτῶν εἶναι ὡς μὴ πάσας ἐχόντων· ἀνάγκη οὖν πάσας κἀκεῖνα
ἔχειν, εἰ μέλλοι τέλεια εἶναι ζῷα. καὶ ὅτι, εἰ μὴ πάσας ἔχῃ, οὐδὲ τῶν ἄλλων
δεηθήσονται· οὐδὲ γὰρ ὄψεως, ἐπεὶ μηδὲ κατὰ κρημνῶν ἐφέροντο ἀμοιροῦντα 5
ὄψεως· οὐδὲ ἀκοῆς δεῖται, ἵνα ἐξαγγέλλῃ τὰ νοήματα ἀλλήλοις. τινὲς δὲ καὶ
τὴν φυτικὴν βούλονται αὐτὰ ἔχειν, εἴ γε ἀεὶ συνέχεται. ταῦτα ἔχει ἡ θεωρία.

---

§ 9.　7 *ἥπερ* Fh: *εἴπερ* M
§ 10.　4 *ἔχῃ*] -*ηι* in ras. Mᶜ　—　6 *ἐξαγγέληι* M

W. Haase, *Ein vermeintliches Aristoteles-Fragment bei Joh. Philop.*, Synusia, Festgabe
für W. Schadewaldt, Pfullingen 1965, 354, n. 78, rightly discard the supposed
frgs. 47–48 R.³ (=De philos. 24–25 Ross) as inferences based on the De anima
passages.
2–4.　**Dam. I § 83.**
6–8.　**Dam. I § 84.**
§ 10. 6–7.　*καὶ τὴν φυτικήν* : Porph. (*ap.* Pr., *Tim.* II 282.15–18) explains the
μέσον of *Tim.* 36e1 as the *φυτικόν* of the world-soul. Dam., *princ.* 39.10–12: the
cosmos has vegetative life. Steph., *an.* 597.31–37: according to the ‘Platonists’
the celestial bodies have *ἐπιθυμία*, not *θυμός*.

have vegetative souls, as there must be a force that preserves them forever. Thus far the survey.

11. Then, as regards the attainment of insight itself [65a9]: It seems strange that Socrates should speak of 'insight', when the subject in hand is the philosopher in the stage of purification, of which knowledge is characteristic, whereas insight belongs to the statesman, whose concern is action. The explanation is that, immediately before, the argument was about pleasure and pain, which require insight to discern them and to determine their measure, for they too lie in the sphere of action. For the man who has attained the stage of purification will not choose pleasure and pain at all, because his object is freedom from affects, while the statesman, who aims at moderation of affects, will admit them within narrow limits.

12. Is there any truth in sight [65b1-2]: The 'any' is well added, since sight is neither completely false nor completely truthful.

13. The poets too tell us over and over again [65b3]: The poets he means are Parmenides, Empedocles, Epicharmus; it is they who say that sense-perception yields no accurate knowledge, Epicharmus for example in the line [frg. 12] 'Mind sees and mind hears, all the rest is deaf and blind'. Homer too [*Iliad* 5.127-128] says about Diomedes:
'She took the mist away that had clouded his eyes,
    that he might clearly know';
for if he had not met Athena, he would not have seen anything clearly.

14. Must it not be in reasoning, if at all [65c2]: Reasoning is the proper activity of the soul, which apprehends reality separately, not integrally, as the intelligence does, for reasoning (reckoning) is distinguishing: 'he counted us in with the seals', as the poet says [*Od.* 4.452]; number falls under the category of the discrete. If Plato says in the *Timaeus* [30b1] that the Creator 'reasons', this describes an activity which is the cause of all reasoning.

15. And having as little communion with it as possible [65c8-9]: When a man whose goal is purification shuns the body, this very act of shunning the body is a relation to it, and he knows what he is shunning. As for the contemplative philosopher, he neither shuns nor knows the body; for he does not know where in the world he is, and he is unaware that he does not know.

---

§ 11. 3-4. Ar., *eth. Nic.* VI 5, 1140b5-6, defines φρόνησις as ἕξις ἀληθὴς μετὰ λόγου πρακτικὴ περὶ τὰ ἀνθρώπῳ ἀγαθὰ καὶ κακά.
7. Cf. *supra* § 3.14.
§ 13. 1-2. Parmenides and Empedocles are listed as sceptics by Cic., *Acad.* I 12,44; II 5,14; 23,74; as rejecting sense-perception by Dam. I § 80. In the case of Empedocles, the reference is not to frg. B 3.9-13 (where he says that none of the senses should be relied upon in preference to the others), but to his belief that

Τί δὲ δὴ περὶ αὐτὴν τὴν τῆς φρονήσεως κτῆσιν [65a9]: τί δή ποτε 11
φρονήσεως ἐμνημόνευσε καὶ οὐκ ἐπιστήμης, εἴ γε περὶ καθαρτικοῦ φιλοσόφου
ἐστὶν ὁ σκοπός, οἰκεία δὲ ἡ μὲν ἐπιστήμη τῷ καθαρτικῷ, ἡ δὲ φρόνησις τῷ
πολιτικῷ, εἴ γε περὶ τὰ πρακτὰ καταγίνεται; ἢ ἐπειδὴ προσεχῶς περὶ ἡδονῆς
καὶ λύπης ἦν ὁ λόγος, αὗται δὲ φρονήσεως δέονται διακρινούσης αὐτὰς καὶ 5
τὸ μέτρον αὐτῶν· πρακτὰ γὰρ καὶ αὗται. ὁ μὲν γὰρ καθαρτικὸς οὐχ αἱρήσεται
ὅλως ἡδονὴν καὶ λύπην, τέλος γὰρ αὐτοῦ ἡ ἀπάθεια· ὁ δὲ πολιτικὸς ἐπ᾽ ὀλίγον
αἱρήσεται, τέλος γὰρ τούτου ἡ μετριοπάθεια.

Ἆρ᾽ ἔχει ἀλήθειάν τινα ἡ ὄψις [65b1–2]: καλῶς τὸ ᾽τινά᾽, διότι οὐδὲ 12
πάντη ψεύδεται οὐδὲ πάντη ἀληθεύει.

Καὶ οἱ ποιηταὶ ἀεὶ ἡμῖν θρυλοῦσιν [65b3]: ποιητὰς λέγει Παρμενίδην, 13
Ἐμπεδοκλέα, Ἐπίχαρμον· οὗτοι | γὰρ οὐδὲν ἀκριβὲς λέγουσιν εἰδέναι τὴν (28)
αἴσθησιν, καθάπερ Ἐπίχαρμός φησιν [frg. 12] ᾽νοῦς ὁρῇ καὶ νοῦς ἀκούει, τὰ
δὲ ἄλλα πάντα κωφὰ καὶ τυφλά᾽. καὶ οἱ ποιηταὶ δέ φασι [E 127–128] περὶ
τοῦ Διομήδους ὅτι 5
    ᾽ἀχλὺν δ᾽ ἀπ᾽ ὀφθαλμῶν ἕλεν, ἢ πρὶν ἐπῆεν,
    ὄφρ᾽ εὖ γινώσκοι᾽.
εἰ μὴ γὰρ ἔτυχε τῆς Ἀθηνᾶς, οὐκ ἂν ἑώρα τι ἀκριβές.

Ἆρ᾽ οὖν οὐκ ἐν τῷ λογίζεσθαι, εἴπερ που ἄλλοθι [65c2]: οἰκεῖον 14
τὸ λογίζεσθαι τῇ ψυχῇ διακεκριμένως γινωσκούσῃ τὰ πράγματα, καὶ οὐχ
ἡνωμένως καθάπερ ὁ νοῦς. τὸ γὰρ λογίζεσθαι διακρίνειν ἐστίν· ᾽ἐν δ᾽ ἡμέας
λέγε κήτεσσιν᾽, ὁ ποιητής [δ 452]· ὁ γὰρ ἀριθμὸς πρὸς τῷ διωρισμένῳ ἐστίν.
εἰ δὲ καὶ ἐν τῷ Τιμαίῳ [30b1] φησὶ τὸν δημιουργὸν λογίζεσθαι, ἀλλὰ κατ᾽ 5
αἰτίαν λογίζεται.

Καὶ καθ᾽ ὅσον δύναται μὴ κοινωνοῦσα αὐτῷ [65c8–9]: εἰ φεύγει 15
ὁ καθαρτικὸς τὸ σῶμα, καὶ ἐν αὐτῷ τῷ φεύγειν σχέσιν ἔχει πρὸς αὐτὸ καὶ οἶδεν
ὁ φεύγει. ὁ γὰρ θεωρητικὸς οὔτε φεύγει οὔτε οἶδεν τὸ σῶμα· ἀγνοεῖ γὰρ ὅποι
γῆς ἐστιν, καὶ ὅτι ἀγνοεῖ ἀγνοεῖ.

---

§ 11. 1 δέ] δαὶ Pl. BW²
§ 12. 1 ἡ] om. Pl.
§ 13. 1 ἀεὶ ἡμῖν M¹, Pl. TY: ἡμῖν ἀεὶ Mᶜ, Pl. BW

---

coming to-be and passing-away are illusory (frgs. B 11–12; 17).
4–8. The same line is cited and similarly explained Pr., Rep. I 18.25–26; Ascl.,
Nicom. I λα᾽ 15–18; Philop., Nicom. I λβ᾽ 15–17; Ol., Gorg. 142.9–10; Dav. 79.3–5;
Ps.-El. 23,6.
§ 14. Dam. I § 87. Both Ol. and Dam. stress the noetic character of
λογισμός and relate it to the λογίζεσθαι of the Demiurge, Tim. 30b1.
4. Ar., cat. 6, 4b22–23.
5–6. Pr., Tim. I 399.8–28; cf. 398.26–399.1 (Iamblichus).
§ 15. 3–4. Cf. Pl., Theaet. 173e1–174a2; infra 6 § 3.13–14.

5

Lecture **

1. And then, Simmias: do we agree that there is such a thing as the just itself [65d4–66b7].

Our life is threefold: either the soul turns to secondary existents, observing and organizing them, or it reverts upon itself, apprehending itself, or it lifts itself up to the higher levels of existence. Accordingly Socrates has first proved the philosopher's readiness to die from the way in which he deals with inferior things (his avoidance and contempt of the body), next from the way he reverts upon himself (his indifference to the body except in so far as absolutely necessary), and now he shows also from the fact of his reversion upon higher principles that the philosopher will be ready to die.

The philosopher wants to know the ideas, and it is impossible to apprehend these while collaborating with the body or communicating with it in the search. For if sense-perception has a certain indivisibility, as appears from its observing simultaneously that this particular object is, let us say, white, *and* that it is not black (if it knew these facts separately, it would be the same kind of thing as if I were to observe the one and you the other), this must be even more certainly true of rational soul. Rational soul, too, knows sensible things without division and it differs from sense-perception in that sense-perception knows, but does not know that it knows (for it does not revert upon itself, no more than the body does, or anything that has its being in the body), whereas rat'onal soul knows both sensible things and itself, for it knows that it knows. If this be true, the soul will not associate itself in the search with either the body or the senses or the organs of sense, inasmuch as it wants to know indivisible realities and like is known only by like.

Lect. 5. **The third reason for detachment. The path of the true philosopher.** The third καθαρτικὸς λόγος, 65d4–66a10, views the relation between the soul and the ideas, which cannot be apprehended by the senses (§ 1). The two triads of ideas: goodness - justice - beauty, magnitude - health - strength (§§ 2–3). There follows a disquisition on the exact meaning of the words 'closest to knowing', 65e4, and an observation on the 'trail', 66b4 (§ 4).

§ 1. 2–8. Cf. *supra* 4 §§ 2–3.

9–19. The argument *a fortiori*, as presented by Ol., is rather erratic: 'If even sense-perception contains an indivisible element, rational knowledge must all the more certainly be indivisible; therefore only rational knowledge can serve to apprehend indivisible reality.'

10–13. Cf. Pr., *decem dub.* 4.18–21 'sensibilium omnium oportet esse impartibile aliquid iudicatorium, et specierum que ante sensibilia aliud et has discernens—si

5

Πρᾶξις σὺν θεῷ

Τί δὲ δή, ὦ Σιμμία; φαμέν τι εἶναι δίκαιον αὐτό [65d4–66b7]. 1

Τριττῆς οὔσης τῆς ἡμετέρας ζωῆς, — ἡ γὰρ ψυχὴ ἢ πρὸς τὰ δεύτερα ἐπιστρέφει
γινώσκουσα αὐτὰ καὶ κοσμοῦσα, ἢ πρὸς | ἑαυτὴν γινώσκουσα ἑαυτήν, ἢ πρὸς (29)
τὰ κρείττονα ἀνατείνεται, — δείξας ὁ Σωκράτης τὸν φιλόσοφον ἐθέλοντα
ἀποθνήσκειν ἀπό τε τῆς πρὸς τὰ δεύτερα ἐπιστροφῆς, διότι φεύγει τὸ σῶμα 5
καταφρονῶν αὐτοῦ, ἀλλὰ μὴν καὶ ἐκ τῆς πρὸς ἑαυτὸν ἐπιστροφῆς, διότι φροντίδα
⟨οὐ⟩ ποιεῖται τοῦ σώματος ὅ τι μὴ πᾶσα ἀνάγκη, νῦν δείκνυσι καὶ ἐκ τῆς πρὸς
τὰ κρείττω ἐπιστροφῆς ὅτι ἐθελήσει ἀποθνήσκειν.

Ἐθέλει γὰρ εἰδέναι τὰς ἰδέας, ταύτας δὲ ἀδύνατον ἐπίστασθαι ἐνεργοῦντα
μετὰ τοῦ σώματος ἢ ἔχοντα κοινωνὸν τοῦτο ἐν τῇ ζητήσει. εἰ γὰρ ἡ αἴσθησις 10
ἔχει τι ἀμερές, ὡς δηλοῖ τὸ ἅμα εἰδέναι αὐτὴν ὅτι τυχὸν τοῦτο λευκὸν καὶ οὐ
μέλαν (εἰ γὰρ μεριστῶς ταῦτα ᾔδει, ὅμοιον ἦν ὡς εἰ τοῦ μὲν ἐγώ, τοῦ δὲ σὺ
αἴσθοιο), πολλῷ μᾶλλον ἡ λογικὴ ψυχή. οἶδε γὰρ καὶ αὕτη τὰ αἰσθητὰ ἀμερῶς
καὶ διαφέρει τῆς αἰσθήσεως ὅτι ἡ μὲν οἶδεν, οὐ μὴν οἶδεν ὅτι οἶδεν (οὐδὲ γὰρ
ἐπιστρέφει πρὸς ἑαυτήν, ἐπειδὴ μηδὲ τὸ σῶμα ἐπιστρέφει πρὸς ἑαυτό, οὐ τὰ 15
ἐν τῷ σώματι τὸ εἶναι ἔχοντα), ἡ δὲ λογικὴ ψυχὴ οἶδε τὰ αἰσθητὰ καὶ ἑαυτήν,
οἶδε γὰρ ὅτι οἶδεν. εἰ οὖν ταῦτα οὕτως ἔχοι, οὐ συμπαραλήψεται ἐν τῇ ζητήσει
κοινωνὸν ἡ ψυχὴ ἢ τὸ σῶμα ἢ τὰς αἰσθήσεις ἢ τὰ αἰσθητήρια, εἴ γε τὰ ἀμερῆ
βούλεται εἰδέναι, τῷ δὲ ὁμοίῳ τὸ ὅμοιον γινώσκεται.

Ἐφ᾽ οἷς καὶ δύο τριάδας ἰδεῶν ἡμῖν παρατίθεται, μίαν μὲν ἀγαθοῦ δικαίου καλοῦ, 2
ἑτέραν δὲ μεγέθους ὑγιείας ἰσχύος. καὶ οὐ ταύτῃ διαφέρουσιν αἱ τριάδες αὗται
ἀλλήλων, ὥς τινες ᾠήθησαν, τῷ τὴν μὲν πρώτην περὶ ψυχὴν καταγίνεσθαι, τὴν

---

§ 1.   1 δὲ] δαὶ Pl. BY | post δή] τὰ τοιάδε mg. add. Mᶜ (Pl.) — 5 δεύτερα] in spat.
2 litt. ex corr. Mᶜ — 7 οὐ Nv (Fh): om. M — 10 κοινωνὸν Fh (cf. Pl. 65b1): κοινὸν M —
13 λογικὴ Wk (cf. lin. 16): ὁλικὴ M — 15 οὐ] οὔ Nv

enim alio aliud, dicit aliquis, simile ac si hoc quidem ego, illud autem tu sentias',
i.e. τῶν αἰσθητῶν πάντων εἶναι δεῖ ἀμερές τι κριτήριον, καὶ τῶν πρὸ αὐτῶν εἰδῶν ἄλλο
καὶ ταῦτα διακρῖνον—εἰ γὰρ ἄλλῳ ἄλλο, φησί τις (Ar., an. III 2, 426b19), ὅμοιον ὡς
εἰ τοῦ μὲν ἐγώ, τοῦ δὲ σὺ αἴσθοιο (Greek text partly extant).
13. λογικὴ ψυχή : M and the editions have ὁλικὴ ψυχή. But a 'total soul' (opp.
μερική) is the soul of a sphere or element, a notion which has no relevancy here.
A blurring of the λ would be sufficient to make λογική look like ὁλική. Cf. line 16.
19. τῷ δὲ ὁμοίῳ τὸ ὅμοιον γινώσκεται : Empedocles frg. B 109 (=Ar., an. I 2,
404b8–15; met. B 4, 1000b5–9); according to Theophr., de sensu 1, also a tenet of
Parmenides (=frg. A 46) and Plato (cf. Posidonius on the *Tim.* ap. Sext. Emp., adv.
math. 7,93). It is the basis for the Neoplatonic theories about levels of cognition:
Porph., sent. 25; Iambl., comm. math. 38.6–8.
§ 2. Dam. I §§ 96–97.
3. ὥς τινες ᾠήθησαν : this is the opinion expressed by Dam., though he qualifies

2. After this Socrates cites as examples two triads of ideas, one consisting of the good, the just and the beautiful, another of magnitude, health and strength. The difference between these triads is not, as some have thought, that the former relates to soul, the latter to body; rather, both pervade all being. The good pervades all being, because the Creator 'is good, and no one who is good ever feels envy about anything' [*Tim.* 29e1–2], he will therefore create things after his own likeness; further because, as it is said in the *Republic* [II 379b1–11], one who is good does not call into existence anything that is evil; and because . . . But the same is true of justice also, since everything is clearly distinct from everything else, and marking boundaries between things and keeping within one's own bounds is the function of justice. It is equally true of beauty, as there is a kind of communion and union among things, and beauty is closely connected with union. But magnitude, too, pervades everything: even in the intelligible world there is continuous quantity, though not in the usual sense, but in so far as intelligible reality is multiplied and is not identical with the One; everything, indeed, that comes after the One participates in quantity and in that sense it has magnitude. It is the same with health: because everything consists of elements that maintain the right proportion to each other, there is health in everything. And strength, too, in so far as things are not vanquished by what is inferior to them.

3. In the *Philebus* [20d1–11] Socrates mentions another triad of ideas, the desirable, the perfect, the adequate; the perfect differs from the adequate in that the adequate is productive, so that it can share itself with others, while the perfect is sufficient to itself. The perfect corresponds to justice, because, in a way of speaking, it keeps within its own bounds; the adequate to goodness, because it communicates itself to others; and the desirable to beauty.

4. Next, Socrates says that a man who is active in this way comes 'closest' to knowing the truth [65e4]. What does this mean? Does he not know truth himself? We answer that he comes only 'closest' as compared to the contemplative philosopher; or else it is because Socrates is speaking of discursive reasoning, which is no more than close to the truth, if compared to intellective activity.

He goes on to say that we should follow this 'trail' [66b4], not the

---

it by adding μᾶλλον. In § 96 he describes the all-pervading character of the first triad in much the same way as Ol. does. Pr., *Alc.* 319.12–321.3 (explaining the ἀγαθόν - καλόν - δίκαιον in Pl., *Alc. I* 115a1–116d4) says that both in the highest principles and in their lowest derivatives, the good is more comprehensive than the beautiful, the beautiful more so than the just, but at the level of soul they coincide. Ol., *Alc.* 109.15–110.6 follows Pr.; this, however, is not irreconcilable with the present passage, which uses the two triads as examples of the inter-penetration of forms.

α' δὲ δευτέραν περὶ σῶμα· ἑκατέρα γὰρ | διὰ πάντων τῶν ὄντων διῆλθεν. καὶ γὰρ (30)
καὶ τὸ ἀγαθὸν διῆλθε διὰ πάντων, εἴ γε ὁ δημιουργὸς 'ἀγαθός ἐστιν, ἀγαθῷ 5
δὲ οὐδεὶς περὶ οὐδενὸς ἐγγίνεται φθόνος' [Tim. 29e1–2], ὅμοια ἄρα ἑαυτῷ
παράξει· καὶ ὅτι, ὡς ἐν Πολιτεία εἴρηται [II 379b1–11], ἀγαθὸς οὐ δίδωσι
β' τῷ φλαύρῳ ὑπόστασιν· καὶ ὅτι **. ἀλλὰ καὶ ἡ δικαιοσύνη, εἴ γε ἕκαστον
ἀσύγχυτόν ἐστιν πρὸς τὸ λοιπόν, τὸ δὲ διορίζειν τὰ πράγματα καὶ ἰδιοπραγεῖν
γ' δικαιοσύνης. ἀλλὰ καὶ τὸ κάλλος, εἴ γε κοινωνίαν τινὰ καὶ ἕνωσιν ἔχει τὰ 10
α' πράγματα, τὸ δὲ κάλλος πρὸς τῇ ἑνώσει. καὶ τὸ μέγεθος δὲ διὰ πάντων διῆλθεν·
ἔστι γὰρ καὶ ἐν τοῖς νοητοῖς οὐχ ἁπλῶς τὸ ποσὸν τὸ συνεχές, ἀλλὰ καθὸ
πεπλήθυνται καὶ οὐκ ἔστιν ὅπερ τὸ ἕν· πᾶν γὰρ τὸ μετὰ τὸ ἓν πλήθους μετέχει
β' καὶ ταύτῃ μέγεθος ἔχει. ἀλλὰ καὶ ὑγίειαν· ὡς γὰρ ἐκ στοιχείων ἕκαστον
γ' συγκείμενον συμμετρίαν σῳζόντων πρὸς ἄλληλα ὑγίειαν ἔχει. ἀλλὰ καὶ ἰσχύν, 15
καθὸ οὐ κρατεῖται ὑπὸ τῶν χειρόνων.

Ἐν δέ γε τῷ Φιλήβῳ [20d1–11] ἄλλην τριάδα φησὶν εἶναι ἰδεῶν, ἐφετοῦ 3
α' τελείου ἱκανοῦ· καὶ διαφέρει τὸ τέλειον τοῦ ἱκανοῦ, ὅτι τὸ μὲν ἱκανὸν γόνιμόν
β' ἐστιν, ὡς καὶ ἄλλοις μεταδιδόναι ἑαυτοῦ, τὸ δὲ τέλειον αὔταρκές ἐστι. καὶ
τὸ μὲν τέλειον πρὸς τῇ δικαιοσύνῃ ἐστίν, οἷον γὰρ ἰδιοπραγεῖ· τὸ δὲ ἱκανὸν
γ' πρὸς τῷ ἀγαθῷ, καὶ ἄλλοις μεταδιδοῦν· τὸ δὲ ἐφετὸν πρὸς τῷ κάλλει. 5

Εἶτα καί φησιν ὅτι οὕτως ἐνεργῶν 'ἐγγύτατά' ἐστι τοῦ εἰδέναι τὸ ἀληθές 4
[65e4]. τί φῄς; τί οὖν οὐκ αὐτὸ τὸ ἀληθὲς οἶδεν; ἢ ἐγγύτατα ὡς πρὸς παραβολὴν
τοῦ θεωρητικοῦ· ἢ ὅτι περὶ διανοητικῆς ἐνεργείας, αὕτη δὲ ἐγγύς ἐστι τοῦ
ἀληθοῦς παραβαλλομένη ὡς πρὸς τὴν νοερὰν ἐνέργειαν.

Εἶτα καί φησιν ὅτι ταύτην τὴν 'ἀτραπὸν' ἰτέον [66b4], οὐ τὴν λεωφόρον, 5
τουτέστι καθαρτικῶς ζητέον· ἀτραπὸς γὰρ ἡ ὁδός, τουτέστιν ἡ κάθαρσις ἡ
ἐπὶ τὴν θεωρίαν ἄγουσα. οὐ τὴν λεωφόρον δὲ δεῖ ἰέναι, τουτέστι τὴν | τῶν (31)

---

§ 2. 8 lac. stat. Nv — 14 ὑγίειαν] -α Nv — 15 ἰσχύν] -ύς Nv

---

9. ἰδιοπραγεῖν: cf. note at 2 § 14.2–3.
10–11. On beauty and union cf. Pr., Alc. 322.11–17.
§ 3. On the triad of Phil. 20d1–10, τέλεον - ἱκανόν - ἐφετόν, cf. Dam., Phil. §§ 77
and 241, with notes. Pr. had a predilection for parallels of this kind. The obvious
correspondences are ἐφετόν=ἀγαθόν, ἱκανόν=κάλλος (γόνιμον), τέλεον=δίκαιον.
5. μεταδιδοῦν: not unusual in later Greek. A. N. Jannaris, An Historical Greek
Grammar, London 1897, § 996,51, cites NT, Apoc. 22,2.
§ 4. 5–11. Dam. I § 101, who explains that the 'trail' is the inevitable conclusion
from the foregoing reflections.

highway, that is, we should lead the life of purification; for the 'trail' is the road of purification, which leads to contemplation. The highway that we must avoid is the way of the masses; for there was also a Pythagorean precept to shun the highways, as in the lines [Callim. frg. 1.25–26]:

> 'The paths where no wagons pass,
> tread those, and do not follow in the tracks of others'.

Thus far the survey.

5.   Do we agree that there is such a thing as the just itself, or do we not? [65d4–5]: The 'just itself' is his term for the idea. It must necessarily exist, because things in this world are approximate, not exact, and prior to the undefined the exact must exist. For instance, the spherical shape in this world is not accurate: if we take away a quantity the size of a grain of sand, it nevertheless presents itself to us in the same shape. Nor are the qualities in this world unalloyed, but the heat of fire is combined with dryness, and prior to these the unadulterated forms must exist.

6.   Yes we do, by Zeus [65d6]: Simmias unhesitatingly assents to the doctrine of ideas, because he had connections with the Pythagoreans, who held that doctrine. That is why he confirms his statement by an oath, swearing very properly by Zeus, who as the Creator has the ideas in himself.

7.   Seen with your eyes [65d9]: Above Socrates spoke of sight and hearing [65b2], here of eyes and ears [66a4]. This explains why Plato dreamed that he had a third eye, when he had found the theory of ideas.

8.   Is the complete truth of them beheld through the body [65e1–2]: Sense-perception apprehends through the body. For the knower is either completely different from the known (as in the case of sense-perception, which knows objects different from itself); or completely identical with it (as intelligence by knowing itself knows intelligible reality) or different at the outset and later identical, as in the case of the soul: when it knows external things, the known is different from the knower, but when it knows itself, the two are identical.

9.   Nor dragging along any other sense [65e8–66a1]: The attempt to be active separately is a kind of violence done to the sense and a dragging along of it.

10.   Tries to hunt down [66a3]: 'Hunting down' is the appropriate term where intelligible things are concerned, because they are apprehended

---

8.   Aelian., *var. hist.* 4,17; Diog. Laert. 8,17; Porph., *vit. Pyth.* 42; Iambl., *vit. Pyth.* 18,83; *protr.* 21, p. 111.17–28; Eustath., *Il.* 23.585; Pr. *Parm.* 685, 35-36.
§ 5.   Cf. Dam. I § 94.3–5.
2–5.   Cf. *infra* 11 § 7.10–11; 12 § 1.11–13.
§ 6.   2–4.   See note on 1 § 20.5–6.

πολλῶν· καὶ Πυθαγόρειον γὰρ ἦν παράγγελμα φεύγειν τὰς λεωφόρους, ὥσπερ τὸ [Callim. frg. 1.25–26]

'τὰ μὴ πατέουσιν ἄμαξαι,   10

τὰ στείβειν, ἑτέρων δ' ἴχνια μὴ καθ' ὁμά'.

ταῦτα ἔχει ἡ θεωρία.

Φαμέν τι εἶναι δίκαιον αὐτὸ ἢ οὐδέν; [65d4–5]: αὐτοδίκαιον καλεῖ 5
τὴν ἰδέαν. ἀνάγκη δὲ εἶναι τοῦτο· τὰ γὰρ τῇδε παχυμερῆ ἐστιν καὶ οὐκ ἀκριβῆ, δεῖ δὲ πρὸ τῶν ὁλοσχερῶν τὰ ἀκριβῆ εἶναι. τὸ γὰρ τῇδε σχῆμα τῆς σφαίρας ὂν οὐκ ἔστιν ἀκριβές· εἰ γὰρ ψαμμιαῖον μέγεθος ἀφέλοιμεν ἐξ αὐτῆς, οὐδὲν ἧττον τὸ τοιοῦτο φαίνεται σχῆμα. καὶ αἱ ποιότητες δὲ αἱ τῇδε οὐκ ἀμιγεῖς 5
εἰσιν, ἀλλὰ συνέζευκται τῇ θερμότητι τοῦ πυρὸς ξηρότης, καὶ δεῖ πρὸ τούτων τὰ ἀνόθευτα εἶναι.

Φαμέν τοι, νὴ Δία [65d6]: ὁ Σιμμίας ἑτοίμως συγκατατίθεται τῷ περὶ 6
τῶν ἰδεῶν λόγῳ ὡς συνήθης Πυθαγορείοις τὰς ἰδέας πρεσβεύουσι. διὸ καὶ μεθ' ὅρκου τοῦτο προήγαγεν, καὶ τὸν οἰκεῖον θεὸν ὄμνυσι, τὸν Δία· ἐν τούτῳ γὰρ αἱ ἰδέαι εἰσὶν ὡς δημιουργῷ.

Τοῖς ὀφθαλμοῖς εἶδες [65d9]: ἄνω ἔλεγεν 'ὄψει καὶ ἀκοῇ' [65b2], νῦν 7
'ὀφθαλμοῖς καὶ ὠσίν' [66a4]· διὸ καὶ τριόφθαλμον ἑαυτὸν ἐθεάσατο, ἡνίκα τὰς ἰδέας ηὗρεν.

Διὰ τοῦ σώματος τὸ ἀληθέστατον αὐτῶν θεωρεῖται [65e1–2]: 8 (32)
ἡ γὰρ αἴσθησις διὰ τοῦ σώματος γινώσκει. τὸ γὰρ γινῶσκον ἢ πάντῃ ἕτερόν ἐστι τοῦ γινωσκομένου, καθάπερ ἡ αἴσθησις οἶδε τὰ αἰσθητὰ ἕτερα ὄντα· ἢ πάντῃ ταὐτόν, ὥσπερ ὁ νοῦς ἑαυτὸν γινώσκων οἶδε τὰ νοητά· ἢ κατ' ἀρχὰς μὲν ἕτερον, ὕστερον δὲ ταὐτόν, ὥσπερ ἡ ψυχὴ ἡνίκα μὲν οἶδε τὰ ἔξω, ἕτερόν 5
ἐστι τὸ γινωσκόμενον τοῦ γινώσκοντος, ἡνίκα δὲ ἑαυτήν, ταὐτόν.

Μήτε ἄλλην αἴσθησιν ἐφέλκων [65e8–66a1]: βία γάρ ἐστι καὶ ὁλκὴ 9
τῆς αἰσθήσεως τὸ πειρᾶσθαι χωριστῶς ἐνεργεῖν.

Ἐπιχειροῖ θηρεύειν [66a3]: οἰκεῖον τὸ 'θηρεύειν' ἐπὶ τῶν νοητῶν, 10
διότι ἀφανεῖ δυνάμει τῆς ψυχῆς γινώσκεται ταῦτα, καθάπερ καὶ οἱ θηραταὶ ἀφανεῖς σπεύδουσιν εἶναι τοῖς θηράμασιν.

Ἀπαλλαγεὶς ὅτι μάλιστα ὀφθαλμῶν τε καὶ ὤτων [66a3–4]: οὐχ 11

---

§ 4. 11 καθομα M
§ 5. 6 ante ξηρότης] ÷ in ras. Mˣ (ἡ ξηρότης M¹?)
§ 6. 1 τοι] τι Pl. Y, μέντοι Pl. B — 3 καὶ τὸν μ: καίτοι M
§ 7. 1 ἴδες M
§ 8. 1 τὸ ἀληθέστατον αὐτῶν M¹, Pl. Y: αὐτῶν τὸ ἀληθέστατον Mᶜ, Pl. BTW —
6 γινωσκόμενον Wk: γινῶσκον M (γινωσκομένου pro γινώσκοντος Fh)
§ 9. 1 post μήτε] τινὰ Pl. BW

3–4. The forms in the Demiurge: Pr., theol. III 12, 269.3–9.
§ 7. 2–3. Proleg. 5.40–42 ἀμέλει γοῦν καὶ φασὶν αὐτὸν εὑρηκότα τὰς ἰδέας ἑωρακέναι ἑαυτὸν τρίτον ἔχοντα ὀφθαλμόν. Origen, c. Cels. VI 8, p. 78.15–16. The scholion in M (infra p. 185) may derive directly from the Proleg.
§ 8. Dam. I § 99; supra 4 § 7.
§ 11. Infra 6 § 9.

by a hidden faculty of the soul, just as the huntsman tries to hide from his prey.

11. **Freeing himself, as far as possible, from eyes and ears [66a3–4]**: 'Freeing himself', not in the sense that one should take one's own life (for that is forbidden), but in the sense of living separately.

12. **'Exceedingly true', said Simmias [66a9]**: The word 'exceedingly' is well-chosen, because the subject, intelligible reality, is one that exceeds human nature.

13. **Will not genuine philosophers come to hold this sort of belief [66b1–2]**: Not the belief that derives its content from the lower functions, but a belief that is the outcome of thought; for belief exists in two kinds. 'Genuine philosophers' as opposed to statesmen.

14. **As it were a trail that we have to follow [66b3–4]**: Not to our ruin, to which some trails lead, but to happiness.

15. **Our souls are contaminated [66b5–6]**: The question is who the speakers are. If they are the philosophers, how can their souls be contaminated by the body? If laymen, why did he speak of philosophers first? It is the philosophers who are speaking, but they are comparing their life here below with the life that preceded it.

16. **By so evil a thing, we shall never acquire [66b6]**: In what sense does he call the body an evil? It is relatively evil: to the man whose object is purification it is an obstacle which precludes independent activity; as for the statesman, he even needs it, as an instrument.

6

Lecture **

1. **For the body is the cause of countless distractions [66b7–67b6]**.

The philosophers are still talking to each other. Socrates, after showing from the three ways of life that the philosopher will be ready to die, had concluded that it is impossible for the human soul to attain its desire as long as it is contaminated by the body. This very point they now

---

§ 13. 1–3. Dam. I § 103; cf. § 125.

2. δεχομένην : cf. Plot. V 5,1.63 ὅτι παραδεχομένη καὶ διὰ τοῦτο δόξα. Etym. magn. 283.15 δόξα· παρὰ τὸ δέχω δέξω, δέξα καὶ δόξα.

2–3. Rational and irrational opinion: Dam. I § 103; § 125; Dav. 47.1–15; 79.16–19; Ps.-El. 17,16–17; note on Dam., *Phil.* § 225.1–7.

3. To Ol. apparently the 'genuine philosophers' are the καθαρτικοί. See § 15.

§ 15. Dam. I § 100.

§ 16. Dam. I § 102.

Lect. 6. Reflections of the true philosophers. The ways in which the body disturbs the functioning of the mind are grouped on much the same plan as in Dam. I § 108;

ὅτι δεῖ ἐξάγειν ἑαυτόν (ἀθέμιτον γὰρ τοῦτο), διὰ τοῦτο 'ἀπαλλαγείς', ἀλλὰ χωριστῶς ζήσας.

Ὑπερφυῶς, ἔφη ὁ Σιμμίας [66a9]: καλῶς τὸ 'ὑπερφυῶς', διότι καὶ 12
περὶ τούτων ὁ λόγος, περὶ γὰρ νοητῶν.

Παρίστασθαι δόξαν τινὰ τοῖς γνησίως φιλοσοφοῦσιν [66b1-2]: 13
δόξαν οὐ τὴν κάτωθεν δεχομένην, ἀλλὰ τὴν διανοίας οὖ|σαν ἀποτελεύτησιν· (33)
διττὴ γὰρ ἡ δόξα. 'γνησίοις' δὲ 'φιλοσόφοις' εἶπεν διὰ τοὺς πολιτικούς.

Ὥσπερ ἀτραπὸς ἐκφέρειν ἡμᾶς [66b3-4]: ἀλλ' οὐκ ἐπὶ κακῷ, καθάπερ 14
ἔνιαι τῶν ἀτραπῶν, ἀλλ' ἐπ' ἀγαθῷ.

Συμπεφυρμένη ἡμῶν ἡ ψυχή [66b5-6]: τίνες ταῦτα λέγουσιν, ἄξιον 15
ζητῆσαι. εἰ μὲν οἱ φιλόσοφοι, καὶ πῶς συμπέφυρται αὐτῶν ἡ ψυχὴ τῷ σώματι;
εἰ δὲ οἱ πολλοί, καὶ πῶς εἶπεν 'οἱ φιλόσοφοι'; ἢ οἱ φιλόσοφοι ταῦτα λέγουσι
παραβάλλοντες τὸν τῇδε αὐτῶν βίον πρὸς τὸν προηγησάμενον.

Μετὰ τοῦ τοιούτου κακοῦ, οὐ μήποτε κτησόμεθα [66b6]: πῶς 16
κακὸν λέγει τὸ σῶμα; ἢ πρός τι κακόν· τῷ γὰρ καθαρτικῷ ἐμποδὼν γίνεται
χωριστῶς ἐνεργεῖν, ἐπεὶ τοῦ πολιτικοῦ καὶ ὄργανόν ἐστιν.

6

Πρᾶξις σὺν θεῷ

Μυρίας μὲν γὰρ ἡμῖν ἀσχολίας παρέχει τὸ σῶμα [66b7-67b6]. 1
Ἔτι πρὸς ἀλλήλους οἱ φιλόσοφοι διαλέγονται. δείξαντος γὰρ τοῦ Σωκράτους
ἐκ τῆς τριττῆς ζωῆς ὅτι ὁ φιλόσοφος ἐθελήσει ἀποθνήσκειν, συμπέρασμα συνῆγεν
ὅτι ἀδύνατόν | ἐστι τὴν ἡμετέραν ψυχὴν τυχεῖν οὗ ἐφίεται συμπεφυρμένην τῷ (34)
σώματι. τοῦτο οὖν αὐτὸ διὰ παραδειγμάτων ἐκτραγῳδοῦσιν ἀφηγούμενοι τὰ 5
συμβαίνοντα ἐμπόδια τῇ ψυχῇ ἀπὸ τοῦ σώματος καὶ κατὰ φύσιν ἔχοντος ἐν

---

§ 13. 1 post δόξαν] τοιάνδε ins. Mᶜ (Pl.) | φιλοσοφοῦσιν] φιλοσόφοις Pl.
§ 14. ἀτραπὸς] ἀτραπός τις Pl. BW² | ἐκφέρειν ἡμᾶς M¹, Pl. BTY: ἡμᾶς ἐκφέρειν Mᶜ, Pl. W
§ 15. 1 post συμπεφυρμένη] ἦν ins. Mᶜ, ἦ Pl.
§ 16. 1 τοῦ] om. Pl. B¹ | κτησόμεθα] -σώμεθα Pl.

§ 1. 3 τριττῆς Fh: τρίτης M

---

in Ol. the principle of classification is indicated more clearly (§ 1). Imagination is the ἔσχατος χιτών in knowledge, as ambition is in emotional life, Dam. I § 111 (§ 2). The question whether in this world a life of continuous contemplation is attainable, is answered in the affirmative (§ 3).

§ 1. 5-12. Dam. I § 108.1-5. Dam. lists the same points, but takes c3-4 καὶ εἰδώλων παντοδαπῶν καὶ φλυαρίας ... πολλῆς as already relating to imagination (ὅσα τῆς αἰσθητικῆς καὶ φανταστικῆς γνώσεως εἴδωλα καὶ φλυαρήματα, lines 3-4), while Ol. (cf. §§ 6-7) includes them among the irrationalities of emotional life. This makes for a clear structure: (i) the body, in its normal and abnormal state, (ii) irrational soul in its vital functions, directed either toward the body or toward external things, and (iii) in its cognitive function. The same classification is referred back to at § 4.

exemplify in dramatic terms, setting forth the inconveniences to which
the soul is subjected by the body, both when in its normal state, through
the necessity of food [66b7–c1], and when in an abnormal condition,
during illness [c1–2]. Then there is also the inconvenience caused by
irrationality, on the one hand in the vital faculties (where it is twofold,
either stemming from the body only, e.g. fear, desire, love [c2–3], or
provoked by external factors, such as war and greed for money [c5–d2]),
on the other hand in the field of knowledge, where imagination always
gets in the way of our thinking [d3–7].

2. There are two affects, indeed, that are hard to wipe out, among
the cognitive faculties imagination, and in the vital faculties ambition;
for what the soul puts on first, it strips last. The first garment of the soul,
where the vital faculties are concerned, is ambition, because it is the
will to rule that decided the human soul to descend into genesis; even
if we seem to have no ambition, ambition is the motive behind it, and
we have again failed to escape from this passion. In knowledge the most
persistent affect is imagination; therefore Odysseus needed the moly of
Hermes, right reason, to escape from Calypso, who is imagination and
who like a cloud covers the sun of reason; imagination, indeed, is a veil
(kalymma), hence someone has spoken of it as 'Fancy, with thy flowing
robes'. This explains also why Odysseus first lands on the island of Circe,

---

§ 2. **Dam. I § 111.** The aphorism on ambition as the garment shed last comes
from Dioscurides ap. Athen. XI 507D (Jacoby IIIB 594): ἦν δὲ ὁ Πλάτων πρὸς
τῇ κακοηθείᾳ καὶ φιλόδοξος, ὅστις ἔφησεν 'ἔσχατον τὸν τῆς δόξης χιτῶνα ἐν τῷ θανάτῳ
αὐτῷ ἀποδυόμεθα, ἐν διαθήκαις, ἐν ἐκκομιδαῖς, ἐν τάφοις,' ὥς φησι Διοσκουρίδης ἐν τοῖς
ἀπομνημονεύμασι. Pr., Alc. 138.12–13; Ol., Alc. 50.25–51.10; 98.16–20; 101.3–7;
Simpl., Epict. 47.1–5; 118.54–119.3. – In the passage 66d2–7 the distorting influence
of the 'body' upon our attempts at contemplation is currently identified as φαντασία
(Philop., an. 2.29–3.5; Ps-Them., parva nat. 3.16–17; Michael Ephes., parva nat. 10.22–25;
Sophon., an. 120.9–15; Pr. Parm. 1025.8–15), and it seems to be the purely accidental use
of ἔσχατον by Pl. at d3 which invited the parallel drawn between ambition and
imagination by Dam. I § 111 and Ol., h.l. and Alc. 51.11–15 ἰστέον δὲ ὅτι τὸ φιλότιμον
πάθος ἐν ταῖς ζωτικαῖς ἡμῶν δυνάμεσίν ἐστι δυσαπόβλητον, ἡ δὲ φαντασία ἐν ταῖς
γνωστικαῖς· πάρεστι γὰρ ἀεὶ τῇ ἡμετέρᾳ ψυχῇ ἡ φαντασία, τύπους ἀναπλάττουσα ὧν ἀγνοεῖ
ἡ ψυχὴ καὶ τοῖς ἀσωμάτοις σχήματα καὶ μεγέθη καὶ σώματα περιτιθεῖσα καὶ τόπῳ
περιορίζουσα τὸν θεόν. With explicit reference to the Ph.: Philop., aet. 116.25–117.2
ἐν τῇ περὶ τοῦ θείου νοήσει οὐκ ἐξισχύει μὲν ἡ ἡμετέρα διάνοια ἀφαντάστως αὐτὸ θεωρεῖν,
ἀλλ' ὡς καὶ ὁ Πλάτων φησί, συμπαραθεῖ πάντως ταῖς περὶ θεοῦ ἐννοίαις ἡ φαντασία
τύπους ἡμῖν καὶ ὄγκους περὶ αὐτοῦ νοεῖν ὑπολαμβάνουσα. Anal. pr. 3.8–12 παρεμπίπτουσα
αὕτη (=ἡ φαντασία), ὡς καὶ ὁ Πλάτων φησί, ταράττει τοὺς μὴ παιδευθέντας αὐτὴν τῶν
λογικῶν ἐνεργειῶν διακρίνειν τὰ τῆς αἰσθήσεως ὑπάρχοντα καὶ τοῖς νοητοῖς περιάπτουσα,
οἷον, εἰ τύχοι, τοῖς ἀσωμάτοις μορφὴν καὶ σχῆμα καὶ ὄγκον, τοῖς ἐξ ἀφαιρέσεως εἴδεσιν
ὕλην πάντως ὑποβάλλουσα. An. 2.29–3.5 δ καὶ ὁ Πλάτων ἐν τῷ Φαίδωνι λέγει, ὅτι τοῦτό
ἐστι τὸ χαλεπώτατον τῶν ἐν ἡμῖν, ὅτι ὅταν καὶ σχολὴν ἀπὸ τῶν περιολκῶν τοῦ σώματος
μικρὸν ἀγάγωμεν καὶ θελήσωμεν τῇ θεωρίᾳ τῶν θείων σχολάσαι, παρεμπίπτουσα ἡ
φαντασία θόρυβον ἡμῖν κινεῖ, ὑπονοεῖν διδοῦσα ὅτι σῶμά ἐστι τὸ θεῖον, καὶ μέγεθος ἔχει

ταῖς ἀναγκαίαις τροφαῖς [66b7–c1] καὶ παρὰ φύσιν ἐν ταῖς νόσοις [c1–2].

ἀλλὰ μὴν καὶ ἡ ἀλογία ἐμποδὼν γίνεται, ἥ τε ζωτική — διττὴ δὲ αὕτη, ἡ περὶ
τὸ σῶμα μόνον θεωρουμένη, ὥσπερ φόβοι καὶ ἐπιθυμίαι καὶ ἔρωτες [c2–5],
ἡ περὶ τὰ ἔξω, οἷον πόλεμοι καὶ φιλοχρηματίαι [c5–d2]· — ἀλλὰ μὴν καὶ ἡ   10
γνωστικὴ ἐμποδὼν γίνεται, ὥσπερ ἡ φαντασία ἀεὶ ἐμποδὼν γινομένη ταῖς
ἡμετέραις νοήσεσι [d3–7].

Δύο γὰρ δυσέκνιπτα πάθη, ἐν μὲν γνώσεσιν ἡ φαντασία, ἐν δὲ ζωαῖς ἡ φιλοτιμία.   2
ἃ γὰρ πρῶτα ἐνδύεται, ταῦτα καὶ ὕστερον ἀποτίθεται. πρῶτος δὲ χιτὼν τῆς
ψυχῆς ἐν ζωαῖς ἡ φιλοτιμία, ὡς γὰρ φίλαρχος ἡ ἡμετέρα ψυχὴ ᾑρήσατο κατελθεῖν
εἰς γένεσιν· εἰ γὰρ καὶ δοκοῦμεν μὴ εἶναι φιλότιμοι, ἀλλὰ δι' αὐτὸ τοῦτο, διὰ
φιλοτιμίαν, ὥστε πάλιν οὐκ ἐξεφύγομεν τὸ πάθος. ἐν δὲ γνώσεσιν ἡ φαντασία·   5
διὸ καὶ ὁ Ὀδυσσεὺς μῶλος ἐδεήθη Ἑρμαϊκοῦ καὶ λόγου ὀρθοῦ πρὸς τὸ ἐκφυγεῖν
τὴν Καλυψὼ φαντασίαν οὖσαν καὶ δίκην νέφους ἐμποδὼν γενομένην τῷ λόγῳ
ἡλίῳ ὄντι· κάλυμμα γὰρ αὕτη, διὸ καί τις ἔφη 'Φαντασίη τανύπεπλε'. διὸ καὶ
πρῶτον κατήχθη ὁ Ὀδυσσεὺς ἐπὶ τὴν Κίρκην αἴσθησιν οὖσαν ὡς θυγατέρα
τοῦ Ἡλίου. παρεμποδὼν οὖν ἡ φαντασία γίνεται ταῖς νοήσεσιν ἡμῶν. διὸ καὶ   10
ἐν τῷ ἐνθουσιᾶν ἐὰν φαντασθῶμεν, παύεται ἡ ἐνθουσιαστικὴ ἐνέργεια· ἐναντίως (35)
γὰρ ἔχει ἐνθουσιασμὸς καὶ φαντασία. διὸ καὶ Ἐπίκτητος [man. 1,5] ἐκέλευσεν
ἡμᾶς ἐπιλέγειν ἑαυτοῖς 'φαντασία, φαντασία εἶ καὶ οὐ πάντως τὸ φαινόμενον'.

καὶ σχῆμα, καὶ οὐκ ἐᾷ ἡμᾶς ἀσωμάτως καὶ ἀσχηματίστως περὶ τοῦ θεοῦ ἐννοεῖν. Steph.,
an. 542.10–12 καὶ ὅτε γὰρ περὶ τὰ θεῖα ἐνεργεῖ, παρειστρέχει ἡ φαντασία, τύπον ἐντιθεῖσα
τοῖς ἀτυπώτοις, καὶ διὰ τοῦτο ὁ Πλάτων ἔσχατον αὐτὴν λέγει κακόν. Correspondences
in the wording between Ol. and Philop. suggest the influence of Amm., though not
necessarily of his commentary on the Ph., since this is clearly a commonplace.

6–10. On allegorical interpretations of the Odyssey see Norvin 1915, 80–81;
Pépin 107; 110–111; 200. Circe is usually pleasure; in Ps.-Plut., vit. Hom. 126,
she is ἡ τοῦ παντὸς ἐγκύκλιος φορά, Stob. I 49,60 she stands for τὴν ἐν κύκλῳ περίοδον
καὶ περιφορὰν παλιγγενεσίας. Calypso too is generally explained as pleasure; as the body
by Eustath., Od. 1.51; as φαντασία Pr. Eucl. 55.18-23. The epistemological approach
is probably Porphyry's, cf. sent. 40 (p. 48.6–7) ἑαυτὸν δὲ ἀπέστρεψας κάλυμμα λαβὼν
τὴν ὑποδραμοῦσαν τῆς ὑπονοίας φαντασίαν, where we find the two metaphors, the veil
and the cloud, combined as in Ol. Cf. Beutler, RE art. Porphyrios (21) 308.19–67.

6. The moly is out of place; Ol.'s source must have mentioned Hermes' visit
to Ogygia (Od. 5.43–148).

8. Φαντασίη τανύπεπλε : the quotation (modeled on Λαμπετίη τανύπεπλος, Od.
12.375) may be from Crates, who has some very similar personifications (Εὐτελίη
frg. 2.2 Diehl, ἀθάνατον βασίλειαν Ἐλευθερίαν frg. 7.4); we would then have to assume
that the early Cynics had already developed a notion of φαντασία resembling the
later Stoic one; the evidence for this depends on the origin of Diog. Laert. 6,70;
see D. R. Dudley, A History of Cynicism, London 1937, 216–220. – Another
possibility is Timon of Phlius.

10–11. Cf. Ol., Alc. 8.11–14 κατὰ γὰρ τὸ ἐν ἡμῖν θεῖον ἐνθουσιῶμεν, ἁπλοῦν ὂν
ὥσπερ καὶ τὸ θεῖον αὐτό. διὰ τοῦτο γὰρ καὶ οἱ παῖδες μᾶλλον καὶ οἱ ἐν ἀγροῖς διατρίβοντες,
ὡς ἀφελεῖς καὶ ἁπλοῖ, ἐνθουσιῶσιν· ἀφαντασίαστος γὰρ ὁ ἐνθουσιασμός, διὸ καὶ φαντασίᾳ
λύεται ὡς ἐναντίᾳ οὔσῃ. Infra § 12.3–4.

who, as the daughter of the Sun, stands for sense-perception. Imagination, then, gets in the way of our thinking. For the same reason an ecstatic condition is interrupted, if during it we form a mental picture, for ecstasy and imagination are contraries. Because of all this Epictetus [*Enchir.* 1, 5] tells us to repeat to ourselves continually: 'Fancy, you are only a fancy, and not necessarily what you appear to be'. This, the influence of imagination upon their thought, also caused the Stoic community to think of God as corporeal, for it is imagination that clothes incorporeal realities in bodies. What does Plato mean then? Is there no thought unaccompanied by imagination? Yes, there is; when the soul apprehends universals, imagination has no part in its activity.

3. But let us consider this question by itself, whether it is possible, while in the body, to lead an uninterrupted life of purification or of contemplation. The ancients do not grant this, and Plato too seems to deny it, since he says that it will never be possible, as long as we are in the body, to know the truth. Our own professor, however, maintains that it is possible: if one can share in the life of a community when outside the body, why should a life of purification and contemplation be impossible, while still in the body? Another point: in the *Phaedrus* [248d2–e3], where he mentions various ways of life, Plato does not speak of a lifetime of continuous ecstasy, but he does refer to the contemplative life, because it is not possible to spend one's whole life in ecstasy, but there is nothing to prevent us from spending it in purification and contemplation. For though we partake of food, we do so in a spirit of purification, that the soul should not be impeded in its activities by the body. Therefore the man who has dedicated himself to purification or contemplation pays attention to the body as to a talkative neighbor, so as not to be disturbed in his thoughts; this is what Plato says about the perfect philosopher, that he does not know where in the world he is, and is unaware that he does not know [*Theaet.* 173c6–174a2]. Here we find a double ignorance that is superior to knowledge. Thus far the survey.

14–15. *SVF* II frgs. 1028–1048. Similar comments on the crudity of Stoic materialism: El., *isag.* 47.29–48.8; Dav. 111.3–18; Ps.-El. 29,18–22.

14. Cf. Galen, *nat. fac.* I 3, 8.6 K. ὁ ἀπὸ τῆς Στοᾶς χορός.

15–17. Cf. Dam. I §§ 112–113. Ar., *an.* III 7, 431a16–17 διὸ οὐδέποτε νοεῖ ἄνευ φαντάσματος ἡ ψυχή. Porph., *sent.* 16 αἱ νοήσεις οὐκ ἄνευ φαντασίας. Simpl., *an.* 268.8–25 rejects the 'Peripatetic' interpretation of Ar., which relates his statement to θεωρητικὴ γνῶσις and to νοῦς.

§ 3. Dam. I § 115. Pr. denies the possibility of an entire life spent in contemplation: *Rep.* II 276.18–25 μὴ γὰρ οὐδὲ δυνατὸν ἢ βίον ἕνα πάσης ἀρετῆς ἄμοιρον γενέσθαι καὶ τοὐναντίον πάσης ἀρετῆς μέτοχον· ἀλλ' ὃ μέν τις μᾶλλον ὃ δὲ ἧττον ἀρετῆς μέτοχός ἐστιν, ἥκιστα δὲ ἢ μάλιστα ἀδύνατον (follows a reference to *Ph.* 66b3–d7); *prov.* 49.14–18 διὸ καὶ ὁ φιλόσοφος χορὸς ὁ τῶν Στωϊκῶν διὰ τὸ κατὰ φαντασίαν ἐνεργεῖν σῶμα τὸν θεὸν ὑπέλαβον· αὕτη γὰρ τοῖς ἀσωμάτοις σώματα περιτίθησιν. τί 15 οὖν φησιν; οὐκ ἔστι νόησις ἀφαντασίαστος; ἢ ἡνίκα τὰ καθόλου γινώσκει ἡ ψυχή, τότε ἄνευ φαντασίας ἐνεργεῖ.

Φέρε δὲ τὸ πρόβλημα αὐτὸ ἐξετάσωμεν καθ᾿ αὐτό, ἆρά ἐστιν ἐν τῷ σώματι 3 ὄντα διόλου καθαρτικῶς ἢ θεωρητικῶς ζῆν. οἱ μὲν οὖν παλαιοὶ οὐ βούλονται τοῦτο, φαίνεται δὲ καὶ ὁ Πλάτων μὴ βουλόμενος, εἴ γέ φησιν ὅτι οὐ μή ποτε δυνατὸν ἐν τῷ σώματι ὄντας γνῶναι τὸ ἀληθές. ὁ δὲ φιλόσοφος ὁ καθ᾿ ἡμᾶς φησιν ὅτι δυνατόν· εἰ γάρ ἐστιν ἔξω τοῦ σώματος ὄντα πολιτικῶς ἐνεργῆσαι, 5 διὰ τί μὴ καὶ ἐν τῷ σώματι καθαρτικῶς ἢ θεωρητικῶς; καὶ εἰ ἐν τῷ Φαίδρῳ [248d2–e3] μεμνημένος βίων ἐνθουσιαστικὸν οὐ λέγει παρ᾿ ὅλον τὸν χρόνον βίον εἶναι, θεωρητικοῦ δὲ μέμνηται βίου, διότι παρ᾿ ὅλον μὲν τὸν βίον ἐνθουσιαστικῶς οὐκ ἔστιν ἐνεργῆσαι, καθαρτικῶς δὲ καὶ θεωρητικῶς τί κωλύει; εἰ γὰρ καὶ τρεφόμεθα, ἀλλ᾿ ὡς καθαρτικοί, ἵνα γὰρ μὴ παραποδίζηται ἡ ψυχὴ 10 ἐν ταῖς ἐνεργείαις τοῦ σώματος ἐμποδίζοντος. οἷον οὖν φλύαρον γείτονα τὸ σῶμα θεραπεύει ὁ καθαρτικὸς καὶ θεωρητικός, ἵνα ἐν ταῖς νοήσεσιν ἀκώλυτος ᾖ· ὥσπερ φησὶν περὶ τοῦ κορυφαίου φιλοσόφου ὅτι ἀγνοεῖ ὅποι γῆς ἐστιν, καὶ ἀγνοεῖ ὅτι ἀγνοεῖ [Theaet. 173c6–174a2]. καὶ εὗρεν ὁ λόγος διπλῆν ἀμαθίαν ἐπιστήμης κρείττονα. ταῦτα ἔχει ἡ θεωρία. 15

Μυρίας μὲν γὰρ ἀσχολίας παρέχει τὸ σῶμα [66b7–8]: εἰκότως 4 ᾿μυρίας᾿, διότι, ὡς εἴρηται [§ 1], καὶ κατὰ φύσιν ἔχον καὶ | παρὰ φύσιν ἐμποδὼν (36) γίνεται· καὶ οὐ μόνον τὸ σῶμα, ἀλλὰ καὶ ἡ ἀλογία, καὶ αὕτη πολλαχῶς.

---

§ 3. 7 βίων Wk: βίον M | ἐνθουσιαστικὸν] -κὸν in ras. Mᶜ — 13 περὶ] in ras. Mᶜ
§ 4. 1 post γὰρ] ἡμῖν ins. Mᶜ (Pl.) — 2 ὡς] ᾿ex ⸗, seq. ÷ ÷ in ras. Mᶜ (ὥσπερ M¹?) —
3 αὕτη M¹: αὐτὴ Mᶜ

'speculativum autem rursum fieri perfecte impossibile est propter causas quas ipse in Fedone docet...' According to Dam. l.c. this includes the impossibility of a life devoted entirely to purification; Dam. himself believes that both can be realized in this world, though in a lesser degree than in the hereafter.

2–3. οἱ ... παλαιοί : as far as the contemplative life is concerned, this includes Porphyry; cf. sent. 32 (p. 31.9–10) ἐπιμελητέον οὖν μάλιστα τῶν καθαρτικῶν ἡμῖν σκεψαμένοις ὅτι τούτων μὲν ἡ τεῦξις ἐν τῷ βίῳ τούτῳ. The term 'the ancients' is applied to the school of Plot. by Pr., theol. I 10, 42.4.

4. ὁ φιλόσοφος ὁ καθ᾿ ἡμᾶς : presumably Ol. himself, though Amm. cannot be excluded entirely.

8–9. Infra § 12.3–4.

11. φλύαρον γείτονα : above 4 § 3.14–16.

4. **For the body is the cause of countless distractions [66b7–8]:** 'Countless' indeed, because, as we said already [§ 1], it is a hindrance both in its normal and in an abnormal condition; and not only the body, but the irrational functions of the soul as well, and this in many different ways.

5. **With loves and desires [66c2]:** The plural is aptly used to express removal from the One. 'Love' is a strong desire.

6. **And fears and phantasms of all sorts [66c2–3]:** Fear manifests itself in the three parts of the soul: desire fears loss of property, spirit disgrace, reason error, which may be caused either by a false argument or by ignorance. 'Phantasms' he calls the pleasures of this world as compared to divine leisure; how indeed can pleasure here below be pleasure, mingled as it is with the discomfort that is its counterpart? For if it were not linked with the extreme discomfort caused by thirst, the extreme pleasure caused by drinking would not follow.

7. **It overwhelms us with absurdities [66c3–4]:** Plato applies the word 'absurdities' to everything that is superfluous, not only in words, but also in actions; here he uses it of the body and the things of the body, i.e. irrational activities.

8. **For all wars are fought for the sake of riches [66c7–8]:** How can he say that the object of all wars is to acquire riches? Are not wars also fought for the sake of beauty, as the Trojan war was because of Helen? Some explain that without money no war is fought: 'We must have money, and without it no necessary action can be taken' [Demosth. 1, 20]. This, however, is not what the text says: it says that the object of wars is to acquire riches. Others say that Plato uses the word 'riches' of all property; all wars take place for the sake of some kind of property, and a woman is property too. We object that war can be waged also to escape slavery. The answer must be, therefore, that we should not divide man, as it is currently done, into soul and body and external things (or myself, what is mine, and that which belongs to what is mine), but into soul and external things, the body also being external in its relation to the soul; the division to be adopted, then, is into 'myself' and 'that which belongs to what is mine', and since riches are admittedly external things, Socrates really says that all wars are because of external

---

§ 5. 2–3. Pr., *Alc.* 328.15 ἔστι γὰρ ὁ ἔρως ἔφεσίς τινος ἐρρωμένη καὶ σύντονος, cf. 329.19–21; 336.23. Dam., *Phil.* § 16.5–6 ἡ σύντονος ὄρεξις ἔρως. Cf. Pl., *Laws* V 734a4 συντόνους δὲ καὶ οἰστρώδεις ἐπιθυμίας τε καὶ ἔρωτας.

§ 6. 4. τὴν θείαν ῥᾳστώνην : Pl., *Laws* X 903e3 ἧπερ ἂν ἔχοι ῥᾳστώνης ἐπιμελείας θεοῖς τῶν πάντων. Occurrences listed Dam., *Phil.* § 154.9 note and index s.v. ῥᾳστώνη ; add: Pr., *Tim.* III 280.11–13; Ol., *Alc.* 7.7–8; schol. Pl. 468.5–9.

5–7. Pl., *Ph.* 60b3–c7; *Rep.* IX 583c3–584a11; *Phil.* 46b5–50d6.

5. τῇ οἰκείᾳ λύπῃ : either a copyist's mistake, or more probably a condensed

Ἐρώτων δὲ καὶ ἐπιθυμιῶν [66c2]: εἰκότως πληθυντικῶς ταῦτα προ- 5
ήγαγεν ἐνδεικνύμενος τὴν ἀπόστασιν τὴν ἀπὸ τοῦ ἑνός. ἔρως δέ ἐστι σύντονος
ἐπιθυμία.

Καὶ φόβων καὶ εἰδώλων παντοδαπῶν [66c2–3]: ὁ φόβος ἐν τῇ 6
τριμερείᾳ τῆς ψυχῆς θεωρεῖται. φοβεῖται γὰρ ἡ μὲν ἐπιθυμία ἀφαίρεσιν χρημάτων,
ὁ δὲ θυμὸς ἀτιμίαν, ὁ δὲ λόγος ἀπάτην· ἀπατᾶται δὲ ἢ ὑπὸ ψευδοῦς λόγου ἢ
διὰ ἄγνοιαν. 'εἴδωλα' δὲ καλεῖ τὰς τῇδε ἡδονὰς ὡς πρὸς τὴν θείαν ῥαστώνην
παραβάλλων αὐτάς· πῶς γὰρ ἡδονὴ ἡ τῇδε, ἢ συμμιγής ἐστι τῇ οἰκείᾳ λύπῃ; 5
εἰ μὴ γὰρ τῇ μεγίστῃ λύπῃ συνῆν τῇ ἀπὸ τοῦ διψῆν, οὐδὲ ἐπηκολούθει ἡ ἀπὸ
τοῦ πίνειν μεγίστη ἡδονή.

Καὶ φλυαρίας ἐμπίπλησιν ἡμᾶς [66c3–4]: φλυαρίαν καλεῖ ὁ Πλάτων 7
πᾶν τὸ περιττόν, οὐ μόνον τὸ ἐν λόγοις, ἀλλὰ καὶ τὸ ἐν ἔργοις· ὥσπερ νῦν τὸ
σῶμα καὶ τὰ περὶ τὸ σῶμα, τουτέστι τὰς ἐνεργείας τὰς ἀλόγους, φλυαρίας
ἐκάλεσεν.

Διὰ γὰρ τὴν τῶν χρημάτων κτῆσιν πάντες οἱ πόλεμοι γίνονται 8
[66c7–8]: τί φής; διὰ τὴν τῶν χρημάτων κτῆσιν πάντες οἱ πόλεμοι γίνονται;
οὐ γίνονται οὖν πόλεμοι καὶ διὰ κάλλος, ὡς ὁ Τρωϊκὸς διὰ τὴν Ἑλένην; τινές
φασιν ὅτι ἄνευ χρημάτων πόλεμος οὐ γίνεται· 'δεῖ δὲ χρημάτων, καὶ ἄνευ
τούτων οὐδέν ἐστι γενέσθαι τῶν δεόντων' [Demosth. 1,20]. ἀλλ' οὐ τοῦτό 5
φησιν ἡ λέξις, | ἀλλ' ὅτι διὰ τὰ χρήματα οἱ πόλεμοι γίνονται. ἄλλοι φασὶν ὅτι (37)
χρήματα καλεῖ ὁ Πλάτων πάντα τὰ κτήματα· πάντες οὖν οἱ πόλεμοι διά τι
τῶν κτημάτων γίνονται, κτῆμα δὲ καὶ ἡ γυνή. πρὸς οὓς φαμεν ὅτι 'ἀλλὰ γίνεται
πόλεμος καὶ διὰ τὸ μὴ δουλεῦσαι'. ῥητέον οὖν ὅτι οὐ διαιρετέον, ὡς οἱ πολλοί,
τὸν ἄνθρωπον εἰς ψυχὴν καὶ τὸ σῶμα καὶ τὰ ἐκτός, οἷον ἐγὼ καὶ τὸ ἐμὸν καὶ 10
τὰ τοῦ ἐμοῦ, ἀλλ' εἰς ψυχὴν καὶ τὰ ἐκτός, καὶ τὸ σῶμα γὰρ τῶν ἐκτὸς ὡς πρὸς
τὴν ψυχήν· διαιρετέον οὖν εἰς τὸ ἐγὼ καὶ τὰ τοῦ ἐμοῦ, καὶ ἐπειδὴ τὰ χρήματα
ὁμολογουμένως ἐκτός ἐστιν, διὰ τοῦτό φησιν πάντας τοὺς πολέμους διὰ τὰ ἐκτὸς
γίνεσθαι. ἄλλοι φασὶν ὅτι πάντες οἱ πόλεμοι διὰ χρήματα γίνονται, τουτέστι
διὰ λάφυρα· ἀλλὰ γίνονται πόλεμοι καὶ διὰ φιλοτιμίαν, εἰ μὴ ἄρα τις καὶ ταύτην 15
ἐθέλει λέγειν λάφυρον.

---

§ 5. 1 δὲ] τε Pl. TY
§ 6. 5 λύπῃ] fort. στερήσει vel στερήσει τῇ λύπῃ — 6 διψῆν: -εῖν M | οὐδὲ Fh: οὐδὲν M
§ 8. 1 post πόλεμοι] ἡμῖν Pl. W (ante οἱ Pl. B²) | γίγνονται Mᶜ — 8 ὅτι Mᶜ: om.
M¹ — 13 ἐκτὸς²] immo χρήματα

---

expression, for τῇ ⟨οἰκείᾳ στερήσει τῇ⟩ λύπῃ. Cf. Dam., Phil. § 33.2–3.
§ 7. Ol., Gorg. 105.16–20.
§ 8. Dam. I § 110.1–5.
3–5. τινές : the 'Attic commentators' of Dam.
6–8. Longinus (Dam., lines 4–5).
9–11. Ol., Alc. 3.11–12; 197.13–16; 200.5–10; 228.17–18. Cf. Pl., Alc. I 130d8–131c10.
13. διὰ τὰ ἐκτός : read διὰ τὰ χρήματα.
14–15. Harpocratio (Dam., line 4).

things. Others, again, take the view that all wars are fought for the sake of glory; unless one wants to call this, too, a kind of booty.

9. **We must free ourselves from it [66e1]**: Not that we should take our own life; the meaning is that we must seek to detach ourselves.

10. **Either knowledge is not to be attained at all, or after death [66e6]**: Socrates proposes the following dilemma: 'Either it is impossible for the philosopher while imprisoned in the body to possess knowledge of intelligible things, or it is possible; it cannot be impossible, since philosophers aspire to such knowledge, and Nature would not have created in them a vain longing for the unattainable, while on the other hand any longing that is not abnormal <must be due to Nature>; it remains that it is possible to know intelligible things while still imprisoned in the body'.

11. **We shall come closest to knowledge [67a3]**: 'Closest' because of contemplative knowledge, which is the final goal.

12. **If, as far as feasible, we avoid all contact with the body [67a3–4]**: That is, affective contact, for it is possible, even while in the body, to devote one's entire life to purification. The state of ecstasy cannot continue throughout life, because it is interrupted by imagination, which is contrary to the ecstatic condition. Sneezing, too, is an action incompatible with imagination; if a mental picture is formed, the sneeze is suppressed; hence the saying 'May you live', implying that our animal part needs imaginative activity and that its existence is in danger.

13. **Until God himself releases us [67a6]**: The God to whom he is referring here is Dionysus, who is in charge both of life and of death, of life because of the Titans, of death because of the gift of prophecy that we receive when death draws near. For he is the patron of all Bacchic rapture; therefore he is the guardian not only of comic poets, whose object is pleasure, but also of tragic poets, whose concern is with sorrow and death.

---

§ 9. *Supra* 5 § 11.

§ 10. Dam. I § 118; cf. § 179; Ol. 12 § 1.23–25. The original form of the argument is found in Dam.: either the truth cannot be attained at all (which is unthinkable), or it can be known in this life (which is not true), or it can be known after death (so this must be the case). In this form, it is based on Pr.'s view, criticized in § 3, that a contemplative life in the body is impossible; Ol. adapts it to his own position.

4–5. Ar., *cael.* I 4, 271a33 ὁ δὲ θεὸς καὶ ἡ φύσις οὐδὲν μάτην ποιοῦσιν (II 11, 291b13–14 of Nature only); cf. *infra* 12 § 1.23–25; Dam. I § 179.

§ 11. Cf. Dam. I § 116.2–3.

§ 12. 1–2. *Supra* § 3.

5–7. The observation on sneezing makes little sense as it stands: in the first place the forming of a mental picture evidently does not help to suppress a sneeze, secondly the explanation of the apotropaic ζῆθι implies that the sneeze interrupts the imaginative process, not conversely, and this view is much more understandable.

'Απαλλακτέον αὐτοῦ [66e1]: οὐχ ὅτι δεῖ ἐξάγειν ἑαυτούς, ἀλλὰ τουτέστι   9
χωρισμὸν ζητητέον.

Ἢ οὐδαμοῦ ἐστι κτήσασθαι τὸ εἰδέναι ἢ τελευτήσασιν [66e6]:   10
διλήμματον πλέκει τοιοῦτον ἐνταῦθα ὁ Σωκράτης. 'ἢ ἀδύνατον τὸν φιλόσοφον
ἐν τῷ σώματι κατεχόμενον εἰδέναι τὰ νοητὰ ἢ ἐνδέχεται· ἀλλὰ μὴν οὐκ ἀδύνατον,
διότι ἐφίενται οἱ φιλόσοφοι τῆς τοιαύτης γνώσεως, οὐκ ἂν δὲ τοὺς φιλοσόφους
ὀρεκτικοὺς μάτην ἐποίησεν ἡ φύσις τῶν ἀδυνάτων ὀρεγομένους, καίτοι ἐφ'   5
ὧν οὐκ εἰσὶν ἀλλόκοτοι αἱ ὀρέξεις **· ἐνδέχεται ἄρα εἰδέναι τὰ νοητὰ ἐν τῷ
σώματι κατεχόμενον'.

'Εγγυτάτω ἐσόμεθα τοῦ εἰδέναι [67a3]: 'ἐγγυτάτω' διὰ τὴν θεωρη-   11(38)
τικὴν γνῶσιν· αὕτη γὰρ τέλος.

'Εὰν ὅτι μάλιστα μηδὲ ὁμιλῶμεν τῷ σώματι [67a3–4]: κατὰ   12
σχέσιν, ἐπεί ἐστι καὶ ἐν τούτῳ ὄντας καθαρτικῶς παρ' ὅλον τὸν βίον ζῆν.
ἐνθουσιαστικῶς μὲν γὰρ ἐν ὅλῳ τῷ βίῳ οὐκ ἔστι ζῆσαι, διότι διακόπτεται
ὑπὸ τῆς φαντασίας· ἐναντίως γὰρ ἔχει αὕτη πρὸς ἐνθουσιαστικὴν ἐνέργειαν.
οὕτω καὶ ἐν τῷ πτάρνυσθαι ἀφαντασιάστως ἐνεργοῦμεν· εἰ γὰρ φαντασθῶμεν,   5
διακόπτεται καὶ ὁ πταρμός· διὸ καὶ 'ζῆθι' φαμέν, ὡς τοῦ ζῴου δεομένου κατὰ
φαντασίαν ἐνεργεῖν καὶ κινδυνεύοντος μὴ εἶναι.

Ἕως ἂν ὁ θεὸς αὐτὸς ἀπολύσῃ [67a6]: θεὸν ἐνταῦθα καλεῖ τὸν Διό-   13
νυσον, διότι οὗτος ἔφορος καὶ ζωῆς καὶ θανάτου, ζωῆς μὲν διὰ τοὺς Τιτᾶνας,
θανάτου δὲ διὰ τὴν μαντείαν τὴν περὶ τὸν θάνατον. ἔφορος γὰρ πάσης βακχείας·
διὸ οὐ μόνον κωμικῶν ἔφορός ἐστιν ὡς περὶ ἡδονὰς καταγινομένων, ἀλλὰ καὶ
τραγικῶν περὶ λύπας καὶ θανάτους καταγινομένων.   5

Ὡς τὸ εἰκός [67a7–8]: οὐκ ἐνδοιάζον τὸ 'εἰκός', ἀλλὰ τουτέστι τὸ ἐοικός.   14
ἐπάγει δὲ τὸ 'ἴσως τὸ ἀληθὲς γνωσόμεθα' δι' εὐλάβειαν· ἐπεὶ αὐτός ἐστιν ὁ

---

§ 10.   6 lac. stat. Wk
§ 12.   1 μηδὲ] μηδὲν Pl.
§ 13.   1 αὐτός] om. Pl. B¹
§ 14.   2 τό¹ M¹: τῶι Mᶜ

The meaning intended would then be εἰ γὰρ πτάρωμεν, διακόπτεται καὶ ἡ φαντασία.
It is true that on this assumption the connection between the two observations
becomes a purely associative one: ecstasy cannot coexist with imagination (because
imagination disturbs it); nor, for that matter, can sneezing (because imagination
is disturbed by it). Also, the text as we have it is supported by the καί before
ὁ πταρμός (the sneeze is interrupted by φαντασία, *as is the ecstatic condition*), so
that it seems to go back at least as far as the reportator, possibly to Ol.
   6.   ζῆθι: only found here; other formulas in A. S. Pease, *The Omen of Sneezing*,
Class. Journ. 6, 1911, 429–433 (Ζεῦ σῶσον *Anthol. Pal.* 11,268.3; 'salve' in Latin).
§ 13.   Cf. *supra* 1 § 6.1–5; *infra* 7 § 10.14–15.
§ 14.   On εἰκός and ἴσως cf. note at 2 § 6. – The same quotation from Pl. in
the same modified form and in the same context: *infra* 8 § 17; El., *cat.* 110.18–20;
cf. Ol., *Gorg.* 239.26–27. Pl., *Rep.* X 618e4–619a1 uses the adverb: ἀδαμαντίνως δὴ
δεῖ ταύτην τὴν δόξαν ἔχοντα εἰς Ἅιδου ἰέναι.

14. We may expect [67a7–8]: 'May expect' does not express a doubt but it is equivalent to 'we have a right to expect'. The following words 'perhaps we shall know the truth' are prompted by discretion; for Socrates himself has said [*Rep.* X 618e4–619a1] that we must 'take this with us down to Hades as an iron-bound conviction'.

7

Lecture **

1. 'Well then', said Socrates, 'if that is true, my friend' [67b7–68c4].
After concluding in general that the philosopher will be ready to die, Socrates now draws the same conclusion [67b7–c4], without adding anything to it, and yet without repeating himself; for above he made the point in general terms, here he applies it to an example and makes it more particular by referring to himself: 'Therefore Socrates will be ready to die with good hope of gaining what he has desired so long; consequently Euenus too, if a philosopher, will be ready to follow Socrates in his willingness to die'.

By 'hope' we must here [67b8] understand, not the hope that Herodotus calls 'a dream of the waking', which has its origin in sensible things, but divine hope, which derives from intelligence and is certain, the hope of which the Oracle [frg. 47] says:
              'Let fire-borne hope sustain thee',
'fire-borne' standing for divine, because the ancients compared the divine to fire.

2. 'It is suitable, when setting out for that other world, to occupy oneself with these things'. Socrates calls his departure to the other world a 'setting out' (*apodêmia*) because it is a taking leave of the crowd (*dêmos*); the crowd is the whole world of sense-perception with its instability and its fluctuations, and therefore the journey thither is a taking leave of

---

Lect. 7. **Socrates' conclusion as to his own fate.** After a very short summary of the pericope (§ 1.1–8), Ol. discusses two isolated words, 'hope' 67b8 and ἀποδημία 67c1 (§ 1.9–§ 2.6). He then returns to the more general point, in what respect the second definition of death differs from the first (§ 2.7–§ 3.7). There follows another separate note on the word 'ridiculous' at 67d12 (§ 3.8–15). Socrates' remark on those who die to join their loved ones leads to a disquisition on the state of souls in the hereafter (§ 4.1–12); then there is a paragraph on the inconvertibility of the proposition 'The philosopher does not fear death' (§ 4.13–17) and one on the omission of the 'pleasure-seeker' at 68b7–c3 (§ 5).

§ 1. 9–13. **Dam.** I § 125. Cf. Dam. I § 48; *Phil.* § 178; Ol., *infra* § 6.1–10; *Alc.* 27.23–28.1. – The aphorism 'Hope is a day-dream' is attributed to Anacreon (*Gnomol. Vat.* 375), Pindar (Stob. IV 47,12), Plato (Aelian., *var. hist.* 13,29), Aristotle (Diog. Laert. 5,18), Herodotus (Ol., *Alc.*). – The new content of the word in the

λέγων ὅτι ʻἀδαμαντίνοις δεσμοῖς δεῖ ταῦτα ἔχοντα κατιέναι εἰς ʺΑιδουʼ [Rep. X 618e4–619a1].

7

Πρᾶξις σὺν θεῷ (39)

Οὐκοῦν, ἔφη ὁ Σωκράτης, εἰ ταῦτα ἀληθῆ, ὦ ἑταῖρε [67b7–68c4]. 1
Συναγαγὼν ὁ Σωκράτης διὰ τοῦ καθόλου λόγου ὅτι ὁ φιλόσοφος ἐθελήσει
ἀποθνῄσκειν, τὸ αὐτὸ νῦν συνάγει [67b7–c4]· καὶ οὐδὲν πλέον προστίθησιν καὶ
οὐ ταυτολογεῖ· ἀνωτέρω μὲν γὰρ ἐπὶ τοῦ καθόλου τὸν λόγον προήγαγεν,
νῦν δὲ ὡς ἐπὶ παραδείγματος αὐτὸν προάγει καὶ μερικώτερον τὸν λόγον ποιεῖ 5
ἐφʼ ἑαυτοῦ λέγων· ʻΣωκράτης ἄρα ἐθελήσει ἀποθνῄσκειν μετὰ ἀγαθῆς ἐλπίδος
τεύξεσθαι οὗ πάλαι ἐπεθύμει· οὐκοῦν καὶ Εὔηνος, εἰ φιλόσοφος, ἐθελήσει
κατακολουθῆσαι Σωκράτει ἀποθνῄσκειν ἐθέλοντιʼ.
ʺΕλπίδαʼ δὲ ἀκουστέον ἐνταῦθα [67b8] οὐ τὴν παρὰ ʻΗροδότῳ, τὴν ʻἐγρηγο-
ρότων ἐνύπνιονʼ, τὴν ἀπὸ αἰσθητῶν γινομένην, ἀλλὰ τὴν θείαν καὶ ἀπὸ νοῦ 10
κατιοῦσαν καὶ βεβαίαν, περὶ ἧς τὸ λόγιον ἔφη [frg. 47]
ʻἐλπὶς δὲ τρεφέτω σε πυρίοχοςʼ·
πυρίοχον γὰρ καλεῖ τὴν θείαν, ἐπειδὴ οἱ παλαιοὶ πυρὶ ἀπείκαζον τὸ θεῖον.
ʻΠρέπει δὲ ἐκεῖσε ἀποδημοῦντα τὰ τοιαῦτα πραγματεύεσθαι.ʼ ʻἀποδημίανʼ 2
δὲ ἐκάλεσε τὴν ἐκεῖσε πορείαν ὡς ἀπὸ τοῦ δήμου οὖσαν· δῆμος γὰρ πᾶν τὸ
αἰσθητὸν διὰ τὸ ἀστάθμητον αὐτοῦ καὶ ῥευστόν· ἀποδημία οὖν ἡ ἐκεῖσε ⟨πορεία⟩·
ʻπατὴρ γὰρ ἡμῶν καὶ πατρὶς ⟨ἐκεῖ⟩ʼ [Plot. I 6,8.21]. τί δὲ δηλοῖ ἄρα τὸ ʻπραγμα-
τεύεσθαιʼ; ἢ οὐ δεῖ λόγῳ μόνῳ ἄνω καὶ κάτω θρυλεῖν τὰς καθαρτικὰς 5
ἀρετάς, ἀλλὰ καὶ ἔργῳ αὐτὰς δεικνύναι.

---

3 κατιέναι] -τ- in ras. Mᶜ (καὶ ἰέναι M¹)
§ 1. 12; 13 πυρήοχος scr. Kroll (item 7 § 6.2)
§ 2. 3 πορεία Wk: om. M — 4 ἐκεῖ Wk (cf. 1 § 13.9; 16.4): om. M — 5 θρυλλεῖν M¹

Chaldean Oracles is discussed by Lewy 147, nn. 296–297 (Iambl., myst. 83.2–5;
Pr., Tim. I 212.22–24).
12. Kroll (followed by Lewy and Des Places) writes πυρήοχος metri causa, on
the analogy of πυρητόκος. The MSS., however, have -ι- also in Pr., Tim. II 107.10.
Not in LSJ.
13. οἱ παλαιοὶ πυρὶ ἀπείκαζον τὸ θεῖον: not the Oracles themselves, which are
never quoted as οἱ παλαιοί, but in the first place Heraclitus (A 8, B 64, B 67),
further Empedocles (A 31, cf. B 6) and Hippasus (A 8).
§ 2. 1–4. Cf. supra 1 § 16. – Quoting from memory, Ol. substitutes 61e1–2 for
67b7–c2; the discussion of πραγματεύεσθαι (lines 4–6) refers to πραγματεία 67b10.
2–3. Demosth., or. 19,136 ὡς ὁ μὲν δῆμός ἐστιν ἀσταθμητότατον πρᾶγμα τῶν πάντων
καὶ ἀσυνθετώτατον ὥσπερ ἐν θαλάττῃ πνεῦμα ἀκατάστατον, ὡς ἂν τύχῃ, κινούμενος
(Norvin).
4. Supra 1 § 13.10.

the crowd, for 'our Father and our fatherland are yonder' [Plot. I 6, 8.21]. And what is expressed by 'occupying oneself?' That one should not just talk at length about purificatory virtues, but practice them.

Next Socrates defines death as purification of the soul from the body [67c5–d6]. But why, having defined death before [64c4–8], does he do so again now? This is another instance of passing from the more general to the more particular: above he defined death as a separation of the soul from the body and of the body from the soul (and we observed [3 § 4] that he had a good reason for mentioning both); here, however, he defines death as only a purification of the soul from the body; now death is more general than purification, because one who is purified necessarily dies also, whereas one who dies is not necessarily purified, witness those body-loving souls that hover about their graves even after death. Thus we have acquitted Socrates of the charge of repeating himself.

3. He then gives another proof that the philosopher will be ready to die [67d7–68a3], as follows: 'The philosopher shuns the sensible and pursues the intelligible; one who does this detaches himself from the body; one who detaches himself is willing to die; and the conclusion is obvious'. Though he has mentioned this before [64a4–66a10], yet there is no pointless repetition: above the major was simple, 'the philosopher shuns the sensible', here it is composite, 'the philosopher shuns the sensible and pursues the intelligible'.

He adds that it is 'ridiculous' to be willing to die all one's life, and then to be afraid when death does come [67d12]. Since he uses the word both above and here, let us ask ourselves what the ridiculous is according to Plato. Ridiculous is the ugly when it is powerless; therefore Thersites was ridiculous, 'the ugliest man that had come to Troy' [Il. 2, 216]. Both are properties of matter: ugliness in so far as it is devoid of form and beauty, powerlessness in so far as it is unable to be anything that exists. And when the human soul fears death, the cause is either ignorance, i.e. ugliness, or weakness and cowardice.

4. There follows another argument to show that philosophers are

---

7–§ 3.7. A comparison between 64a4–66a10 and 67c5–68b7. The second passage is not a mere repetition of the first, since (1) it limits the definition of death to voluntary death; (2) it adds love of wisdom to detachment from the body as the philosopher's aim.

9. *Supra* 1 § 12.14–17.

12–15. **Dam.** I §§ 126–127.

14–15. *Ph.* 81c11–d2; *supra* 3 § 4.3–4.

§ 3. 8. The word γελοῖον does not occur, instead Pl. writes ἄτοπον (64a7).

9–12. Cf. Pr., *Rep.* II 319.2–7.

10–11. Pl., *Phil.* 49c4–5 ἡ δ' ἀσθενὴς (scil. ἄγνοια) ἡμῖν τὴν τῶν γελοίων εἴληχε τάξιν τε καὶ φύσιν.

11–12. αἶσχος as ὕλη οὐ κρατηθεῖσα εἴδει Plot. I 8,5.23–24; Pr., *Alc.* 326.10–13;

'Εφ' οἷς ὁρίζεται τὸν θάνατον κάθαρσιν ψυχῆς ἀπὸ σώματος [67c5–d6].
καὶ διὰ τί καὶ πάλαι ὁρισάμενος τὸν θάνατον [64c4–8] καὶ νῦν τοῦτο ποιεῖ;
ἢ πάλιν ἀπὸ τοῦ καθολικωτέρου ἐπὶ τὸ μερικώτερον προῆλθεν· πάλαι μὲν γὰρ
ὡρίζετο τὸν θάνατον χωρισμὸν ψυχῆς ἀπὸ σώματος καὶ σώματος ἀπὸ ψυχῆς   10
(καὶ ἐλέγομεν [3 § 4] ὅτι οὐ μάτην τῶν δύο | ἐμνημόνευσε), νῦν δὲ τὸν θάνατον (40)
ὁρίζεται κάθαρσιν μόνον ψυχῆς ἀπὸ σώματος· καὶ καθολικώτερος ὁ θάνατος
τῆς καθάρσεως, διότι ὁ μὲν καθαιρόμενος πάντως καὶ ἀποθνῄσκει, οὐ μὴν
ὁ ἀποθνῄσκων καὶ καθαίρεται διὰ τὰς φιλοσωμάτους ψυχὰς περὶ τοὺς τάφους
καὶ μετὰ τὸν θάνατον εἰλουμένας. καὶ οὕτως ἠλευθερώσαμεν αὐτὸν ἀδολεσχίας.   15
Εἶτα δείκνυσι πάλιν ὅτι ὁ φιλόσοφος ἐθελήσει ἀποθνῄσκειν, οὕτως· 'ὁ   3
φιλόσοφος φεύγει τὰ αἰσθητὰ καὶ διώκει τὰ νοητά, ὁ τοιοῦτος χωρίζει ἑαυτὸν
τοῦ σώματος, ὁ χωρίζων ἑαυτὸν ἀποθνῄσκειν ἐθέλει, καὶ δῆλον τὸ συμπέρασμα'.
εἰ δὲ καὶ ἀνωτέρω [64a4–66a10] τούτου ἐμνημόνευσεν, ἀλλ' οὐκ ἀδολεσχεῖ·
ἀνωτέρω μὲν γὰρ ἁπλοῦν ἦν τὸ συνημμένον, ἔλεγε γὰρ 'ὁ φιλόσοφος φεύγει   5
τὰ αἰσθητά', ἐνταῦθα δὲ σύνθετόν ἐστιν, ἔφη γὰρ ὅτι 'ὁ φιλόσοφος φεύγει τὰ
αἰσθητὰ καὶ διώκει τὰ νοητά'.
Εἶτά φησιν ὅτι 'γελοῖόν' ἐστι παρ' ὅλον τὸν βίον ἐθέλειν ἀποθνῄσκειν,
ἥκοντος δὲ τοῦ θανάτου δεδιέναι [67d12]. ἀλλ' ἐπειδὴ καὶ ἀνωτέρω καὶ ἐνταῦθα
γελοίου ἐμνημόνευσεν, τί τὸ γελοῖον παρὰ Πλάτωνι; γελοῖον τοίνυν ἐστὶν   10
αἰσχρὸν ἀσθενές· διὸ καὶ ὁ Θερσίτης γελοῖος ἦν, 'αἴσχιστος' γὰρ 'ἀνὴρ ὑπὸ
Ἴλιον ἦλθεν' [B 216]. οἰκεῖον δὲ τῇ ὕλῃ καὶ τὸ αἰσχρὸν ὡς ἀνειδέῳ καὶ ἀκαλλεῖ·
ἀλλὰ μὴν καὶ τὸ ἀδύναμον, διότι ἀδυναμίαν ἔχει πάντων τῶν ὄντων. καὶ ἡ
ἡμετέρα δὲ ψυχὴ δέδιεν τὸν θάνατον ἢ διὰ ἄγνοιαν καὶ αἶσχος ἢ διὰ ἀσθένειαν
καὶ δειλίαν.   15
Εἶτα καὶ ἄλλως κατασκευάζει ὅτι οἱ φιλόσοφοι ἀποθνῄσκειν ἐθέλουσιν   4
[68a3–b4]. εἰ γὰρ οἱ παρ' ἡμῖν ἀνθρωπίσκοι τελευτᾶν βούλονται ἐρῶντές τινων,

---

§ 3. 14 δὲ M^c: om. M¹

(with the example of Thersites) Ol., *Gorg*. 39. 17–21; 75.27–76.1.
§ 4. 1–12. The whole paragraph must come from Pr., who has a very similar
passage relating the lives of individuals to their several ἀγελάρχαι *Crat*. 37.28–38.15.
The word ἀγελάρχης derives ultimately from Pl., *Polit*. 271d6–7 καὶ δὴ καὶ τὰ ζῷα
κατὰ γένη καὶ ἀγέλας οἷον νομῆς θεῖοι διειλήφεσαν δαίμονες, cf. Pr., *Crat*. 38.2 ἀγελάρχαις
καὶ νομεῦσιν. The compound occurs in Philo, *somn*. II 152 (leader of a flock) and
153 (leading principle in the soul); Plut., *Rom*. 6 (leader of a group); Pr., *Parm*.
686.24 (id.). Elsewhere in Pr., it has a terminological sense, in which the *Polit*.
passage is combined with *Tim*. 42d2–e4: the ἀγελάρχαι are in the first place planetary
deities, Pr., *Tim*. III 132.2–4 ἐξ ὧν ἁπάντων δῆλον, ὅπως ἀληθὲς καὶ τῶν πλανωμένων
ἕκαστον ἀγελάρχην εἶναι πολλῶν θεῶν συμπληρούντων αὐτοῦ τὴν ἰδίαν περιφοράν. 265.6–10
the notion is extended to elemental Gods: καὶ γὰρ ἄτοπον, εἰ περὶ μόνα διανενέμηνται
τὰ ἰδίως καλούμενα ἄστρα μερικαὶ ψυχαί, οἱ δὲ ἄλλοι θεοὶ μὴ εἶεν ἀγελάρχαι ψυχῶν,

willing to die [68a3–b4]: worthless people in this world want to die when
they are in love, thinking that in the hereafter they are going to see
their beloved and be with them, though as a matter of fact this will
not necessarily come true, because they may belong to the spheres of
different divine herdsmen – some souls indeed, belong to the Healing
Powers, others to the Moon; for, as Plato says in the *Timaeus* [42d4–5],
the Creator scattered the souls on the Sun and the Moon; and from this
comes failure or success in our enterprises, because our actual condition
is often at variance with our original choice; lives of great men show
great achievements because their condition tallies with their chosen
destination, while failure is the result of the reverse: many a Plato digs
the soil, as somebody has said; – so if this is true, it is even more true
that philosophers are willing to die, as they know for certain that in
the hereafter they will attain the object of their desire.

Socrates says [68b5–c4] that, if a man is a philosopher, he is unafraid
of death, but he does not add that one not afraid of death is also a
philosopher, for many are willing to die out of rashness and recklessness
without being philosophers. If, then, a man is a philosopher, he is also

---

οἱ καθ' ἕκαστον στοιχεῖον ἐκείνοις ἀνὰ λόγον ὄντες, ἀέριοι καὶ ἐνύδριοι καὶ χθόνιοι.
308.24–27 πᾶσαι οὖν τοῦ κόσμου μερίδες ὑπεδέξαντο μερικὰς ψυχὰς ἐσπαρμένας καὶ πᾶς
ἐγκόσμιος θεὸς ἀγελάρχης ἐστὶ ψυχῶν μερικῶν καὶ νεμηθεισῶν καὶ ἐσπαρμένων περὶ
αὐτὸν κατὰ τὸν νοῦν τὸν δημιουργικόν. At *theol.* VI 17, 394.28, Pr. applies the word
to the ἀπόλυτοι θεοί (those ranking immediately above the intramundane Gods),
but they are only οἷον ἀγελάρχαι τινὲς ἐπιβεβηκότες τοῖς πᾶσι καὶ οἷον δαίμονες θεοί.
The same qualification οἷον ἀγελάρχαι τινές applies to demons (who in their turn
are dependent upon their own ἀγελάρχαι, Pr., *Rep.* II 297.24; *Alc.* 70.11–13):
decem dub. 44.30–32 (the common fate of large groups of people who perish or
are saved together) 'aut in eam que secundum substantiam communionem aut
in ydemptitatem utentium ipsis demonum *velut gregis principum quorundam* possibile
reducere.' Though I have not found this special sense before Pr., it is probably
at least as old as Porphyry, since Eusebius already uses it of angels (*demonstr. evang.*
IV 6,9 ὥσπερ τινὰς ἀγελάρχας καὶ ποιμένας θείους ἀγγέλους κατεστήσατο, obviously
referring to the *Polit.* myth). If so, its content appears to have been somewhat
different than in Pr., judging from the divergent accounts that Porph., Iambl.
and Syrianus give of the caste of herdsmen in Egypt (*Tim.* 24a7) as reported by
Pr., *Tim.* I 152.10–155.2. According to Porph., they are analogous τοῖς ἐπὶ ταῖς
τῶν ζῴων ἀγέλαις τεταγμένοις (scil. δαίμοσι), οὓς δι' ἀπορρήτων ψυχὰς εἶναι λέγουσιν
ἀποτυχούσας μὲν τοῦ ἀνθρωπικοῦ νοῦ, πρὸς δὲ τὰ ζῷα ἐχούσας διάθεσιν· ἐπεὶ καὶ ἀνθρώπων
ἀγέλης ἐστι τις κηδεμὼν καὶ μερικοί τινες, οἱ μὲν ἔθνη, οἱ δὲ πόλεις, οἱ δὲ καὶ τοὺς
καθ' ἕκαστον ἐπισκοποῦντες. The scholiast (467.14; possibly Simplicius) paraphrases
ἀγελάρχαι τῶν ζῴων δαίμονες, but he can hardly have had independent authority
for doing so, so that it must remain doubtful if Porphyry actually used the compound
in this context. If he did, it meant to him, in the first place, a class of sublunary
demons in charge of animal life and, by extension, demons (or Gods) watching
over mankind and over specific communities and individuals; at least the one
supreme ἀνθρώπων ἀγέλης κηδεμών must have had the status of a God. The relation

οἰόμενοι ἐκεῖσε ὄψεσθαι τὰ παιδικὰ καὶ συνέσεσθαι τούτοις, καίτοι μὴ πάντως
θεώμενοι διὰ τὸ ὑπὸ διαφόρους ἀγελάρχας τελεῖν· — αἱ | μὲν γὰρ τῶν ψυχῶν (41)
Παιώνιοι, αἱ δὲ Σεληναῖαι· ὡς γάρ φησιν ἐν Τιμαίῳ [42d4–5], ἐγκατέσπειρεν ὁ   5
δημιουργὸς Ἡλίῳ καὶ Σελήνῃ τὰς ψυχάς· διὸ καὶ ἀποτυχίαι ἢ ἐπιτυχίαι ἐν
τοῖς ἐπιτηδεύμασι γίνονται διὰ τὸ ἀσύμφωνον εἶναι πολλάκις τὴν προβολὴν
ταῖς ἐξ ἀρχῆς αἱρέσεσιν· αἱ γὰρ μεγαλουργοὶ ζωαὶ καὶ μεγάλα κατορθώματα
ἔχουσι σύμφωνον ἔχουσαι τῇ αἱρέσει τὴν προβολήν, αἱ δὲ ἀποτυχίαι διὰ τὸ
ἀνάπαλιν γίνονται, 'πολλοὶ γὰρ Πλάτωνες τὴν γῆν σκάπτουσιν', ὡς ἔφη τις· —   10
πολλῷ οὖν μᾶλλον οἱ φιλόσοφοι ἐθέλουσιν ἀποθνήσκειν, εἰδότες ἀκριβῶς ὅτι
τεύξονται ἐκεῖσε τοῦ ἐφετοῦ.

Καί φησιν [68b5–c4] ὅτι εἰ φιλόσοφος, ἀδεὴς περὶ τὸν θάνατον, οὐκ εἶπεν
δέ, εἰ ἀδεὴς περὶ τὸν θάνατον, καὶ φιλόσοφος· πολλοὶ γὰρ διὰ θράσος καὶ προπέ-
τειαν ἐθέλουσιν ἀποθνήσκειν μὴ ὄντες φιλόσοφοι. εἰ οὖν φιλόσοφος, καὶ ἀδεὴς   15

---

§ 4. 5 ἐγκατέσπειρεν Wk: συγκατέσπειρεν M — 9 τῇ μ: τὴν M | αἱρέσει Mᶜ: αἵρεσιν M¹

---

with the planetary Gods is not mentioned, but may be implied; cf. Porphyry's
doctrine that the irrational soul and the 'vehicle' are accretions acquired in the
course of the soul's descent through the spheres (Pr., *Tim.* III 234.18–32). To Iambl.,
the Egyptian castes all represent δεύτεραι οὐσίαι καὶ δυνάμεις, the herdsmen standing
for πᾶσι τοῖς ἐν τῷ κόσμῳ τὴν ἐπιστασίαν λαχοῦσι τῆς εἰς τὸ σῶμα ῥεπούσης ζωῆς καὶ
τῶν ἀλογίστων δυνάμεων καὶ ταύτας ἐν τάξει διανέμουσι (153.15–18). Syrianus, finally,
equates them to divine powers: τὸ δὲ νομευτικὸν ἐν τοῖς τὰ εἴδη πάντα τῆς ζωῆς
διακεκριμένως ἐπιτροπεύουσι τὰ ἐν τῇ γενέσει φερόμενα· καὶ γὰρ ἐν τῷ Πολιτικῷ νομέας
θείους τινὰς αὐτὸς ἡμῖν παραδέδωκε (154.8–11).
3–6.   Souls belonging to different spheres: Pr., *Alc.* 113.6–10.
5.   Παιώνιοι ... Σεληναῖαι : Παιώνιοι seems not quite appropriate, since it does
not denote a particular divine character, but rather is a δύναμις (cf. Pr., *elem.*
151–159, Dodds p. 278), common to different Gods: Apollo (Pr., *Crat.* 100.15),
Helios (*Tim.* III 262.27). The Παιώνιος σειρά (*Tim.* II 63.10) is of the same nature
as the ζωογόνος σειρά, *elem.* 155; similarly παιώνιοι θεοί *Rep.* II 3.22 as distinguished
from δημιουργικοί etc.; Ol., *Gorg.* 244.6–7 δύναμις νοερά ... ζωοποιός ... παιωνία,
and Pr., *Tim.* III 140.28 παιώνιοι καὶ κριτικαὶ δυνάμεις, *Rep.* II 153.26 παιώνιοι
δυνάμεις. Further παιώνιος ἰατρική *Tim.* I 158.18, *Rep.* II 118.10, and παιώνιος
πρόνοια *Dam.* II § 157.
ibid.   ἐγκατέσπειρε : a correction for the συγκατέσπειρεν of M, which would mean
'sowed or planted them together with the Sun ...'; ἐγκατασπείρειν occurs, though
in different contexts, Pr., *Tim.* II 76. 26 and Ol., *Gorg.* 200.2. In the *Tim.* text Pl.
has ἔσπειρεν, Pr., *Crat.* 38.3, in a related passage, ἐνσπειρομένων.
7, 9.   τὴν προβολήν : from the verb προβάλλειν or προβάλλεσθαι, 'activate (a faculty),
actualize (a potentiality)' usually with reference to modes of life or to λόγοι. Examples
in indices Pr., *Alc.*, *Rep.*, *Tim.*, *prov.*, *mal. subs.*, *Dam.*, *Ph.*, *Phil.*, *Ol.*, *Alc.*, *Gorg.*, *Ph.*
10.   I cannot identify the quotation; the mannered ἔφη τις may indicate any
author down to Pr. (e.g. Ol., *Alc.* 189.16).
13–17.   **Dam. I § 136.**

unafraid of death, and if he is not unafraid of death, he is not a philosopher or 'lover of wisdom', but a lover of the body, and such a man must be either a lover of riches or of glory.

5. Why does Plato fail to include the pursuit of pleasure [68b7–c3]? Harpocratio [frg. 4] raised the problem without solving it. Proclus says he does not mention it because he had already insisted before [64d1–4] that we should avoid pleasures. But this is not relevant to the question why he does not mention the love of pleasure. According to the philosopher Ammonius, however, the reason is that he does not intend to distinguish the philosopher from the non-philosopher, but from the pretended philosopher, who, even if he loves pleasure, will try to conceal his pleasures and feign temperance, whereas he will probably not conceal his greed for money or his ambition, but use certain plausible pretexts, as Zeno did when he said he took fees from his students either to teach them contempt of money or to dispense it to their poorer fellow-students; as for ambition, he professes that it serves him to stir his disciples to imitation, and accordingly he called ambition a wholesome passion, though still a passion. Thus far the survey.

6. There is every reason to hope that, when I have reached the place where I am going [67b8]: 'Hope' in the sense of divine hope, of which it is said: 'Let fire-borne hope sustain thee' [*Chald. Or.* frg. 47]. According to Plato [*Phil.* 32b9–c2] and Aristotle [*mem.* 1, 449b10–13] hope is a belief, from which it follows that only rational beings hope, irrational beings do not, because hope (*elpis*) has absent things for its objects, being as it were a 'taker of faith' (*helepistis*), while irrational creatures

---

§ 5. **Dam. I § 137.** Dam. ascribes the first solution (Pr.) to Harpocratio, the second (Amm.) to Paterius, adopting it himself, too. Cf. Beutler, art. Ol. 214.52–215.35.

9–12. The story of Zeno illustrates how exegetical ingenuity can create facts out of nothing. The starting-point is Pl., *Alc. I* 119a1–6, where it is said that Zeno charged a fee of 100 minas for his courses. Since Zeno on account of his role in the *Parm.* had been canonized as a true philosopher, who, moreover, symbolized in that dialogue either the participated divine Intelligence or the divine Life (Pr., *Parm.* 628.6–19), and since the official view at Athens was still that a philosopher would take no payment for his teaching, the solution was found (by Pr. ?) that Zeno, while pretending to accept the money for himself, spent it on behalf of needy students (Ol., *Alc.* 140.7–16). Evidence for his talent for dissimulation was discovered in his attitude before the tyrant Nearchus, in the story about Pericles cited below, and in the epithet ἀμφοτερόγλωσσος in Timon of Phlius (frg. B 45, cf. El., *cat.* 109.6–15), for which a new meaning was all the more welcome as the obvious one of 'in utramque partem disputans' clashed with the Neoplatonic interpretation of the *Parm.* (another expedient in Pr., *Parm.* 684.26–28). Ol. now adds a further complication: Zeno is only pretending that he is pretending. This may be a mischievous invention of Amm., who had his financial problems (Dam., *vit. Isid.*

περὶ τὸν θάνατον, καὶ εἰ μὴ ἀδεὴς περὶ τὸν θάνατον, οὐ φιλόσοφος, ἀλλά τις φιλοσώματος· ὁ τοιοῦτος δὲ ἢ φιλοχρήματός ἐστιν ἢ φιλότιμος. Καὶ διὰ τί τὸ φιλήδονον παρῆκεν [68b7–c3]; ὁ μὲν Ἁρποκρατίων [frg. 4] 5
ἀπορήσας οὐκ ἐπελύσατο· ὁ δέ γε Πρόκλος φησὶν ὅτι φιληδόνου οὐκ ἐμνημόνευσεν, διότι ἀνωτέρω [64d1–4] εἶπεν ὅτι δεῖ φεύγειν τὰς ἡδονάς. οὐδὲν δὲ πρὸς τὸ προκείμενον· διὰ τί γὰρ φιληδόνου οὐκ ἐμνημόνευσεν; ὁ δέ γε φιλόσοφος Ἀμμώνιός φησιν ὅτι ἐπειδὴ σκοπὸς αὐτῷ διακρῖναι οὐ φιλόσοφον ἀπὸ μὴ 5
φιλοσόφου, ἀλλὰ ἀπὸ προσποιουμένου εἶναι φιλοσόφου, ὁ δὲ τοιοῦτος κἂν φιλήδονος ᾖ συγκρύψει μὲν τὰς ἡδονὰς καὶ προσποιήσεται σωφρονεῖν, τὸ δὲ φιλοχρήματον οὐ συγκρύψει ἴσως οὐδὲ τὸ φιλότιμον, ἀλλὰ προφασίσοιτο εὐλόγους τινὰς αἰτίας, | καθάπερ καὶ Ζήνων ἔλεγεν λαμβάνειν ἐκ τῶν μαθητῶν (42)
ἢ ἐθίζων αὐτοὺς καταφρονεῖν μισθοῦ ἢ διὰ τὸ μεταδιδόναι τοῖς ἀπορωτέροις· 10
φιλοτιμίας δέ φησιν ἀντέχεσθαι διὰ τὸ εἰς ζῆλον κινῆσαι τοὺς μαθητάς, διὸ τὴν φιλοτιμίαν ἀγαθὸν ἐκάλει πάθος, πάθος δὲ ὅμως. ταῦτα ἔχει ἡ θεωρία.

Πολλὴ ἐλπὶς ἀφικομένῳ οἷ ἐγὼ πορεύομαι [67b8]: ἐλπὶς ἡ θεία, 6
περὶ ἧς ἔφη 'ἐλπὶς δὲ τρεφέτω σε πυρίοχος' [Or. Chald. frg. 47]. καὶ ἔστιν κατὰ Πλάτωνα [Phil. 32b9–c2] καὶ Ἀριστοτέλην [mem. 1, 449b10–13] ἡ ἐλπὶς δόξα· διὸ τὰ λογικὰ μόνα ἐλπίζει, τὰ δὲ ἄλογα οὐκ ἐλπίζει, διότι ἡ ἐλπὶς τῶν ἀπόντων ἐστίν, οἷον ἐλεπίστις, τὰ δὲ ἄλογα τοῦ παρόντος μόνου συναισθά- 5

---

§ 5. 5 ἀμμώνιος (ut semper) M — 6 κἂν Nv: καὶ M — 7 ᾖ Nv: ἢ M
§ 6. 5 ἐλεπίστις mg. Mᶜ: ἐλπίστις M¹ —

---

p. 105.18–22; 250.2–3) and could not share the high principles of the wealthy Athenian school (ibid. p. 212.1–5; 213.7–14; Ol., Alc. 141.1–3). It is no doubt also Amm. who found the formula used by Ol., Alc. 140.18–141.1 and Gorg. 226.24–26: while no fee is required, students will feel morally obliged to contribute toward the needs of their teacher.

11–12. Cf. Plut., Pericl. 5,3 (=Zeno A 17) τοὺς δὲ τοῦ Περικλέους τὴν σεμνότητα δοξοκοπίαν τε καὶ τῦφον ἀποκαλοῦντας ὁ Ζήνων παρεκάλει καὶ αὐτούς τι τοιοῦτο δοξοκοπεῖν, ὡς τῆς προσποιήσεως αὐτῆς τῶν καλῶν ὑποποιούσης τινὰ λεληθότως ζῆλον καὶ συνήθειαν. Ol. knew Plutarch's Lives, also that of Pericles, see indices Alc. and Gorg.
§ 6. 1–10. Cf. Dam. I § 48; § 173; Ol. supra § 1.9–13.
2–4. The reference for Pl. is no doubt Phil. 32b9–c2 τίθει τοίνυν αὐτῆς τῆς ψυχῆς κατὰ τὸ τούτων τῶν παθημάτων (scil. λύπης τε καὶ ἡδονῆς) προσδόκημα τὸ μὲν πρὸ τῶν ἡδονῶν ἐλπιζόμενον ἡδὺ καὶ θαρράλεον, τὸ δὲ πρὸ τῶν λυπηρῶν φοβερὸν καὶ ἀλγεινόν (Dam., Phil. § 147 comments: ὅτι αἱ μὲν ἐλπίδες δόξαι τινές, θάρρος δὲ καὶ φόβος πάθη τινὰ τῆς ζωῆς). The only passage in Ar. to be considered is mem. 1, 449b10–13 οὔτε γὰρ τὸ μέλλον ἐνδέχεται μνημονεύειν, ἀλλ' ἔστι δοξαστὸν καὶ ἐλπιστόν (εἴη δ' ἂν καὶ ἐπιστήμη τις ἐλπιστική, καθάπερ τινές φασι τὴν μαντικήν), οὔτε τοῦ παρόντος, ἀλλ' αἴσθησις (cf. 25–28).
4–6. Dam., Phil. § 178 distinguishes three kinds of anticipation: of reason, of irrational life (the donkey who smells the stable) and of the two jointly.

are conscious only of what is present, not of what is absent. But in Plato's opinion hope is a belief pertaining to the vital faculties, and this may be gathered from what he says in the *Philebus* [40a6–7], that it resembles a syllogism: if he says that it resembles a syllogism, but is not one in the strict sense, he must mean that it is a vital faculty. Aristotle, on the other hand, holds that it is cognitive belief. The expressions 'when I have reached' and 'where I am going' are appropriate to soul, which apprehends things in time, not out of time, and fragmentarily, not undividedly and simultaneously, as intelligence apprehends them, without transition and eternally and simultaneously. Motion, indeed, is proper to soul, because the first of motions is locomotion and the first thing moved is the self-moved; for anything must be one of these three: unmoved, self-moved, or moved from without. Hence these expressions 'when I have reached' and 'where I am going', which are appropriate, as we said, to locomotion.

7. **In adequate measure there [67b8]:** The adequate has the power to produce its like.

8. **To any man [67c2]:** Socrates does not confine himself to the individual case, though this was the subject under discussion, for such a procedure is unphilosophical; rather, he reduces it to the general rule.

9. **That his thought is prepared and as it were purified [67c2–3]:** thought is characteristic of the life of purification, as intelligence is of contemplative life. He adds 'as it were' because of contemplative life, in which purification is truly attained.

10. **To assemble and gather itself together, and dwell [67c8–9]:** What is the meaning of this pleonasm? Surely the words are not linked together for nothing, nor does Plato want to make a stylistic display; 'to assemble itself' means to turn away from the influence of the body, and 'gather itself together' is to turn away from unreasoned belief. Is it not evident, further, that Plato is adapting elements from the well-known Orphic myth [frg. 211]? The myth tells how Dionysus is torn to pieces by the

---

7–9. This inference as to Pl.'s opinion based on a non-existent quotation can be explained as follows: Ol. remembered the sentence *Phil.* 40a6–7 λόγοι μήν εἰσιν ἐν ἑκάστοις ἡμῶν ἃς ἐλπίδας ὀνομάζομεν; vaguely as ἡ ἐλπίς ἔοικε συλλογισμῷ. He also remembered that according to the commentators anticipation in Pl. is a vital, not a cognitive function, an inference drawn by Dam., *Phil.* § 147 (cited above) and founded upon the fact that Pl. discusses it in that context (32b9–c2 anticipation of pleasure and pain taking the form of confidence and fear; 35e7–36c1 thirst and the expectation of a drink; 39c7–40c3 expectations of the just and daydreams of the wicked). Trying to find some proof for this assertion, he discovers it in the ἔοικε which in his recollection was part of the Pl. text. – The contrary statement as regards Ar. must be derived from the fact that in him anticipation is juxtaposed with perception and memory.

10–16. Any verb expressing motion lends itself to this kind of interpretation, e.g. ἴθι *Alc. I* 108c6, d9: Pr., *Alc.* 208.1–4 τὸ μὲν 'ἴθι' συνεχῶς ὑπὸ τοῦ Σωκράτους

νεται, οὐ μὴν τοῦ ἀπόντος. ἀλλὰ κατὰ μὲν Πλάτωνα δόξα ἐστὶν ζωτικὴ ἡ ἐλπίς,
καὶ τοῦτό ἐστιν ἑλεῖν ἐκ τῶν εἰρημένων αὐτῷ ἐν τῷ Φιλήβῳ [40a6–7]· ἔφη
γὰρ αὐτὴν ἐοικέναι συλλογισμῷ· εἰ δὲ ἐοικέναι εἶπεν, οὐ μὴν αὐτόθεν συλλογισμόν, ζωτικὴν ἄρα δόξαν αὐτὴν βούλεται. ὁ δέ γε Ἀριστοτέλης δόξαν αὐτὴν
βούλεται εἶναι γνωστικήν. οἰκεῖον δὲ τὸ 'ἀφικομένῳ' καὶ 'πορεύομαι' τῇ ψυχῇ,   10
ἐγχρόνως καὶ οὐκ ἀχρόνως, καὶ μεριστῶς, οὐκ ἀμερίστως ἢ ἀθρόως γινωσκούσῃ
τὰ πράγματα, καθάπερ ὁ νοῦς ἀμεταβάτως καὶ αἰωνίως καὶ ἀθρόως γινώσκει.
οἰκεία γὰρ ἡ κίνησις τῇ ψυχῇ, διότι πρώτη τῶν κινήσεων ἡ κατὰ τόπον, πρῶτον
δὲ τῶν κινουμένων τὸ αὐτοκίνητον· τρία γάρ ἐστιν, ἀκίνητον, αὐτοκίνητον,
ἑτεροκίνητον. διὸ καὶ τὸ 'ἀφικομένῳ' καὶ 'πορεύομαι', ὅπερ οἰκεῖον, ὡς εἴρηται,   15
τοπικῇ κινήσει.

Ἱκανῶς ἐκεῖ [67b8]: τὸ ἱκανὸν οἷόν τέ ἐστιν ἀπογεννῆσαι καὶ ἄλλα τοιαῦτα.   7

Καὶ ἄλλῳ ἀνδρί [67c2]: οὐκ ἐνέμεινε τοῖς κατὰ μέρος, καὶ ταῦτα τοῦτον 8 (43)
ἔχων σκοπόν, ἐπειδὴ ἀφιλόσοφον τοῦτο, ἀλλὰ ἀνῆλθεν ἐπὶ τὸ καθόλου.

Παρεσκευάσθαι τὴν διάνοιαν ὥσπερ κεκαθαρμένην [67c2–3]:   9
οἰκεία ἡ διάνοια τῇ καθαρτικῇ ζωῇ, ὥσπερ ὁ νοῦς τῇ θεωρητικῇ. τὸ δὲ 'ὥσπερ'
εἶπεν διὰ τὸν θεωρητικὸν βίον, ἐκεῖνος γὰρ κατὰ ἀλήθειάν ἐστι κεκαθαρμένος.

Συναγείρεσθαί τε καὶ ἀθροίζεσθαι καὶ οἰκεῖν [67c8–9]: τί βούλεται   10
ὁ ἐπαναδιπλασιασμὸς τῶν λέξεων τούτων; οὐ γὰρ μάτην εὔρονται οὐδὲ ἐπίδειξιν
λέξεως νῦν σκοπὸν ἔχει ποιήσασθαι ὁ Πλάτων, ἀλλὰ διὰ μὲν τοῦ 'συναγείρεσθαι'
τουτέστιν ἀπὸ τῆς σωματοειδοῦς ζωῆς ἐπιστρέφεσθαι, διὰ δὲ τοῦ 'ἀθροίζεσθαι'
τουτέστιν ἀπὸ τῆς δοξαστικῆς. πῶς δὲ ἄρα οὐ τὰ Ὀρφικὰ ἐκεῖνα [frg. 211]   5

10; 15 τὸ Mˣ: τῷ M¹ | πορεύομαι] accent. add., -αι seq. ~ in ras. scr. Mˣ (πορευομένωι
ut vid. M¹)
§ 7. 1 ἱκανῶς ἐκεῖ] ἐκεῖ ἱκανῶς Pl. B
§ 9. 1 παρεσκευάσθαι] παρασκευάσασθαι Pl. W

λεγόμενον φατέον οἰκειότατον εἶναι τῇ γνώσει τῆς ἡμετέρας ψυχῆς· ἐν κινήσει γάρ ἐστι
καὶ οὐκ ἀθρόως οὐδὲ ἀμεταβλήτως ὑφέστηκεν, ὥσπερ ἡ τοῦ νοῦ μόνιμος καὶ διαιώνιος
ἐνέργεια (Ol., Alc. 78.26–79.2; 82.22–83.2). Dam. I § 173.2–3.
13. Pr., Tim. III 239.17–20 διότι γὰρ ἀρχὴ κινήσεώς ἐστιν, ἀνάγκη τῆς πρωτίστης
εἶναι κινήσεως ἀρχὴν αὐτὴν τοῖς ζῴοις. πρωτίστη δὲ ἡ κατὰ τόπον τῶν ἄλλων, ὡς καὶ
Ἀριστοτέλης (phys. VIII 7, 260a26–29) ἔδειξεν. Ibid. III 123.31–124.3.
14–15. Pr., elem. 14.
§ 7. Derived from the current interpretation of the ἱκανόν of Phil. 20d4–6;
e.g. Pr., theol. I 22, 102.27–103.28; Dam., Phil. § 77.
§ 8. Supra § 1.2–8.
2. Cf. Ol.'s favorite maxim φιλοκαθόλου οἱ φιλόσοφοι: Alc. 160.16; mete. 2.11;
El., cat. 130.28–29; [Amm.,] anal. pr. 53.32–33.
§ 9. 1–2. Cf. Dam. I § 99.
§ 10. 1–5. Dam. I § 128.

Titans and is made whole by Apollo; so 'assembling and gathering itself together' means passing from the Titanic life to the unitary life. And there is Kore, too, who has to descend into Hades, but is brought up again by Demeter to dwell in her ancient home, which accounts for the 'dwelling'; Plato, indeed, borrows from Orpheus everywhere. In the sequel [69c8–d1], he even quotes a line by him [frg. 235]:

'Many carry the thyrsus, few become Bacchus'.

Those who carry the thyrsus without becoming Bacchus are philosophers still involved in civic life, while the thyrsus-bearers and Bacchants are those on the way to purification. This is why Dionysus, as we said already [1 § 6; 6 § 13], is the cause both of life and of death: of death as the patron of prophecy, which excludes imagination; therefore the poets call Sleep the brother of Death [Il. 14.231], because sleep, too, detaches us from sense-perception, though not from imagination, as death does.

11.   Always above all and alone of all, the seekers for wisdom [67d7–8]: 'Always' describes the life of purification as continuous, 'above all' as strenuous; for these two factors lend force to our efforts, the continuity of the action and its energy.

12.   A man who prepares himself [67d12–e1]: It is ridiculous indeed to long for this all one's life, then, when the fulfillment has come, to be angry or sad. It would be as if fire, while aspiring to that upper region which is the cause of its motion, were to refuse to abide in it.

13.   If he has an uncompromising quarrel with the body [67e6–7]: The middle form *diabeblêtai* can be used in an active sense also, as in this passage, where it is equivalent to *diaballei*. Note the construction with the dative.

14.   A human being, boy-friend or wife [68a3–4]: the other argument, that worthless people in this world are willing to die, as for example Euadne, who flung herself on a funeral pile in the belief that she would join her dead husband.

6–10.   Dam. I §§ 129–130.

10–18.   *Infra* 8 § 7.

10–12.   *Infra* 10 § 3.13–15.

15.   Cf. *supra* 6 § 12.3–4.

§ 11.   Dam. I § 132.

§ 12.   Dam. I § 134.

παρῳδεῖ νῦν ὁ Πλάτων, ὅτι ὁ Διόνυσος σπαράττεται μὲν ὑπὸ τῶν Τιτάνων, ἐνοῦται δὲ ὑπὸ τοῦ Ἀπόλλωνος; διὸ 'συναγείρεσθαι' καὶ 'ἀθροίζεσθαι' τουτέστιν ἀπὸ τῆς Τιτανικῆς ζωῆς ἐπὶ τὴν ἐνοειδῆ. καὶ ἡ Κόρη δὲ κατάγεται μὲν εἰς Ἅιδου, ἀνάγεται δὲ πάλιν καὶ οἰκεῖ ἔνθα πάλαι ἦν ὑπὸ τῆς Δήμητρος· διὸ καὶ τὸ 'οἰκεῖν'· παρῳδεῖ γὰρ πανταχοῦ τὰ Ὀρφέως. διὸ καὶ στίχον αὐτοῦ [frg. 235]   10 φησιν ἐφεξῆς [69c8–d1]·

'πολλοὶ μὲν ναρθηκοφόροι, παῦροι δέ τε Βάκχοι'.

καὶ ναρθηκοφόροι μέν, οὐ μὴν Βάκχοι, οἱ πολιτικοὶ φιλόσοφοι, ναρθηκοφόροι δὲ Βάκχοι οἱ καθαρτικοί. διὸ καὶ ζωῆς καὶ θανάτου, ὡς εἴρηται [1 § 6; 6 § 13], ὁ Διόνυσος αἴτιος· θανάτου γὰρ ὡς μαν|τείας ἔφορος ἀφαντάστου οὔσης·   15 (44) διὸ καὶ τὸν ὕπνον ἀδελφὸν τοῦ θανάτου φασὶν οἱ ποιηταὶ καὶ 'κασίγνητον' [Hom. Ξ 231], διότι χωρίζει ἡμᾶς καὶ οὗτος ἀπὸ τῆς αἰσθήσεως, εἰ καὶ μὴ ἀπὸ φαντασίας, καθάπερ ὁ θάνατος.

Ἀεὶ μάλιστα καὶ μόνοι οἱ φιλοσοφοῦντες [67d7–8]: διὰ μὲν τοῦ   11 'ἀεί' τὸ ἀδιάκοπον ἐδήλωσε τῆς καθάρσεως, διὰ δὲ τοῦ 'μάλιστα' τὸ σύντονον. δύο γὰρ ταῦτα ⟨τὰ⟩ ἐπιτηδεύματα συνίστησιν, τὸ ἀδιάκοπον τῆς ἐνεργείας καὶ τὸ σύντονον.

Ἄνδρα παρασκευάζοντα ἑαυτόν [67d12–e1]: γελοῖον γάρ ἐστι παρ'   12 ὅλον μὲν τὸν χρόνον ἐφίεσθαι τούτου, ἥκοντος δὲ τοῦ ἐφετοῦ χαλεπῶς ἢ δυσφόρως φέρειν, ὡς εἰ καὶ τὸ πῦρ ἐφιέμενον τοῦ ἄνω τόπου, δι' ὃν κινεῖται, μὴ ἐθέλειν δὲ ἐν τούτῳ εἶναι.

Εἰ γὰρ διαβέβληται πανταχῇ τῷ σώματι [67e6–7]: τὸ 'διαβέβληται'   13 μέσον ὂν δύναται καὶ ἐπὶ ἐνεργείας λαμβάνεσθαι, ὥσπερ ἐνταῦθα, ἀντὶ τοῦ 'διαβάλλει'. σημειωτέον δὲ τὴν σύνταξιν, ὅτι πρὸς δοτικὴν ἀποδέδοται.

Ἡ ἀνθρωπίνων μὲν παιδικῶν καὶ γυναικῶν [68a3–4]: τὸ ἄλλο ἐπιχεί-   14 ρημα, ὅτι οἱ παρ' ἡμῖν ἀνθρωπίσκοι ἐθέλουσιν ἀποθνήσκειν, καθάπερ ἡ Εὐάδνη, ἡ ἐν πυρκαϊᾷ ἐνέβαλλεν ἑαυτὴν διὰ τὸ οἴεσθαι συνεῖναι τῷ ἀνδρὶ τελευτήσαντι.

---

§ 10. 9 δημη~τρος, ~τρ- in ras. Mˣ (fort. ex δημητερος)
§ 11. 3 τὰ Nv: om. M
§ 12. 3 ἐθέλοι ci. Fh, lac. post κινεῖται statuit Nv
§ 13. 1 διαβέβληται] -νται Pl. | ante πανταχῇ] μὲν Mᶜ, Pl.

---

3. Finckh proposed ἐθέλοι, but the careless construction may be original.
§ 13. Ol. can hardly have thought that the pass. perf. διαβέβληται c. dat. equals διαβάλλει c. acc., 'defames'. Rather he must be trying to distinguish the purely passive meaning 'is thought of badly (by or among)' from the intransitive meaning 'has a quarrel (with)'.
§ 14. 2–3. Eurip., Suppl. 990–1030; Apollod. III 79.

8

Lecture **

1. And, Simmias, is not what we call courage also [68c5–69e5].

Socrates had already made insight a characteristic of the life of
purification, when he said: 'And next, in what position will they be as
regards the attainment of insight itself?' [65a9], and he now proceeds
to do the same for courage and temperance; the obvious reason why
he does not mention justice is that it superimposes itself on the other
virtues. He began with insight because in purification a man's first task
is to turn towards himself, while insight is an emanation of intelligence
reverting upon itself. Others see a resemblance between courage and
purification in unflinching resistance against the inferior; for such is
courage, unwavering before lower forces; such, too, is Socrates, who
remains unmoved by Xanthippe and his crying child and does not suffer
himself to be upset by them [60a1–8].

2. Since, however, we have touched upon the subject of virtues, let

---

Lect. 8.　**Virtue as purification.** After a short introductory paragraph on virtue
as purification in the *Ph.* (§ 1), Ol. deals at length with the Neoplatonic scale of
virtues: natural, moral, social, purificatory, contemplative, exemplary (or theurgical)
(§ 2–§ 4.4). He then tries to define the spurious virtues of 68c2–69b2 in relation
to this scale (§ 4.5–§ 6). In the last paragraph of the *theoria* the Orphic allusions
of 69c3–d2 are discussed (§ 7).

§ 1. 2–3. *Supra* 4 § 11.

4–5.　**Cf. Dam. I** § 163.3; there is a direct reference to him *infra* § 9.7–9.

8.　A reminiscence of Plot. II 3,11.8–9 νοῦ ἀπόρροια πανουργίαν (scil. εἰργάσατο),
cited by Pr., *Alc.* 34.13–14; *Rep.* I 105.2–3; *Tim.* III 314.3–4.

7–9.　Cf. *infra* § 3.8–10=Pr. ap. Dam. I § 152.1–3.

§§ 2–3. Dam. I §§ 138–144. Further texts: Porph., *sent.* 32; Macrob., *somn.Scip.*
I 8,5; Hierocl., *carm. aur.* 422b5–9; Marin., *vit. Pr.* 3; Amm., *int.* 135.19–32; Philop..
cat. 141.25–142.3; Ol., *Alc.* 4.15–8.14; *supra* 1 § 5; *Proleg.* 26.24–25; El., *isag,*
19.30–20.15; Dav. 38.32–39.13; Ps.-El. 14,24–25; Psell., *omnif. doctr.* 67; 69.
Literature: H. van Lieshout, *La théorie plotinienne de la vertu,* Fribourg-Paris
1926; O. Schissel von Fleschenberg, *Marinos von Neapolis und die neuplatonischen
Tugendgrade,* Athens 1928; Lewy 465–468. – Plot., trying to define the virtues
that make man Godlike (*Theaet.* 176b1–d1), starts from the cardinal virtues of *Rep.* IV
434d2–444a9, which he calls πολιτικαὶ ἀρεταί (3.8) referring to *Rep.* 430c3 (where
Pl. contrasts the πολιτικὴ ἀνδρεία of the guards with the θηριώδης and ἀνδραποδώδης
aggressivity of others; at *Ph.* 82a11–b1 Pl. understands by δημοτικὴ καὶ πολιτικὴ
ἀρετή what the Neoplatonists call ἠθικὴ ἀρετή, i.e. ἐξ ἔθους τε καὶ μελέτης γεγονυῖαν).
To these Plot. opposes the virtues of *Ph.* 68c5–69e5, which, though they are called
by the same (four) names, are different in nature, being καθάρσεις. In each he
distinguishes two aspects, the process of purification on the one hand, the state
of purity and contemplation on the other (4–6). The forms of virtue in the intelligence

8

Πρᾶξις σὺν θεῷ   (45)

Ἄρα οὖν, ἔφη, ὦ Σιμμία, οὐ καὶ ἡ ὀνομαζομένη ἀνδρεία[68c5–69e5].   1
Ἀποδοὺς ὁ Σωκράτης τὴν φρόνησιν τῇ καθαρτικῇ ζωῇ, ἡνίκα ἔλεγεν 'τί
δὲ δή; περὶ αὐτὴν τὴν τῆς φρονήσεως κτῆσιν πῶς ἕξουσιν·' [65a9] ἐντεῦθεν
βούλεται καὶ ἀνδρείαν καὶ σωφροσύνην ἀποδοῦναι τῇ καθαρτικῇ ζωῇ· δικαιοσύνης
δὲ εἰκότως οὐκ ἐμνημόνευσεν ὡς ἐπιφαινομένης ταῖς ἄλλαις ἀρεταῖς. ἤρξατο   5
δὲ ἀπὸ τῆς φρονήσεως, διότι καθαρτικοῦ ἔργον τὸ πρὸς ἑαυτὸν ἐπιστρέφειν,
νοῦ δὲ ἀπόρροια καὶ ἡ φρόνησις τοῦ πρὸς ἑαυτὸν ἐπιστρέφοντος. ἄλλοι δὲ τὴν
ἀνδρείαν ἀπεικάζουσιν τῇ καθαρτικῇ διὰ τὸ πρὸς τὰ δεύτερα ἀμάλθακτον·
τοιαύτη γὰρ καὶ ἡ ἀνδρεία, ἀρρεπὴς οὖσα περὶ τὰ δεύτερα· οὕτω δὲ καὶ ὁ Σωκράτης
οὐδὲν πέπονθεν ὑπὸ Ξανθίππης καὶ τοῦ παιδίου κλάοντος, ἀλλ' ἀκλινῶς ἔσχε   10
πρὸς αὐτούς [60a1–8].
Ἀλλ' ἐπειδὴ ἀρετῶν ἐμνημονεύσαμεν, φέρε εἴπωμεν τοὺς βαθμοὺς τῶν   2

---

§ 1. 1 ἀνδρία (ut semper) M¹

are mentioned in connection with the question of ἀντακολούθησις (mutual implication)
of virtues, not as a higher degree in a scale (7). – In Porph., the two aspects of
κάθαρσις appear as two distinct levels of virtue, καθαρτικαί and θεωρητικαί ἀρεταί.
Though this is clearly a further formalization, it is not so gross a distortion of
Plot.'s view as F. Heinemann (Plotin, Leipzig 1921, 131) thinks, since Plot. himself
already describes the virtues corresponding to each of the two stages separately
and in different terms (3.13–19 and 4.11–27). A more radical change is that the
archetypes in intelligence are now no longer transcendent, but become παραδειγματικαί
ἀρεταί, which can be exercised by man and make him a 'father of Gods' (sent.
p. 31.8; cf. Dam. I § 143). – It must have been Iambl. in his Περὶ ἀρετῶν who
lengthened the scale both downwards and upwards. Dam. I §§ 143–144 ascribes
the exemplary and the hieratic virtues to him, while the natural and moral virtues
appear in Proleg. 26 in connection with his system of the Platonic dialogues
(cf. ibid., Introd. p. XXXIX). Natural virtue, name and notion, comes from Ar.,
eth. Nic. VI 13, 1144b3–9 (cf. Plot. I 3,6.18–24); and so does ἠθικὴ ἀρετή, as far as
Ar.'s description goes (ἡ δ' ἠθικὴ ἐξ ἔθους περιγίνεται, eth. Nic. II 1, 1103a17), though
the actual content is what Pl. calls τὴν δημοτικὴν καὶ πολιτικὴν ἀρετήν . . ., ἣν δὴ
καλοῦσι σωφροσύνην τε καὶ δικαιοσύνην, ἐξ ἔθους τε καὶ μελέτης γεγονυῖαν ἄνευ φιλοσοφίας
τε καὶ νοῦ (Ph. 82a11–b3). – As regards the παραδειγματικαί and θεουργικαί (or
ἱερατικαί) ἀρεταί the sources disagree. In Ol., the παραδειγματικαί correspond to
θεουργία (line 20), and this must be the original version, for the 'father of Gods'
in Porphyry can be hardly anything but a θεουργός. Marinus and Psellus, omnif.
doctr. 67, have only the θεουργικαὶ ἀρεταί instead, while adding the archetypes not
as a degree of virtues, but as transcendent principles; the μανικαὶ ἀρεταί of Psellus 69
must be identical with the θεουργικαί, which, in 67, are said to cause the θεία μανία.
Dam., then, is the only one of our texts to draw a clear line between παραδειγματικαί
and ἱερατικαὶ ἀρεταί: the παραδειγματικαί, he says, not quite correctly (I § 143),
are an innovation of Iambl., while the ἱερατικαί, already hinted at by Iambl., are

us enumerate the degrees of virtues. They are five. Virtues are either
(1) natural, resulting from our temperament, or (2) moral, i.e. due to
habituation. Natural virtues are especially proper to brute animals, as
they are the outcome of a temperament: all lions are constitutionally
courageous and so is all their offspring (which cannot be said to hold
true of us humans), all cattle are temperate, all storks just, all cranes
clever. Moral virtues mainly belong to ourselves and to such of the other
animals as have a more highly developed imagination that is amenable
to habituation (Aristotle calls it 'teachable'). As for rational virtues, they
either (3) deal with tripartite soul and moderation of the passions (civic
virtues), or they do not, in which case they either (4) aim at freedom
from passions (purificatory virtues), or (5) have attained this freedom
(contemplative virtues). Plotinus [I 2, 7.2–6] holds that there is another
degree of virtues, that of the ideal examples. There are, indeed, also
exemplary virtues; for just as our eye, when illuminated by the sunlight,
is at first different from the source of the light, as its recipient, but is
afterwards somehow united with it and joined to it, and becomes as it
were one with it and 'sun-like', so our soul is at first illuminated by
intelligence and its actions are directed by the contemplative virtues,
but afterwards it becomes in a way identical with the source of the
illumination and acts in union with the One by the exemplary virtues.
The object of philosophy is to make us intelligence, that of theurgy to
unite us with the intelligible principles and conform our activity to the
ideal examples.

3. As possessors of natural virtues we have knowledge of the corporeal
things of this world, because the range of these virtues is also limited
to the corporeal; as possessors of moral virtues we know the fatality
that links the universe, because this fatality rules irrational forms of
life only (rational soul is not subject to fate) and moral virtues are also
irrational; by the civic virtues we know all intra-mundane reality; by
the purificatory virtues supra-mundane reality; as possessors of

---

described more distinctly by οἱ περὶ Πρόκλον (I § 144). The obscure point in Iambl.
seems to have been precisely whether the παραδειγματικαί and ἱερατικαί were identical
or not. The purpose of the distinction made by Pr. was obviously to complete
the parallel with levels of knowledge: contemplative virtue corresponds to intelligence,
archetypal virtue to the intelligible, hieratic virtue to the unitary or divine. The
wavering in our texts may be explained as due to inconsistency in Pr. himself,
on whom the others (Marinus, Ol., Psellus) must depend.

§ 2. 3.　συνηθισμοῦ and συνηθίζεσθαι (8): the form (influenced by συνήθης) may
have been used in the 6th cent.

3–7.　On the supposed characters of animals see Ar., hist. an. I 1, 488b12–28.
Some of the instances cited here: Aelian., nat. an. 2,1; 3,23; 10,16; Philop., cat.
141.25–27; Ol., Alc. 110.6; 232.11–12; El., isag. 19.35–20.1; Dav. 39.5–9; Ps.-El. 14,25.

7–9.　Cf. Ar., an. III 10, 433b29 φαντασία δὲ πᾶσα ἢ λογιστικὴ ἢ αἰσθητική. The

α' ἀρετῶν. πέντε τοίνυν βαθμοὶ τῶν ἀρετῶν εἰσιν. ἢ γὰρ φυσικαί εἰσιν, αἱ ἀπὸ
β' κράσεως ἐπιγίνονται ἡμῖν· ἢ ἠθικαί, ὡς αἱ ἀπὸ συνηθισμοῦ. καὶ οἰκεῖαι αἱ μὲν
φυσικαὶ μάλιστα τοῖς ἀλόγοις ζώοις, αἳ ἀπὸ κράσεώς εἰσιν· πάντες γὰρ οἱ λέοντες
ἀνδρεῖοι διὰ τὴν κρᾶσιν καὶ οἱ ἀπὸ τούτων πάντες, ὅπερ οὐκ ἔστιν εὑρεῖν 5
σωζόμενον ἐφ' ἡμῶν, πάντες οἱ βόες σώφρονες, πάντες οἱ πελαργοὶ δίκαιοι,
πᾶσαι αἱ γέρανοι φρόνιμοι. αἱ δὲ | ἠθικαὶ οἰκεῖαι μάλιστα ἡμῖν καὶ τῶν ἄλλων (46)
ζώων ὅσα τελειοτέραν ἔχει φαντασίαν καὶ συνηθίζεσθαι δυναμένην, ἣν καλεῖ
γ' διδακτικὴν ὁ Ἀριστοτέλης. εἰ δὲ λόγῳ χρῶντο αἱ ἀρεταί, ἢ τῇ τριμερείᾳ
⟨χρῶνται⟩ τῆς ψυχῆς καὶ τοῖς πάθεσι μεμετρημένοις, ὡς αἱ πολιτικαί· ἢ οὐ 10
δ' ε' χρῶνται, καὶ ἢ φεύγουσι τὰ πάθη, ὡς αἱ καθαρτικαί, ἢ πεφεύγασιν, ὡς αἱ
ϛ' θεωρητικαί. ὁ δέ γε Πλωτῖνος [I 2,7.2–6] καὶ ἄλλον βαθμὸν βούλεται εἶναι
ἀρετῶν παρὰ ταύτας, τὸν τῶν παραδειγμάτων. εἰσὶ γὰρ καὶ παραδειγματικαὶ
ἀρεταί· ὥσπερ γὰρ τὸ ἡμέτερον ὄμμα πρότερον μὲν φωτιζόμενον ὑπὸ τοῦ
ἡλιακοῦ φωτὸς ἕτερόν ἐστι τοῦ φωτίζοντος ὡς ἐλλαμπόμενον, ὕστερον δὲ 15
ἑνοῦταί πως καὶ συνάπτεται καὶ οἷον ἓν καὶ ἡλιοειδὲς γίνεται, οὕτω καὶ ἡ ἡμετέρα
ψυχὴ κατ' ἀρχὰς μὲν ἐλλάμπεται ὑπὸ νοῦ καὶ ἐνεργεῖ κατὰ τὰς θεωρητικὰς
ἀρετάς, καὶ ὕστερον οἷον ὅπερ τὸ ἐλλάμπον γίνεται καὶ ἑνοειδῶς ἐνεργεῖ κατὰ
τὰς παραδειγματικὰς ἀρετάς. καὶ φιλοσοφίας μὲν ἔργον νοῦν ἡμᾶς ποιῆσαι,
θεουργίας δὲ ἑνῶσαι ἡμᾶς τοῖς νοητοῖς, ὡς ἐνεργεῖν παραδειγματικῶς. 20

Καὶ ὡς μὲν φυσικὰς ἀρετὰς ἔχοντες γινώσκομεν τὰ ἐγκόσμια σώματα, 3
σώματα γὰρ καὶ τὰ ὑποκείμενα ταῖς τοιαύταις ἀρεταῖς· ὡς δὲ ἠθικὰς ἀρετὰς
ἔχοντες τὴν εἱμαρμένην ἴσμεν τοῦ παντός, διότι καὶ αὕτη περὶ ἀλόγους ζωὰς
καταγίνεται, οὐ γὰρ ἡ λογικὴ ψυχὴ ὑπὸ εἱμαρμένην ἐστίν, καὶ αἱ ἠθικαὶ δὲ
ἀρεταὶ ἄλογοί εἰσι· κατὰ δὲ τὰς πολιτικὰς τὰ ἐγκόσμια ἴσμεν· κατὰ δὲ τὰς 5
καθαρτικὰς τὰ ὑπερκόσμια· ὡς δὲ θεωρητικὰς ἔχοντες τὰ νοερά· ὡς δὲ παραδειγματικὰς τὰ νοητά.

---

§ 2. 3 συνηθισμοῦ] συνεθισμοῦ Fh (item lin. 8 συνεθίζεσθαι) — 10 χρῶνται Wk: om.
M — 13 τὸν Fh: τὴν M | παραδειγμάτων] -ατικῶν Fh

φαντασία διδακτή (I have retained διδακτική because the error may have been made
by Ol. or the reportator, either of whom could have been vaguely familiar with
its opposite, φ. ἀναμνηστική) derives from Plutarch of Athens. Cf. Simpl., an. 292.31–35
(at Ar. 432b13–19) ἀλλὰ διὰ τὸ ἀόριστον αὐτῶν τῆς φαντασίας πολλαχοῖ καὶ ὁ
Ἀριστοτέλης καὶ ἐν τούτοις ὁ φιλόσοφος Πλούταρχος οὐκ ἀξιοῖ φαντασίαν τοῖς τοιούτοις
ἀποδιδόναι ζώοις, τὸ τῆς φαντασίας ὄνομα οὐκ ἐπὶ τῆς ὡρισμένης μόνης φέρων, ἀλλὰ
καὶ ἐπὶ τῆς διδάσκεσθαι δυναμένης. Steph., an. 495.25–29 (at Ar. 427b27–428a1) πρὸς
ἣν ἐροῦμεν ὅτι διττὴ ἡ φαντασία, ἡ μὲν ἀναμνηστικὴ ἡ δὲ διδακτή, καθ' ἣν διδασκόμεθα,
ἣν καὶ ψιττακὸς ἔχει· κατ' αὐτὴν γὰρ διδάσκεται τοὺς ἀνθρωπείους λόγους. ποίαν οὖν
ἄρα φαντασίαν ἀπὸ τούτων τῶν ζώων ἀφαιρεῖται ὁ Ἀριστοτέλης; καὶ λέγομεν ὅτι οὐ
τὴν ἀναμνηστικήν, ἀλλὰ τὴν διδακτήν.
10. ⟨χρῶνται⟩: cf. infra line 11; § 6.7.
§ 3. 1–7. Correspondence between levels of virtue and degrees of reality.
3–4. Fate as a reflection of Providence on the material plane: Pr., prov. 10–14.

contemplative virtues the intellective world; as possessors of ideal virtues the intelligible world.

Temperance is characteristic of the moral virtues, justice of the civic virtues (in view of commercial relations), courage of the purificatory virtues (because these require unwavering firmness towards the material), and insight of the contemplative virtues.

4. The following question is worth asking: it is Platonic doctrine that virtues are modes of life, in which respect they are contradistinguished from knowledge, which is cognitive; but how can insight be a mode of life? The answer is that insight is choice and avoidance in the sphere of action, not merely judgment cognitive of things as such or not such.

Plato calls the natural virtues 'slavish' inasmuch as even slaves can possess them, and the moral virtues 'shading effects' because they have to do only with the *that*, and the *that* is a shadow of the *because*.

Another problem worth discussing is to what kind of virtues Plato refers when he says that they exchange affects for affects and that they avoid great passions to choose the smaller ones, exchanging, in a manner of speaking, 'gold for bronze' [Hom., *Il.* 6.236]. Some of the commentators have thought that he means the natural and moral virtues. **5.** This, however, is not true, for these virtues do not exchange affects for affects, since they operate by being simply what they are. The philosopher Proclus says that the allusion is to virtues that are not constant throughout life

---

8–10. Dam. I § 152.1–3. Correspondence between levels of virtue and the several cardinal virtues. Pr., *Rep.* I 12.25–13.6 (referring to his commentary on the *Ph.*) καὶ γὰρ αὖ καὶ ὡς ἐν ἄλλοις διείλομεν, ἡ μὲν σωφροσύνη μάλιστα χαρακτηρίζει τὴν ἠθικὴν ἀρετήν . . ., ἡ δὲ δικαιοσύνη τὴν πολιτικήν . . ., ἡ δὲ ἀνδρεία τὴν καθαρτικήν . . ., ἡ ⟨δὲ⟩ φρόνησις τὴν θεωρητικήν . . . *Supra* § 1.7–9.

§ 4. 1–4. What Ol. marks as δόγμα Πλατωνικόν is usually Neoplatonic inference: *Alc.* 89.19–20 Πλατωνικὸν δόγμα, ὅτι ἐκ ψευδῶν προτάσεων οὐδὲν ἀναγκαῖον συνάγεται. 145.6–7 δόγμα Πλατωνικόν, ὅτι βούλεται οὐχ ὡς 'Αριστοτέλης τὸν νοῦν ἀρχὴν εἶναι, ἀλλὰ τὸ ἀγαθόν. 213.18–19 δόγμα Πλατωνικόν, ὅτι οὐ βούλεται τῶν τεχνητῶν εἶναι λόγους. *Infra* 13 § 2.39–40 δόγμα γὰρ Πλατωνικὸν τὸ αὐτοπαραγωγὸν εἶναι τὴν ψυχήν. Here, we have really a δόγμα Πρόκλειον : cf. Pr., *Rep.* I 206.13 ταύτην (i.e. virtue properly so called) οὖν ζωτικὴν μὲν εἶναι πάντως φήσομεν. The parenthesis at line 2 is not an attempt to find support in Pl. for this doctrine, since the contrast knowledge - virtue is hardly found in Pl. in this form (cf., though, *Menex.* 246e7–247a2); rather, it looks like an appeal to *communis opinio*.

3. ἐκλογὴ καὶ ἀπεκλογή : these Stoic terms also Pr., *Rep.* II 73.10.

3–4. Cf. *supra* 4 § 11.3–4 note.

5–§ 6.17. Dam. I §§ 145–148; cf. § 164.6–12. – Ol. begins (§ 4.5–7) by stating that by 'slavish virtues' Pl. means the natural virtues, by 'shading effects' the moral virtues, which was, at least as regards the first half of the statement, the current explanation in Ol.'s school (Ol. *infra* § 9.5–6; *Alc.* 30.4–8; El., *isag.* 20.9–10; *cat.* 228.19; Dav. 39.1–3; Ps.-El. 14,24). Then, after a fresh start, he takes this back (§ 4.10–§ 5.2) and proceeds to outline the highly complicated interpretation of the passage by Pr. (§ 5.2–§ 6.17), which was adopted by Dam. too. This view identifies (i) 'slavish' virtue with spurious virtue (virtue mixed with its opposite,

Οἰκεία δὲ ἡ μὲν σωφροσύνη ταῖς ἠθικαῖς ἀρεταῖς, ἡ δὲ δικαιοσύνη ταῖς πολιτικαῖς διὰ τὰ συναλλάγματα, ἡ δὲ ἀνδρεία ταῖς καθαρτικαῖς διὰ τὸ ἀρρεπὲς τὸ πρὸς τὴν ὕλην, ἡ δὲ φρόνησις ταῖς θεωρητικαῖς.   10

Ἐκεῖνο δὲ ἄξιον ἀπο|ρῆσαι· εἰ δόγμα Πλατωνικόν ἐστι τὸ τὰς ἀρετὰς ζωὰς 4 (47) εἶναι (ταύτῃ γὰρ καὶ ἀντιδιῄρηνται τῇ ἐπιστήμῃ γνωστικῇ οὔσῃ), πῶς ἡ φρόνησις ζωή ἐστιν; λύσις, ὅτι ἐκλογὴ καὶ ἀπεκλογὴ τῶν πρακτῶν ἡ φρόνησις, ἀλλ' οὐχ ἁπλῶς κρίσις γνωστικὴ τῶν τοιούτων ἢ μή.

Καλεῖ δὲ ὁ Πλάτων τὰς μὲν φυσικὰς ἀρετὰς 'ἀνδραποδώδεις' ὡς καὶ ἀνδραπό- 5 δοις δυναμένας ὑπάρχειν· τὰς δὲ ἠθικὰς 'σκιαγραφίας', τὸ ὅτι γὰρ μόνον ἔχουσιν, σκιὰ δὲ τὸ ὅτι τοῦ διότι.

Ἐκεῖνο δὲ ἄξιον ζητῆσαι, τίνας ἐν τῇ λέξει ὁ Πλάτων ἀρετάς φησιν πάθη παθῶν ἀνταλλαττομένας καὶ τὰ μεγάλα πάθη φεύγειν, τὰ δὲ ἐλάττω αἱρεῖσθαι, οἷον 'χρύσεα χαλκείων' [Hom. Z 236] ἀμειψαμένας. τινὲς μὲν οὖν τῶν ἐξηγητῶν 10 ταῦτα ᾠήθησαν ἐπὶ τῶν φυσικῶν καὶ ἠθικῶν ἀρετῶν λέγεσθαι. τὸ δὲ οὐχ οὕτως· 5 οὐδὲ γὰρ αὗται πάθη παθῶν ἀνταλλάττονται τῷ εἶναι αὐτῷ ποιοῦσαι. ἀλλὰ ταῦτα ὁ φιλόσοφος Πρόκλος λέγεσθαί φησιν ἐπὶ ἀρετῶν οὐ διὰ βίου τοιούτων, ἀλλ' ἔν τινι χρόνῳ διὰ ἀνάγκην τινά, οἷον πολλοὶ δειλίᾳ ἀνδρίζονται καὶ ἀκολασίᾳ

§ 4. 9 καὶ M: del. Nv

e.g. courage resulting from fear); (ii) ἐσκιαγραφημένη ἀρετή with natural and moral virtue; (iii) τῷ ὄντι and ἀληθὴς ἀρετή with civic virtue; (iv) ἀληθὴς τῷ ὄντι ἀρετή with purificatory virtue; (v) 'living with the Gods' with contemplative virtue. – Pr.'s analysis of the text can be reconstructed as follows: (A) [68d2–69a5] The virtue of most people is preposterous, their courage is fear of something worse, their temperance is pursuit of the maximum pleasure [Ol. § 6.1–4; § 11: distinction between spurious virtues on the one hand and natural and moral virtues on the other]. (B) [69a6–b5] Such exchange of affect against affect will never lead to virtue, which can *really* (τῷ ὄντι b2) be bought for insight only; this holds for courage, temperance, justice, and for all *true* (ἀληθής b3) virtue generally: none can ever exist without understanding [Ol. § 6.4–6; § 11: distinction between spurious virtues and civic virtues]. (C) [69b5–8] If (1) severed from insight and (2) made an object of barter, virtue will be (1) only a 'shading effect' and (2) fit for slaves, neither sound nor genuine [(1)=natural and moral virtues, which, though not based on insight, are nevertheless shadowings of the higher virtues; (2)=sham virtues, mixed with their opposites]. (D) [69b8–c3] *Really true* virtue (ἀληθὲς τῷ ὄντι b8), whether temperance, justice, courage, or insight itself, is purification [purificatory virtues]. (E) [69c3–d2] The end of the journey is living with the Gods, *theoria* [Ol. § 15.3–5: contemplative virtues].

10. χρύσεα χαλκείων : the quotation had become proverbial for a bad bargain, and is therefore not very apposite here.

ibid. τινὲς ... τῶν ἐξηγητῶν : if the natural and moral virtues were referred to in those terms and in the context of the Iamblichean scale, the commentators to be considered would be Iambl., Theodorus of Asine, Paterius and Plutarch of Athens.

but appear temporarily under the pressure of certain circumstances; thus many people act bravely out of cowardice and restrain themselves out of intemperance, for many, though cowards, prefer to die bravely for fear of greater evils, for instance slavery, thus exchanging affects for affects (death for slavery); others do not eat to satiety, though intemperate, for the sake of greater pleasures to be enjoyed in good health. These are the virtues Plato describes as spurious and as exchanging affects for affects.

6. He distinguishes natural and moral virtues from spurious virtues by the fact that the former operate by simply being what they are, in the same way as God and Nature operate by being what they are, while false virtues, because they are assumed, do not act spontaneously, but deliberately pretend to be what they are not. Again, the mark by which he distinguishes false virtues from civic virtues is that civic virtues do not exchange affects for affects, but, unlike spurious virtues, have only one aim, the good. He also sets the civic virtues apart from purificatory and contemplative virtues: (1) civic virtues deal with tripartite soul [69b4–5], purificatory and contemplative virtues do not; (2) civic virtues are 'really' virtues [b2] and 'true' virtues [b3], but not both together, 'really true' virtues, as purificatory and contemplative virtues are [b8]; compare the passage in the *Alcibiades* [129a8–b1], where Plato calls the soul the 'self', but the rational soul the 'self itself': in the same way he now calls civic virtues 'real' virtues only, and purificatory and contemplative virtues 'really true' virtues; (3) another distinction he makes is that civic virtues do not have the character of an initiation, as purificatory and contemplative virtues have [c3–d2]; their very names bear upon this, 'purificatory' from the purifying rites we use in initiation, 'contemplative' from the contemplation of divine things.

7. It is in view of this that Plato paraphrases the Orphic saying [frg. 235] according to which in Hades the uninitiated among us will (figuratively) lie in mud, the initiation being the rapture of virtue; and he goes on:
          'Many carry the thyrsus, few become Bacchus',
meaning by those who carry the thyrsus without becoming Bacchus

---

§ 5. 8. ψευδωνύμους : the word is meant to make explicit what Pl. is supposed to express by ἄτοπος (68b3) and οὐδὲν ὑγιὲς οὐδ' ἀληθὲς ἔχη (69b8). It was already used by Harpocratio, if the account of his view by Dam. § 147 is an accurate one, which is not certain.

§ 6. 1–4. The subject of διακρίνει is Pl., since all this is believed to be said in 68d2–69a5 (cf. § 11). The spontaneous activity of natural and moral virtues (αὐτῷ τῷ εἶναι ποιοῦσι, cf. Pr., *elem.* 122 and Dodds' index s.v. εἶναι) is contrasted with the factitious character of the ψευδώνυμοι.

6–8. Cf. *infra* § 15.2–3. The connection with tripartite soul is elicited from b3–5: μετὰ φρονήσεως (reason), καὶ προσγιγνομένων καὶ ἀπογιγνομένων καὶ ἡδονῶν (desire) καὶ φόβων (spirit).

8–13. Cf. *infra* § 14.

σωφρονοῦσι· πολλοὶ γὰρ δειλοὶ ὄντες δέει μειζόνων κακῶν, οἷον τοῦ δουλεύειν, 5
αἱροῦνται ἀνδρείως ἀποθανεῖν, πάθη παθῶν ἀνταλλαττόμενοι, οἷον τὸν θάνατον
δουλείας, καὶ πολλοὶ οὐκ εἰς κόρον ἐσθίουσιν ἀκόλαστοι ὄντες διὰ τὸ μειζόνων
ἡδονῶν ἀπολαῦσαι ἐν τῇ ὑγιείᾳ. ταύτας οὖν λέγει ὁ Πλάτων ψευδωνύμους
ἀρετὰς καὶ πάθη παθῶν ἀνταλλαττομένας.

Διακρίνει δὲ τὰς φυσικὰς καὶ ἠθι|κὰς τῶν ψευδωνύμων, ὅτι αὗται μὲν 6 (48)
αὐτῷ τῷ εἶναι ποιοῦσι, καθάπερ καὶ ὁ θεὸς καὶ ἡ φύσις τῷ εἶναι ποιοῦσιν,
αἱ δὲ ψευδώνυμοι ἐπίπλαστοι οὖσαι οὐκ αὐτῷ τῷ εἶναι, ἀλλὰ μετὰ βουλῆς
ὑποκρίνονται ὃ μή εἰσιν. ταύτας δὲ διακρίνει τῶν πολιτικῶν, ὅτι αἱ μὲν πολιτικαὶ
οὐ πάθη παθῶν ἀνταλλάττονται, εἴ γε ἐκεῖναι ἕνα σκοπὸν ἔχουσι τὸ ἀγαθὸν 5
α′ καὶ οὐ καθάπερ αἱ ψευδώνυμοι. διακρίνει δὲ πολιτικὰς καθαρτικῶν καὶ θεωρητικῶν, ὅτι αἱ μὲν πολιτικαὶ τῇ τριμερείᾳ τῆς ψυχῆς χρῶνται [69b4–5], αἱ δὲ
β′ καθαρτικαὶ καὶ θεωρητικαὶ οὐχ οὕτως· καὶ ὅτι αἱ μὲν πολιτικαὶ 'τῷ ὄντι' [b2]
εἰσὶν ἀρεταὶ καὶ 'ἀληθεῖς' [b3], οὐ μὴν ἄμφω, τῷ ὄντι ἀληθεῖς, αἱ δὲ καθαρτικαὶ
καὶ θεωρητικαὶ ἅμα ἄμφω εἰσίν, 'τῷ ὄντι ἀληθεῖς' [b8]· ὥσπερ γὰρ ἐν τῷ 10
Ἀλκιβιάδη [129a8–b1] ἔλεγεν 'αὐτὸ' μὲν τὴν ψυχήν, 'αὐτὸ' δὲ 'τὸ αὐτὸ' τὴν
λογικὴν ψυχήν, οὕτω καὶ νῦν 'τῷ ὄντι' μόνον καλεῖ τὰς πολιτικὰς ἀρετάς, 'τῷ ὄντι'
γ′ δὲ 'ἀληθεῖς' τὰς καθαρτικὰς καὶ θεωρητικάς· διακρίνει δὲ αὐτὰς καὶ ἄλλως,
ὅτι αἱ μὲν πολιτικαὶ οὐκ εἰσὶ τελεστικαί, αἱ δὲ καθαρτικαὶ καὶ θεωρητικαὶ
τελεστικαί εἰσι [c3–d2]· διὸ καὶ τὸ ὄνομα τοιοῦτον ἔχουσι, καθαρτικαὶ μὲν ἀπὸ 15
τοῦ καθαρμοῦ, ᾧ ἐν ταῖς τελεταῖς χρώμεθα, θεωρητικαὶ δὲ ἀπὸ τοῦ τὰ θεῖα
ὁρᾶν.

Διὸ καὶ παρῳδεῖ ἔπος Ὀρφικὸν [frg. 235] τὸ λέγον ὅτι 'ὅστις δ' ἡμῶν 7
ἀτέλεστος, ὥσπερ ἐν βορβόρῳ κείσεται ἐν Ἅιδου', τελετὴ γάρ ἐστιν ἡ τῶν
ἀρετῶν βακχεία· καί φησιν
'πολλοὶ μὲν ναρθηκοφόροι, παῦροι δέ τε Βάκχοι',
ναρθηκοφόρους οὐ μὴν Βάκχους τοὺς πολιτικοὺς καλῶν, ναρθηκοφόρους δὲ 5
καὶ Βάκχους τοὺς καθαρτικούς. καὶ γὰρ ἐνδούμεθα μὲν τῇ ὕλῃ ὡς Τιτᾶνες διὰ

---

§ 6. 1 ὅτι αὗται μέν mg. M^c: om. M¹ — 4 ὑποκρίνονται M^c: ἀποκρίνονται M¹

10–12. Cf. Ol., Alc. 4.7–13; 209.15–21; 222.4–14. Ol. h.l. follows the interpretation of Pr. (αὐτό=τριμέρεια τῆς ψυχῆς governed by civic virtues, αὐτὸ τὸ αὐτό=
λογικὴ ψυχή governed by purificatory and contemplative virtues), whereas in the
commentary on the Alc. he seems to prefer that of Dam. (αὐτό=rational soul,
αὐτὸ τὸ αὐτό=the highest, suprarational function of the soul).
16–17. θεωρητικαὶ ἀπὸ τοῦ τὰ θεῖα ὁρᾶν : Ol., Gorg. 143.5–6; Ps.-El. 23,3. Cf. Alex.,
top. 236.24=Suda Θ 214 θεωρία περὶ τὰ θεῖα.
§ 7. Dam. I §§ 165–166. Cf. Ol. 7 § 10.10–18.
1–4. Infra 10 § 3.13–15.
5–9. Cf. Dam. I § 171, which explains the capital in Βάκχοι here and elsewhere,
and the translation 'become Bacchus'.

philosophers still involved in civic life, while the thyrsus-bearers and Bacchants are those on the way to purification. We are chained to matter as Titans by extreme partition, in a world where mine and thine prevail, but we are resuscitated as Bacchus; hence we become more receptive to the gift of prophecy as death draws near, and Dionysus is the patron of death because he is the patron of ecstasy in any form. It is an admirable detail that this part of the conversation begins with a God (in the passage 'The esoteric reason, that we are in a sort of prison' [62b2–4]) and ends with the same God with whom it began, that is, Dionysus. Here, with God's help, ends the first section, to be followed by the arguments on the immortality of the soul. Thus far the present survey.

8. **Is not what is called courage . . . to those so minded [68c5]:** 'What is called': by the crowd, who use the same word while differing as to the thing, for they are ignorant of true virtues.

9. **Who disdain the body and spend their lives in the pursuit of wisdom [68c11–12]:** The commentators wonder why justice is the only virtue that he does not mention. Proclus says that there is no clearly defined temperament to which justice belongs; it is not the same with justice as it is with the other virtues, where we can find a definite temperament corresponding to each; for justice is not a physical virtue, as the others, which Plato calls 'slavish' in the present passage. This, however, is not a plausible explanation; rather we should give the reason stated in the survey [§ 1], that he leaves out justice because it superimposes itself on the other virtues, which was the solution of Damascius [I § 163].

10. **'You know', he said, 'that all other people consider death a great evil?' [68d5–6]:** Suppose someone were to ask us: 'Did Socrates consider death an evil or not? If he did, he is not a philosopher; if he did not, he shows no courage by meeting a fate that he does not consider an evil, for a man cannot be called brave because he is not afraid of things that hold no terror for him'. We can reply that his courage consisted precisely in this, that what terrified other people was not terrible to him; all courage, after all, consists in this.

11. **Yes, my blessed Simmias, I am afraid that this is not [69a6]:** The word 'blessed' is well applied here, because Socrates is raising Simmias to a higher kind of virtues, the civic ones, whose proper characteristic

---

7. *Supra* 1 § 5.11.

8–9. *Supra* 1 § 6.1–5; 6 § 13.

9–12. It is a great beauty in a discourse when it returns to its starting-point, thus moving in that most perfect of shapes, the circle (cf. El., *isag.* 23.26–27; Dav. 45.27–46.1; Ps.-El. 17,1; Steph., *aphor.* I 25, f. 28ᵛ). Here we have the even greater beauty that this circle coincides with the cyclic motion of the soul (Dam. I § 166).

τὸν πολὺν μερισμόν — πολὺ γὰρ τὸ ἐμὸν καὶ σόν, — ἀνεγειρόμεθα δὲ ὡς Βάκχοι·
διὸ καὶ περὶ τὸν θάνατον μαντικώτεροι γινόμεθα, καὶ ἔφορος δὲ τοῦ θανάτου
ὁ Διόνυσος, διότι καὶ πάσης βακχείας. καὶ εὖ γε τοῦ λόγου, διότι καὶ ἀπὸ | θεοῦ   (49)
ἤρξατο, ἡνίκα ἔλεγεν 'ὁ μὲν ἐν ἀπορρήτοις περὶ αὐτῶν λεγόμενος λόγος, ὡς   10
ἔν τινι φρουρᾷ ἐσμεν [62b2–4], καὶ εἰς θεὸν κατέληξεν ἐξ οὗ καὶ ἤρξατο, λέγω
δὴ τὸν Διόνυσον. ἐν οἷς σὺν θεῷ τὸ πρῶτον τμῆμα· διαδέχονται γὰρ οἱ περὶ
ἀθανασίας τῆς ψυχῆς λόγοι. ταῦτα ἔχει ἡ παροῦσα θεωρία.

Οὐ καὶ ἡ ὀνομαζομένη ἀνδρεία τοῖς οὕτω [68c5]: 'ὀνομαζομένη'   8
ὑπὸ τῶν πολλῶν· ὀνόματος γὰρ μόνου κοινοῦ μετέχουσιν [[ἢ]] περὶ τὸ πρᾶγμα
διαφερόμενοι, ἀγνοοῦσι γὰρ τὰς ἀληθεῖς ἀρετάς.

Ὀλιγωροῦσί τε καὶ ἐν φιλοσοφίᾳ ζῶσιν [68c11–12]: ζητοῦσιν οἱ   9
ἐξηγηταὶ τί δή ποτε δικαιοσύνης οὐκ ἐμνημόνευσε μόνης τῶν ἄλλων ἀρετῶν.
καὶ ὁ μὲν Πρόκλος φησὶν ὅτι οὐκ ἔστιν ἐναργῶς κρᾶσις ᾗ ἕπεται ἡ δικαιοσύνη·
οὐδὲ γάρ, ὥσπερ ἐπὶ τῶν ἄλλων ἀρετῶν ἐστιν εὑρεῖν κρᾶσιν ἀφωρισμένην
ἑκάστῃ τῶν ἀρετῶν, οὕτως ἐστὶν εὑρεῖν καὶ ἐπὶ τῆς δικαιοσύνης· οὐ γάρ ἐστιν   5
αὕτη σωματικὴ ἀρετή, καθάπερ αἱ ἄλλαι, ἃς νῦν ἀνδραποδώδεις λέγει. τοῦτο
δὲ οὐ πιθανόν, ἀλλὰ μᾶλλον ῥητέον τὸ ἐν τῇ θεωρίᾳ [§ 1] εἰρημένον, ὅτι ὡς
ἐπιφαινομένην ταῖς ἄλλαις ἀρεταῖς παρῆκεν τὴν δικαιοσύνην, τοῦτο δὴ τὸ
τοῦ Δαμασκίου [I § 163].

Οἶσθα, ἦ δ' ὅς, ὅτι τὸν θάνατον ἡγοῦνται πάντες οἱ ἄλλοι τῶν   10
μεγάλων κακῶν; [68d5–6]: εἰ οὖν τις ἡμᾶς ἔροιτο, 'πότερον ὁ Σωκράτης
κακὸν ἡγεῖτο τὸν θάνατον ἢ οὐ κακόν; εἰ μὲν οὖν κακόν, οὐ φιλόσοφος· εἰ δὲ
οὐ κακόν, οὐκ ἀνδρεῖος, οἷς μὴ ἡγεῖται κακοῖς ἐπιβατεύων, οὐ γὰρ ἀνδρεῖος
ὁ τὰ ⟨μὴ⟩ φοβερὰ μὴ δεδιώς'; ἢ κατ' αὐτὸ | τοῦτο ἀνδρεῖος, διότι τὰ τοῖς   5 (50)
ἄλλοις φοβερὰ οὐ φοβερὰ ᾤετο, ἐπεὶ καὶ πᾶσα ἀνδρεία ἐν τούτῳ θεωρεῖται.

Ὦ μακάριε Σιμμία, μὴ γὰρ οὐκ αὐτή [69a6]: προσφόρως νῦν τὸ   11
'ὦ μακάριε', διότι ἀνάγει ἐπὶ μείζους ἀρετάς, τὰς πολιτικάς, αἷς οἰκεῖον τὸ
μακαριστόν. διὰ δὲ τῶν εἰρημένων διακρίνας τὰς ψευδωνύμους ἀρετὰς τῶν
ἠθικῶν καὶ φυσικῶν ἐντεῦθεν τὰς πολιτικὰς διακρίνει καὶ τῶν ψευδωνύμων.

---

§ 8. 1 ἀνδρία M — 2 ἢ M: del. Fh
§ 10. 2 μεγάλων κακῶν M, Pl. B, T v.l.: μεγίστων κακῶν εἶναι Pl. B²TWY —
5 μὴ¹ Wk: om. M — 6 ἀνδρία M
§ 11. 1 γὰρ] om. Pl. TY | οὐκ αὐτή] οὐχ αὕτη Pl. — 3 μακάριστον M

---

§ 9. Dam. I § 163. Cf. supra § 1.4–5. – Dam. first reports Pr.'s answer
(ἢ ὅτι οὐκ ἔχει πάθη σωματικά, οἷς ἐμφανίζεται), then adds his own in the very much
abridged form: ἢ ὅτι μᾶλλον τῶν τριῶν ἦν μορίων. – More on the relation between
justice and the other cardinal virtues in El., isag. 18.29–19.2, with ἐποχεῖσθαι instead
of the ἐπιφαίνεσθαι here (line 8).
§ 10. Dam. I § 157.
§ 11. 1–3. A different explanation of ὦ μακάριε Ol., Alc. 171.6–9.
3–4. Supra § 6.1–5.

is that they entitle a man to be qualified as happy. In the preceding passage Socrates has distinguished the spurious virtues from the moral and natural ones; he now proceeds to make a further distinction between civic and spurious virtues.

12. **As though they were coins, when there is in fact only one right sort of coin [69a9–10]**: When referring to the exchange of spurious virtues he rightly uses the plural 'coins', but the civic virtues he calls 'coin' in the singular, because unity is more proper to the latter than to the former.

13. **When bought and sold [69b1–2]**: Socrates keeps up the metaphor of currency by mentioning purchase and sale.

14. **And true virtue in general [69b3]**: As we said [§ 6], he calls the civic virtues 'really' virtues separately and 'true' virtues separately, but to describe the purifying virtues he uses the words in combination.

15. **But the really true thing is a purification from all this [69b8–c1]**: 'Purification' is a derivative from the 'purificatory' life. In this passage Socrates distinguishes the purifying virtues from the civic ones, after which he further distinguishes between purifying and contemplative virtues, in that the former avoid affects and those who possess them are still in search of wisdom, while the latter are already secure from emotions.

16. **And it may well be that those to whom our initiatory rites [69c3–4]**: At first sight they may seem contemptible because they express themselves in mythical language.

17. **And whether I have had any success, I shall know for certain when I have arrived in that other land [69d5]**: Not that Socrates did not know, nor does he say this because in doubt; rather, his motive is philosophical caution, since it is bad taste to praise oneself. For the same reason he said above [63b9–c4]: 'That I am going to good masters, I know for a certainty, but if I shall come also to good men, is still unsure'. Some maintain that Plato is sceptical as regards the immortality of the soul and that this explains these words of Socrates. The philosopher Ammonius, however, has written a monograph on our passage to defend him. How, indeed, could he be sceptical, when in the sequel he proves the eternity of the soul by unshakable arguments, and when he has said elsewhere [*Rep.* X 618e4–619a1] that we must take this down to Hades with us as an iron-bound conviction?

18. **If you find my defense more convincing [69e3–4]**: It was of course

---

§ 14. *Supra* § 6.8–13.
§ 15. 2–3. *Supra* § 6.6–8.
3–5. The achieved result (πεφεύγασιν) is supposed to be expressed in the perfects κεκαθαρμένος τε καὶ τετελεσμένος (c6–7) and πεφιλοσοφηκότες (d2). Cf. Porph., *sent.* 32 (pp. 25.10–26.4) on the distinction between purificatory and contemplative virtues: ἐπεὶ δὲ καὶ κάθαρσις ἡ μέν τις ἦν καθαίρουσα ἡ δὲ κεκαθαρμένων, αἱ καθαρτικαὶ ἀρεταὶ κατ' ἄμφω θεωροῦνται τὰ σημαινόμενα τῆς καθάρσεως· καθαίρουσί τε γὰρ τὴν ψυχὴν

"Ωσπερ νομίσματα, ἀλλ᾽ ἢ ἐκεῖνο μόνον νόμισμα ὀρθόν [69a9–10]:   **12**
τὰς μὲν καταλλαγὰς τῶν ψευδωνύμων ἀρετῶν πληθυντικῶς 'νομίσματα' καλεῖ,
τὰς δὲ πολιτικὰς ἀρετὰς ἑνικῶς 'νόμισμα'· οἰκεῖον γὰρ αὐταῖς τὸ ἓν ἧπερ ταύταις.
᾽Ωνούμενά τε καὶ πιπρασκόμενα [69b1–2]: ἐνέμεινε τῇ μεταφορᾷ   **13**
τοῦ νομίσματος μνησθεὶς ὠνῆς καὶ πράσεως.

Καὶ ξυλλήβδην ἀληθὴς ἀρετή [69b3]: ἰδοὺ ἐπὶ τῶν πολιτικῶν 'τῷ   **14**
ὄντι' ἰδίᾳ καὶ 'ἀληθεῖς' ἰδίᾳ, οὐ μὴν ἅμα ἄμφω, ἐπὶ δὲ τῶν καθαρτικῶν ἅμα
ἄμφω.

Τὸ δὲ ἀληθὲς τῷ ὄντι ἢ κάθαρσίς τις τῶν τοιούτων [69b8–c1]:   **15**
παρωνύμως ἀπὸ τῆς καθαρτικῆς ζωῆς 'κάθαρσις'. διακρίνει δὲ διὰ τούτων
τὰς καθαρτικὰς ἀρετὰς τῶν πολιτικῶν· εἶτα καὶ ταύτας διακρίνει τῶν θεωρητικῶν, ὅτι αἱ μὲν φεύγουσι τὰ πάθη καὶ φιλοσοφοῦσιν οἱ ταύτας ἔχοντες, αἱ δὲ
πεφεύγασιν.   5

Καὶ κινδυνεύουσι καὶ οἱ τὰς τελετὰς ἡμῖν οὗτοι [69c3–4]: κινδυ-   **16**
νεύουσι φαῦλοι εἶναι διὰ τὸ μυθώδη λέγειν.

Καί τι ἠνύσαμεν, ἐκεῖσε ἐλθόντες σαφές [69d5]: οὐχ ὅτι ἠγνόει **17** (51)
ὁ Σωκράτης καὶ διστάζων ταῦτα λέγει, ἀλλὰ τοῦτο διὰ φιλόσοφον εὐλάβειαν·
φορτικὸν γὰρ τὸ ἑαυτὸν ἐπαινεῖν. οὕτω δὴ καὶ ἀνωτέρω [63b9–c4] ἔλεγεν
'ὅτι παρὰ δεσπότας ἀγαθοὺς ἄπειμι, ἀκριβῶς οἶδα, εἰ δὲ παρὰ ἀνδράσιν
ἀγαθοῖς, οὔπω δῆλον'. τινὲς δέ φασιν ὅτι ἀμφιβάλλει ὁ Πλάτων εἰ ἀθάνατος   5
ἡ ψυχή, διὸ ταῦτα λέγει ὁ Σωκράτης. ὁ δέ γε φιλόσοφος ᾽Αμμώνιος μονόβιβλον
ἔγραψεν εἰς τὸ χωρίον ἀπολογούμενος ὑπὲρ αὐτοῦ. πῶς δὲ ἀμφιβάλλειν εἶχεν
ὁ ἐφεξῆς διὰ ἀρραγῶν λόγων δεικνὺς τὴν ψυχὴν ἀίδιον καὶ ὁ ἀλλαχοῦ [Rep. X
618e4–619a1] εἰπὼν ὅτι 'δεῖ ἀδαμαντίνοις δεσμοῖς ταῦτα ἔχοντα κατιέναι
εἰς "Αιδου';   10

Εἴ τι οὖν ὑμῖν πιθανώτερός εἰμι ἐν τῇ ἀπολογίᾳ [69e3–4]: εἰκὸς   **18**
γὰρ ἦν αὐτὸν πιθανώτερον εἶναι παρὰ τοῖς μαθηταῖς ἢ παρὰ τῷ δήμῳ, διότι
διδασκαλικῇ πειθοῖ οὐκ ἦν χρήσασθαι ἐπὶ δήμου. καὶ ὅτι παρὰ μὲν τῷ δήμῳ

---

§ 12. 1 ἀλλ᾽ ἢ M, Pl. B (ἀλλὴ T): ἀλλ᾽ ἢ Pl. WY | νόμισμα] τὸ νόμισμα Pl.
§ 15. 1 ἢ] post κάθαρσις Pl. B²W
§ 16. 1 κινδυνεύουσι] -ωσι Pl.
§ 17. 1 καί τι] καὶ τί M | σαφές M¹: τὸ σαφές Mᶜ, Pl.

καὶ καθαρθείσῃ σύνεισι. τέλος γὰρ τὸ κεκαθάρθαι τοῦ καθαίρειν. Porph. paraphrases
Plot. I 2,4.1–5, who seems to have had Ph. 69c2–d2 in mind.
§ 17. Some of the arguments from Amm.'s monobiblos on Ph. 69d5, proving
that Pl. was not a sceptic, may be extant supra 2 § 16; 6 § 14; infra 10 § 15; El.,
cat. 110.12–28; Proleg. 10–11.
§ 18. Dam. I § 174. Cf. supra 2 § 16.
3. Pl., Gorg. 455a1.

to be expected that Socrates would find more belief with his disciples than with the people of Athens, since a crowd would not have been open to persuasion by instruction. Besides, the trial before the people dealt with his life as a member of the community, that before his disciples with his progress to purification, and the greater the degree of exactitude of the one subject as compared with the other, the greater, we may assume, the degree of probability too.

9

Lecture **

1. To this speech of Socrates Cebes replied [69e6–70c5].

In his proof that the philosopher is fearless of death because he is in hopes of going to better masters and friends, Socrates has introduced these two topics, first, the existence of a providence that determines what is due to each, if the philosopher is to meet the destiny he deserves, and, secondly, the immortality of the soul, if he is to obtain his due; Cebes makes no difficulties as to the first, the existence of a providence, because he is convinced of that, but he questions the immortality of the soul, and this gives rise to the subsequent arguments on immortality. Socrates now demonstrates that the soul is immortal by the following reasoning: 'If the living and the dead proceed from each other, it follows that our souls continue to exist in Hades; the former is true; therefore so is the latter'.

2. In order that we can grasp this argument, let us start a little farther back. Plato acknowledges two kinds of opposites, the qualities themselves and the substances that possess them [103a11–c2]; the qualities themselves, he holds, do not pass into each other, but they succeed each other (no part of whiteness is involved in the change into black), while

---

Lect. 9. **The argument from opposites: Cebes' question; preliminaries and objections.** The most striking feature in Ol.'s treatment of the argument from opposites is the absence of any allusion to Dam.'s entirely new approach. Either Ol.'s text of Dam. did not include the *monobiblos* that contains so signal a contribution to the question (Dam. I §§ 207–252) or he preferred to simplify things by ignoring it. The main contents of the *theoria* are the following: If Socrates' confident expectation of a better fate after death is to be justified, there must be a life after death, and Socrates now proceeds to prove this by the argument from opposites (§ 1). Of the two kinds of opposites in *Ph.* 103a11–c2 (forms, or accidents), Socrates is now concerned with accidents, which require a permanent substrate; since the body is not permanent, this must be the soul (§ 2). Objection: the conclusion would apply to the vegetative soul also (§ 3). Objections against the premise that opposites proceed from each other: asleep and awake, young and old, do not fit the rule (§§ 4–5). At the end there is an unexpected criticism of the doctrine of reincarnation (§ 6).

περὶ τῆς πολιτικῆς αὐτοῦ ζωῆς ἐκρίνετο, παρὰ δὲ τοῖς μαθηταῖς περὶ τῆς
καθαρτικῆς, καὶ ἀκριβέστερον τοῦ ὑποκειμένου τὸ ὑποκείμενον· διὸ εἰκὸς 5
καὶ πιθανώτερον.

9

Πρᾶξις σὺν θεῷ

Εἰπόντος δὲ τοῦ Σωκράτους ταῦτα ὑπολαβὼν ὁ Κέβης [69e6–70c5]. 1
Δείξας ὁ Σωκράτης ὅτι ὁ φιλόσοφος ἀδεὴς περὶ τὸν θάνατον διότι ἐλπίζει
παρὰ κρείττοσι δεσπόταις καὶ φίλοις ἀπιέναι, ἐπειδὴ δύο ταῦτα εἰσήγαγεν,
α′ καὶ τὸ εἶναι πρόνοιαν τὸ κατ᾽ ἀξίαν ἑκάστῳ ἀφορίζουσαν, ἵνα καὶ λήξεων
β′ προσ|ηκουσῶν τύχῃ ὁ φιλόσοφος, ἔτι μὴν καὶ τὸ τὴν ψυχὴν ἀΐδιον εἶναι, ἵνα 5(52)
τύχῃ τῶν κατ᾽ ἀξίαν, ὁ Κέβης πρὸς μὲν τὸ πρῶτον, τὸ εἶναι πρόνοιαν, οὐκ
ἀπορεῖ ἅτε δὴ πεπεισμένος τούτῳ, ἐπιζητεῖ δὲ εἰ ἡ ψυχὴ ἀθάνατος· διὸ διαδέχονται οἱ περὶ ἀθανασίας τῆς ψυχῆς λόγοι. δείκνυσιν οὖν ὁ Σωκράτης ὅτι ἡ
ψυχὴ ἀθάνατος διὰ λόγου τοιούτου· ʽεἰ τὸ ζῶν καὶ τὸ τεθνεὸς ἐξ ἀλλήλων,
εἰσὶν ἄρα ἡμῶν αἱ ψυχαὶ ἐν ῞Αιδου· ἀλλὰ μὴν τὸ πρῶτον· καὶ τὸ δεύτερον ἄρα᾽. 10
῞Ινα δὲ τούτῳ παρακολουθήσωμεν, ἄνωθέν ποθεν ἀρξώμεθα. ἰστέον τοίνυν 2
ὅτι διττὰ τὰ ἐναντία βούλεται εἶναι ὁ Πλάτων, ἢ γὰρ αὐτὰς τὰς ποιότητας ἢ
τὰ ἔχοντα τὰς ποιότητας [103a11–c2]· καὶ αὐτὰς μὲν τὰς ποιότητας οὐ βούλεται
μεταβάλλειν εἰς ἀλλήλας, ἀλλὰ μετὰ ἀλλήλας αὐτὰς βούλεται, διότι οὐδὲν
μέρος τῆς λευκότητος ἐν τῇ μεταβολῇ τῇ εἰς τὸ μέλαν, τὰ δέ γε δεδεγμένα 5
σώματα βούλεται μεταβάλλειν εἰς ἄλληλα, διότι μένει ⟨τι⟩ ἐν τῇ μεταβολῇ τῶν
ἐναντίων, οἷον τὸ σῶμα. τούτων οὕτως ἐχόντων, ἐπειδὴ καὶ ζωὴ καὶ θάνατος
ἐναντία ἐστί (καὶ τοῦτο δείκνυσιν ὁ Πρόκλος ἤτοι ὁ Συριανός· συντάττει γὰρ
αὐτὰ τοῖς οἰκείοις ὑπομνήμασιν, λέγω δὴ τὰ Συριανοῦ, μὴ γράφων εἰς αὐτὰ
ὡς τοῦ διδασκάλου γράψαντος· δείκνυσιν οὖν τοῦτο οὕτως· ʽζωὴ καὶ θάνατος 10

---

§ 1. δὲ M¹: δὴ Mᶜ, Pl.
§ 2. 4 post βούλεται] εἶναι add. Nv (sed cf. 10 § 14.2) — 6 τι Wk: om. M (διό τι
scr. Nv) —

§ 1. 2–8. Cf. supra 2 § 7.
8–10. Dam. I § 184. Infra 10 § 3.6–8.
§ 2. 1–3. Dam. I § 189.
3–7. Dam. I § 190.1–3. Simpl., phys. 182.19–23 ἀλλὰ πῶς τὰ ἐναντία οὐκ ἐξ
ἀλλήλων; αὐτὸ γὰρ τοὐναντίον δειχθήσεται, ὅτι ἐξ ἀλλήλων τὰ ἐναντία, ἐκ γὰρ μέλανος
τὸ λευκὸν καὶ ἐξ ἀμούσου τὸ μουσικόν. ἢ ὡς μὲν μετ᾽ ἄλληλα γινόμενα ἐξ ἀλλήλων λέγοιτο,
ὡς δὲ ἐκ στοιχείων καὶ ὑπομενόντων (ὡς ἐκ ξύλου κλίνη λέγεται γίνεσθαι), οὐκ ἂν γένοιτο
τὸ ἐναντίον ἐκ τοῦ ἐναντίου. Philop., phys. 111.30–112.1 ἐξ ἀλλήλων δὲ πάλιν λέγεται
τῷ μετ᾽ ἄλληλα εἶναι, ὥσπερ ὁ Πλάτων ἐν τῷ Φαίδωνι κυριώτερον ὠνόμασε ʽμετ᾽ ἄλληλα᾽
αὐτὰ εἰρηκώς, διότι μετὰ τὸ λευκὸν τὸ μέλαν εὐθὺς γίνεσθαι πέφυκε, καὶ πάλιν φθαρέντος
τοῦ μέλανος τὸ λευκόν, καὶ ἐπὶ πάντων ὁμοίως.
6. ⟨τι⟩ : cf. line 13.
7–11. Dam. I § 185.
8–10. See Introduction pp. 17–18.
10–11. Cf. infra 10 § 3.20–22.

the recipients in his opinion actually pass into each other, since there is a constant element in the succession of opposites, viz. the body itself. This being so, inasmuch as life and death, too, are opposites (as is shown by Proclus, or rather by Syrianus, whose work Proclus has incorporated in his own commentary, dismissing the subjects already treated by his master; the argument runs 'Life and death are integration and dissociation, these are opposites, and the inference is obvious'); inasmuch, furthermore, as these two pass into each other in the way qualities do, that is to say, they succeed each other, it follows that in the process of their change there must be something constant, as there is in every change; and since the body does not remain, but is dissolved into its elements, the only other possibility is that the soul remains; and if it remains always, it follows that the soul is everlasting.

3.   However, on this line of reasoning, vegetative soul also is immortal, seeing that it is integrated with the plant and dissociated from it. No, for this is not integration or dissociation properly so called, because the thing that is integrated has to exist before the integration, and the thing that is dissociated similarly, a condition which is not fulfilled in the case of vegetative soul. If someone should object that this point is not granted with regard to rational soul either, viz. that it exists before the integration and after the dissociation, so that Plato is begging the question, we answer that the point *is* granted by the interlocutor himself. Cebes, in fact, has asked if the soul after leaving the body vanishes as smoke or air let out of a bag: now if he compares it to air and smoke, his opinion must be that it continues to exist after the separation from the body.

4.   Some object that not all opposites proceed from each other: e.g. the sleeping proceeds from the waking, but the waking does not necessarily proceed from the sleeping, because a child is born waking without having slept before; why, then, should it be absurd to suppose

---

12–15.   Dam. I § 190.3–8.

12.   The insertion of the negative by M^c (prompted by 3–4) spoils the sense: the sequel shows that a change *is* assumed, but one that consists in a succession of different accidents (ἤτοι . . .).

§ 3.   The objection that, if the argument holds, vegetative soul too must be immortal (recapitulated *infra* 10 § 5.1–4) is found neither in Syrianus (Dam. I §§ 193–201; 243–251) nor in Dam. (I §§ 209–220) nor in Strato (Dam. II § 63), and is therefore probably a contribution of Amm. Cf. the passage from Philop. cited above at 3 § 4.8, where it is said that vegetative soul is the life of the 'earthly' body, as irrational soul is of the pneumatic body. Both Syrianus and Dam. discuss the case of irrational soul, which they consider separable (Dam. I §§ 199; 217; 239; 250), and they omit vegetative soul apparently on the same ground on which Ol. here declares it not to be a case in point, viz. because there is no real being joined or separated.

3–4.   ὡσαύτως τε καὶ τὸ διακρινόμενον : scil. εἶναι μετὰ τὴν διάκρισιν. – Cf. *supra* 3 § 4.8–10: what is really separable not only can be separated, but can also exist

σύγκρισις καὶ διάκρισίς ἐστιν, ταῦτα ἐναντία, καὶ δῆλον τὸ συμπέρασμα') — ἐπειδὴ ταῦτα [οὐ] μεταβάλλει εἰς ἄλληλα ὡς αἱ ποιότητες, ἤτοι μετ' ἀλλήλά εἰσιν, δεῖ ἄρα ἐν τῇ μεταβολῇ τούτων εἶναί τι τὸ μένον, διότι καὶ ἐν πάσῃ μεταβολῇ· καὶ ἐπειδὴ τὸ σῶμα οὐ μένει, ἀναστοιχειοῦται γάρ, ὑπόλοιπόν ἐστι τὴν ψυχὴν μένειν· καὶ εἰ ἀεὶ μένει, ἀεὶ ἄρα ἐστὶν ἡ ψυχή.   15
᾽Αλλ' ὅσον ἐπὶ τούτῳ, καὶ ἡ φυτικὴ ψυχὴ ἀθάνατός ἐστιν, εἴ γε καὶ συγκρίνεται   3
τῷ φυτῷ καὶ | διακρίνεται. ἡ οὐκ ἀκριβὴς αὕτη ἡ σύγκρισις οὐδὲ ἡ διάκρισις·   (53)
δεῖ γὰρ τὸ συγκρινόμενον εἶναι πρὸ τῆς συγκρίσεως, ὡσαύτως τε καὶ τὸ διακρινόμενον, ὅπερ οὐκ ἔστιν εἰπεῖν ἐπὶ τῆς φυτικῆς ψυχῆς. εἰ δέ τις λέγοι
'ἀλλ' οὐδὲ ἐπὶ τῆς λογικῆς ὡμολόγηται ὅτι ἐστὶ πρὸ τῆς συγκρίσεως καὶ μετὰ   5
τὴν διάκρισιν, καὶ τὸ ἐν ἀρχῇ αἰτεῖται ὁ Πλάτων', ῥητέον ὅτι τοῦτο ὁμολογούμενον ἐξ αὐτοῦ τοῦ προσδιαλεγομένου. ὁ γὰρ Κέβης ἠρώτησεν εἰ καθάπερ
καπνὸς ἢ πνεῦμα ἐξιὸν ἐξ ἀσκοῦ μετὰ τὴν ἔξοδον φθείρεται· εἰ δὲ πνεύματι
αὐτὴν ἀπείκασεν καὶ καπνῷ, δῆλος ἄρα ἐστὶ βουλόμενος καὶ μετὰ τὴν ἔξοδον
ὑφεστάναι αὐτήν.   10
᾽Αποροῦσι δέ τινες λέγοντες ὅτι οὐ πάντα τὰ ἐναντία ἐξ ἀλλήλων γίνεται·   4
ἰδοὺ γὰρ τὸ καθεῦδον μὲν ἐκ τοῦ ἐγρηγορότος γίνεται, οὐ πάντως δὲ καὶ τὸ
ἐγρηγορὸς ἐκ τοῦ καθεύδοντος, τὸ γὰρ παιδίον ἐγρηγορὸς γεννᾶται μὴ πρότερον
καθευδῆσαν· τί οὖν ἄτοπον καὶ τὸν θάνατον μὲν ἐκ τῆς ζωῆς γίνεσθαι καὶ τὸ
ζῶν εἰς τὸ τεθνεὸς μεταβάλλειν, οὐκέτι δὲ καὶ τὸ ἀνάπαλιν; διὰ τί γὰρ ὁ Πλάτων   5
συνέταξε ζωὴν καὶ θάνατον τοῖς μεταβάλλουσιν ἄμφω εἰς ἄλληλα ἐναντίοις, οὐ μὴν
ὕπνῳ καὶ ἐγρηγόρσει;

---

12 οὐ ins. Mᶜ: del. Wk
§ 3. 6 διάκρισιν Wk: σύγκρισιν M
§ 4. 4 ἄτοπον mg. Mᶜ: om. M¹

---

separately.
5–11. **Dam. I § 185.** Cf. § 223.
6. αἰτεῖται : the middle in the logical sense e.g. Ar., top. VIII 13, 163a20; 23.
§§ 4–5. **Dam. I §§ 195–196.** The objections are numbers (v) and (vi) of Syrianus (ap. Dam.) and the solutions are also his; there is no question of those given by Dam. I §§ 246–247. It is hard to guess how number (v) came to be split up into two separate objections (§ 4.8–9 and 10–11, answers § 5.7–9 and 10–23). There can be no textual error, since in both cases the wording of the question is confirmed by the answer; besides, there is nothing in all the available material (Syr.-Pr., Dam., Strato) that is close enough to have been replaced by either one of these ἀπορίαι. A possible solution is that Ol. presented the question as one, but gave two answers (out of four in Syr.-Pr. ap. Dam. I § 196), the first in combination with the point of sleeping and waking (§ 5.7–9, similar to, though not identical with, Dam. I § 196.1–2), the second separately (§ 5.10–23=Dam. I § 196.4–6). The reportator, deceived by an apparent difference between οὐ γίνεται νεώτερον ἐκ πρεσβυτέρου and τὸ πρεσβύτερον οὐ μεταβάλλει εἰς τὸ νεώτερον might then have made two questions out of one. In the recapitulation at 10 § 5.7–11 there is only one.

that death comes from life and the living passes into the dead, but not the other way? Why, indeed, does Plato class life and death with those opposites that pass into each other, and not with sleep and waking?

Again, they say that the older comes from the younger, not, however, the younger from the older.

A third difficulty they raise is that younger changes into older, but older does not change into younger.

5. To the first and second objections Proclus (i.e. Syrianus) [Dam. I § 195] replies that the waking is not created by nature as a primary end, but as a concomitant; if nature produced it for its own sake, it would certainly have proceeded from the sleeping. We can compare it to the shavings that result as a by-product of planing when the carpenter dresses a plank, without his intending to produce them: in the same way the waking state is a concomitant not aimed at by nature. For the same reason the younger does not come from the older, because it has not been created by nature as a primary end, otherwise it would certainly have come from the older.

To the third objection, that opposites do not necessarily pass into each other, since we observe that the older does not pass into the younger, Syrianus [Dam. I § 196] answers that there is a way in which even the older can pass into the younger, and the solution he finds is this: suppose A is seven years old and B is newly born, then A begins by being a whole lifetime older than B (seven exceeds zero by all its seven units); as time goes on, A turns eight, B one, and instead of being a whole lifetime older, A now exceeds B by a fraction of his own age (eight exceeds one by a fraction, not by the whole of itself); and so, in the course of time, the proportion of eight to one diminishes and becomes smaller, which means that older passes into younger; A becomes relatively younger as compared with the original proportion. This is also true in actual fact: when a child is just born, we see a great distance between ourselves and it, then as time goes on, we see the excess decrease and the relative difference between the ages become smaller.

---

§ 5. 5. ἕλικες : cf. Origen, c. Cels. 6,56 κακὰ τοίνυν . . . ὁ θεὸς οὐ πεποίηκεν, ἀλλὰ τοῖς προηγουμένοις αὐτοῦ ἔργοις . . . ἐπηκολούθησεν, ὥσπερ ἐπακολουθεῖ τοῖς προηγουμένοις τοῦ τέκτονος ἔργοις τὰ ἑλικοειδῆ ξέσματα καὶ πρίσματα.

10–23. Recapitulated at 10 § 5.7–13, where there is a reference to *Parm.* 152a5–7, which shows that Syrianus' solution was suggested by that dialogue. Cf. Pr., *Parm.* 1231.5–14 εἰ δὲ καὶ ἄλλος τις τρόπος ἐστὶ τοῦ καὶ πρεσβύτερον ἑαυτοῦ τι γιγνόμενον

Πάλιν φασὶν ὅτι τὸ μὲν πρεσβύτερον ἐκ νεωτέρου γέγονεν, οὐκέτι δὲ καὶ τὸ νεώτερον ἐκ τοῦ πρεσβυτέρου.

Ἐκ τρίτου δὲ ἀποροῦσι λέγοντες ὅτι τὸ μὲν νεώτερον μεταβάλλει εἰς τὸ 10 πρεσβύτερον, οὐκέτι δὲ καὶ τὸ πρεσβύτερον εἰς τὸ νεώτερον.

Πρὸς μὲν οὖν τὸ πρῶτον καὶ τὸ δεύτερόν φησιν ὁ Πρόκλος ἤτοι ὁ Συριανὸς 5 [Dam. I § 195] ὅτι τὸ ἐγρηγορὸς οὐ κατὰ πρῶτον λόγον ἐκ τῆς φύσεως γίνεται, ἀλλὰ παρέπεται τοῦτο· ἐπεὶ εἰ προελομένης τῆς φύσεως τοῦτο ἐγίνετο, πάντως ἂν ἐκ καθεύδοντος ἐγεγόνει. ἀλλ᾽ ὥσπερ ἐν τῷ ἀποξέειν τὸν τέκτονα τὸ ξύλον ἕλικες παρακολουθοῦσιν ἐν τῇ ξέσει τοῦ τέκτονος μὴ | προελομένου ταύτας 5 (54) ποιῆσαι, οὕτω καὶ ἐπὶ τοῦ ἐγρηγορότος παρακολούθημά ἐστι τοῦτο τῆς φύσεως οὐ προελομένης. οὕτω δὲ καὶ νεώτερον γίνεται οὐκ ἐκ πρεσβυτέρου, διότι οὐ κατὰ πρῶτον σκοπὸν τοῦτο ὑπὸ τῆς φύσεως ἐγένετο, ἐπεὶ πάντως ἂν ἐκ πρεσβυτέρου ἐγεγόνει.

Πρὸς δὲ τὸ τρίτον τὸ λέγον ὅτι οὐκ ἀνάγκη μεταβάλλειν τὰ ἐναντία εἰς 10 ἄλληλα, ἰδοὺ γὰρ τὸ πρεσβύτερον οὐ μεταβάλλει εἰς τὸ νεώτερον, φησὶν [Dam. I § 196] ὅτι δυνατὸν τῷ τρόπῳ τούτῳ μεταβάλλειν καὶ τὸ πρεσβύτερον εἰς τὸ νεώτερον, καὶ μηχανᾶται τρόπον τοιοῦτον· ἐὰν γάρ, φησίν, ὑποθώμεθά τινα ζ᾽ χρόνων ὄντα καί τινα νεωστὶ τεχθέντα, οὗτος κατ᾽ ἀρχὰς μὲν ὅλῳ ἑαυτῷ ὑπερέχει τοῦ τεχθέντος (τὰ γὰρ ἑπτὰ τοῦ μηδενὸς ὅλῳ ὑπερέχει), προκόπτοντος 15 δὲ τοῦ χρόνου ὁ μὲν ὀκτὼ ἐτῶν γίνεται, ὁ δὲ ἐνιαυτοῦ, καὶ μεταβάλλει ἐκ τοῦ ὅλῳ ἑαυτῷ ὑπερέχειν εἰς τὸ μέρει τινὶ ἑαυτοῦ ὑπερέχειν (τὰ γὰρ ὀκτὼ τοῦ ἑνὸς μέρει καὶ οὐχ ὅλῳ ἑαυτῷ ὑπερέχουσιν), καὶ οὕτω προκόπτοντος τοῦ χρόνου καθαιρεῖται ὁ ὀκταπλασίων λόγος καὶ ἐλάσσων γίνεται, ὥστε μεταβάλλειν τὸ πρεσβύτερον ἐπὶ τὸ νεώτερον, κατὰ μέρος γὰρ νεώτερος γίνεται ὡς πρὸς τὸν 20 ἐξ ἀρχῆς παραβαλλόμενος. οὕτω δὲ ἔχει καὶ τὰ πράγματα· ὁρῶμεν γάρ τινος ἄρτι τεχθέντος ὑπερβάλλοντας ἡμᾶς πολλῷ, εἶτα προϊόντος τοῦ χρόνου καθαιρουμένην τὴν ὑπεροχὴν καὶ ἐλάττονα τὸν λόγον τῆς αὐξήσεως γινόμενον.

---

§ 5. 7 οὗ¹ ins. Mᶜ: om. M¹ — 18 ἑαυτῷ Nv: -ῶν M — 21 παραβαλλόμενος Nv: -ον M

ἅμα γίγνεσθαι καὶ νεώτερον, ἡ δευτέρα ὑπόθεσις ἡμᾶς ἀναδιδάσκει· ἡ γὰρ αὐτὴ πρόσθεσις (πρόθεσις edd.) κατὰ μὲν τὴν ἀριθμητικὴν μεσότητα ἑαυτοῦ ποιεῖ πρεσβύτερον τὸ τὴν προσθήκην τοῦ χρόνου ταύτην λαβόν, κατὰ <δέ> γε τὴν γεωμετρικὴν τὸ αὐτὸ νεώτερον ἐλασσούμενον κατὰ τὸν λόγον, ὡς ἐν ἐκείνοις ἔσται καταφανές. Pr. is commenting upon 141c1–4, but refers to the second hypothesis 152a5–7 ἆρ᾽ οὖν μεμνήμεθα ὅτι νεωτέρου γιγνομένου τὸ πρεσβύτερον πρεσβύτερον γίγνεται;

6. So much for the objections. Since, however, there is the vexed question of Plato's belief in metempsychosis (or more correctly reincarnation, because we do not have a plurality of souls informing one body, which would be metempsychosis, but one soul vesting itself in one body after another), let us prove that the doctrine of metempsychosis (or reincarnation, which comes to the same thing after all) is false. The question that Plato himself [87b2–88b8] raises with regard to rational soul, whether it is not possible that, like a weaver who wears out many garments and finally dies himself, the soul after wearing many bodies may be destroyed herself afterwards – this question can be asked for even better reason concerning irrational soul: since it continues to exist after separation from the body, we cannot tell whether, after wearing many bodies, it will not be destroyed itself finally. Now if we denied [§ 3?] that irrational soul is reincarnated, though it continues to exist after the separation, we must deny this even more strongly of rational soul, and Plato will either have to grant the reincarnation even of irrational soul, or have to deny it in the case of rational soul too. Thus far the survey.

7. And has a certain power and understanding [70b3–4]: i.e. 'has some kind of life and cognitive ability', for 'power' means vital activity, 'understanding' means disposition to knowledge.

8. Shall we then continue our story [70b6]: Does this really mean that what Socrates says is a story? The answer is that Socrates uses the word 'story-telling' for a demonstration based on something derivable, as in the present argument, where he proves the immortality of the soul not

---

§ **6.** What this puzzling paragraph is intended to express, seems to be roughly this: If there is any truth at all in Cebes' suggestion of a limited number of reincarnations followed by final extinction, it applies to irrational, not to rational soul; we denied reincarnation in the case of irrational soul; therefore there is no reincarnation at all. Not only is the argument logically deficient, but it cannot represent the view of Ol., who believed in reincarnation, cf. *infra* 10 § 1; 12 § 2.15–18; *Gorg.* 97.4–9; 97.26–98.2; 109.18–21; *Alc.* 27.10–16; *mete.* 147.24–148.6. The passage 10 § 5.4–6, in particular, indicates that he followed the doctrine of Pr. (above 3 § 4.8, note): rational soul and the luminous body, which it animates, are immortal; irrational soul survives as long as the pneumatic body does, through a number of incarnations; vegetative soul dies with the 'shell-like' body. The whole of 10 § 5 is, in fact, a summary of 9 §§ 3–5 (and 6), either as Ol. himself arranged the material, or as he found it arranged in his source: (1) objections against the συνημμένον : (a) vegetative and (b) irrational soul; (2) objections against the πρόσληψις : (a) awake and asleep, (b) old and young. One possible reconstruction of what happened is the following: Ol. dealt with the objections in the order mentioned, but reserved the question of irrational soul for separate discussion at the end of the *theoria*, in the context of reincarnation generally. In § 6 he went on to discuss the terms μετεμψύχωσις and μετενσωμάτωσις (lines 1–6; he refers back to this at 10 § 1.2), then the extent of reincarnation, concluding that what Cebes suggests in the case

Καὶ ταῦτα μὲν ὡς πρὸς τὰς ἀπορίας. ἀλλ' ἐπειδὴ εἴωθεν ἄνω καὶ κάτω 6
⟨θρυλεῖσθαι⟩ ὡς εἰσάγει ὁ Πλάτων τὴν μετεμψύχωσιν — ἤτοι τὴν μετενσω-
μάτωσιν, διότι οὐ πολλαὶ ψυχαὶ ἓν σῶμα εἰδοποιοῦσιν, ἐπεὶ αὕτη μετεμψύχωσις
ἦν, ἀλλὰ μία ψυχὴ διάφορα σώματα μεταμπίσχεται, — φέρε δείξωμεν ψευδῆ
ὄντα τὸν περὶ τῆς μετεμψυχώσεως λόγον (ἤτοι μετενσωματώσεως· ταὐτὸν 5
γὰρ σημαίνει). ὁ γὰρ αὐτὸς ἐπὶ τῆς λογικῆς ἀπορεῖ [87b2–88b8], λέγων ὅτι
ζητητέον μήποτε ἡ ψυχή, δίκην ὑφάντου πολλὰ ἱμάτια κατατρίψαντος καὶ
ὕστερον φθαρέντος, οὕτω | καὶ ἡ ψυχὴ πολλὰ σώματα ἐνδυσαμένη ὕστερον καὶ (55)
αὐτὴ διεφθάρη, τοῦτο οὖν ἐστιν εὐλογώτερον ἐπὶ τῆς ἀλόγου ἁρμόσαι· ἐπειδὴ
γάρ ἐστι καὶ μετὰ τὸν χωρισμὸν τοῦ σώματος, ἄδηλον μήποτε πολλὰ σώματα 10
ἐνδυσαμένη ὕστερον διαφθαρῇ. εἰ οὖν μὴ ἐλέγομεν [§ 3?] τὴν ἄλογον μετεμψυχοῦσθαι καίτοι οὖσαν μετὰ τὸν χωρισμόν, πολλῷ μᾶλλον οὐδὲ τὴν λογικήν,
καὶ ἢ δώσει ὁ Πλάτων καὶ ἐκ τῆς ἀλόγου μετεμψύχωσιν ἢ οὐδὲ ἐκ τῆς λογικῆς.
ταῦτα ἔχει ἡ θεωρία.

Καί τινα δύναμιν ἔχει καὶ φρόνησιν [70b3–4]: τινὰ ζωὴν ἔχει καὶ 7
γνωστικὴν †ἐπιστήμηγν† ἡ μὲν γὰρ 'δύναμις' τὴν ζωτικὴν ἐνέργειαν δηλοῖ,
ἡ δὲ 'φρόνησις' τὴν ἐπιστημονικὴν ἕξιν.

Βούλει οὖν διαμυθολογῶμεν [70b6]: τί οὖν; μῦθος τὰ λεγόμενα ὑπὸ 8
τοῦ Σωκράτους; ἢ τὴν ἐξ ἑπομένου πίστιν μυθολογίαν ἐκάλεσεν ὁ Σωκράτης,
οἷός ἐστιν ὁ προκείμενος λόγος· κατασκευάζει γὰρ τὴν ἀθανασίαν τῆς ψυχῆς
οὐκ ἐκ τῆς οὐσίας ὁρμώμενος, ἀλλ' ἔκ τινος ἑπομένου, τοῦ μεταβάλλειν τὸν
θάνατον καὶ τὴν ζωὴν εἰς ἄλληλα. ταύτην οὖν μυθολογίαν εἶπεν. 5

---

§ 6. 2 θρυλεῖσθαι Nv: om. M — 7 ὑφαντοῦ M — 9 αὐτὴ μ: αὕτη M
§ 7. 1 τινὰ μ: τίνα M — 2 ἐπιστήμην] aut ἐνέργειαν aut ἕξιν leg.
§ 8. 1 βούλῃ M¹ | οὖν om. Pl. | διαμυθολογῶμεν Mᶜ, Pl.: -οῦμεν M¹

---

of rational soul, i.e. that after wearing out a succession of bodies it may be doomed
ultimately to perish itself, applies in reality to irrational soul; it survives, but
not forever (10 § 5.4–6). The reportator, probably (at least there is no evidence
that a third person handled the text), then tried to turn this into an argument
against reincarnation; identifying the vegetative soul of § 3 with the irrational soul
of the present paragraph, he introduced the fallacious *a fortiori* reasoning outlined
above.

1–2. ἄνω καὶ κάτω ⟨θρυλεῖσθαι⟩ : cf. 7 § 2.5.

2–4. The objection against the term μετεμψύχωσις formulated here (certainly
not for the first time) must have led to the coining of the word μετενσωμάτωσις
and the revival of παλιγγενεσία. Logically, it is valid only as far as the passive
form of the verb is concerned; the *nomen actionis*, as well as the (non-existent)
active and middle, could denote a change of the object animated, just as
μεταμπίσχεσθαι a change of the garment worn. Occurrences listed in *LSJ*, cf. *ibid.*,
Preface ix, n. 1; H. Dörrie, *Kontroversen um die Seelenwanderung im kaiserzeitlichen
Platonismus*, Hermes 85, 1957, 414–435 (428, n. 4).

§ 7. 2. ἐπιστήμην must have replaced ἐνέργειαν or a similar word under the
influence of ἐπιστημονικόν in the next line.

§ 8. Cf. 10 § 3, where the same διαμυθολογῶμεν is made to apply to formal
deductive proof (i.e. proof ἐκ τῆς οὐσίας).

on the ground of its essence, but of the accidental fact that death and life pass into each other. This is what he means by a 'story'.

9. That anyone overhearing us, even if he were a comic poet [70b10–c1]: What is the point of Plato's reference to the comic poets here? What it amounts to is: 'I shall not give the comic poets an excuse to jeer at me'. This because Eupolis [frg. 352] says of Socrates:

"And what about this shabby jabberer,
who is expert at everything, . . .
the only thing that he forgets is how to earn a living."

'This time he will have no reason to say this of me, now that I am endeavoring to learn whether our souls continue to exist in Hades or not, for this is a question of practical importance'. We must admire Plato for turning the lines of Eupolis to account so opportunely; the power of opportunity is great indeed: 'Opportunity is the soul of treatment' and 'Opportunity is time with rightness added'. Note, however, that he mentions him only in passing and does not quote the passage at length.

10

Lecture **

1. Now there is this ancient doctrine which I remember [70c5–72e2].

The doctrine of metempsychosis, or reincarnation, is inevitable if we start from these two premises, the eternity of the world and the immortality of the soul: if both are to be maintained, there must necessarily be metempsychosis, or else the infinite will exist actually. Therefore the question is raised if Aristotle, who teaches that the world

---

§ 9. 4–7. Ascl., *met.* 135.23–24 cites the lines in the form: μισῶ δὲ καὶ Σωκράτη τὸν πτωχὸν ἀδολέσχην, / ὃς τῶν ἄλλων μὲν πεφρόντικεν, / πόθεν δὲ φάγῃ, τούτου κατημέληκεν (first line confirmed by Pr., *Parm.* 656.24). Both Ascl. and Ol. must have the quotation from Amm., hence the incomplete second line in both.

10–11. Cf. Pr., *Alc.* 120.14–15 τὸ τὰς ψυχὰς εἶναι τοὺς καιροὺς τῶν θεραπειῶν . . ., ὅ φησιν ὁ τῶν Ἀσκληπιαδῶν Ἱπποκράτης (where ψυχάς is the predicate, so that τάς should probably be dropped, cf. *decem dub.* 51.6 λέγοντες εἶναι ψυχὰς θεραπειῶν τοὺς καιρούς). Ol., *Alc.* 39.7 ψυχαὶ γὰρ τῶν θεραπειῶν οἱ καιροί. Steph., *aphor.* I 1, f. 3ʳ αἱ ψυχαὶ τῶν βοηθημάτων οἱ καιροί εἰσιν. The closest approach in Hippocrates is *de morbis* I 5 (VI 146–148 L.): (cases of immediate danger) ὁ μέντοι καιρός ἐστιν ἐπὴν πάθῃ τι τούτων ὤνθρωπος· ὅ τι ἄν τις πρὸ τοῦ τὴν ψυχὴν μεθεῖναι ὠφελήσῃ, τοῦθ' ἅπαν ἐν καιρῷ ὠφέλησεν, where, however, there is no question of the use of ψυχή as the essence of things (as in 'brevity is the soul of wit'; some examples in *LSJ* s.v. ψυχή IV 6). *CPG*, Apostol. 9,42 καιρὸς ψυχὴ πράγματος, a proverb which, without being derived from the passage in Hippocr., may have influenced the form Pr. gave to it.

11. Ol., *Alc.* 39.8–9 (after the words quoted above) καὶ ὡς Ἀριστοτέλης φησί, 'καιρός ἐστι χρόνος προσλαβὼν τὸ δέον' καὶ 'χρόνος προσλαβὼν τὸ εὖ.' Ar., *anal. pr.* I 36, 48b35–36 πάλιν ὅτι ὁ καιρὸς οὐκ ἔστι χρόνος δέων (Philop., *anal. pr.* 342.8 τινὲς γὰρ

Εἰπεῖν τινα συνακούσαντα, οὐδὲ εἰ κωμῳδοποιὸς εἴη [70b10–c1]: 9
τί βούλεται ἐνταῦθα τῷ Πλάτωνι ἡ μνήμη τῶν κωμῳδοποιῶν; ἢ τὸ λεγόμενον
τοῦτό ἐστιν, ὅτι 'οὐ δώσω χώραν τοῖς κωμῳδοποιοῖς διαλοιδορεῖσθαί μοι'·
ὁ γὰρ Εὔπολίς φησιν [frg. 352] *περὶ τοῦ Σωκράτους·*
  'τί δῆτα ἐκεῖνον τὸν ἀδολέσχην καὶ πτωχόν, 5 (56)
  ὃς τἆλλα μὲν πεφρόντικεν,
  ὁπόθεν ⟨δὲ⟩ καταφαγεῖν ἔχοι, τούτου κατημέληκεν'.
'νῦν οὖν οὐκ ἐρεῖ ταῦτα περὶ ἐμοῦ ζητοῦντος μαθεῖν εἰ εἰσὶν αἱ ψυχαὶ ἡμῶν
ἐν Ἅιδου ἢ μή, χρειώδης γὰρ ἡ τοιαύτη ζήτησις'. καὶ εὖ γε τοῦ Πλάτωνος
ἐν καιρῷ παρῳδήσαντος τὰ Εὐπόλιδος· μέγιστα γὰρ δύναται ὁ καιρός· 'ψυχαὶ 10
γὰρ 'τῶν θεραπειῶν οἱ καιροί', καὶ ἔστιν ὁ καιρὸς 'χρόνος προσλαβὼν τὸ εὖ'.
ὅρα δὲ ὅτι ἐπ' ὀλίγον αὐτοῦ ἐμνημόνευσεν καὶ οὐκ ἐνέμεινεν παρῳδῶν τοῦτο.

10

Πρᾶξις σὺν θεῷ

Παλαιὸς μὲν οὖν ἐστί τις ὁ λόγος οὗτος οὗ μεμνήμεθα [70c5–72e2]. 1
ā *Ὁ περὶ μετεμψυχώσεως λόγος ἤτοι μετενσωματώσεως ἀναγκαῖός ἐστι*
δύο τούτων προληφθέντων, τοῦ τὸν κόσμον ἀίδιον εἶναι καὶ τοῦ τὴν ψυχὴν
ἀθάνατον εἶναι· εἰ γὰρ ἄμφω σῴζεται, ἀνάγκη μετεμψύχωσιν εἶναι, ἵνα μὴ
τὸ ἄπειρον ὑποστῇ ἐνεργείᾳ. διὸ καὶ Ἀριστοτέλης ἀμφιβάλλεται, λέγων τὸν 5
κόσμον ἀίδιον, μήποτε τὴν ψυχὴν θνητὴν λέγει, διὰ τὸ ἐπιτωθάζειν αὐτὸν ἐν
τῇ Περὶ ψυχῆς [I 3, 407b22] *τῇ μετεμψυχώσει λέγοντα· 'κατὰ γὰρ τοὺς*

§ 9. 1 συνακούσαντα Μ¹: νῦν ἀκούσαντα Μᶜ, Pl. | κωμῳδοποιὸς Μ¹ (Pl. TW):
κωμῳδιοποιὸς Μᶜ (Pl. BT²Y) — 7 δὲ Wyttenbach: om. Μ
§ 1. 1 ὁ λόγος οὗτος Μ, Pl. B²T²W: λόγος οὗτος infra § 6.1 Μᶜ, Pl. TY: λόγος
infra § 6.1 Μ¹, Pl. B

οὕτως ὁρίζονται τὸν καιρόν, ὅτι ἔστι χρόνος δέων); eth. *Nic.* I 4, 1096a26–27 (τἀγαθόν)...
ἐν χρόνῳ καιρός. Cf. also Pr.*Parm.*1224.40
12. The rule is stated by Hermog., *meth.* 30; cf. Ol., *Alc.* 104.3–6; *Gorg.* 142.10–12.
Lect. 10. The argument from opposites: analysis and objections. Metempsychosis
is the inevitable corollary of three essential Platonic doctrines (§ 1.2–10). The
purpose of the argument is not, as Iambl. thought, to prove the soul's immortality,
but its survival (§ 1.11–20). Three prevalent opinions: (1) the soul perishes with
the body, because it is the harmony of the body, (2) it perishes with the body,
because it is material, (3) it may survive the body for some time (§ 2). Formal
analysis of the argument (§§ 3–4). Objections repeated from the preceding lecture:
vegetative and irrational soul; waking and sleeping, young and old (§ 5). The whole
theoria runs almost exactly parallel with Dam., who in this part follows Syr.-Pr.
with very rare variations. The first paragraph, though without a counterpart in
Dam., must also come from Pr., see note below.
§ 1. 2–10. Pr., *Rep.* II 338.21–28 (speaking of reincarnation in human form)
τοῦτο δὲ οὐδ' ἂν Ἀριστοτέλης ἀπαγορεύσειεν, εἴπερ ἀθανάτους τε εἶναι δίδωσιν τὰς ψυχὰς
καὶ τῷ πλήθει πεπερασμένας καὶ τὸν κόσμον ἀίδιον· ὧν τὸ μὲν καὶ λέγει καὶ δείκνυσιν,
ἀίδιον εἶναι τὸν κόσμον (cael. I 10–12)· τὸ δὲ ὁμολογεῖ σαφῶς, ὅταν λέγῃ περὶ τοῦ δυνάμει
νοῦ 'καὶ τοῦτο μόνον τῶν ἐν ἡμῖν ἀθάνατον' (an. III 5, 430a23)· τὸ δὲ ἀναγκάζεται
συγχωρεῖν, τὸ πᾶν ἀίδιον πλῆθος εἶναι πεπερασμένον (cf. cael. I 5–7).

is eternal, does not hold the soul to be mortal, since in the *De anima*
[I 3, 407b22] he ridicules metempsychosis, saying 'According to
Pythagorean myths the living comes back to life from what is dead'.
As he calls it a myth, he clearly does not believe in metempsychosis,
and this is the strongest argument against Aristotle to prove that he
must deny the immortality of the soul.

This is the first point we want to make; the second is that the aim of
the present argument is not to prove that the soul is immortal, but that
it continues to exist for some time after the separation from the body,
and Iamblichus is wrong in supposing that each argument taken separately
proves its immortality. This is characteristic of the ardor of Iamblichus,
who from his high coign of vantage looks down in ecstasy, but it does
not suit the context: for neither does the questioner define the problem
that way, nor does the respondent prove that the soul is immortal. Cebes,
in fact, asked if it is possible for the soul when separated from the body
to continue to exist and not to be dispersed like breath, and Socrates
shows that it survives for some time after the separation from the body,
but not that it does so for good. Note that these statements hold good
of irrational soul also, and as far as the present argument goes, it too
will be everlasting.   2.   There have been the following three false beliefs
about soul: (1) the soul is destroyed with the body, as in the doctrine
that soul is harmony, which was held by Simmias [85e3–86d4] and certain
Pythagoreans; (2) soul, being a kind of tenuous body, like smoke, is
dispersed and annihilated upon leaving the body, which was the belief
of Homer

('His soul leaving the body flew away to Hades' [*Il.* 16.856; 22.263];
and

'Gibbering it went underground, like smoke' [*Il.* 23.100–101]).
It is also the opinion of Cebes, who is now raising the objection, and
Socrates refutes it by showing that the soul survives for some time;
(3) the ignorant soul is destroyed immediately upon leaving the body,
while the soul of the wise, tempered by the virtues, survives until the

---

11–20.   Dam. I § 183.1–6.

13–16.   Dam. I § 207.1–6; cf. *infra* 11 § 2.1–5; 13 § 4.6–18.

13–14.   Iambl., *Ph.* frg. 1.

14.   ἐνθουσιῶν ὡς κατὰ περιωπήν: Norvin's conjecture ἐνθουσιῶν ὡς (instead of
ἐνθουσιῶντος) is supported by Pr., *Rep.* II 154.23–24 ἐντεῦθεν γὰρ ὡς ἐκ περιωπῆς
ὅλον τὸν κόσμον καὶ τὰ ἐν αὐτῷ καθορᾶν. The alternative is deleting φησιν.

ibid. The quotation from Homer, *Il.* 18.262, is used in the same context by
Dam. I § 207.4 and, in a different one, *vit. Isid.* p. 82.8. Since there is no other
evidence that Ol. knew Dam.'s monograph (I §§ 207–252), we must assume that
both Dam. and Ol. took it from Syrianus, who must also have discussed Iambl.'s
view in his introduction.

19–20.   Dam. I § 199; *supra* 9 § 6.6–13; *infra* § 5.

§ 2.   Dam. I § 183.6–8; § 178.1–5.

Πυθαγορείους μύθους τὸ ζῶν ἐκ τοῦ τεθνεῶτος ἀναβιώσκεται'. εἰ οὖν μῦθον ἐκάλεσεν, δῆλός ἐστι μὴ δοξάζων μετεμψύχωσιν, καὶ μέγιστον τοῦτο ἐπιχείρημα κατὰ 'Αριστοτέ|λους ἀναγκαστικὸν τοῦ τὴν ψυχὴν μὴ λέγειν ἀθάνατον.　10 (57)

β　Πρῶτον τοῦτο, ‹β' δὲ› ὅτι ὁ σκοπὸς τῷ προκειμένῳ λόγῳ δεῖξαι οὐκ ἀθάνατον τὴν ψυχήν, ἀλλ' ἐπιδιαμένουσαν χρόνον τινὰ μετὰ τὸν χωρισμὸν τοῦ σώματος, καὶ οὐ καθάπερ 'Ιάμβλιχος οἴεται, ἕκαστον λόγον δεικνύναι τὴν ἀθανασίαν τῆς ψυχῆς. ταῦτα γὰρ ἐνθουσιῶν ὡς κατὰ περιωπήν φησιν, 'οἷος ἐκείνου θυμός', οὐ μὴν τῇ λέξει ταῦτα οἰκεῖα· οὐδὲ γὰρ ὁ ἐρωτῶν τοῦτο ὥρισεν τὸ πρόβλημα　15 οὔτε ὁ ἀποκρινόμενος ἔδειξε τὴν ψυχὴν ἀθάνατον. ὁ μὲν γὰρ Κέβης ἠρώτησεν εἰ δυνατὸν τὴν ψυχὴν χωρισθεῖσαν ἀπὸ τοῦ σώματος ἐπιδιαμένειν καὶ μὴ δίκην πνεύματος διασκορπίζεσθαι, καὶ ὁ Σωκράτης δείκνυσιν ὅτι ἐπιδιαμένει χρόνον τινὰ μετὰ τὸν χωρισμὸν τοῦ σώματος, οὐ μὴν ὅτι καὶ ἀεὶ ἔδειξεν. καὶ ὅτι ταῦτα καὶ τῇ ἀλόγῳ ὑπάρχει, καὶ ὅσον ἐπὶ τούτῳ ἔσται καὶ αὕτη ἀίδιος. τρεῖς γὰρ　2 α' αὗται δόξαι ψευδεῖς περὶ ψυχῆς γεγόνασι, μία μὲν ἡ λέγουσα ἅμα φθείρεσθαι τῷ σώματι τὴν ψυχήν, ὡς ἡ λέγουσα τὴν ψυχὴν ἁρμονίαν, ἧς δόξης ἦν ὁ β' Σιμμίας [85e3–86d4] καί τινες τῶν Πυθαγορείων. δευτέρα δὲ ἡ λέγουσα τὴν ψυχὴν οἷον σῶμα οὖσαν λεπτομερὲς καὶ καπνῷ ἐοικυῖαν μετὰ τὴν ἔξοδον τὴν　5 ἀπὸ τοῦ σώματος σκεδάννυσθαι καὶ φθείρεσθαι, ἧς δόξης ἦν καὶ ὁ ποιητὴς ('ψυχὴ δὲ ἐκ ῥεθέων πταμένη "Αϊδόσδε βεβήκει' [Π 856, X 362] καὶ

'ᾤχετο τετριγυῖα κατὰ χθονὸς ἠΰτε καπνός' [Ψ 100–101]).

ταύτης τῆς δόξης καὶ ὁ νῦν ἀπορῶν Κέβης ἐστί, πρὸς ἣν καὶ ἐνίσταται ὁ　10 γ' Σωκράτης δεικνὺς ὅτι ἐπιδιαμένει χρόνον τινά. τρίτη δόξα ἡ λέγουσα τὴν μὲν ἀπαίδευτον ψυχὴν ἐξιοῦσαν τοῦ σώματος εὐθὺς φθείρεσθαι, τὴν δὲ πεπαιδευμένην στομωθεῖσαν ταῖς ἀρεταῖς ἐπιμένειν τὴν ἐκπύρωσιν τοῦ παντὸς κόσμου, ἧς δόξης ἦν καὶ ὁ Ἡράκλειτος.

---

11 β' δὲ Wk: om. M — 14 ἐνθουσιῶν ὡς Nv: ἐνθουσιῶντος Μ

---

3. Cf. Philolaus A 23; Echecrates 4; Pythagoreans B 41.

4–11. See note on Dam. I § 222.1–4.

7. The critic of Pl. in Athenaeus XI 507e says that he stole his notion of immortality from Homer, Il. 18.856.

11–14. The metaphor of the hardening of the soul is not used in Von Arnim's fragments on the survival of the souls of the wise (SVF II frgs. 809–811); it is standard, however, in the description of the soul as pneuma hardened by cold (II frgs. 804, 806). The terms πεπαιδευμένος and ἀπαίδευτος are also Stoic: cf. Aristo, I frg. 396 and Epict., man. 5 (cited by Pr., Alc. 287.9–12).

14. Heraclitus: probably inferred (on the analogy of the Stoic view) from frg. B 77: 'wet souls die' (and therefore fiery souls survive). His supposed doctrine of a world conflagration (A 1, p. 141.20–22; A 5, p. 145.21–22) would imply the limited survival of individuals, again on the analogy of Stoic doctrine.

universal conflagration, which was the opinion, for example, of Heraclitus.

3. The third point we must examine is the logical progress of the argument, which is called a 'story' in the text [70b6]; the word 'story' is applied to ratiocinative knowledge inasmuch as it is attained by means of a middle term and is not a direct vision of reality, just as intellection could be called knowledge from images and is only a 'story' as compared to archetypal knowledge; and thus we see that the syllogistic method, of which the Peripatos is so proud, is called 'story-telling' by Plato. The reasoning, however, runs as follows: 'If the living and the dead proceed from each other, it follows that our souls continue to exist in Hades; the former is true; therefore so is the latter'. That the living and the dead do proceed from each other is corroborated in the text by the testimony of the ancient poets, of Orpheus in particular, who says [frg. 224a]:

'The same inhabit the house as fathers and sons,
as respected wives and cherished daughters.'

(Everywhere indeed Plato borrows from Orpheus, thus when he said above [62b2–3] 'The esoteric reason for this' and again [69c8–d1]

'Many carry the thyrsus, few become Bacchus'.)

But Empedocles, too, says [frg. B 117]:

'At one time I was a youth and a maiden,
a bird, a shrub, a swift fish in the sea [rising from the sea].'

Proclus, however (i.e. Syrianus) presents the demonstration that the living and the dead proceed from each other in this form: 'Life and death are integration and dissociation, these two are opposites, and opposites pass into each other; therefore the living and the dead also pass into each other.' 4. The thesis that opposites pass into each other is proved in the text on three grounds. In the first place by induction: Socrates cites a great many examples of opposites and shows that they pass into

---

§ 3. 1–6. Cf. *supra* 9 § 8. Usually myths are supposed to appeal to the imagination (Ol., *Gorg*. 239.19–30), but since myth is essentially an image of reality, any section of the line in the *Rep*. (VI 509d1–511e5) can be called a 'myth' in relation to the preceding one, in this case ratiocinative knowledge as compared to intellection.

5–6. The Platonists are always on the defensive against the Peripatetic claim to superiority in logic: Alcin., *did*. 6; Hermias 51.32–52.1; Pr., *Alc*. 339.11–14; Amm., *int*. 83.8–21; 201.15–19; Ol., *Alc*. 118.12–15; 121.16–18; *Gorg*. 27.9–11; 128.11–15; *cat*. 17.37–18.10.

6–8. **Dam.** I § 184; cf. Ol. 9 § 1.8–10. Philop., *anal. pr*. 358.14–17 ὁ γοῦν Πλάτων λαβὼν ὅτι εἰ τὸ ζῶν καὶ τὸ τεθνηκὸς ἐξ ἀλλήλων, εἰσὶν ἡμῶν αἱ ψυχαὶ ἐν Ἅιδου, ἀλλὰ μὴν τὸ πρῶτον, καὶ τὸ δεύτερον ἄρα, οὐ μόνον τὴν πρόσληψιν, ἀλλὰ καὶ τὸ συνημμένον κατεσκεύασε.

8–18. With the exception of the parenthesis at 13–15 the paragraph is from Syr.-Pr.; cf. Pr., *Rep*. II 338.11–339.16, with the same quotation from the *Orphica* (frg. 224a) for reincarnation in human shape and a second (frg. 224b) for reincarnation in animals; the fragment of Empedocles occurs *ibid*. 333.6–10 as an instance of

γ̄   Τρίτον ζητήσωμεν τίς ἡ συλλογιστικὴ ἀγωγὴ τοῦ ἐπιχειρήματος, ἦν καὶ   3
μῦθον καλεῖ ἡ λέξις [70b6], | τὴν διὰ συλλογισμοῦ γνῶσιν μῦθον καλέσασα (58)
ὡς διὰ μέσου ὅρου γινομένην καὶ μὴ αὐτοπτοῦσαν τὰ πράγματα, καθάπερ ἡ
νοερὰ οἷον ἐξ εἰκόνων ἐστὶν γνῶσις καὶ μῦθός ἐστιν παραβαλλομένη πρὸς τὴν
παραδειγματικήν· ὥστε τὴν συλλογιστικὴν μέθοδον, ἐφ᾽ ᾗ ὁ Περίπατος σεμνύ-   5
νεται, μῦθον ὁ Πλάτων ἐκάλεσεν. ἔστι δὲ ὁ λόγος οὗτος· 'εἰ τὸ ζῶν καὶ τὸ
τεθνεὸς ἐξ ἀλλήλων, εἰσὶν ἄρα ἡμῶν αἱ ψυχαὶ ἐν Ἅιδου· ἀλλὰ μὴν τὸ πρῶτον·
καὶ τὸ δεύτερον ἄρα᾽. καὶ ὅτι τὸ ζῶν καὶ τὸ τεθνεὸς ἐξ ἀλλήλων, κατασκευάζει
ἡ λέξις ἐκ τῆς μαρτυρίας τῶν παλαιῶν ποιητῶν, ἀπὸ Ὀρφέως, φημί, λέγοντος
[frg. 224a]·   10
      'οἱ δ᾽ αὐτοὶ πατέρες τε καὶ υἱέες ἐν μεγάροισιν
      ἠδ᾽ ἄλοχοι σεμναὶ κεδναί τε θύγατρες᾽.
(πανταχοῦ γὰρ ὁ Πλάτων παρῳδεῖ τὰ Ὀρφέως· οὕτω γοῦν καὶ ἀνωτέρω [62b2–3]
ἔλεγεν 'ὁ μὲν οὖν ἐν ἀπορρήτοις περὶ αὐτῶν λεγόμενος᾽ καὶ πάλιν [69c8–d1]
      'πολλοὶ μὲν ναρθηκοφόροι, παῦροι δέ τε Βάκχοι᾽.)   15
ἀλλὰ μὴν καὶ ὁ Ἐμπεδοκλῆς ἔφη [frg. B 117]·
      'ἤδη γάρ ποτ᾽ ἐγὼ γενόμην κοῦρός τε κόρη τε
      θάμνος τ᾽ οἰωνός τε καὶ εἰν ἁλὶ νήχυτος [ἔξαλος ἄμφορος] ἰχθύς᾽.
ὁ δέ γε Πρόκλος ἤτοι ὁ Συριανὸς κατασκευάζει ὅτι τὸ ζῶν καὶ τὸ τεθνεὸς ἐξ
ἀλλήλων, ὅτι 'ἡ ζωὴ καὶ ὁ θάνατος σύγκρισις καὶ διάκρισις, ταῦτα δὲ ἐναντία, 20
τὰ δὲ ἐναντία μεταβάλλει εἰς ἄλληλα· ὥστε καὶ τὸ ζῶν καὶ τὸ τεθνεὸς μεταβάλλει εἰς ἄλληλα᾽. ὅτι γὰρ τὰ ἐναντία μεταβάλλει εἰς ἄλληλα, δείκνυσιν ἡ   4
α᾽ λέξις τριχόθεν. πρῶτον μὲν ἐκ τῆς ἐπαγωγῆς· παρατίθεται γὰρ πολλὰ ἐναντία,
β᾽ ἃ δείκνυσι μεταβάλλοντα εἰς ἄλληλα [70d7–71a11]. δεύτερον ἐκ τῶν γενέσεων
αὐτῶν καὶ τῶν ὁδῶν· εἰ γὰρ αἱ ὁδοὶ μεταβάλλουσιν εἰς ἀλλήλας, οἷον ἡ λεύκανσις

---

§ 3.   1 τρίτον] ex corr. in spat. 2 litt. Mᶜ — 12 ἠδ᾽ μ: εἰ δ᾽ M — 18 ἔξαλλος ἄμφορος
(sic) M: secl. Fh

---

the belief of reincarnation in plants.
   12.   Pr., *Rep. l.c.* has the correct reading εὔκοσμοί τ᾽ ἄλοχοι καὶ μητέρες ἠδὲ θύγατρες.
The intrusive κεδναί is of course Homeric (*Od.* 1.432, 10.8), the σεμναί *might be*
Biblical (from *1 Tim.* 3,11 γυναῖκας ὡσαύτως σεμνάς); see other instances of Biblical
language, Ol., *Alc.*, Introd. p. IX.
   13–15.   Cf. *supra* 7 § 10.10–12; 8 § 7.1–4.
   18.   The numerous variants in this line are reported by Diels, *Poetarum
philosophorum fragmenta*, Berlin 1901, 153–154. Ol. cited εἰν ἁλὶ νήχυτος, of which
εἰν ἁλί is supported by Clement and Cyril (against ἔξαλος or ἐξ ἁλός in all the other
witnesses); νήχυτος 'flowing' is unsupported and obviously due to association with
νήχειν. A reader wrote the text as known to him in the margin (ἔξαλλος ἄμφορος),
and this reading was added to our text. Its first part is standard (apart from the
spelling); the second part, ἄμφορος, which could mean ἀνάφορος=ἀνώφορος, 'rising
from the sea', is not an uninteresting variant beside ἔμπνοος, ἔμπορος, ἔμπυρος
and φαίδιμος.
   19–22.   Dam. I § 185. *Supra* 9 § 2.10–11.
   § 4.   1–11.   Dam. I § 186.

each other [70d7–71a11]. Secondly, from their processes of becoming and the ways that lead to them: if the processes pass into each other, e.g. whitening and blackening, the results (white and black) must even more certainly pass into each other [71a12–72a10]. Thirdly, by the argument that Nature will be lame, if either one of a pair of opposites passes into the other, while the other remains unchanged, and eventually one of the pair would run out and the remaining one would be an opposite no longer, having nothing into which to change; if, for example, waking were to change into sleep, but sleep no longer into waking, we shall find the story of Endymion utterly pointless, because not only he but everybody else will sleep forever. (This was a man who was said to be always asleep, because he spent his life in astronomical observation in a solitary place, and so he was described as a lover of the Moon. The same is said of Ptolemy, who lived for forty years in the so-called Wings of Canobus devoting himself to astronomy, hence the stone tablets there, in which he had his astronomical discoveries engraved.) Similarly, if dissociation changes into integration, everything will be integrated at last and the word of Anaxagoras [frg. B 1] will come true, 'All things were together' [72a11–d5].

5. We have already discussed [9 § 3] an objection against the hypothetical syllogism, viz. that, as far as this argument goes, vegetative soul will also be immortal, and so will irrational soul, so that the latter too will be reincarnated; we have answered this by alleging, as regards vegetative soul, that it cannot be said to be integrated or dissociated at all, and as regards irrational soul that, according to Plato, it *is* subject to metamorphosis and after wearing out many 'shell-like' bodies, like a weaver who has worn out many garments, is ultimately destroyed itself.

We have discussed also [9 § 4] the objections against the minor premise based on the instances of waking and sleeping, younger and older (if any one should say that these are not opposites but correlatives, the answer is that young and aged in any case are not correlatives but opposites in their own right). Our solution [9 § 5] has been that these conditions are not created by Nature for their own sake, but are by-products comparable to wood-shavings. This is the solution we find offered by Plato in the *Parmenides* [152a5–7] and Syrianus appropriately uses it here, because it is relevant and really Platonic. Thus far the survey; and this, with God's help, is also the end of the argument from the opposites.

11–13. Endymion was rationalized into an astronomer by Mnaseas (*FHG* III p. 149: schol. Apoll. Rhod. 4.264; schol. Germanic., Aratea, ed. Breysig, Berlin 1867 [repr. Hildesheim 1967], 201.6–10; Fulgent., *mythol.* 2,16). Cf. Plin., *nat. hist.* 2,6,43; Lucian., *de astrol.* 18; Nonnus, *Dionys.* 41.379–381.

13–15. F. Boll, *Studien über Cl. Ptolemäus*, Jahrb. für class. Philol., Suppl. 21, 1894, 49–244 (65–66), rejects this as an inference from the Tablets of Canobus

εἰς τὴν μέλανσιν, πολλῷ μᾶλλον καὶ τὰ τέλη μεταβάλλουσιν εἰς ἄλληλα, οἷον 5
γ′ τὸ λευκὸν καὶ τὸ μέλαν [71a12–72a10]. τρίτον ὅτι χωλεύει ἡ φύσις, εἰ ἓν
μὲν | τῶν ἐναντίων μεταβάλλει εἰς τὸ ἄλλο, ἓν δὲ οὐ μεταβάλλει, καὶ τῷ χρόνῳ (59)
ἐπιλείποι θάτερον τῶν ἐναντίων, καὶ οὐδὲ ἐναντίον ἔσται τὸ λοιπόν, μηδὲν
ἔχον εἰς ὃ μεταβαλεῖ, — καὶ τὸ ἐγρηγορέναι, εἰ τύχοι, μεταβάλλοι εἰς τὸ
καθεύδειν, οὐκέτι καὶ τὸ καθεύδειν εἰς τὸ ἐγρηγορέναι, λῆρον τὸν Ἐνδυμίωνα 10
ἀποδείξομεν· οὐδὲ γὰρ μόνος οὗτος, ἀλλὰ πάντες ἀεὶ καθευδήσουσιν. ἐλέγετο
δὲ οὗτος ἀεὶ καθεύδειν, διότι ἀστρονομῶν ἐπ’ ἐρημίας διέτριβεν, διὸ καὶ φίλος
τῇ Σελήνῃ. ὃ καὶ περὶ Πτολεμαίου φασίν· οὗτος γὰρ ἐπὶ μ′ ἔτη ἐν τοῖς λεγομένοις
Πτεροῖς τοῦ Κανώβου ᾤκει ἀστρονομίᾳ σχολάζων, διὸ καὶ ἀνεγράψατο τὰς στήλας
ἐκεῖ τῶν εὑρημένων αὐτῷ ἀστρονομικῶν δογμάτων. καὶ εἰ ἡ διάκρισις εἰς τὴν 15
σύγκρισιν μεταβάλλει, τῷ χρόνῳ πάντα συγκριθήσεται, καὶ ἀληθὲς ἔσται τὸ
Ἀναξαγόρου [frg. B 1] τὸ ‘ἦν ὁμοῦ πάντα χρήματα’ [72a11–d5].

Ἠπορήσαμεν δὲ ἡμεῖς [9 § 3] καὶ πρὸς τὸ συνημμένον λέγοντες ὅτι ὅσον ἐπὶ 5
τούτῳ καὶ ἡ φυτικὴ ψυχὴ ἀθάνατος ἔσται καὶ ἡ ἄλογος, καὶ ἔσται καὶ αὕτη
μετεμψυχουμένη· καὶ ἐπελυσάμεθα ἐπὶ μὲν τῆς φυτικῆς ψυχῆς, ὅτι οὐ λέγεται
αὕτη ὅλως συγκρίνεσθαι ἢ διακρίνεσθαι, ἐπὶ δὲ τῆς ἀλόγου, ὅτι βούλεται καὶ
ταύτην ὁ Πλάτων μετεμψυχοῦσθαι καὶ πολλὰ ὀστέινα σώματα κατατρίψασαν 5
δίκην ὑφάντου πολλὰ ἱμάτια κατατρίψαντος ὕστερον καὶ αὐτὴν διαφθαρῆναι.

Ἠπόρηται δὲ [9 § 4] καὶ πρὸς τὴν πρόσληψιν ἐκ τοῦ ἐγρηγορέναι καὶ καθεύδειν
καὶ νεωτέρου καὶ πρεσβυτέρου· εἰ γάρ τις λέγει ταῦτα μὴ ἐναντία | ἀλλὰ πρός (60)
τι, ἀλλὰ τὸ νέον καὶ γεγηρακὸς οὐ πρός τι ἀλλὰ καθ’ αὑτὰ ἐναντία. καὶ λέλυται
[9 § 5] ὅτι οὐ κατὰ προηγούμενον σκοπὸν ταῦτα ὑπὸ τῆς φύσεως γίνεται, ἀλλὰ 10
παρέπεται ἑλίκων δίκην. ταύτην δὲ τὴν λύσιν ὁ Πλάτων ἐν τῷ Παρμενίδῃ
[152a5–7] φαίνεται λέγων, ἐπικαίρως δὲ ὁ Συριανὸς ἐνταῦθα αὐτῇ χρῆται
ὡς οἰκείᾳ ⟨καὶ⟩ κατὰ ἀλήθειαν Πλατωνικῇ οὔσῃ. ταῦτα ἔχει ἡ θεωρία· ἐν οἷς
σὺν θεῷ καὶ ὁ περὶ ἐναντίων λόγος.

---

§ 4. 8 οὐδὲ Wk: οὐδὲν M | μηδὲν μ: μηδὲ M — 9 καὶ] καὶ ⟨εἰ⟩ Fh
§ 5. 6 ὑφαντοῦ M — 13 καὶ Wk: om. M

(text of which in *Ptolemaei opera*, ed. Heiberg, II pp. 147–155) and thinks that
Ptolemy worked in Alexandria; he sees no explanation for the forty years.
§ 5. 3–6. Cf. *supra* § 1.19–20; 9 § 6.6–13; Dam. I § 250.
5. ὀστρέινα : see note on Dam. I § 168.6–7.
11–13. The reference to the *Parm.* does not fit the solution of the wood-shavings
(9 § 5.1–9), but the alternative solution offered at 9 § 5.10–23 (see note).
12–13. Dam. I § 196.4–6.

6. Now there is an ancient doctrine which I remember [70c5–6]: i.e. an Orphic and Pythagorean doctrine.

7. 'Consider this,' Socrates said, 'in relation not only to man' [70d7]: Some, deceived by this passage, have thought that Plato declares all soul immortal. For what does he say? 'Consider this point in relation not only to man, but to brute animals and plants as well,' which seems to imply that he regards even irrational and vegetative soul as immortal. To establish this, they argue that all soul as the giver of life is insusceptible of death, since nothing is susceptible of the opposite of that which it brings about: fire, the giver of heat, is not susceptible of cold; in the opinion of Iamblichus, indeed, it is not even susceptible of what it brings about, for while providing heat it does not receive heat. The philosopher Ammonius, however, gives a better account of the passage: Plato says this with a view to the following argument which shows that opposites pass into each other, and in this context the words occur 'And in short, everything that comes into being,' that is to say, all these things pass into each other, not only man, but also the other animals and plants.

8. And just to unjust, and a thousand other cases [70e3–4]: It is to be noted in this sentence that Plato considers greater and smaller as opposites, which therefore pass into each other, and that he does not think, as the Peripatos does [Ar., *cat.* 6, 5b15–6a4], that they are correlatives. If the question is asked: 'How, being correlatives, can they also be opposites and pass into each other?' we must answer that in so far as they participate in opposites, they pass into each other, even though they are correlatives; for in the same way as hotter and colder are both correlatives and opposites, because hot and cold are opposites participated by the correlatives, and similarly more just and more unjust, so great and small have an existence of their own as opposites, apart from the correlatives, since they are opposite forms; great and small are definite realities, in which greater and smaller share, so that they are

---

§ 6. **Dam.** I § 203. A different interpretation is given by Hermias 42.19–20 (παλαιός = ἀίδιος).

§ 7. There is no trace in either Syr.-Pr. or Dam. of the misinterpretation of 70d7–e4 cited and rejected here by Amm. The obvious meaning as defended by Amm. at 9–13 is explicitly stated by Dam. (I § 207) and implied by Syr.-Pr. (Dam. I § 186.1–2). The doctrine as such, of course, is not uncommon: it is ascribed to Harpocratio (Hermias 102.13–15) and Numenius (Dam. I § 177.1–2). It could refer, not only to the much-discussed ψυχὴ πᾶσα ἀθάνατος of *Phaedr.* 245c5, but also to the final argument of the *Ph.* : soul is the origin of life, therefore it cannot die (lines 5–9). The inference that this would include animal and vegetative soul was already drawn by Strato (Dam. I §§ 434–437).

8–9. Iambl., *Ph.* frg. 2. Priscian., *solut.* 47.12–15 ascribes this variant to Plot.: 'addidit autem quidam quondam sapientum, magnus inquam Plotinus, et quod eo maius: si igitur neque ipsam quam infert vitam anima potest iterum recipere,

Παλαιὸς μὲν οὖν τις λόγος οὗ μεμνήμεθα [70c5–6]· Ὀρφικὸς γάρ 6
ἐστι καὶ Πυθαγόρειος.

Μὴ τοίνυν κατὰ ἀνθρώπων, ἦ δ' ὅς, σκόπει μόνον τοῦτο [70d7]· 7
τινὲς ἐκ τούτου τοῦ ῥησιδίου ἀπατηθέντες ᾠήθησαν τὸν Πλάτωνα πᾶσαν ψυχὴν
ἀπαθανατίζειν. σκόπει γὰρ τί φησιν· 'μὴ μόνον κατὰ ἀνθρώπων σκόπει μοι
τὸν λόγον, ἀλλὰ καὶ κατὰ ἀλόγων καὶ φυτῶν', ὡς ἂν καὶ τὴν ἄλογον ψυχὴν
καὶ τὴν φυτικὴν ἀθάνατον αὐτοῦ βουλομένου. καὶ κατασκευάζουσι τοῦτο οὕτως, 5
ὅτι πᾶσα ψυχὴ ζωῆς οὖσα χορηγὸς οὐκ ἐπιδέχεται θάνατον, οὐδὲν γὰρ ᾧ ἐπάγει
τὸ ἐναντίον ἐπιδέχεται· οὐδὲ γὰρ τὸ πῦρ θερμότητα ἐπάγον ψύξεώς ἐστι δεκτικόν,
ὅπου γε, ὥς φησιν ὁ Ἰάμβλιχος, οὐδὲ ὃ ἐπάγει δέχεται, οὐδὲ γὰρ θερμότητα
χορηγοῦν θερμότητα δέχεται. ἄμεινον δὲ ὁ φιλόσοφος Ἀμμώνιος ἐξηγήσατο
τὸ χωρίον τοῦτο λέγων ὅτι τοῦτό φησιν πρὸς τὸ ἐφεξῆς ἐπιχείρημα τὸ κατα-   10
σκευάζον ὅτι τὰ ἐναντία μεταβάλλει εἰς ἄλληλα, ὅ φησιν ὅτι 'καὶ ξυλλήβδην
ὅσαπερ ἔχει γένεσιν'· ταῦτα γὰρ πάντα μεταβάλλει εἰς ἄλληλα, καὶ οὐ μόνον
ἄνθρωπος, ἀλλὰ καὶ τὰ ἄλλα ζῷα καὶ φυτά.

Καὶ δίκαιον ἀδίκῳ καὶ ἄλλα δὴ μυρία [70e3–4]· σημειωτέον διὰ 8 (61)
τούτων ὅτι βούλεται ὁ Πλάτων τὸ μεῖζον καὶ ἔλαττον ἐναντία εἶναι καὶ μεταβάλλειν εἰς ἄλληλα, καὶ οὐ καθάπερ ὁ Περίπατος [Ar., cat. 6, 5b15–6a4] πρός
τι αὐτὰ οἴεται. εἰ δὲ λέγοι τις 'καὶ πῶς πρός τι ὄντα ἐναντία ἐστὶν καὶ μεταβάλλει εἰς ἄλληλα;' λεκτέον 'καθὸ ἐναντίων μετέχει, κἂν πρός τί ἐστι, μετα-   5
βάλλει εἰς ἄλληλα· ὥσπερ γὰρ τὸ θερμότερον καὶ ψυχρότερον καὶ πρός τί ἐστι
καὶ ἐναντία, διότι τὸ θερμὸν καὶ ψυχρὸν ἐναντία ἐστίν, ὧν τὰ πρός τι μετέχει,
καὶ ὥσπερ τὸ δικαιότερον καὶ ἀδικώτερον, οὕτω καὶ καθ' αὐτά ἐστιν ἐναντία
ἀποκεκριμένα τῶν πρός τι μέγα καὶ μικρόν, ἅπερ ἐναντία εἴδη ἐστίν· ὥρισται
γὰρ τῇ φύσει τὸ μέγα καὶ μικρόν, ὧν μετέχει καὶ τὸ μεῖζον καὶ ἔλαττον, καὶ   10
πρός τι ὄντα ἐναντία ἐστίν. ἐκεῖνο δὲ ἄξιον ζητῆσαι, περὶ ποίων ἄρα ἐναντίων

---

§ 6. 1 παλαιὸς Mᶜ: πάλαι M¹ | τις M¹: ἐστί τις Mᶜ, supra 10 § 1.1 M, Pl. | λόγος]
v. supra 10 § 1.1

§ 7. 6 οὐδὲν Fh: οὐδὲ M — 8 γε Nv: γὰρ M | ὥς] ὡς ins. Mᶜ: om. M¹ — 11 ὅ] διό
Nv; an οὖ? — 12 ὅσαπερ ἔχει Mᶜ (Pl.): ὅσα περιέχει M¹

§ 8. 10 post καὶ³] ÷ in ras. 2 litt. Mᶜ

---

multo magis contrarium vitae, ipsam mortem.' Priscianus' source is a lost treatise
by Pr. on Plato's three proofs of immortality (Introd. p. 18). The argument is
not found in the Enneads, and Pr. may have known it from Iambl.'s commentary
on the Ph. (either in the present passage, or in the final argument); another
possibility is that in this particular sentence Priscianus depends directly on Iambl.,
de anima, which he cites as another of his sources. Non-Enneadic tradition in
Iambl. is also possible, infra 13 § 4.

§ 8. 1–11. Apparently the aim of this section is from the very beginning to
discuss the character of 'large' and 'small' (forms, or correlatives, cf. Ar., cat. 6,
5b15–6a4), not that of 'larger', which is a relative in any case (cat. 7, 6b36–39).

11–18. Dam. I § 191 (=Syr.-Pr., closely followed by Ol.). The starting-point
is the classification of ἀντικείμενα, Ar., cat. 10, 11b16–23: πρός τι (double/half),
ἐναντία (evil/good), στέρησις καὶ ἕξις (blindness/sight), κατάφασις καὶ ἀπόφασις (is/is not).

simultaneously correlatives and opposites. A relevant question is, to what kind of opposites Plato refers here. Is it opposites properly so called? But why, in that case, does he mention some correlatives, which are not opposites in the strict sense, as changing into each other? If, on the other hand, he means contraries in the widest acceptation, it is not necessarily true that they pass into each other: possession changes into privation, but not conversely. Our conclusion must be, then, that he is referring to opposites in the proper sense, and if he includes some correlatives as well, this is because, as we said already [§ 5], they pass into each other thanks to their participation in opposites.

9. **And of course from stronger to weaker [71a3]:** If in every case of change the weaker changes and the stronger remains, the stronger must remain also in the change from life to death, in other words, the soul. Some say that it is possible to suppose another surviving element, so that the conclusion that the soul remains is not inevitable: the body as such remains, and so does its prime matter. We can refute this by saying that the body does not remain as matter after the separation, for after the separation both the matter as matter and the form as form (i.e. animation) are destroyed.

10. **And then, is there not the further fact that between any pair of opposites [71a12-13]:** Here begins the second argument, the one derived from the processes: if the processes are opposites and pass into each other, all the more so do the results. A corollary from this is that in Plato's view all opposites have intermediate terms. There is no ground to contest, as a matter of fact, not only that they have intermediate terms, but also that these are infinite in number, if we take it that Nature having proceeded to motion, can arrest its movement at any point. If this movement is infinitely divisible, as continuous quantity is by definition, opposites will have an infinite number of intermediate terms. Then why do we speak of two processes only, and not of an infinite number? Because, as Aristotle says [*phys.* V 1, 224b30-35], they all unite for the conflict: whatever exists besides white appears as black in contrast with the white.

15-16. Ol., *cat.* 135.9-11 ἡ γὰρ ἕξις μεταβάλλει μὲν εἰς στέρησιν, ἡ δὲ στέρησις οὐ μεταβάλλει εἰς ἕξιν.

§ 9. The point that soul is stronger than body and therefore the permanent substrate in the alternation of life and death, is made by Syr.-Pr. (Dam. I § 190.5-8; § 202.2) and rightly rejected by Dam. (I § 215) as alien to the argument and anticipating upon the proof from similarity to things invisible (80c2-81e1, cf. 87a5-6). Syr. may already have used the chance reference here to strong and weak (one instance in the inductive argument) in support of this view.

5. ἡ πόρρω ὕλη : though the notion is Aristotelian, the term is not. See Alex., *met.* 583.8-9; 618.20; Ol., *mete.* 168.28 foll.; [Amm.,] *anal. pr.* 47.6.

§ 10. 2-4. *Supra* § 4.3-6.

ταῦτα λέγει ὁ Πλάτων. ἆρα περὶ τῶν κυρίως ἐναντίων; ἀλλὰ πῶς καὶ τῶν πρός
τι μέμνηται, ἅπερ οὐ κυρίως ἐναντία ἐστίν, καὶ ταῦτα λέγει μεταβάλλειν εἰς
ἄλληλα; εἰ δὲ περὶ τῶν ἁπλῶς ἀντικειμένων, ἀλλὰ ταῦτα οὐ πάντως μεταβάλλουσιν εἰς ἄλληλα· ἡ μὲν γὰρ ἕξις εἰς τὴν στέρησιν μεταβάλλει, οὐ μὴν ἡ   15
στέρησις εἰς τὴν ἕξιν. λεκτέον οὖν ὅτι περὶ τῶν κυρίως ἐναντίων ἐστὶν αὐτῷ
ὁ λόγος· εἰ δὲ καὶ τῶν πρός τι μέμνηται, ἀλλὰ ταῦτα, ὡς εἴρηται, τῇ μεθέξει
τῶν ἐναντίων μεταβάλλει εἰς ἄλληλα.

Καὶ μὴν ἐξ ἰσχυροτέρου γε τὸ ἀσθενέστερον [71a3]: εἰ ἐν πάσῃ   9
μεταβολῇ τὸ μὲν ἀσθενέστερον μεταβάλλει, τὸ δὲ ἰσχυρότερον μένει, μετα-
βαλλούσης ἄρα τῆς ζωῆς εἰς τὸν θάνατον τὸ ἰσχυρότερον μένει, οἷον ἡ ψυχή.
τινὲς δέ φασιν ὅτι δυνατὸν ἄλλο τι ὑποθέσθαι μένον, καὶ οὐκ ἀνάγκη τὴν | ψυχὴν (62)
μένειν· τὸ γὰρ σῶμα ὑπομένει, μένει γὰρ ὡς σῶμα· ἀλλὰ καὶ ἡ πόρρω ὕλη μένει.   5
λυτέον οὖν ὡς οὐ μένει τὸ σῶμα ὡς ὕλη μετὰ τὸν χωρισμόν· ἔφθαρται γὰρ
μετὰ τὸν χωρισμὸν καὶ ἡ ὕλη ὡς ὕλη καὶ τὸ εἶδος ὡς εἶδος, οἷον ἡ ἐμψυχία.

Τί δὲ αὖ; ἔστιν καὶ τοιόνδε ἐν αὐτοῖς, οἷον μεταξὺ ἀμφοτέρων   10
πάντων [71a12–13]: ἐντεῦθεν τὸ δεύτερον ἐπιχείρημα τὸ ἐκ τῶν ὁδῶν, ὅτι
εἰ αἱ ὁδοὶ ἐναντίαι εἰσὶν καὶ μεταβάλλουσιν εἰς ἀλλήλας, πολλῷ μᾶλλον καὶ
τὰ τέλη. καὶ ἔχεις ἐντεῦθεν πόρισμα, ὅτι πάντα τὰ ἐναντία ἔμμεσα βούλεται
εἶναι ὁ Πλάτων. τί γὰρ κωλύει οὐ μόνον ἔμμεσα αὐτὰ εἶναι, ἀλλὰ καὶ ἄπειρα   5
εἶναι τὰ μέσα, τὴν γὰρ φύσιν προελθοῦσαν καὶ κινηθεῖσαν ἐν ὁτῳοῦν μέρει
τῆς κινήσεως ἠρεμῆσαι; καὶ εἰ ἡ κίνησις ἐπ’ ἄπειρόν ἐστι διαιρετὴ λόγῳ τῶν
συνεχῶν, καὶ τὰ μέσα τῶν ἐναντίων ἄπειρα ἔσται. καὶ διὰ τί δύο μόνας λέγομεν
εἶναι ὁδοὺς καὶ μὴ ἀπείρους; ἢ ὥς φησιν Ἀριστοτέλης [phys. V 1, 224b30–35],
διότι πάντα ὡς ἓν μάχεται· τὰ γὰρ παρὰ τὸ λευκὸν ὡς μέλανα τῷ λευκῷ μάχεται.   10
οὐκ ἄρα ἐστίν, ὡς ὁ Περίπατος οἴεται, ἄμεσα ἐναντία.

---

§ 9. 1 γε] om. Pl. BW — 5 μένει¹] -έν- in ras. 3 litt., -ει ex εἰ, Mᶜ
§ 10. 1 ἔστιν M¹: ἐστίν τι Mᶜ, Pl. BTY: ἔστιν ἔτι Pl. B² W — 7 ἠρεμῆσαι μ: ἠρέμησε M

4–11. **Dam. I § 192.** On the rejection of ἄμεσα ἐναντία, probably by Pr., see
note on Dam.

5–8. The proof that all opposite qualities have an infinite number of inter-
mediates is entirely based on Ar.'s *Physics* and not unworthy of the author of
the *Institutio physica* : (i) Nature is the principle of motion and rest, III 1, 200b12–13;
(ii) all qualitative change is motion between opposites, I 5, 205a6–7; (iii) all change
takes place in a continuum, VI 5, 235b24–25; (iv) the continuum is infinitely
divisible, I 2, 185b10–11.

9–10. Cf. Ar., *phys.* V 1, 224b30–35 ἐκ δὲ τοῦ μεταξὺ μεταβάλλει· χρῆται γὰρ
αὐτῷ ὡς ἐναντίῳ ὄντι πρὸς ἑκάτερον· ἔστι γάρ πως τὸ μεταξὺ τὰ ἄκρα. διὸ καὶ τοῦτο
πρὸς ἐκεῖνα κἀκεῖνα πρὸς τοῦτο λέγεταί πως ἐναντία (examples from tones and colors).
Similarly V 5, 229b14–22.

Therefore opposites without intermediate terms, as posed by the Peripatos, do not exist.

11. **They come into being from each other, and for each there is a process of becoming [71b9–10]**: Plato is not just repeating himself: 'they come into being from each other' refers to the processes, 'for each there is a process of becoming' to the results.

12. **The one of the pairs I mentioned just now [71c9]**: The sense is this: 'There are two pairs, one of which I shall mention to you', says Socrates, 'and then you must tell me the other. We have as opposite results sleeping and waking, and as the processes leading to these dozing off and waking up, of which waking up belongs to being awake and dozing off' (*katadarthanein*, an ancient word for being nearly asleep) 'belongs to sleep; now you must give names to the other pair of contrasts connected with life and death'. These two are the opposite resulting states, and the processes leading to them are revival on the side of life, and on the side of death the death-struggle.

13. **But is Nature to be lame on that side [71e9]**: The other argument: 'Suppose the change were ever to come to an end, because the one passed into the other, but not conversely'.

14. **If there were only a rectilinear process from the one thing to its contrary [72b1–3]**: If he holds that all that lives comes from the dead and conversely, an ensuing corollary is that Plato does not teach eternal punishment, but thinks that the souls of the lawless return to life. When he speaks of eternal punishment elsewhere [*Gorg.* 525c6; e1], he means by eternity (*aiōn*) a certain period and a complete revolution; cf. Homer [*Il.* 24.725], who calls the individual life *aiōn*: 'Husband, you have gone from this life too young'; so, too, in 'Experience causes our life to proceed by design' [*Gorg.* 448c5–6]. On the other hand, he holds that even the souls of theurgists do not always remain on the intelligible plane, but that they too descend into genesis, those of whom the Oracle [frg. 138] says 'In the abode of the angels'.

15. **And in agreeing on this we do not deceive ourselves [72d7]**: Consequently Plato is not a Sceptic, since he makes a positive statement as to the immortality of the soul and says that he is not deceived; if,

---

§ 13. *Supra* § 4.6–11.

§ 14. On the subject of eternal punishment cf. Pr., *Rep.* II 179.9–26; Dam. I §§ 492 and 547; Ol., *Gorg.* 263.17–264.26. The disquisition on αἰών is relevant to the τὸν ἀεὶ χρόνον of *Gorg.* 525c6 and e1, not to the οὔποτε of *Ph.* 113e6. But Ol. is really reporting the discussion on περίοδος, cf. Ol., *Gorg.*, and Dam.

5. ἀποκατάστασιν : the word is used as a synonym for περίοδος by Pr., *elem.* 199–200.

6. πάρος for νέος (νέον Zenodotus) may be a real variant in Homer (cf. *Il.* 23.474 πάρος='too soon'), but is more probably a simple error.

8–10. The theurgists for good in the Intelligible: Psell., *orac. Chald.* 1153A11–16

Γίνεσθαί τε αὐτὰς ἐξ ἀλλήλων γένεσίν τε εἶναι ἑκατέροις 11
[71b9–10]: οὐκ ἀδολεσχεῖ ὁ Πλάτων, ἀλλὰ τὸ μὲν 'γίνεσθαι αὐτὰς ἐξ ἀλλήλων'
περὶ τῶν ὁδῶν εἴρηται, τὸ δὲ 'γένεσιν εἶναι ἑκατέροις' περὶ τῶν τελῶν.

Τὴν μὲν τοίνυν ἑτέραν συζυγίαν ὧν νυνδὴ ἔλεγον [71c9]: τὸ12(63)
λεγόμενον τοιοῦτόν ἐστιν, ὅτι 'δύο οὐσῶν συζυγιῶν τὴν μὲν μίαν', φησίν, 'ἐγώ
σοι ἐρῶ', ὁ Σωκράτης, 'τὴν δὲ ἄλλην σὺ ἀπόκριναι.

ἐπειδὴ γὰρ ἐναντία τέλη
ἐστὶ τὸ καθεύδειν τῷ ἐγρηγορέναι καὶ εἰσὶν ὁδοὶ τούτων τὸ καταδαρθάνειν
καὶ ἐγείρεσθαι, πρὸς μὲν τῇ ἐγρηγόρσει τὸ ἐγείρεσθαι, πρὸς δὲ τῷ καθεύδειν 5
τὸ καταδαρθάνειν· — τοῦτο γὰρ καλοῦσιν οἱ παλαιοὶ τὸ ὅσον οὔπω καθεῦδον· —
εἰπὲ δὲ σὺ τὴν λοιπὴν ἀντίθεσιν τὴν περὶ ζωῆς καὶ θανάτου'. ἔστιν γὰρ ἐναντία
ταῦτα τέλη, ὁδοὶ δὲ πρὸς μὲν τῇ ζωῇ τὸ ἀναβιώσκεσθαι, πρὸς δὲ τῷ θανάτῳ
τὸ ψυχορραγεῖν.

'Ἀλλὰ ταύτῃ χωλὴ ἔσται ἡ φύσις [71e9]: τὸ ἄλλο ἐπιχείρημα, ὅτι 13
'εἰ ἐπιλείποι ποτὲ ἡ μεταβολὴ τοῦ ἑνὸς εἰς τὸ λοιπὸν μεταβάλλοντος, οὐκέτι
δὲ καὶ τὸ ἀνάπαλιν'.

'Ἀλλ' εὐθεῖά τις εἴη ἡ γένεσις ἐκ τοῦ ἑτέρου εἰς τὸ καταντικρύ 14
[72b1–3]: εἰ βούλεται τὰ ζῶντα πάντα ἐκ τῶν τεθνεώτων καὶ ἀνάπαλιν, πόρισμα
ἔχεις ἐντεῦθεν ὅτι οὐ βούλεται ὁ Πλάτων εἶναι ἀίδιον κόλασιν, ἀλλὰ πάλιν
ἔρχεσθαι εἰς βίον τὰς ἀκολάστους ψυχάς. εἰ δὲ καὶ ἀλλαχοῦ [Gorg. 525c6; e1]
λέγει αἰώνιον τὴν κόλασιν, ἀλλ' οὖν αἰῶνα καλεῖ περίοδόν τινα καὶ ἀποκατάστασιν· 5
οὕτω γὰρ καὶ ὁ ποιητὴς τὸν μερικὸν βίον αἰῶνα ἐκάλεσεν ('ἄνερ, ἀπ' αἰῶνος πάρος
ὤλεο' [Ω 725]), | καὶ 'ἐμπειρία μὲν ποιεῖ τὸν αἰῶνα ἡμῶν πορεύεσθαι κατὰ (64)
τέχνην' [Gorg. 448c5–6]. ἀλλὰ μὴν οὐδὲ τὰς τῶν θεουργῶν ψυχὰς βούλεται
μένειν ἀεὶ ἐν τῷ νοητῷ, ἀλλὰ καὶ κατιέναι εἰς γένεσιν· περὶ ὧν φησι τὸ λόγιον
'ἀγγελικῷ ἐνὶ χώρῳ' [frg. 138].   10

Καὶ ἡμεῖς ταῦτα οὐκ ἐξαπατώμενοι ὁμολογοῦμεν [72d7]: οὐκ 15
ἐφεκτικὸς ἄρα ὁ Πλάτων, εἴ γε ἀποφαίνεται περὶ τῆς ἀθανασίας τῆς ψυχῆς
καὶ λέγει μηδὲ ἐξηπατῆσθαι· εἰ δὲ καὶ ἀνωτέρω [69d5–6] λέγει ἀμφιβάλλων ὅτι
'ἐκεῖσε ἐλθόντες τὸ σαφὲς εἰσόμεθα', τοῦτο περὶ τῆς ἑαυτοῦ λήξεως ἔλεγεν ὁ
Σωκράτης, οὐ περὶ τῆς ἀθανασίας.   5

---

§ 11. 1 γίγνεσθαι Mᶜ | αὐτὰς M¹: αὐτὰ Mᶜ, Pl. | ἑκατέροις M¹: -ον Mᶜ, Pl. TY:
ἐξ ἑκατέρου Pl. BW
§ 12. 3 σοι Nv (Pl.): εὖ M | post ἐρῶ] ras. 1 litt. M — 6 καθεῦδον] καθεύδειν Fh
§ 14. 1 post ἑτέρου] μόνον ins. Mᶜ (Pl.) — 2 post τεθνεώτων] εἶναι add. Nv (cf. 9 § 2.4)
— 9 μένειν ἀεὶ] accentus mut., -εὶ ex -ι fecit Mᶜ (μὲν εἶναι ut vid. M¹)
§ 15. 1 ταῦτα] αὐτὰ ταῦτα Pl. B, τὰ αὐτὰ ταῦτα Pl. TWY | οὐκ om. Pl. Y¹

ἀποκαθιστῶσι δὲ τὰς ψυχὰς μετὰ τὸν λεγόμενον θάνατον κατὰ τὰ μέτρα τῶν οἰκείων
καθάρσεων ἐν ὅλοις τοῖς τοῦ κόσμου μέρεσιν· τινὰς δὲ καὶ ὑπὲρ τὸν κόσμον ἀναβιβάζουσι.
Porph. ap. Augustin., civ. X 30: 'mundatam ab omnibus malis animam et cum
Patre constitutam nunquam iam mala mundi huius passuram esse confessus est'
(scil. Porphyrius). Ibid. XII 21; XXII 27. Iambl., myst. 69.7–15 ... ἐπὶ μείζονά
τε τάξιν τὴν ἀγγελικὴν ἀναγομένη. Contradicted by Pr., elem. 206; cf. Dam. I § 204;
§ 492. Cf. Lewy pp. 219–222; F. W. Cremer, Die chaldäischen Orakel und Jamblich
de mysteriis, Meisenheim am Glan, 1969, 64.
§ 15. Supra 8 § 17.
4–5. Cf. supra 7 § 4.4–5.

above [69d5–6], Socrates shows himself uncertain when he says 'I shall know for sure when I have arrived there', he refers to his own destined abode, not to immortality.

16. **And that the good souls have a better lot than the wicked [72e1–2]:** From this you can derive another corollary, viz. that for the good it is better to be dead than to be alive, for the wicked, on the contrary, it is better to be alive than to be dead. For if the soul were destroyed with the body, it would be better for the good to be alive and for the wicked not to exist; since, however, it is not destroyed with the body, it is better for the wicked to be alive, because so long as they are alive they may well mend their ways, with the help of books and teachers, and become better men, so that they can depart this life with purified minds. This, with God's help, is the end of the argument from the opposites.

THE ARGUMENT FROM RECOLLECTION

11

Lecture **

1. **'Besides', Cebes rejoined, 'according to that other theory, too'** [72e3–74a9].

Having first proved by the argument from the living and the dead that the soul survives after the separation from the body, in other words that it is post-existent, Socrates now proves its pre-existence also, by the present argument that learning is recollection, so that from the two arguments together it can be concluded that the soul has a longer life than the body, since it consists both before and after the body.

2. There are three current interpretations of these two arguments. Iamblichus believes that each by itself proves the immortality of the soul; 'for if,' he says, 'the living and the dead originate from each other, and if they do so always, it follows that the soul is eternal; similarly, if learning is always recollection, the soul must be eternal on this ground too'. Others arrive at the immortality of the soul as the collective result of the two arguments: the first argument, by demonstrating that our

---

§ 16. 2–5. Pl., *Ph.* 107c5–d2 (slightly different; cf. Dam. I § 475); *Gorg.* 512b1–2 (the opposite).

Lect. 11. The argument from recollection: relation to the other proofs; characteristics of recollection. Purpose of the argument (§ 1). According to Iambl. it is by itself a complete proof of immortality; according to 'some', it is so if combined with the preceding; according to Ol., the two taken together prove only (limited) pre-existence and survival (§ 2). Definitions and etymologies of memory, recollection and oblivion (§§ 3–4). The five characteristics of recollection according to *Ph.* 73c1–74a8 (§ 5); though two of them do not necessarily apply to *all* recollection, they

Καὶ ταῖς μὲν ἀγαθαῖς ἄμεινον εἶναι, ταῖς δὲ κακαῖς κάκιον 16
[72e1–2]: καὶ ἐντεῦθεν ἄλλο πόρισμα κέρδανον, τοῖς μὲν ἀγαθοῖς κρεῖττον
εἶναι τὸ τεθνάναι τοῦ ζῆν, τοῖς δὲ κακοῖς ἀνάπαλιν ἄμεινόν ἐστιν εἶναι ἢ τεθνάναι.
εἰ μὲν γὰρ συνεφθείρετο ἡ ψυχὴ τῷ σώματι, καὶ τοῖς ἀγαθοῖς ἄμεινον ἦν τὸ
ζῆν καὶ τοῖς κακοῖς τὸ μὴ εἶναι· ἐπειδὴ δὲ οὐ συμφθείρεται, ἄμεινόν ἐστι τοῖς 5
κακοῖς ζῆν, εἰκὸς γὰρ αὐτοὺς ζῶντας προκόπτειν καὶ βιβλία ἔχοντας καὶ
διδασκάλους καὶ ἀμείνονας ἑαυτῶν γίνεσθαι, ὡς κεκαθαρμένους ἐκεῖσε ἀπιέναι.
ἐν οἷς σὺν θεῷ ὁ ἐκ τῶν ἐναντίων λόγος.

Ὁ ἐκ τῶν ἀναμνήσεων λόγος σὺν θεῷ   (65)

11

Πρᾶξις σὺν θεῷ

Καὶ μήν, ἔφη ὁ Κέβης ὑπολαβών, καὶ κατ' ἐκεῖνόν γε τὸν λόγον 1
[72e3–74a9].

Δείξας ὁ Σωκράτης ἐκ τοῦ ζῶντος καὶ τοῦ τεθνεῶτος ὅτι ἐπιδιαμένει ἡ
ψυχὴ μετὰ τὸν χωρισμὸν τοῦ σώματος, τουτέστιν ὅτι μεθυπάρχει, δείκνυσι
διὰ τοῦ προκειμένου λόγου ὅτι καὶ προϋπάρχει ἡ ψυχὴ τοῦ σώματος ἐκ τοῦ 5
τὰς μαθήσεις ἀναμνήσεις εἶναι· ὡς ἐξ ἀμφοτέρων τῶν λόγων συνάγεσθαι ὅτι
πολυχρονιωτέρα ἡ ψυχὴ τοῦ σώματος, εἴ γε καὶ προϋπάρχει αὐτοῦ καὶ μεθυπάρχει.
α′   Καὶ τρεῖς ἐκδοχαὶ φέρονται τῶν δύο τούτων λόγων. ὁ μὲν γὰρ Ἰάμβλιχος 2
οἴεται ἑκάτερον λόγον καθ' αὑτὸν δεικνύναι τὴν ἀθανασίαν τῆς ψυχῆς· 'εἰ γάρ',
φησί, 'τὸ ζῶν καὶ τεθνεὸς ἐξ ἀλλήλων καὶ ἀεὶ ἐξ ἀλλήλων, ἀίδιος ἄρα ἡ ψυχή·
ἀλλὰ μὴν καὶ εἰ ἀεὶ αἱ μαθήσεις ἀναμνήσεις, ἀίδιος ἄρα καὶ κατὰ τοῦτον τὸν
β′ λόγον ἡ ψυχή'. ἄλλοι δὲ διὰ ἄμφω τῶν λόγων ἐρανίζονται τὴν ἀθανασίαν τῆς 5
ψυχῆς· ὁ μὲν γὰρ πρῶτος λόγος ὁ δεικνὺς ὅτι εἰσὶν ἡμῶν αἱ ψυχαὶ ἐν Ἅιδου
δείκνυσιν αὐτὴν ἄφθαρτον, ὁ δέ γε παρὼν λόγος ὁ ἐκ τῶν ἀναμνήσεων ἀγένητον,

---

§ 16.   1 μὲν] μέν γε Pl. BW

---

certainly do so to Platonic anamnesis (§§ 6–8).
§ 1. Dam. I § 252.1–6.
§ 2. The first view is that of the doxographical period, when doctrines and
arguments led a life of their own independent of the context: it is apparently
represented by Strato (Dam. II §§ 63–65) and explicitly by Alcin., did. 25; Iambl.
then tried to make true its general validity. The second view is close to Pl.'s (77c6–d4),
although taken in its narrowest sense this passage need not say more than what
Ol. makes it say. The third view is that of Pr., Parm. 698.36–699.7; cf. Simpl.,
phys. 440.35–441.2; also Dam. I §§ 264–265.
1–5. Iambl., Ph. frg. 3. Cf. Dam. I § 207.3–5; supra 10 § 1.13–14.

souls continue to exist in Hades, proves it imperishable, the present
argument from recollection proves it ungenerated, and so, if you combine
the two, you will conclude that the soul is both ungenerated and
imperishable. The philosopher, however, says that this is not compatible
with the text: in our view neither the one of the arguments nor the
two together can prove its immortality, but only that it is pre-existent
and post-existent for a certain length of time. Therefore Plato, being
well aware that he has not yet proved his point adequately, adds other
arguments to establish the same thesis, and only the fifth of these, the
one based on the essence of soul, affords proof positive of its immortality;
also, it is said in the text [73a2–3] that each of the two arguments has
shown it to be 'something immortal', which implies that he has not
strictly demonstrated that the soul is immortal.

3. But since the subject is recollection, and recollection is closely
connected with memory, and the opposite of memory is oblivion, let us
define each of these three, recollection, memory, oblivion, taking the
words themselves as starting-points. Recollection (*anamnêsis*), then, is a
renewal of memory (*ananeôsis mnêmês*), as the word indicates, memory
(*mnêmê*) is preservation of intelligence (*monê tou nou*), oblivion (*lêthê*) is
a kind of rheum (*lêmê*), for as rheum is a hindrance to sight, so is oblivion
to human knowledge, which is comparable to sight. Memory is preservation
of intelligence, because it is seen primarily in intelligence, for memory
is a fixation of knowledge: just as sempiternity is the solid state of being
(the sempiternal, *aïdion*, is that which always is, *aei on*) and as immortality
(or life inextinguishable) is the solid state of life, so memory is the solid
state of knowledge. 4. Recollection occurs only when there is a break
caused by oblivion, and therefore recollection is especially appropriate
to human beings, because our soul, though having an infinite capacity
of life, has no infinite power of knowledge, and consequently, when
oblivion has intervened, there is as it were a rebirth of knowledge,
recollection. This is a second knowledge of the same object; for knowledge
is acquired either by a first act of apprehension, as when we see Socrates

---

14–15. Cf. *infra* § 10.

§ 3. 3–6. For the etymologies cf. Pl., *Crat.* 437b3 (μνήμη=μονή), Ar., *top.* IV 4,
125b6 (μονὴ ἐπιστήμης), Dam. I § 257.6 (ὁ νοῦς μένει), El., *isag.* 2.9 (μονὴ νοῦ). –
Dam. I § 253.3–4 (ἀνάμνησις=ἀνανέωσις μνήμης); El., *isag.* 2.9–10. – Hermias 63.7–9
ἐπειδὴ γὰρ τὰς μαθήσεις ἀναμνήσεις βούλεται εἶναι, οἶον δὲ ὑπό τινων λημῶν ἐπεσκιάσθαι
τὸ τῆς ψυχῆς ὄμμα ὑπὸ τῆς γενέσεως, τούτου χάριν τὰ ἐμπόδια μόνον ὑπεξαιρεῖ. Pr.,
Tim. III 153.5 τὸ ὄμμα τῆς ψυχῆς λήθην ἴσχει καὶ ἀορασίαν.

6–9. **Dam.** I § 256; II § 8.3–5. Dam., after repeating the parallel between everlasting being, immortality and memory, then proceeds to give some criticisms
and qualifications of his own (§ 257); in particular he denies that memory can be
a function of νοῦς (below § 4).

§ 4. 1–9. The argument of Pr. (§ 3.7–9) continued: since the essence of soul

ὥστε εἰ συνῆς ἄμφω τοὺς λόγους ἀγένητον συνάξεις τὴν ψυχὴν καὶ ἄφθαρτον.
γ′ ταῦτα δέ, φησὶν ὁ φιλόσοφος, οὐκ οἰκεῖα τῇ λέξει· οἰόμεθα γὰρ μηδὲ ἕνα τῶν
λόγων μηδὲ ἄμφω δεικνύναι αὐτὴν ἀθάνατον, ἀλλὰ καὶ προϋπάρχουσαν χρόνον 10
τινὰ καὶ μεθυπάρχουσαν. διὸ καὶ ὁ Πλάτων αἰσθόμενος ὅτι οὔπω ἱκανῶς τὸ
προκείμενον ἀπέδειξεν ἐπάγει καὶ ἄλλους λόγους τοῦ αὐτοῦ κατασκευαστικούς,
καὶ μόνος ὁ ε′ ὁ ἐκ τῆς οὐσίας τῆς ψυχῆς κυρίως τὴν ἀθανασίαν αὐτῆς δείκνυσιν·
καὶ ὅτι ἐν τῇ λέξει φησὶν [73a2–3] ἄμφω τοὺς λόγους 'τὶ ἀθάνατον' δεδειχέναι,
ὡς ἂν μὴ κυρίως δείξας ὅτι ἀθάνατος ἡ ψυχή. 15
Ἀλλ' ἐπειδὴ περὶ ἀναμνήσεως ὁ λόγος, παράκειται δὲ τῇ ἀναμνήσει ἡ μνήμη, 3 (66)
ἀντίκειται δὲ τῇ μνήμῃ ἡ λήθη, φέρε ἕκαστον τῶν τριῶν ὁρισώμεθα, τί ἀνάμνησις,
τί μνήμη, τί λήθη, ἐκ τῶν ὀνομάτων. ἀνάμνησις τοίνυν ἐστὶν ἀνανέωσις μνήμης,
ὡς τοὔνομα δηλοῖ· μνήμη δὲ μονὴ τοῦ νοῦ· λήθη δὲ οἷον λήμη τις, ὡς γὰρ ἡ
λήμη ἐμπόδιόν ἐστι τῆς ὄψεως, οὕτω καὶ ἡ λήθη οἷον λήμη ἐστὶν τῆς ἡμετέρας 5
γνώσεως οἷον [τῆς] ὄψεως. ἡ γὰρ μνήμη μονὴ τοῦ νοῦ, πρώτως γὰρ ἐν τῷ
νῷ θεωρεῖται· πῆξις γὰρ τῆς γνώσεως ἡ μνήμη· ὡς γὰρ παγίωσίς ἐστι τοῦ
ὄντος τὸ ἀεί (ὃν γὰρ ἀεί ἐστι τὸ ἀΐδιον), τῆς δὲ ζωῆς πῆξις ἡ ἀθανασία (ζωὴ
γὰρ ἄσβεστός ἐστιν), οὕτω καὶ [ἡ] πῆξις τῆς γνώσεως ἡ μνήμη. ἡ γὰρ ἀνάμνησις 4
λήθης διακοπτούσης· διὸ οἰκεία ἡμῖν μάλιστα ἡ ἀνάμνησις· ἐπειδὴ γὰρ οὐκ
ἀπειροδύναμος ἡ ἡμετέρα ψυχὴ κατὰ γνῶσιν, εἰ καὶ κατὰ ζωὴν ἀπειροδύναμός
ἐστι, διὰ τοῦτο [οἷον] λήθης διαδραμούσης οἷον παλιγγενεσία τις τῆς γνώσεώς
ἐστιν ἡ ἀνάμνησις. δευτέρα γὰρ γνῶσις τοῦ αὐτοῦ ἐστιν· ἡ γὰρ γνῶσις ἢ κατὰ 5
πρώτην ἐπιβολήν ἐστιν, ὡς ἡνίκα θεασώμεθα Σωκράτην μηδέποτε αὐτὸν
θεασάμενοι, καὶ λέγεται μάθησις· ἢ κατὰ δευτέραν, καὶ ἢ λήθης μεταξὺ γινομένης, ὡς ἡνίκα Κέβητα θεασάμενοι εἰς ἀνάμνησιν ἔλθωμεν Σιμμίου διὰ τὸ
συνεῖναι αὐτὸν τῷ Σιμμίᾳ, ἢ μὴ διαδραμούσης λήθης, καὶ λέγεται μνήμη. καὶ
ἐπέκεινα μνήμη τῆς ἀναμνήσεως· ἡ γὰρ μνήμη πρώτως μὲν ἐν τῷ νῷ ἐστι, 10
διότι οὗτος ἀεὶ ἑαυτὸν νοεῖ καὶ μένει ἐν ἑαυτῷ, δευτέρως δὲ ἐν ταῖς ψυχαῖς

---

§ 3. 6 τῆς M: del. Wk — 9 ἡ M: del. Nv
§ 4. 4 οἷον¹ M: del. Wk — 6 post μηδέποτε] ∼ ∼ in ras. Mˣ — 8 τὸ M¹: τῶι M

---

is life, it has an unlimited power of life; knowledge, the next function in the series
being - life - intelligence, has a more limited range, and not being inherent in all
soul is absent from some, intermittent in others.

4. λήθης διαδραμούσης: not a chance metaphor, but a technical term, firmly
embedded in the definition of recollection (§ 5.16–19) and occurring no less than
seven times in this lecture and the following (also § 4.9; 13; § 5.9; 10; § 8.6; and
12 § 2.6). Therefore the οἷον is out of place and must be a duplication of the next οἷον.

10–13. Cf. Dam. I § 259. Ol. follows Pr. (Dam. I § 256.2) without, however,
adding Pr.'s restriction that intelligence has memory not as thinking itself, but
as thinking intelligible reality beyond it (§ 256.2–4; § 257.4–5). Dam. I § 257.10–14,
following a shift of viewpoint in Pr., argues that memory belongs to the level of soul.

11. ἐν ταῖς ὅλαις or τελείαις or α′ ψυχαῖς should be either inserted or understood,
cf. Dam. I § 257.13; II § 6.1–3.

without having seen him before, and this is called learning; or by a second act of apprehension, in which case either oblivion has intervened (as when seeing Cebes we remember Simmias, in whose company he was), or there is no intervening oblivion, and then we speak of memory. Memory is superior to recollection, because memory exists primarily in intelligence, which always thinks itself and abides in itself, secondarily also in souls, inasmuch as they pass from one object to another and do not know all things simultaneously and timelessly, and in a third mode it exists also in human souls, in which there are also interruptions by oblivion; memory is superior also because it is similar to eternity, being always directed to the same object, whereas recollection resembles time because of its transitional character; thirdly, because there is memory also where there is no forgetting, but recollection exists only where oblivion occurs; finally, because the more efficacious causes communicate themselves to a greater number, while the weaker ones have a more limited range of communication, and for this reason memory is found in irrational animals too, while recollection goes no farther than rational souls.

5. These five elements must concur, if there is to be recollection: (1) The recollection must be a second knowledge: if, indeed, recollection is a renewal of memory, and only that which has suffered from age can be renewed, it must be a second knowledge; further because knowledge is achieved either by a first act of apprehension, in which case it is learning, or by a second, in which case it is recollection [73c1–2]. (2) There must be a passing on from one kind of knowledge to another and from one object to another. For example, someone who sees Cebes remembers Simmias; here you have a transition from one kind of knowledge to another, from sense-perception to imagination, since occupation with the absent is proper to imagination; but there is also a transition from one object to another, from Cebes to Simmias [73c4–d11]. (3) Recollection

---

15–16. **Dam. I § 258; II § 4.5–6; 6.5–6.**

16–18. **Dam. I § 272; II § 22.** The general principle stated here, that the influence of the higher powers extends farther downward than that of the lower ones, is a well-known rule of Pr. (*elem.* 57; cf. Ol., *Alc.* 109.18–21). The minor (memory appears first in intelligence, recollection in soul) is also a view held by Pr. (see above, lines 11–14). The inference seems obvious that the conclusion (memory, as coming from intelligence, reaches down as far as irrational animals, while recollection begins and ends in rational soul) must derive also from Pr.'s commentary. It is all the more surprising to find that El., *isag.* 2.6–25, cites exactly the opposite opinion from Pr.'s commentary on the *Ph.*: μόνος γὰρ τῶν ζῴων ἄνθρωπος ἀναμιμνήσκεται τῶν ἀλόγων μνήμην ἐχόντων μόνον, ὡς δηλοῖ ὁ κύων τοῦ Ὀδυσσέως ὁ Ἄργος φυλάξας τὴν μνήμην εἰς εἴκοσιν ἔτη. οὐ ταὐτὸν δὲ μνήμη καὶ ἀνάμνησις· μνήμη μὲν γάρ ἐστι μονὴ νοῦ, ἀνάμνησις δὲ ἀπολομένης μνήμης ἀνανέωσις. καὶ ἡμεῖς μὲν οὕτως (i.e. El. and no doubt also Ol. in his lost commentary on the *Isagoge*). ὁ δὲ φιλόσοφος Πρόκλος βούλεται ἐν τοῖς εἰς Φαίδωνα ὑπομνήμασιν ἔχειν καὶ τὰ ἄλογα ἀνάμνησιν· ὑπερβαίνει γάρ, φησίν, τὴν ἐκείνων ζωὴν τὸ ἀμετάπτωτον τῆς γνώσεως· τὸ γὰρ διὰ παντὸς μεμνῆσθαι αὐτὰ καὶ μὴ ἐπιλανθάνεσθαι ὑπὲρ τὴν ἐκείνων φύσιν ἐστί· τοῖς γὰρ ἀνθρώποις

ὡς μεταβαινού|σαις καὶ μὴ ἀθρόως πάντα καὶ ἀχρόνως γινωσκούσαις, τρίτως (67)
δὲ καὶ ἐν ταῖς ἡμετέραις ψυχαῖς, ἐν αἷς καὶ λήθη διατρέχει· καὶ ὅτι ἡ μὲν μνήμη
αἰῶνι ἔοικεν ἀεὶ περὶ τὸ αὐτὸ οὖσα, ἡ δὲ ἀνάμνησις χρόνῳ διὰ τὴν μετάβασιν·
καὶ ὅτι ἡ μὲν μνήμη καὶ ⟨ἐν⟩ τοῖς μὴ ἐπιλανθανομένοις ἐστίν, ἡ δὲ ἀνάμνησις   15
ἐν οἷς μόνοις λήθη ἐστίν· καὶ ὅτι τὰ ἰσχυρότερα αἴτια πλείοσιν μεταδιδόασιν
ἑαυτῶν, τὰ δὲ ἀσθενέστερα συνεσταλμένην ἔχει τὴν μετάδοσιν, διὸ μνήμη μὲν
καὶ ἐν τοῖς ἀλόγοις ζῴοις, ἡ δὲ ἀνάμνησις μέχρι τῶν λογικῶν ψυχῶν ἵσταται.

α′   Ε′ δὲ τούτων συνδραμόντων γίνεται ἀνάμνησις. δεῖ γὰρ τὴν ἀνάμνησιν   5
δευτέραν εἶναι γνῶσιν· εἰ γὰρ ἀνανέωσίς ἐστι μνήμης ἡ ἀνάμνησις, ἀνανεοῦται
δὲ τὸ παλαιωθέν, δευτέρα ἄρα γνῶσίς ἐστι· καὶ ὅτι ἡ γνῶσις ἢ κατὰ πρώτην
ἐπιβολὴν γίνεται, ὡς ἡ μάθησις, ἢ κατὰ δευτέραν, ὡς ἡ ἀνάμνησις [73c1–2].
β′   δεύτερον δεῖ μετάβασιν εἶναι ἀπὸ γνώσεως ἐπὶ γνῶσιν καὶ ἀπὸ γνωστοῦ ἐπὶ   5
γνωστόν. οἷον ὁ Κέβητα θεασάμενος εἰς ἀνάμνησιν ἔρχεται Σιμμίου, καὶ ἰδοὺ
ἀπὸ γνώσεως ἐπὶ γνῶσίν ἐστιν ἡ μετάβασις, ἀπὸ γὰρ αἰσθήσεως ἐπὶ φαντασίαν,
φαντασίας γὰρ τὸ περὶ τὸ ἀπὸν ἐνεργεῖν· ἀλλὰ καὶ ἀπὸ γνωστοῦ ἐπὶ γνωστόν,
γ′   ἀπὸ γὰρ Κέβητος ἐπὶ Σιμμίαν [73c4–d11]. τρίτον λήθης διαδραμούσης δεῖ
μεταξὺ γίνεσθαι τὴν ἀνάμνησιν· εἰ γὰρ μὴ διαδράμοι, οὐ λέγεται τὸ τοιοῦτο   10

κρείττοσιν οὖσιν οὐχ ὑπάρχει τοῦτο. ἐπιλανθάνεται δὲ καὶ τὰ ἄλογα· δεινοῖς γάρ ποτε
περιπεσόντα αὖθις τοῖς αὐτοῖς περιπίπτει καὶ τὰ πρότερον σαίνοντα μετὰ χρόνον ὑλακτεῖ
καὶ ἀγριαίνει πρὸς τοὺς ποτε συνήθεις. ὅθεν δῆλον ὅτι ἐπιλανθάνεται καὶ ἀναμιμνήσκεται.
ὅτι δὲ ἔχει ἀνάμνησιν, δῆλον κἀντεῦθεν, ἐκ τοῦ μὴ ὁμοίως εἰς συνήθειαν ἄγεσθαι τῷ
προορ... καὶ τῷ πάντη ξένῳ· θᾶττον γὰρ ἐν συνηθείᾳ γίνεται τοῦ προορ..., ὡς
φυλάξας δῆλον ὅτι τύπον τινὰ καὶ δι' αὐτοῦ λαβὼν ἀφορμὴν ἀναμνήσεως. πλὴν εἰ καὶ
ἐπὶ ἀμφοτέρων ἐστὶν ἀνάμνησις, ἀλλ' οὖν διαφορά τίς ἐστιν· ἐπὶ μὲν γὰρ ἀνθρώπου σὺν
τῇ ἀναμνήσει ἐστὶ καὶ τὸ συναισθάνεσθαι αὐτοὺς τῆς ἀναμνήσεως, ἐπὶ δὲ τῶν ἀλόγων
οὐκ ἔστι τοῦτο· οὐδὲ γὰρ συναισθάνεται ἐκεῖνα ὅτι ἀνεμνήσθη· ὥσπερ γὰρ ἡ ὄψις ὁρᾷ
μέν, οὐκ οἶδεν δὲ ὅτι ὁρᾷ, οὕτως καὶ ἐπ' ἐκείνων ἐστίν. This final conclusion is repeated
without comment by Dam. at I § 272 and II § 22, which usually means that he
is reporting Pr., and this seems to bear out the substantial correctness of El.'s
account. The view mentioned first by El. and marked by him as his own position,
is the one adopted here (and in the commentary on the *Isag.*) by Ol. and deduced
from a canon of Pr., either by Amm. or by Ol.
    § 5. Dam. I § 262, § 253; II § 13, cf. § 4.

must be preceded by a break caused by oblivion; if there is no such break, we do not speak of recollection, but of memory [73e1–3]. (4) The transition must be either from similar to similar or from dissimilar to dissimilar: a man who sees the portrait of Socrates and is reminded of Socrates, passes from similar to similar, one who is reminded by Simmias of Cebes passes from dissimilar to dissimilar [73e5–74a4]. (5) In the case of recollection by transition from similar to similar, we must also be able to supply what is missing [74a5–8]. This being so, we conclude that recollection is a second knowledge achieved by passing from one kind of knowledge to another and from one object to another after an interval of oblivion, the transition starting either from the similar or the dissimilar, with the further condition, in the former case, that something can be supplied.

6. But let us discuss objections against two of the assumptions cited above. Against the second it may be alleged that recollection does not necessarily pass from one kind of knowledge to another and from one object to another: there may be transition neither in the kind of knowledge nor in its object, e.g. if somebody has seen Socrates before but forgotten him, then, upon seeing him again, remembers him. Clearly there is no transition in the kind of knowledge, since in both cases we have to do with sense-perception; but neither is there transition from one object to another, for Socrates was the object both before and now. Another assumption which can be questioned is that the transition must be from similar to similar or from dissimilar to dissimilar; it may be also from the same to the same, e.g. if having seen Socrates before and having forgotten him, one sees him again now and remembers him: here we have a transition from the same to the same. Must we conclude, then, that Plato's assumptions are false? Yes, if we take them to relate to *all* recollection; since, however, the philosopher is not referring to all recollection, but only to the kind now under discussion, by which he believes that the soul, aroused and awakened by sensory impressions, brings forth the forms that were hidden within, the assumptions are true with this restriction. 7. Because the soul is a 'sacred image that takes all forms', since it possesses the principles of all that is, it can be aroused by sensible things to recollection of the principles that it has within itself and produce them: having observed a thing in this world, the soul realizes its absolute essence. So we have thus far established that in the case of the human soul there is transition from one kind of knowledge to another, from sense-perception to ratiocination; but also from one object to another, from the equal in this world to the absolute equal. Furthermore, it is a transition from similar to similar, from one kind of equality to another. Finally, the transition being from similar to

---

§ 7. 1–2. *Supra* 4 § 2.3.

δ' ἀνάμνησις, ἀλλὰ μνήμη [73e1–3]. τέταρτον τὸ τὴν μετάβασιν γίνεσθαι ἀπὸ
ὁμοίου ἐπὶ ὅμοιον ἢ ἀπὸ ἀνομοίου ἐπὶ ἀνόμοιον· ὁ μὲν γὰρ τὴν εἰκόνα Σωκράτους
θεασάμενος καὶ ἀπ' αὐτῆς ἀναμνησθεὶς τοῦ Σωκράτους ἀπὸ ὁμοίου ἐπὶ ὅμοιον
μετῆλθεν, ὁ δὲ ἀπὸ Κέβητος Σιμμίου ἀναμνησθεὶς ἀπὸ ἀνομοίου ἐπὶ ἀνόμοιον
ε' [73e5–74a4]. πέμπτον, ἡνίκα ἀπὸ ὁμοίου ἐπὶ ὅμοιον ἀνάμνησις γίνεται, δύνασθαι   15
ἡμᾶς καὶ προσθεῖναι τὸ λεῖπον [74a5–8]. τούτων οὕτως ἐχόντων ἀνάμνησίς
ἐστι δευτέρα γνῶσις ἀπὸ γνώσεως ἐπὶ γνῶσιν καὶ ἀπὸ γνωστοῦ | ἐπὶ γνωστὸν (68)
λήθης διαδραμούσης ἢ ἀπὸ ὁμοίου ἢ ἀπὸ ἀνομοίου τῆς μεταβάσεως γινομένης,
καὶ ἡνίκα ἀπὸ ὁμοίου, δύνασθαί τι καὶ προστιθέναι.

'Αλλὰ ἀπορήσωμεν πρὸς δύο λήμματα τῶν προειρημένων. πρὸς μὲν τὸ β',   6
ὅτι οὐ πάντως ἡ ἀνάμνησις ἀπὸ γνώσεως ἐπὶ γνῶσίν ἐστιν καὶ ἀπὸ γνωστοῦ
ἐπὶ γνωστόν· ἐνδέχεται γὰρ καὶ μὴ μετάβασιν εἶναι μήτε γνώσεως μήτε γνωστοῦ,
οἷον εἴ τις πάλαι Σωκράτην θεασάμενος καὶ αὖθις αὐτὸν ἰδὼν μετὰ τὸ ἐπιλα-
θέσθαι αὐτοῦ εἰς ἀνάμνησιν ἔλθῃ. ἰδοὺ οὐ γέγονε μετάβασις γνώσεως, αἰσθητικὴ   5
γὰρ ἑκατέρα γνῶσις· ἀλλ' οὐδὲ γνωστοῦ γέγονε μετάβασις, Σωκράτης γὰρ ἦν ὁ καὶ
πάλαι καὶ νῦν γινωσκόμενος. ἀλλὰ καὶ πρὸς ἄλλο λῆμμά ἐστιν ἀπορῆσαι, τὸ
λέγον ὅτι ἡ μετάβασις ἢ ἀπὸ ὁμοίου ἐπὶ ὅμοιον γίνεται ἢ ἀπὸ ἀνομοίου ἐπὶ
ἀνόμοιον· ἐνδέχεται γὰρ καὶ ἀπὸ τοῦ αὐτοῦ ἐπὶ τὸ αὐτό, ὥσπερ εἴ τις θεασάμενος
πάλαι Σωκράτην καὶ ἐπιλαθόμενος αὐτοῦ καὶ νῦν θεώμενος αὐτὸν εἰς ἀνάμνησιν   10
αὐτοῦ ἔλθῃ· καὶ ἰδοὺ ἀπὸ τοῦ αὐτοῦ ἐπὶ τὸ αὐτό. τί οὖν; ψεύδεται τὰ Πλατωνικὰ
λήμματα; ἢ εἰ μὲν ἐπὶ πάσης ἀναμνήσεως ἀκούσωμεν τῶν λημμάτων, ψεύδονται·
ἐπειδὴ δὲ οὐ περὶ πάσης ἀναμνήσεως λέγει ὁ φιλόσοφος, ἀλλὰ περὶ τῆς νῦν
προκειμένης, καθ' ἣν ἡ ψυχὴ αὐτῷ νυττομένη καὶ ἐρεθιζομένη ὑπὸ τῶν αἰσθητῶν
ἀποκυΐσκει τὰ ἔνδον ἐν ἑαυτῇ εἴδη, ταύτῃ ἀληθῆ τὰ λήμματα. ἐπειδὴ γὰρ   7
'πάμμορφον ἄγαλμά' ἐστιν ἡ ψυχὴ πάντων τῶν ὄντων ἔχουσα λόγους, ἐρεθιζομένη
ὑπὸ τῶν αἰσθητῶν ἀναμιμνήσκεται ὧν ἔνδον ἔχει λόγων καὶ τούτους προβάλλεται·
β' οἷον θεασαμένη τὸ τῇδε προβάλλεται τὸ ἁπλῶς. καὶ ἰδοὺ τέως ἔχομεν ὅτι ἐπὶ
τῆς ἡμετέρας ψυχῆς μετάβασίς ἐστιν ἀπὸ γνώσεως ἐπὶ γνῶσιν, ἀπὸ γὰρ αἰσθη-   5
τικῆς ἐπὶ διανοητικήν· ἀλλὰ καὶ ἀπὸ γνωστοῦ ἐπὶ γνωστόν, ἀπὸ γὰρ τοῦ τῇδε
δ' ἴσου ἐπὶ τὸ ἁπλῶς ἴσον ἡ μετάβασις γίνεται. ἀλλὰ καὶ ἀπὸ | ὁμοίου ἐπὶ ὅμοιον, (69)
ε' ἀπὸ γὰρ ἴσου ἐπὶ ἴσον. καὶ ἐπειδὴ ἀπὸ ὁμοίου ἐπὶ ὅμοιον γέγονεν ἡ μετάβασις,
δυνάμεθα καὶ προστιθέναι τὸ λεῖπον. τὸ μὲν γὰρ ἐνταῦθα ἴσον οὐκ ἀκριβές
ἐστι· πῶς γὰρ ἀκριβῶς ἴσον τὸ καὶ ψαμμαίου μεγέθους ἀφαιρεθέντος ἢ προσ-   10
τεθέντος ἴσον μεῖναν· 'οὐδὲ' γὰρ 'ὁρῶμεν οὐδὲν ἀκριβὲς οὐδὲ ἀκούομεν' κατὰ
τὸν αὐτοῦ λόγον [65b3–4]· ἀπὸ οὖν τοῦ παχυμεροῦς ἴσου ἐπὶ τὸ ἀκριβὲς ἴσον
ἔρχεται, καὶ ἰδοὺ τὸ λεῖπον προστίθησιν.

---

§ 6. 8–9 ἐπὶ ἀνόμοιον ins. Mᶜ: om. M¹ — 12 ἀκούσωμεν] -μεν in fine lin. ins. Mᶜ —
14 καθ'] -α- in ras. 2 litt. Mᶜ

10–11. Supra 5 § 5.2–5; infra 12 § 1.11–13.

similar, we can also supply what is missing. For the equal in this world is not exactly equal, otherwise it would not remain so after removal or addition of a quantity the size of a grain of sand. In Plato's own words, 'we neither see nor hear anything accurately' [65b3–4]; hence the soul passes from approximate equality to exact equality, in other words, it supplies what was missing.

8. And as regards the two other assumptions concerning recollection, that it is a second knowledge, and that it is interrupted by oblivion, can we maintain them or can we not? The answer is yes, we can. That it is a second knowledge is proved by the very fact of transition and supplementation: if it were the first, we could not supply anything at all, nor would there be transition; a man who sees Socrates' portrait, but has not seen Socrates himself before, cannot go beyond the portrait. That, moreover, there has been an interval of oblivion also, is proved by the fact that when recollecting we are not conscious of having known before. This is really the most evident sign of forgetting, not to be conscious that one knew before, but to think that one has learnt only now. Thus far the survey.

9. **According to that other theory too, Socrates, if it is correct, the one that you are always repeating [72e3–5]:** As a disciple of Socrates, Cebes is readily persuaded that learning is recollection. Socrates proves this in the dialogue *Meno* [81e3–86b6]: he calls Meno's servant and sets him a geometrical problem, and when he answers correctly, Socrates concludes that learning is recollection, because people (when questioned in the right way) could not give true answers if they did not have innate notions of the things about which they are asked. Therefore Cebes attributes the doctrine to Socrates, saying that he had often heard it from him.

10. **The soul seems to be something immortal [73a2–3]:** as we said [§ 2]: 'something immortal', not simply 'immortal'.

11. **Remind me, because at the moment I cannot quite ... [73a5–6]:** i.e. 'Our subject being recollection, you must remind me how it was proved that learning is recollection'.

12. **If the questions are put properly [73a8]:** That is to say, in the right, Platonic way, not as the Peripatetics handle them, nor with an eye to cheap triumphs, but with the readiness to hold out a hand to one's interlocutor, if he stumbles.

---

§ 8. 6–9. *Infra* 12 § 2.6–7.

§ 9. 3–7. **Dam. I** § 300.

§ 10. *Supra* § 2.14–15.

§ 11. The note would have more point if applied to b6–7 αὐτὸ δὲ τοῦτο δέομαι παθεῖν περὶ οὗ ὁ λόγος, ἀναμνησθῆναι. Probably the reportator missed the lemma.

§ 12. Περιπατητικῶς : in the way of Aristotelian dialectic; βωμολόχως : in the

Ἄρα δὲ καὶ τὰ ἄλλα δύο λήμματα τῆς ἀναμνήσεως οὐ σῴζομεν, τὸ δευτέραν **8**
α' εἶναι γνῶσιν καὶ τὸ λήθη μεταξὺ διακόπτεσθαι; ἢ καὶ ταῦτα σῴζομεν. ὅτι
γὰρ δευτέρα ἐστὶ γνῶσις, δηλοῖ αὐτὴ ἡ μετάβασις ⟨καὶ ἡ πρόσθεσις⟩· εἰ γὰρ
πρώτη ἦν, οὐδὲν προστιθέναι ὅλως ἐδυνάμεθα, οὐδὲ μετάβασις ἐγίνετο· ὁ γὰρ
τὴν εἰκόνα Σωκράτους θεασάμενος, μὴ πρότερον δὲ τὸν Σωκράτην θεασάμενος **5**
γ' ἵσταται μέχρι τῆς εἰκόνος. ὅτι δὲ καὶ λήθη διέδραμε μεταξύ, δηλοῖ τὸ μὴ
ἐφιστάνειν ἡμᾶς ἀναμιμνησκομένους ὅτι προῄδειμεν αὐτά· τοῦτο γὰρ μέγιστον
σημεῖον λήθης, τὸ μὴ ἐφιστάνειν ὅτι πρότερον ἤδει αὐτά, ἀλλ' οἴεσθαι νῦν μεμαθη-
κέναι. ταῦτα ἔχει ἡ θεωρία.

Καὶ κατ' ἐκεῖνόν γε τὸν λόγον, ὦ Σώκρατες, εἰ ἀληθής ἐστιν, **9**
ὃν εἴωθας θαμὰ λέγειν [72e3–5]: ὡς Σωκρατικὸς ὁ Κέβης ἑτοίμως ἔχει
περὶ τὸ πεισθῆναι ὅτι αἱ μαθήσεις ἀναμνήσεις εἰσίν. τοῦτο γὰρ ἔδειξεν αὐτῷ
ὁ Σωκράτης ἐν τῷ Μένωνι τῷ διαλόγῳ [81e3–86b6]· λαβὼν τὸν τοῦ Μένωνος
οἰκέτην καὶ ἐρωτήσας γραμμικόν τι κἀκείνου ὀρθῶς ἀποκριναμένου ἔδειξεν **5**
ὅτι αἱ μαθήσεις ἀναμνήσεις, ἐπεὶ οὐκ ἂν ἄλλως τὸ ἀληθὲς ἀπεκρίναντο οἱ ὀρθῶς
ἐρωτώμενοι, εἰ μὴ εἶχον ἐν ἑαυτοῖς τοὺς λόγους ὧν ἠρωτῶντο. διὸ καὶ ὁ Κέβης
ἀνατίθησι τὸ δόγμα Σωκράτει, λέγων θαμὰ ἀκηκοέναι αὐτοῦ τοῦτο λέγοντος.

Ἀθάνατόν τι ἔοικεν ἡ ψυχὴ εἶναι [73a2–3]: ἰδοὺ 'τὶ ἀθάνατον' καὶ **10**(70)
οὐχ ἁπλῶς.

Ὑπόμνησόν με· οὐ γὰρ σφόδρα γε ἐν τῷ παρόντι [73a5–6]: ἀντὶ **11**
τοῦ 'περὶ ἀναμνήσεως ὄντος τοῦ λόγου ἀνάμνησόν με, πῶς ἐδείχθησαν αἱ μαθήσεις
ἀναμνήσεις'.

Ἐάν τις καλῶς ἐρωτᾷ [73a8]: τουτέστιν ὀρθῶς καὶ Πλατωνικῶς, καὶ **12**
μὴ Περιπατητικῶς καὶ μὴ βωμολόχως, ἀλλὰ χεῖρα ὀρέγῃ τοῖς ὀλισθήμασι τῶν
προσδιαλεγομένων.

---

§ 8. 2 ὅτι] -ι in ras. Mᶜ — 3 καὶ ἡ πρόσθεσις Wk: om. M
§ 9. 2 ὃν M¹: ὃν σὺ Mᶜ, Pl. — 5 γραμμικόν Nv: γραμματικόν M — 8 ἀνατίθησι] -α-
in ras., -τι- sscr. et puncto del. Mᶜ (i.e. ἀντιτίθησι M¹)
§ 11. 1 γε] om. Pl.

---

way of eristics such as Euthydemus. Cf. Amm., int. 202. 19–25 οὐ διαγίνεται ὁ παρὰ
Πλάτωνι Σωκράτης ἐν ταῖς πρὸς τοὺς κοινωνοῦντας αὐτῷ τῶν λόγων συνουσίαις κατὰ
τὴν πρόθεσιν τοῦ κατὰ τὸν Ἀριστοτέλην καλουμένου διαλεκτικοῦ· ὁ μὲν γὰρ οὕτω λεγόμενος
διαλεκτικὸς πρὸς νίκην μόνον ὁρᾷ τοῦ προσδιαλεγομένου καὶ τὸ περιαγαγεῖν αὐτὸν εἰς
τὴν ἀντίφασιν, ὁ δέ γε Σωκράτης καὶ πταίοντας τοὺς προσδιαλεγομένους ἐπανορθοῖ καὶ
τέλος τίθεται οὐ τὴν νίκην ἀλλὰ τὴν τῆς ἀληθείας κατάληψιν.

13. If you confront them with geometrical figures [73b1]: Geometry is chosen as the subject for the answers, because there the road is a single and narrow one, of which it is strictly true that it is a 'trail', not a 'highway.'

14. Have known it some time before [73c2]: The first assumption.

15. If a man having seen or heard one thing [73c6]: The second, that there must be a transition from one kind of knowledge, and from one object of knowledge, to another.

16. 'This, then,' said Socrates, 'is a kind of recollection' [73e1]: The beginning of the third assumption, that there must be an interval of oblivion. Oblivion may be brought about by (1) lack of attention, as with the indifferent, (2) time, as with old men, (3) disease, as for example the affection called lethargy by physicians. These are the causes of oblivion: indifference, time, disease.

17. 'Further,' said Socrates, 'is it possible, when seeing a horse . . .' **[73e5]:** Beginning of the fourth assumption.

18. 'But when it is by something similar . . .' [74a5]: Of the fifth.

12

Lecture **

1. Surely we agree that there is such a thing as the equal, not as one stick is equal to another [74a9–].**

The text before us proves two things: that forms exist (not ideas, of course, but forms in the soul) and that learning is recollection; it does so by showing that the five elements of recollection listed above [11 § 5] apply to learning as well. To demonstrate the existence of forms he uses two arguments; that learning is recollection is proved in the way described.

As to the existence of forms there can be no doubt. If the one must exist prior to the manifold and the absolute prior to the particular (in other words, the intelligible must precede things sensible, and the immaterial things material), it follows that forms exist [74a9–b7]. The second argument is that the approximate must be preceded by the exact, and the vague and inaccurate by the well-defined, and the forms in this

---

§ 13. 2–3.   *Supra* 5 § 14.
§§ 14–18.   *Supra* § 5.

Lect. 12.   Forms exist. The five characteristics of recollection are also those of learning. The pericope covered can have ended either at 74e8 or at 75c6. To the two proofs for the existence of forms derived from the text of Pl. (74a9–c6) three additional ones are added to demonstrate the existence of forms in the soul (§ 1). The five characteristics of recollection listed at 11 § 5 are then shown to apply to the process of learning (§ 2). Only a small part of the *lexis* is extant (§ 3). If

Ἐάν τις ἐπὶ τὰ διαγράμματα ἄγῃ [73b1]: ἐν γὰρ τοῖς γεωμετρικοῖς   13
ἡ ἀπόκρισις, διότι μία ἡ ὁδὸς καὶ στενή, καὶ περὶ αὐτῆς κυρίως ἁρμόζει τὸ
'ἀτραπὸς' καὶ οὐ 'λεωφόρος'.

Πρότερόν ποτε ἐπίστασθαι [73c2]: τὸ πρῶτον λῆμμα.   14

Ἐάν τις ἕτερον ἰδὼν ἢ ἀκούσας [73c6]: τὸ δεύτερον, ὅτι δεῖ μετά-   15
βασιν εἶναι καὶ γνώσεως καὶ γνωστοῦ.

Οὐκοῦν, ἦ δ' ὅς, τὸ τοιοῦτον ἀνάμνησίς τίς ἐστιν [73e1]: ἐντεῦθεν 16 (71)
τὸ τρίτον λῆμμα, ὅτι δεῖ καὶ λήθην εἶναι μεταξύ. γίνεται δὲ λήθη ἢ διὰ τὸ
μὴ ἐπισκοπεῖν, ὃ πάσχουσιν οἱ ῥάθυμοι, [ἢ διὰ τὸ μὴ] ἢ διὰ χρόνον, ὡς ἐπὶ
τῶν γερόντων, ἢ διὰ νόσον, ὡς ὁ λήθαργος τὸ παρὰ τοῖς ἰατροῖς πάθος. καὶ
ταῦτα τὰ αἴτια τῆς λήθης· ῥαθυμία, χρόνος, νόσος.   5

Τί δέ; ἦ δ' ὅς· ἔστιν ἵππον [73e5]: ἐντεῦθεν τὸ δ' λῆμμα.   17

Ἀλλ' ὅταν γε, ἔφη, ἀπὸ τῶν ὁμοίων [74a5]: ἐντεῦθεν τὸ πέμπτον.   18

12

Πρᾶξις σὺν θεῷ

Φαμέν πού τι εἶναι ἴσον, οὐ ξύλον λέγω ξύλῳ [74a9–**].   1

Ἡ μετὰ χεῖρα λέξις δύο ταῦτα δείκνυσιν, ὅτι ἐστὶν τὰ εἴδη (οὐ τί φημι
αἱ ἰδέαι, ἀλλὰ τὰ ἐν τῇ ψυχῇ εἴδη) καὶ ὅτι αἱ μαθήσεις ἀναμνήσεις, ἐκ τοῦ
δεικνύναι ἐφαρμόζοντα τῇ μαθήσει τὰ εἰρημένα στοιχεῖα ε' τῆς ἀναμνήσεως
[11 § 5]. καὶ ὅτι μέν εἰσιν εἴδη, δείκνυσι διὰ δύο ἐπιχειρημάτων· ὅτι δὲ καὶ   5
αἱ μαθήσεις ἀναμνήσεις, τῷ εἰρημένῳ τρόπῳ δείκνυσιν.

α'   Ὅτι γάρ εἰσι τὰ εἴδη, δῆλον. εἰ γὰρ δεῖ εἶναι πρὸ τῶν πολλῶν [εἰδῶν] τὸ
ἓν καὶ πρὸ τῶν κατὰ μέρος τὸ ἁπλῶς, δεῖ γὰρ προηγεῖσθαι τῶν αἰσθητῶν τὸ
β'   νοητὸν καὶ τῶν ἐνύλων τὸ ἄυλον, ἔστιν ἄρα | τὰ εἴδη [74a9–b7]. δεύτερον,   (72)
εἰ δεῖ πρὸ τοῦ παχυμεροῦς τὸ ἀκριβὲς καὶ ⟨πρὸ τοῦ⟩ ἀμυδροῦ καὶ ὁλοσχεροῦς   10
τὸ διηρθρωμένον, τὰ δὲ ἐνταῦθα εἴδη οὐκ ἀκριβῆ ἐστιν, διότι ἴσα ἐστὶ τὰ μεγέθη

---

§ 14.   1 πρῶτον Fh: πρότερον M
§ 15.   1 ἕτερον M¹: πρότερον ἢ Mᶜ: τι πρότερον ἢ Pl. BW: τι ἕτερόν τι Pl. TY
§ 16.   3 ἢ διὰ τὸ μὴ M: del. μ
§ 17.   1 δέ] δαὶ Pl. BTW
§ 18.   1 ἔφη] om. Pl.

§ 1.   7 εἰδῶν M: del. Wk — 10 πρὸ τοῦ Nv: om. M

---

the statement of the MS. as to the size of the lacuna (five leaves) is exact, there
are probably two more lectures missing, one dealing with the remainder of the
argument from recollection, the proof that recollection implies pre-existence
(75c7–77a5 ?), the other with the passage leading up to the argument from similarity
(77a6 ?–78b3).

§ 1.   2–3.   Dam. I § 274; II § 15.
7.   The confusing εἰδῶν could be defended on the ground of τὰ ἐνταῦθα εἴδη at
line 11, but cf. § 3.2.
9–12.   Cf. supra 5 § 5.2–5; 11 § 7.9–11.
10.   δεῖ: ⟨εἶναι⟩ to be either inserted or understood from line 7.

world are not exact: two magnitudes that are equal will remain so when a quantity the size of a grain of sand is added or removed [74b7–c6]. Since, however, these arguments prove the existence of ideas no less than that of innate notions in the soul, let us give some additional proof of the existence of such notions in the soul. If the human mind distinguishes between forms in this world and calls the one more beautiful, the other less so, it evidently pronounces these judgments by referring to a certain standard and a certain form; it could not distinguish between things of which it does not have the notions within itself. We should not believe the Peripatos [Ar., *anal. post.* II 19, 99b35] when it declares that we discern these things by means of something called the faculty of judgment: the human soul does not act by mere natural instinct, as a spider makes its web. Besides, if it makes additions and passes from one thing to another, it must evidently have certain forms within itself, otherwise there would be no question of passing on to other things, or of supplying deficiencies, without such forms; a man who sees Socrates' portrait without having seen Socrates before cannot go beyond the portrait. Lastly, if the soul aspires the knowledge of exact forms and no aspiration can be in vain, the cause of this longing can only be the presence of innate forms, which it tries to apprehend clearly.

2. That, secondly, learning is recollection, is proved by the fact that the elements of recollection can be predicated of the human soul: (1) starting from sense-perception, e.g. from equality in this world, we proceed to absolute equality; (2) the transition is effected in this case by something similar; (3) we supply what is missing, since equality here below is not exact; (4) it is, moreover, a second knowledge, otherwise we could not supplement it, for the man who has seen only the portrait of Socrates is unable to go beyond it; (5) finally, there has been an interval of oblivion, the strongest proof of which is that when recollecting we are not conscious of having known these things before. And it is no wonder that this should happen: it is the disturbance caused by the body that prevents us from being aware of having known. As those who are ill do not remember the circumstances of normal health ('The disease made them unable to recognize either themselves or the others', as the historian [Thuc. 2,49,8] says), but when in health we remember the afflictions and sores we suffered during illness, so after separation from the body the

---

14. ἔξωθεν: in this sense also Ol., *Alc.* 74.7; 203.20; *supra* 1 § 3.1.

14–25. Arguments for innate λόγοι or εἴδη in the soul: (1) judging and distinguishing are possible only by virtue of a given standard, not by a mere faculty without a content of its own; (2) completing notions and relating them to others is possible only if the complete notion is already available; (3) the desire for knowledge of the perfect, since natural, must have its ground in the possibility of fulfillment, cf. above 6 § 10 (Dam. I § 179).

17–19. Ar., *anal. post.* II 19, 99b35 ἔχει γὰρ (scil. τὰ ζῷα) δύναμιν σύμφυτον

καὶ ψαμμιαίου τινὸς προστεθέντος αὐτοῖς ἢ ἀφαιρεθέντος ἐξ αὐτῶν ἴσα μένει
[74b7–c6]. ἀλλ' ἐπειδὴ ταῦτα οὐδὲν ἧττον τῶν ἰδεῶν ἢ τῶν ἐν τῇ ψυχῇ λόγων
γ' ἐστὶν κατασκευαστικά, φέρε ἔξωθεν δείξωμεν ὅτι εἰσὶ λόγοι ἐν τῇ ψυχῇ. εἰ
γὰρ διακρίνει ἡ ἡμετέρα ψυχὴ τὰ τῇδε εἴδη καὶ τὸ μὲν λέγει μᾶλλον καλόν,   15
τὸ δὲ ἧττον, δῆλον ⟨ὅτι πρός⟩ τινα ὅρον καὶ πρός τι εἶδος παραβάλλουσα κρίνει
ταῦτα· οὐ γὰρ ἠδύνατο, ὧν μὴ εἶχε λόγους, ταῦτα διακρίνειν. οὐ γὰρ πειστέον
τῷ Περιπάτῳ [Ar., anal. post. II 19, 99b35] λέγοντι ὅτι κριτικῇ τινι δυνάμει
ταῦτα διακρίνει· οὐ γὰρ φυσικῶς ἐνεργεῖ ἡ ἡμετέρα ψυχή, καθάπερ ὁ ἀράχνης
δ' τὸ ἀράχνιον. ἄλλως τε εἰ προστίθησι καὶ μεταβαίνει, δῆλον ἄρα ὅτι ἔχει ἐν   20
ἑαυτῇ εἴδη τινά, ἐπεὶ οὐδὲ τὴν ἀρχὴν μετέβαινεν καὶ τὸ λεῖπον προσετίθει
μὴ ἔχουσα εἴδη· ὁ γὰρ τὴν εἰκόνα Σωκράτους θεασάμενος καὶ μὴ πρότερον
ε' τὸν Σωκράτην μέχρι τῆς εἰκόνος ἵσταται. ἄλλως τε εἰ ἐφίεται γνῶναι τὰ ἀκριβῆ
εἴδη ἡ ψυχὴ καὶ μὴ μάτην ἐστὶν ἡ ἔφεσις, δῆλον ὅτι διὰ τὰ ἐν αὐτῇ εἴδη ἐστὶν
ἡ ἔφεσις· ταῦτα γὰρ βούλεται μαθεῖν.   25

Ὅτι δὲ καὶ αἱ μαθήσεις ἀναμνήσεις, δῆλον ἐκ τοῦ τὰ στοιχεῖα τῆς ἀναμνήσεως   2
ὑπάρχειν τῇ ἡμετέρα ψυχῇ. ἀπὸ γὰρ τῆς αἰσθητικῆς γνώσεως, οἷον ἀπὸ τοῦ
τῇδε ἴσου, ἐρχόμεθα ἐπὶ τὸ ἁπλῶς ἴσον· ἀλλὰ καὶ δι' ὁμοίου ἐνταῦθα συνέβη·
καὶ προστίθεμεν δὲ τὸ λεῖπον, διότι οὐκ ἀκριβὲς τὸ τῇδε ἴσον· ἔτι μὴν καὶ
δευτέρα ἐστὶν γνῶσις, εἴ γε προστίθεμεν, ἐπεὶ ὁ τὴν εἰκόνα Σωκράτους θεασά-   5
μενος ἵσταται μέχρι αὐτῆς· ἀλλὰ μὴν καὶ λήθη διέδραμεν, καὶ τούτου μέγιστον
σημεῖον τὸ ἀναμιμνησκομένους ἡμᾶς μὴ ἐφιστάνειν ὅτι προ|εγνώκειμεν αὐτά. (73)
καὶ οὐδὲν θαυμαστόν, εἰ τοῦτο συμβαίνει· διὰ γὰρ σωματικὸν σάλον οὐκ
ἐφιστάνομεν. ὥσπερ γὰρ οἱ μὲν ἐν νόσῳ ὄντες οὐ μέμνηνται τῶν ἐν τῇ ὑγείᾳ
('σφᾶς τε' γὰρ 'ἑαυτοὺς ὑπὸ τῆς νόσου καὶ τοὺς ἄλλους ἠγνόουν', φησὶν ὁ   10
συγγραφεύς [Thuc. 2, 49, 8]), ἐν δὲ τῇ ὑγείᾳ μεμνήμεθα τῶν ἐν νόσῳ πληγῶν
καὶ τραυμάτων, οὕτω καὶ ἡ ψυχὴ χωρισθεῖσα μὲν τοῦ σώματος διὰ τὸ μὴ

---

16 ὅτι πρός μ: om. M — 17 πιστέον M
§ 2. 9 νόσῳ] -ωι in ras. Mᶜ

κριτικήν, ἣν καλοῦσιν αἴσθησιν. An. III 9, 432a15–17 ἡ ψυχὴ κατὰ δύο ὥρισται δυνάμεις
ἡ τῶν ζῴων, τῷ τε κριτικῷ, ὃ διανοίας ἔργον ἐστὶ καὶ αἰσθήσεως, καὶ ἔτι τῷ κινεῖν τὴν
κατὰ τόπον κίνησιν.
19–20. Ar., phys. II 8, 199a26–27 φύσει τε ποιεῖ καὶ ἕνεκά του ἡ χελιδὼν τὴν
νεοττιὰν καὶ ὁ ἀράχνης τὸ ἀράχνιον.
§ 2. Supra 11 § 5; a résumé of Ph. 73c1–74a8.
6–7. Supra 11 § 8.6–9.
8–18. Dam. I § 269.6–9; II § 19. A well-known quotation from Ar. (frg. 41 R.³=
Eudemus frg. 5 Ross) preserved by Pr., Rep. II 349.13–26; cf. Ol., Gorg. 265.20–24.

soul, being hampered by nothing, can remember the afflictions and sores it incurred while in the body, but so long as it is in the body it cannot remember what happened in former life. And this is not surprising: if we cannot remember the events of one lifetime, but often have forgotten them so completely that in spite of many reminders we fail to recall them and think this is the first time we hear of them, this will be all the more liable to happen in a different life. Thus far the survey.

3. 'May we take it there is such a thing, or not?' – 'We may' [74a12–b1]: This is what we said already [§ 1], that the one must exist prior to the many; mob rule is to be rejected, for here, too, 'the rule of many lords is not a good thing' [Il. 2.204]. Simmias readily admits the existence of forms (so much so that he even swears on it and goes on to say 'Most assuredly I am convinced') because he is familiar with the doctrine of Socrates; for the same reason he said above: 'I am persuaded, but I need to be reminded' [73b6–7].

4. Look at it in this way, too [74b7]: . . . .
. . . .

13

Lecture **

1. 'Well then', said Socrates, 'the kind of question we should ask ourselves is this' [78b4–**].

To enable ourselves to follow the argument from similarity, let us first of all observe that Socrates is contrasting being with genesis (as he does in the *Timaeus* also [27d6–28a1]: 'What is it that always is and has no coming-to-be, and what is it that comes to be but never is?' meaning, by being, exemplary forms, and by coming-to-be the sensible world) and in stating this contrast he points out six properties of each: of being divinity, immortality, accessibility to thought, indissolubility, singleness of form, eternal invariability, and of genesis corporeality (as the opposite of divinity), mortality, incapability of thought, dissolubility, multiformity, complete absence of invariability.

---

§ 3. 1–2. *Supra* § 1.7–8.
2–3. The reference is not directly to Homer, of course, but in the first place to Ar., *met. Λ* 10, 1076a3–4.

Lect. 13. **The argument from similarity: the six attributes of the intelligible; the inference as regards the human soul.** The argument rests on the antithesis of *Tim.* 27d6–28a1, described in six pairs of opposite attributes (§ 1), which are each discussed separately (§ 2). Pl. then establishes that the soul resembles the intelligible more closely than the visible in three respects: it is invisible, it thinks, it rules;

ἐμποδίζεσθαι ὑπό τινος δύναται μεμνῆσθαι τῶν συμβάντων [τῶν] μετὰ τοῦ
σώματος πληγῶν καὶ τραυμάτων, ἐν δὲ τῷ σώματι οὖσα οὐ μέμνηται τῶν ἐν
τῷ προτέρῳ βίῳ. καὶ οὐδὲν θαυμαστόν· εἰ γὰρ ἐν ἑνὶ βίῳ ὄντες οὐ μεμνήμεθα   15
τῶν συμβαινόντων, ἀλλ᾽ οὕτω πολλάκις ἐπιλανθανόμεθα ὡς καὶ πολλῶν ἡμῖν
τεκμηρίων λεγομένων μὴ ἐφιστάνειν, ἀλλ᾽ οἴεσθαι νῦν πρῶτον αὐτὸ μανθάνειν,
πολλῷ μᾶλλον ἐν διαφόρῳ βίῳ τοῦτο συμβήσεται. ταῦτα ἔχει ἡ θεωρία.

Φῶμέν τι εἶναι ἢ μηδέν; Φῶμεν [74a12–b1]: τὸ εἰρημένον [§ 1],   3
ὅτι ἀνάγκη εἶναι πρὸ τῶν πολλῶν τὸ ἕν· οὐδὲ γὰρ ὀχλοκρατίαν εἶναι, ʽοὐκ
ἀγαθὸν᾽ γὰρ οὐδὲ ἐνταῦθα ʽπολυκοιρανίη᾽ [Β 204]. ὁ δὲ Σιμμίας ἑτοίμως
συντίθεται τῷ εἶναι τὰ εἴδη (διὸ καὶ ὅρκον ἐπάγει καί φησιν ὅτι ʽθαυμασίως
πέπεισμαι᾽) ὡς συνήθης τῶν Σωκρατικῶν δογμάτων· διὸ καὶ ἀνωτέρω ἔλεγεν   5
ὅτι ʽπέπεισμαι, ἀλλὰ ἀναμνήσεως δέομαι᾽ [73b6–7].

Σκόπει δὲ καὶ τῇδε [74b7]:   4

. . . .

13

Πρᾶξις σὺν θεῷ   (74)

Οὐκοῦν τοιόνδε τι, ἦ δὲ ὃς ὁ Σωκράτης, δεῖ ἡμᾶς ἀνερέσθαι   1
ἑαυτούς [78b4–**].

Ἵνα τῷ ἐκ τῆς ὁμοιότητος λόγῳ παρακολουθήσωμεν, προλάβωμεν ὅτι
ἀντιδιαιρῶν ὁ Σωκράτης τὴν οὐσίαν τῇ γενέσει, — ὥσπερ καὶ ἐν Τιμαίῳ
[27d6–28a1] ἐποίησεν· ʽτί τὸ ὂν μὲν ἀεί, γένεσιν δὲ οὐκ ἔχον, καὶ τί τὸ γινό-   5
μενον μέν, ὂν δὲ οὐδέποτε;᾽ οὐσίαν μὲν γὰρ τὰ παραδειγματικὰ εἴδη, γένεσιν
δὲ τὸ αἰσθητόν· — ταῦτα ἀντιδιαιρῶν ἐξ ἴδια ἑκάστου παραδίδωσιν, τῆς μὲν
οὐσίας τὸ θεῖον, τὸ ἀθάνατον, τὸ νοητόν, τὸ ἀδιάλυτον, τὸ μονοειδές, τὸ ἀεὶ
κατὰ τὰ αὐτὰ καὶ ὡσαύτως ἔχειν ἑαυτῷ, τῆς δὲ γενέσεως τὸ σωματοειδές
(ἀντίκειται γὰρ τῷ θείῳ), τὸ θνητόν, τὸ ἀνόητον, τὸ διαλυτόν, τὸ πολυειδές,   10
τὸ μηδέποτε κατὰ τὰ αὐτὰ καὶ ὡσαύτως ἔχειν ἑαυτῷ.

---

13 τῶν² Μᶜ: del. Wk — 15 καὶ ins. Μᶜ: om. Μ¹
§ 4. 1 paulo minus una pagina vacat

§ 1. 1 ἀνερέσθαι] ἀνέρεσθαι, -έ- in ras. 2 litt., accentu in alt. -ε- eraso, Μᶜ: ἀνευρέσθαι
Pl. Τ¹, et sic fort. Μ¹

---

therefore it lasts longer (§ 3). This is the opinion of the other commentators as
against Iambl., who argues that it at least contains the material for the complete
proof as constructed by Plotinus (§ 4). The question what forms are meant at
78d1–7 and Pr.'s answer (§ 5). The objection that resemblance is not identity (§ 6).
The *lexis* part of the lecture (§§ 7–20) ought to be complete, or as good as, in
which case the pericope probably ends at 80a9.

§§ 1–2. The six attributes are discussed at length by Pr., *theol.* I 26–27, but
from an entirely different angle: having shown that they apply to everything that
is beyond soul, Pr. deals with them as attributes of the Gods.

§ 1. Dam. I § 312; II § 30.1–6.

2. Let us discuss each of these.

(1) He calls intelligible reality 'divine', because according to Plato it is directly dependent upon God, without being God; so 'divine' equals 'directly dependent upon God'.

(2) It is also 'immortal', because it has inextinguishable life; immortality in the true sense is found in real-existence, which exists eternally and has no was and is and will-be. Sempiternal things are not strictly eternal, since they fall under terms that express time, 'was', 'is', 'will be', and these, the parts of time, past, present and future, are not always, but pass away: the Sun is not always in Aries, but it was and will be there, and it answers a different description when in Aries and when in another zodiacal sign. To real-existents, however, only the 'is' applies, not the 'is' that is contradistinguished from the other indications of time, but the 'is' that denotes subsistence:

'For it was not, nor will it be, but it only is, one simultaneous whole'.

(3) It is also 'accessible to thought', not, however, in the sense that it is the object of thought; for the discussion deals with intellective forms, which think, but are not thought. Intelligible forms are thought, but

---

§ 2. Dam. I §§ 313–324; II § 30.6–12.

2–3. Pr., *theol.* I 26, 114.5–116.3 explains that while the Gods are the henads, the 'divine' is the henad jointly with the being that depends on it (the ἐκθεούμενον) on the different levels of reality. This view was forced upon him by the special requirements of that context; the more natural distinction made here by Ol., and by Dam. I § 313, was no doubt made by Pr. also (cf. Dam. II § 30.7–8 τὸ ἀγαθοειδὲς καὶ ἡνωμένον, with Dam.'s own alternative proposal ἢ μᾶλλον τὸ πρωτουργόν).

2. ἐξῆπται : the expression is already used of the lower principle as depending on its higher correlate by Plot. V 3,16.36; VI 5, 7.9. At least since Hermias (136.4) it occurs regularly as a technical term to express the relation of the successive lower levels in any vertical series (σειρά) to a higher one, usually the henad. There is an obvious connection with Homer, *Il.* 8.19–20 σειρὰν χρυσείην ἐξ οὐρανόθεν κρεμάσαντες πάντες τ' ἐξάπτεσθε θεοὶ πᾶσαί τε θέαιναι, but it is less easy to determine the exact nature of this connection. A metaphysical interpretation of the Golden Cord in Homer (like the one in Psellus, *de aurea catena*) may have existed before Plot. and have influenced him; more probably his occasional use of the word may have helped to suggest such an interpretation to a later Neoplatonist. Cf. Pr., *Tim.* I 314.18–19; II 24.23–29; III 162.15; Ol., *Gorg.* 244.5–6.

4–12. αἰών as the source of immortality: Pr., *theol.* I 26, 117.7–10. The difference between eternal and sempiternal is part of Pl.'s concept of eternity, but the terminological distinction between αἰώνιος and ἀίδιος is late: Pl. uses the two as synonymous, and so does Plot. (e.g. III 7,1.2); Pr.'s usage (e.g. *elem.* 172) follows the distinction as formulated by Ol., *mete.* 146.15–25, according to which αἰώνιος relates to αἰών and ἀίδιος to (endless) time.

6–7. Pl., *Tim.* 37e3–4 ταῦτα δὲ πάντα μέρη χρόνου, καὶ τό τ' ἦν τό τ' ἔσται χρόνου γεγονότα εἴδη.

ibid. χρονικὰ προσρήματα : cf. χρονικὰ ὀνόματα Pr., *Rep.* II 250.9; 30 (i.e. γεγονότα, ὄντα, μέλλοντα in Pl., *Rep.* X 617c4–5).

Ἑκάστου δὲ τούτων τὸν ἀπολογισμὸν εἴπωμεν.　　2

α′　Θεῖον᾽ μὲν οὖν ἐκάλεσεν τὸ νοητόν, διότι θεοῦ ἐξῆπται τοῦτο κατὰ Πλάτωνα, ἀλλ᾽ οὐ θεός ἐστι· θεῖον οὖν ἐστι τὸ θεοῦ ἐξημμένον.

β′　Ἀλλὰ καὶ ἀθάνατον᾽, διότι ζωὴν ἔχει ἄσβεστον· ἡ γὰρ κυρίως ἀθανασία ἐν αὐτῷ ἐστιν ὡς αἰωνίως ὄντι καὶ μὴ ἔχοντι τὸ ἦν καὶ ἔστι καὶ ἔσται. τὰ | 5 μὲν γὰρ ἀίδια οὐδὲ κυρίως ἀεί ἐστιν, διότι ἐστὶν ἐπὶ αὐτῶν τὰ χρονικὰ προσ- (75) ρήματα τὸ ἦν καὶ ἔστιν καὶ ἔσται, ἅπερ οὐκ ἀεί ἐστιν, ἀλλὰ φθείρεται τὰ μέρη τοῦ χρόνου, τὸ ἦν καὶ ἔστιν καὶ ἔσται· ὁ γὰρ ἥλιος οὐκ ἀεὶ ἐν Κριῷ ἐστιν, ἀλλ᾽ ἦν καὶ ἔσται, ἄλλος δέ ἐστι τῷ λόγῳ ἐν Κριῷ ὢν καὶ ἐν ἄλλῳ ζῳδίῳ. ἐπὶ ἐκείνων δὲ τὸ ἔστιν μόνον ἁρμόττει, οὐ τὸ ἀντιδιαιρούμενον τοῖς ἄλλοις χρονικοῖς 10 προσρήμασιν, ἀλλὰ τὸ σημαῖνον ὕπαρξιν· ᾽οὐ γὰρ ἔην, οὐκ ἔσται, ὁμοῦ πᾶν ἔστι δὲ μοῦνον᾽.

γ′　Ἀλλὰ καὶ ᾽νοητόν᾽ ἐστιν, οὐχ ὡς νοούμενον· περὶ γὰρ νοερῶν εἰδῶν ὁ λόγος ἐστίν, ἃ νοεῖ μέν, οὐ νοεῖται δέ. τὰ μὲν γὰρ νοητὰ νοεῖται μέν, οὐ μὴν νοεῖ, ὑπὲρ νοῦν γάρ ἐστι (διὸ καὶ πρόνοια λέγεται ὡς πρὸ τοῦ νοῦ, ὃ καὶ Ὀρφεὺς 15

—

§ 2.　9 ὤν] ὠ- in ras. M^c

8–9. Cf. Ar., phys. IV 11, 219b12–22, where he argues that the present as a moving point of time is in one sense identical with itself, and in another distinct from itself, and that this is equally true of a moving point or object in space, which by the mere fact of its displacement becomes different τῷ λόγῳ. The example of the Sun in the Ram must come from Amm.: cf. Philop. ad loc. (phys. 727.14–15) καὶ τοῦ γενέσθαι τὴν ἀπὸ Κριοῦ ἐπὶ Ταῦρον κίνησιν αἴτιος τυχὸν ὁ ἥλιος ὁ ταύτην κινηθεὶς ἢ ἕτερός τις τῶν ἀστέρων (not in Simpl., phys. 722.35–723.20).

12.　Parm. frg. 8.5, as quoted also by Amm., int. 136.24–25; Ascl., met. 38.7–18; 42.30; 202.16–17; Philop., phys. 65.9. The current text, as handed down by Simpl. (four times; supported by Pr., Parm. 665.26), runs οὐδέ ποτ᾽ ἦν οὐδ᾽ ἔσται, ἐπεὶ νῦν ἔστιν ὁμοῦ πᾶν. See J. Whittaker, God, Time, Being, Oslo 1971, 21–24, who, besides advancing a cautious plea on behalf of the text of the Alexandrians, also points out that their interpretation supposes a comma after ἔσται, not after πᾶν, as in the editions (and also in M). The agreement between the four witnesses, Amm., Ascl., Philop. and Ol., proves only that this is the form in which Amm. happened to remember the line (wrongly or rightly, of course).

13–24.　νοητόν: Pl. can have meant νοητόν (and therefore ἀνόητον also) in the passive sense only, and this is how Pr. takes it theol. I 26, 117.15–118.9, distinguishing different levels of νοητόν ranging from the soul to the One. Cf. Pr., Tim. I 230.22–28: νοητόν in the Ph. includes soul, in the Rep. it denotes everything beyond soul, in the Tim. only the first three triads of being. Ol. gives it the active sense (=νοητικόν) on the strength of the contrast with ἀνόητον and so does Dam. I § 315 and II § 30.9 (though he himself uses ἀνόητος in a passive meaning princ. 10.15); as usual, the obvious inference from their agreement is that Pr. had taken up this position in the commentary on the Ph.

15–19.　The same quotation, with the same explanation of ἀνόμματος, Pr., Tim. III 101.9–24; cf. II 85.24–28.

15.　πρόνοια=πρὸ νοῦ ἐνέργεια: Pr., elem. 120 and 134 (Dodds p. 263); prov. 7.10–12; decem dub. 4.3–4. Cf. already Plot. V 3,10.43–44.

do not think (this is also the origin of the word Providence [*pronoia*], which expresses that it is prior to intelligence [*pro nou*], and Orpheus [frg. 82] hints at the same truth when, intending to describe Eros as intelligible, he says:

'Cherishing in his heart eyeless swift Love';

the eye is the symbol of intelligence because of the rapidity of its action, and consequently 'eyeless' stands for 'not thinking'); it is true that intellective reality is also the object of thought, but from its predominant characteristic it is said to think, not to be thought. That Plato by 'accessible to thought' here means 'thinking', not 'being thought', he shows by contrasting it with 'incapable of thought', which does not mean 'not being thought', but 'not thinking'. In the same way Aristotle [*an*. III 7, 431b26–28] has called 'sensible' what is endowed with sense-perception, as Plato here calls 'accessible to thought' what is endowed with thought.

(4) Further it is 'indissoluble', inasmuch as it does not consist of parts; whatever is dissolved, is dissolved into its own components, but real being, which is non-composite and without parts, cannot be dissolved. All form, even materialized form, is without parts as far as the inherent principles are concerned; when materialized form, though itself without parts, is nevertheless divided, this is due to matter, and while in any part of the seed all the principles are present, as appears from the fact that even if a part of it is taken away, still the animal is shaped without a defect, it is matter that causes the head, the nose, etc., to be separate. It follows that real-existence, if simple, is also indissoluble, according to the Platonic doctrine that the composite can also be dissolved [78c1–2]. Therefore the heavenly bodies, being composite, are dissolved, though not in time, but in virtue of their own nature; having come into being, since anything composite is also subject to the process of becoming and is divisible, they must be dissoluble and perishable. However, they are perishable in the same way in which they come into being: they come into being in the sense that they are caused, since they neither animate themselves nor produce themselves (in Platonic doctrine it is soul that produces itself); in the same way they are perishable by themselves, because they

18. Cf. Dam. I § 413.3–4.

19–20. Iambl. splits the one νοῦς of Plot. into a νοητόν and a νοερόν (Pr., *Tim*. I 307.14–309.13). In Pr., the νοητόν contains a νοῦς νοητός (*theol*. III 14) and, on the other hand, the νοῦς a νοητόν (*ibid*. V 2). This elaboration is left aside here for the sake of the primary distinction.

22–23. Ar., *an*. III 7, 431b26–28 τῆς δὲ ψυχῆς τὸ αἰσθητικὸν καὶ τὸ ἐπιστημονικὸν δυνάμει ταῦτά ἐστι, τὸ μὲν ἐπιστητὸν τὸ δὲ αἰσθητόν. Wyttenbach's correction αἰσθητὸν τὸ agrees with the text of Ar. and is logically necessary in Ol., though of course Ol. himself or the redactor may have made the mistake.

25–40. ἀδιάλυτον should follow μονοειδές, as it does in Pl. and Dam.

30–31. See note above at 4 § 4.13.

[frg. 82] ἐπεσημήνατο, νοητὸν βουλόμενος εἰπεῖν τὸν Ἔρωτα· ἔφη γὰρ
'ποιμαίνων πραπίδεσσιν ἀνόμματον ὠκὺν Ἔρωτα'·
τὸ γὰρ ὄμμα ⟨νοῦ⟩ σύμβολόν ἐστι διὰ τὸ ὀξὺ τῆς ἐνεργείας, ἀνόμματον οὖν
τὸν μὴ νοοῦντα)· εἰ δὲ καὶ νοεῖται τὰ νοερά, ἐκ τοῦ κατ' ἐξαίρετον νοεῖν λέγεται,
οὐ μὴν νοεῖσθαι. ὅτι γὰρ νοητὸν λέγει ὁ Πλάτων ἐνταῦθα τὸ νοοῦν, οὐ μὴν   20
νοούμενον, δῆλός ἐστιν ἀντιτάξας αὐτῷ τὸ ἀνόητον· ἀνόητον γὰρ λέγεται οὐ
τὸ μὴ νοούμενον, ἀλλὰ τὸ μὴ νοοῦν. οὕτω δὲ καὶ Ἀριστοτέλης [an. III 7,
431b26–28] αἰσθητὸν τὸ αἰσθητικὸν ἐκάλεσεν, ὡς καὶ νῦν ὁ Πλάτων νοητὸν
τὸ νοοῦν.

δ′   Ἀλλὰ καὶ 'ἀδιάλυτόν' ἐστιν ὡς μὴ ἐκ μερῶν συγκείμενον· τὸ γὰρ διαλυόμενον   25
εἰς οἰκεῖα μέρη διαλύεται, ἐκεῖνο δὲ ὡς ἀσύνθετον καὶ ἀμερὲς οὐ διαλύεται.
πᾶν γὰρ εἶδος, κἂν ἔνυλον ᾖ, τῷ ἐν αὐτῷ λόγῳ ἀμερές ἐστι· καὶ γὰρ τὸ ἔνυλον
εἶδος ἀμερὲς ὂν μερίζεται διὰ τὴν ὕλην, καὶ ἐν παντὶ μέρει τοῦ σπέρματος
πάντων ὄντων τῶν λόγων, ὡς δηλοῖ | τὸ μέρους αὐτοῦ ἀφαιρεθέντος μηδὲν (76)
ἧττον τέλειον δημιουργεῖσθαι τὸ ζῷον· διὰ δὲ τὴν ὕλην ὡδὶ μὲν κεφαλή, ὡδὶ   30
δὲ ῥίς. εἰ οὖν ἀσύνθετον, καὶ ἀδιάλυτον· δόγμα γὰρ Πλατωνικόν, ὅτι τὸ σύνθετον
καὶ διαλύεται [78c1–2]. διὸ καὶ τὰ οὐράνια σύνθετα ὄντα διαλύεται, οὐ κατὰ
χρόνον ἀλλὰ κατὰ τὸν ἑαυτῶν λόγον· γενητὰ γὰρ ὄντα, ἐπειδὴ πᾶν σύνθετον
καὶ γενητὸν καὶ μεριστόν, καὶ διαλυτά ἐστι καὶ φθαρτά. πλὴν ὡς ἔστι γενητά,
οὕτως ἐστὶ καὶ φθαρτά· γενητὰ τοίνυν ἐστὶ κατ' αἰτίαν, διότι μὴ ἑαυτὰ ζωοῖ   35
μηδὲ ἑαυτὰ παρήγαγεν (δόγμα γὰρ Πλατωνικὸν τὸ αὐτοπαραγωγὸν εἶναι

---

18 νοῦ Wk: om. M — 20 τὸ νοοῦν Forster (Fischer p. 333): τὸν νοῦν M — 23 αἰσθητὸν τὸ
Wyttenbach: τὸ αἰσθητὸν M — 24 τὸ νοοῦν Fh: τὸν νοῦν M — 28 σπέρματος Wk: σώματος
M — 30 ὕλην Fh: κεφαλὴν M — 36 αὐτοπαράγωγον M

32–33. Dam. I § 331; II § 36. Cf. infra § 9. The famous passage on the
indissolubility of the heavens, Tim. 41a7–b6, is discussed at length by Pr., Tim. III
209.27–214.35. Dam. I § 331.1–3 and II § 36.1–8 sums up Pr.'s view as stated
in his commentary on the Ph.: the cosmos is dissoluble in so far as no finite body
can have infinite power, it is everlasting by the will of its Creator, i.e. by a continuous
stream of power which it receives from its cause. This is the opinion adopted here
and rejected by Dam. I § 331.4–8 and II § 36.9–14.
    36–37. The 'Platonic doctrine' must be derived from Phaedr. 245c5–d6: soul is
(1) αὐτὸ κινοῦν, (2) an ἀρχή. This appears to be the only occurrence of αὐτοπαραγωγός
(not in LSJ) instead of the usual αὐθυπόστατος (Pr., elem. 40–51; 189; 191; Tim. I
232.11–18).

cannot maintain their own being, but immortality comes to them as a continuous influx, in accordance with the sound principle of Aristotelian physics, that any finite body has only finite power [phys. VIII 10, 266a24–26].

(5) Real-existents are also 'single in form': single in form, because simple. In the case of simple beings the essence of a thing and the things are identical, in the case of composite beings they are distinct, the former applying to form by itself, the latter to the form present in matter; thus the essence of an animal is different from the existence of an animal. They are further 'single in form' because they do not coexist with their own non-being, but are pure and free from any such admixture; forms here below are contaminated with their own privation.

(6) Finally, it is 'eternally invariable and identical in condition with itself'. The addition 'with itself' is to the point, for reversion upon itself is the proper quality of intelligence, whereas sensible things are never the same, since they differ not only from each other, but also from themselves, being carried in the current of time and motion. In order, then, to express the wide compass of the difference, that existents of the one class revert upon themselves and are eternally invariable and the others differ from this in every respect, Plato adds the words 'with itself.'

3.   Next he divides our own composite being into soul and body and asks which is more similar to the indissoluble entities, the soul or the body. He establishes that the soul is the more similar, by means of three arguments: its invisibility, its capability of discursive thought, and its mastery over the body. These arguments appear to be derived from the substance of the soul: from its being, its knowledge, its life. Invisibility pertains to being, for beings can be classed as either visible (corporeal form) or invisible (form); the point that the soul can reason, while the activity of the body is accompanied by sense-perception, pertains to knowledge; and the argument taken from the mastery of the soul over the body

---

37–40. Ar.'s formula (phys. VIII 10, 266a24–26) runs ὅτι δ' ὅλως οὐκ ἐνδέχεται ἐν πεπερασμένῳ μεγέθει ἄπειρον εἶναι δύναμιν, ἐκ τῶνδε δῆλον. Pr. often refers to it: inst. phys. II 8 τῶν πεπερασμένων κατὰ τὸ μέγεθος σωμάτων οὐκ εἰσὶν αἱ δυνάμεις ἄπειροι. Parm. 1119.26–28; theol. II 2, 18.17–19.2; Tim. I 253.10; 267.13–14; 295.3–4. Various qualifications (such as Parm. l.c. σῶμα ... καθὸ σῶμα δύναμιν ἄπειρον οὐκ ἔχει) prepare the way for the revised formula of elem. 96 παντὸς πεπερασμένου σώματος ἡ δύναμις, ἄπειρος οὖσα, ἀσώματός ἐστιν, cf. Dodds p. 250. Dam. II § 36.9–10 states positively: δύναται γὰρ καὶ ἐν τῷ πεπερασμένῳ σώματι δύναμις εἶναι ἄπειρος, ὡς ἐν ἄλλοις δείκνυται (probably in his own commentary on the Tim.). The gap is not as wide as it might appear to be: if a finite body can be said to have infinite potency (to exist), it is always understood that this potency is adventitious and is bestowed continually by a higher principle, in the measure which the finite body can contain: ἐπιρρέον ἄρα δώσει καὶ ἀεὶ ἐπιρρέον ὅσην δύναται λαμβάνειν (Pr., Tim. I 268.4–5). The neuter subject of δώσει is ἄλλο (the higher principle), so that ἐπιρρεῖν is used here

τὴν ψυχήν)· οὐκοῦν καὶ φθαρτά ἐστιν ὅσον ἐφ' ἑαυτοῖς, οὐ γὰρ ἑαυτὰ συνέχει ἀλλ' ἐπινάεται ἡ ἀθανασία αὐτῶν, κάλλιστα τοῦ Ἀριστοτέλους φυσιολογήσαντος πᾶν σῶμα πεπερασμένον πεπερασμένης εἶναι δυνάμεως [phys. VIII 10, 266a24–26].   40

ε′ ⟨Ἀλλὰ καὶ 'μονοειδῆ'⟩· μονοειδῆ γάρ ἐστι, διότι ἁπλᾶ ἐστιν. ἐπὶ γὰρ τῶν ἁπλῶν ταὐτόν ἐστι τὸ τῇδε εἶναι καὶ τόδε, ἐπὶ δὲ τῶν συνθέτων διάφορον, καὶ τὸ μὲν ἐπὶ τοῦ εἴδους λέγεται μόνου, τὸ δὲ ἐπὶ τοῦ εἴδους τοῦ ἐν τῇ ὕλῃ· ἄλλο γάρ ἐστι τὸ ζῴῳ εἶναι καὶ ἄλλο τὸ ζῷον εἶναι. καὶ ἄλλως δὲ μονοειδῆ ἐστιν ὡς μὴ συνόντα τῷ οἰκείῳ μὴ ὄντι, ἀλλ' εἰλικρινῆ ὄντα καὶ ἀμιγῆ τούτου· τὰ 45 γὰρ ἐνταῦθα εἴδη συναναπέφυρται τῇ οἰκείᾳ στερήσει.

ϛ′ Ἀλλὰ καὶ 'ἀεὶ καὶ ὡσαύτως καὶ κατὰ τὰ αὐτὰ ἔχει ἑαυτῷ'. καὶ καλῶς τὸ 'ἑαυτῷ'· νοῦ γὰρ οἰκεία ἡ πρὸς ἑαυτὸν ἐπιστροφή, τὰ δὲ αἰσθητὰ οὐδέποτέ ἐστιν τὰ αὐτά· οὐ μόνον γὰρ ἀλλήλων διαφέρει, ἀλλὰ καὶ ἑαυτῶν, ἐν ῥευστῷ τῷ χρόνῳ καὶ ἐν κινήσει ὄντα. ἵνα οὖν ἐνδείξηται τὸ πλούσιον τῆς μεταβολῆς, 50 ὅτι τὰ μὲν ἐπέστραπται πρὸς ἑαυτὰ ἀεὶ ὡσαύτως ἔχοντα, τὰ δὲ πάντῃ ἐξήλλακται, διὰ τοῦτο τὸ 'ἑαυτῷ' προσέθηκεν.

Εἶτα διαιρεῖ καὶ τὴν ἡμετέραν σύστασιν εἰς ψυχὴν καὶ σῶμα, καὶ ζητεῖ 3(77) τί μᾶλλον ἔοικε τοῖς ἀδιαλύτοις, πότερον ἡ ψυχὴ ἢ τὸ σῶμα. καὶ κατασκευάζει ὅτι ἡ ψυχὴ μᾶλλον ἔοικε τοῖς ἀδιαλύτοις, διὰ τριῶν ἐπιχειρημάτων· ἐκ τοῦ ἀοράτου, καὶ ἐκ τοῦ διανοητικοῦ αὐτῆς, καὶ ἐκ τοῦ δεσπόζειν τοῦ σώματος. καὶ ἔοικε ταῦτα ἐκ τῆς ψυχικῆς ὑποστάσεως εἰλῆφθαι, ἀπὸ οὐσίας, ἀπὸ γνώσεως, 5 ἀπὸ ζωῆς. τῇ μὲν γὰρ οὐσίᾳ οἰκεῖον τὸ ἀόρατον, διότι διαιροῦνται αἱ οὐσίαι

---

41 Ἀλλὰ καὶ μονοειδῆ Nv: om. M — 44 μονοειδῆ∼, -ῆ∼ in ras. Mᶜ
§ 3. 2–3 πότερον – ἀδιαλύτοις mg. Mᶜ: om. M¹ — 6 οἰκεῖον τὸ ἀόρατον Mᶜ: τὸ ἀόρατον οἰκεῖον M¹

---

causatively as a synonym of ἐπινάειν, a rare word which serves exclusively to describe this particular process, the infinite influx of power into a substance of limited capacity: Pr., Tim. I 279.11; 473.25–27 (schol.); II 100.18–19; 131.3; Ascl., met. 23.5; 120.2; 186.1; Dam. II § 36.7; and Ol. h.l. (the ἐπινεύεται of the editions is a mistake, M has -ά-). There are two ways to explain its origin: (1) Pr. coined it because he was not satisfied with the transitive use of ἐπιρρεῖν, or (2) it occurred in either the Chaldean Oracles or the Orphic epic in a context that would bear this interpretation.
44. Ar., met. Z 6, 1032a4–6 ὅτι μὲν οὖν ἐπὶ τῶν πρώτων καὶ καθ' αὑτὰ λεγομένων τὸ ἑκάστῳ εἶναι καὶ ἕκαστον τὸ αὐτὸ καὶ ἕν ἐστι, δῆλον. Cf. an. III 4, 429b10–22.
46. συναναπέφυρται τῇ οἰκείᾳ στερήσει: cf. note on Dam. I § 94.5.
47. ἀεὶ καὶ ὡσαύτως: the intrusive καί is not uncommon: Pr., Alc. 23.16; Ol., Gorg. 17.12.
§ 3. 1–10. Dam. I § 325; II §§ 32–33.
5–10. On the triad οὐσία - ζωή - γνῶσις see note on 4 § 1.2–4. Ol. again follows Pr. and does not mention the proposal of Dam. II § 33.5–7.

pertains to life, since it is as the formative principle of the body and as self-moved entity that the soul rules the body. It should be clear that the lower phases of soul do not provide life to the body, but are themselves its life, on various levels: irrational soul of the pneumatic body, vegetative soul of the 'shell-like' body. By these three arguments he proves the greater resemblance of the soul to the indissoluble in the following way: (1) 'the soul is invisible, invisibility is more in accordance with the character of things indissoluble'; (2) 'the soul, rather than the body, has the faculty of thought, and this is more in accordance with the character of things indissoluble'; (3) 'the soul has mastery over the body, and this is more in accordance with the character of things indissoluble'. Whereupon he draws his conclusion as follows: 'The soul is in every respect more like the indissoluble than the body is, what is in every respect more like the indissoluble is more indissoluble, therefore the soul is more indissoluble'; 'what is more indissoluble is more durable than the body, therefore the soul is more durable than the body'; 'that which is more durable continues to exist after the separation, since even bodies do not decay at once, but remain for some time (especially if they have been embalmed, as it is done in Egypt), therefore the soul remains after the separation'; and this is precisely the point about which the young men were wondering, whether it is not dispersed and dissolved immediately upon leaving the body.

4. In the commentaries the question is discussed, whether this argument proves the immortality of the soul. Now all the other commentators agree that only the argument from the essence of soul proves its immortality. The argument from recollection has shown that the soul necessarily exists

---

11–12. Cf. note on 3 § 4.8. Ol. anticipates a point that belongs to the argument from the essence of soul, cf. Dam. I § 445.

16–20. Cf. Dam. I § 329; II § 34.

§ 4. Dam. I § 311; II § 29. Iambl. (*Ph.* frg. 4), determined to find a complete proof of immortality in each of the arguments of the *Ph.* (cf. above 11 § 2), was in this case confronted with the obvious limitations of the argument as pointed out by Pl. himself (80a10–b10). He therefore took the position that the complete proof is implicit in the two assumptions that the soul is non-composite and that it dominates the body. The proof based on these premises and attributed to Plot. is found in an almost identical form in Pr., *elem.* 187 πᾶσα ψυχὴ ἀνώλεθρός ἐστι καὶ ἄφθαρτος. πᾶν γὰρ τὸ ὁπωσοῦν διαλύεσθαι καὶ ἀπόλλυσθαι δυνάμενον ἢ σωματικόν ἐστι καὶ σύνθετον ἢ ἐν ὑποκειμένῳ τὴν ὑπόστασιν ἔλαχε· καὶ τὸ μὲν διαλυόμενον, ὡς ἐκ πολλῶν ὑπάρχον, φθείρεται· τὸ δὲ ἐν ἑτέρῳ εἶναι πεφυκὸς τοῦ ὑποκειμένου χωριζόμενον ἀφανίζεται εἰς τὸ μὴ ὄν. ἀλλὰ μὴν ἡ ψυχὴ καὶ ἀσώματός ἐστι καὶ ἔξω παντὸς ὑποκειμένου, ἐν ἑαυτῇ οὖσα καὶ πρὸς ἑαυτὴν ἐπιστρέφουσα. ἀνώλεθρος ἄρα ἐστὶ καὶ ἄφθαρτος. It is an application of prop. 48 πᾶν τὸ μὴ ἀίδιον ἢ σύνθετόν ἐστιν, ἢ ἐν ἄλλῳ ὑφέστηκεν. Again in Philop., *an.* 46.28–34 πᾶν τὸ φθειρόμενον δυσὶ τρόποις φθείρεται, ἢ τῷ ἀναλύεσθαι εἰς τὰ ἑαυτοῦ στοιχεῖα ὡς τὰ ἡμέτερα σώματα, ἢ τῷ ἀποσβέννυσθαι ἐν τῷ ὑποκειμένῳ διὰ τὸ γίνεσθαι αὐτὸ ἀνεπιτήδειον, ὥσπερ ἡ ἁρμονία ἀνεθεισῶν τῶν χορδῶν ἀποσβέννυται. διχῶς οὖν τῆς φθορᾶς οὔσης, ἢ ὡς ἐπὶ σωμάτων ἢ ὡς ἐπὶ ἀσωμάτων ἐν

εἰς ὁρατάς, ὡς τὰ σωματικὰ εἴδη, καὶ ἀοράτους, ὡς τὰ εἴδη· τὸ δὲ ἀπὸ τοῦ
ταύτην μὲν διανοεῖσθαι, τὸ δὲ σῶμα μετὰ τῆς αἰσθήσεως ἐνεργεῖν, ἐκ τῆς
γνώσεως· τὸ δὲ ἀπὸ τοῦ δεσπόζειν τὴν ψυχὴν τοῦ σώματος, ἐκ τῆς ζωῆς, ὡς
γὰρ εἰδοποιοῦσα τὸ σῶμα καὶ αὐτοκίνητος οὖσα δεσπόζει αὐτοῦ. αἱ γὰρ ἄλλαι   10
ψυχαὶ οὐ ζωοποιοῦσιν, ἀλλὰ ζωαὶ αὐτοῦ εἰσιν· ἀλλ' ἡ μὲν ἄλογος τοῦ πνευματικοῦ ζωή ἐστιν, ἡ δὲ φυτικὴ τοῦ ὀστρεΐνου. κατασκευάζει οὖν διὰ τῶν γ'
α' ἐπιχειρημάτων ὅτι μᾶλλον ἔοικεν ἡ ψυχὴ τῷ ἀδιαλύτῳ, οὕτως· 'ἡ ψυχὴ ἀόρατος,
β' τὸ ἀόρατον μᾶλλον πρέπει τοῖς ἀδιαλύτοις'· 'ἡ ψυχὴ νοεῖ μᾶλλον τοῦ σώματος,
γ' τὸ τοιοῦτο πρέπει μᾶλλον τοῖς ἀδιαλύτοις'. 'ἡ ψυχὴ δεσπόζει τοῦ σώματος,   15
τὸ τοιοῦτο πρέπει μᾶλλον τοῖς ἀδιαλύτοις'. ἐφ' οἷς συλλογίζεται τὸ προκείμενον
οὕτως· 'ἡ ψυχὴ κατὰ πάντα μᾶλλον τοῦ σώματος ἔοικε τοῖς ἀδιαλύτοις, τὸ
κατὰ πάντα ἐοικὸς μᾶλλον ἀδιάλυτόν ἐστιν, ἡ ψυχὴ μᾶλλον ἀδιάλυτός ἐστιν'·
'τὸ μᾶλλον ἀδιάλυτον πολυχρονιώτερόν ἐστι τοῦ | σώματος, ἡ ψυχὴ ἄρα   (78)
πολυχρονιωτέρα τοῦ σώματος'· 'τὸ πολυχρονιώτερον ἐπιμένει καὶ μετὰ τὸν   20
χωρισμόν, εἴ γε οὐδὲ αὐτὰ τὰ σώματα εὐθέως φθείρεται ἀλλ' ἐπιδιαμένει (καὶ
μάλιστα εἰ τύχοι ταριχευθέντα, ὡς τὰ παρ' Αἰγυπτίοις σώματα), ἡ ψυχὴ ἄρα
ἐπιδιαμένει μετὰ τὸν χωρισμόν· ὅπερ ἐζήτουν οἱ νεανίαι, μήποτε σκεδάννυται
εὐθὺς καὶ διαλύεται ἐξελθοῦσα τοῦ σώματος.
    Καὶ ζητοῦσιν οἱ ἐξηγηταὶ εἰ δείκνυσιν ὁ λόγος τὴν ἀθανασίαν τῆς ψυχῆς.   4

---

9 ἐκ τῆς] in ras. Mᶜ — 18 μᾶλλον¹] fort. add. τοῖς ἀδιαλύτοις μᾶλλον

ὑποκειμένῳ σώματι ἐχόντων τὸ εἶναι, εἰ ἐδείχθη ἡ ψυχὴ καὶ ἀσώματος οὖσα καὶ χωριστὴ
σώματος, κατ' οὐδένα ἄρα τρόπον φθείρεται. In this concise, stringent form, the argument
does not occur in Plot. The disposition of the main part of *Enneads* IV 7 *Περὶ*
ἀθανασίας ψυχῆς is the following: Soul is not body (2–8³), nor is it the harmony
or entelechy of the body (8⁴⁻⁵), rather it is a substance of an entirely different nature,
the principle of motion and life, in its pure form akin to the divine (9–10) and
therefore immortal, since its life is not adventitious, but essential (11). In ch. 12
the arguments are briefly reviewed again to show that they hold of individual
souls as well as of the universal soul, and here the non-composite character of
the soul is mentioned once more (at 12.13 Henry and Schwyzer refer to Dam. II § 39),
but this is only incidental, and it is clear that the argument as we have it here
either was entirely reshaped by Iambl. or comes from a non-Enneadic source
(see note at 10 § 7.8–9). The comment found in Dam. II § 29.1–7, that Plot.
imagined himself the originator of this proof, though it is essentially identical with
Pl.'s third argument, appears to come also from Iambl. – Pr. (Dam. II § 29.7–11,
cf. I § 311.8–12) accepts the argument as a legitimate interpretation of Pl., but
in defense of his own doctrine of the survival of irrational soul he makes the
reservation that it is not absolute proof, since the possibility remains that the soul,
while detachable from the earthly body, may be an accident of a higher form of
corporeal existence (in other words, the objection of Cebes, 86e6–88b8, is still valid).
Dam. (I § 311.5–8; II 29.12–20) rightly denies the identity of the arguments.

prior to the body, not, however, that it exists always; the present argument shows on the ground of similarity that it is post-existent because more indissoluble and that it survives longer because more durable, but not that it is actually immortal. The philosopher Iamblichus, however, will have it that this argument, too, proves the immortality of the soul completely. As far as the argument from similarity goes, he says, Plato has proved the soul more durable, but from the assumptions made in the text its immortality can be inferred. In them the soul is described as non-composite [78c1-9] and as having mastery over the body [79e8-80a6]; now Plotinus [IV 7, 2-11?] has rightly taught that whatever perishes must perish from either of these two causes, because it is composite, or because it is in a substrate: incorporeal things perish because they are in a substrate, bodies because they are composite. If then the soul is neither composite (this is how Iamblichus argues, and it is also indicated in the text, which never speaks of 'invisible', but only of 'non-composite', the two being apparently considered identical) nor present in a substrate, since it has the mastery over the body, endows it with life and is the cause of its own motion, there will be no manner in which it can perish, neither as composite nor as present in a substrate.

5. Proclus raises the question, to which kind of forms Plato is referring, the absolute forms in the Creator's mind, or those in the human soul. Either view can be defended, the former, that the forms in the Creator's mind are meant, on the ground that Plato speaks of the 'equal itself' and the 'beautiful itself' [78d3], terms which are appropriate to that kind of forms; and because the soul is said to resemble them [79b4-17], whereas, if the reference were to forms in the soul, the soul would not resemble them, but be identical with them. But it is also possible to advocate the opposite view, that forms in the soul are meant, because it says in the text 'the things we have discussed again and again and of which we give an account' [78d1-2]: now the very fact of discussion and scientific knowledge fits this kind of forms, while the other kind is the object of intellective intuition. Proclus' decision is that both are included: since the intellective forms are the prototypes of those in the soul, and these are images of the former, and since prototype and image are correlatives, and correlatives are not known independently of each other, the discussion of the prototypes will inevitably be discussion of the images as well.

2-3. Cf. *supra* 11 § 2.

6-8. *Supra* 10 § 1.14.

15. οὐδαμοῦ γὰρ ʻἀόρατον' αὐτὴν εἶπεν ἀλλὰ ʻἀσύνθετον' : the statement is patently incorrect, unless taken in a very narrow literal way (cf. 79b4-17); only if we read οὗ μὲν γὰρ ʻἀόρατον' . . . οὗ δὲ ʻἀσύνθετον' does it warrant the conclusion ὡς ἂν ταὐτοῦ ὄντος.

§ 5. Cf. Dam. I § 274; II § 15. – In the Procline system, form is manifest at every level of reality: in the νοητόν the archetypes of the *Tim.* (παραδείγματα or

πάντες μὲν οὖν οἱ ἐξηγηταὶ μόνον τὸν ἐκ τῆς οὐσίας λόγον φασὶ τῆς ψυχῆς
δεικνύναι τὴν ἀθανασίαν αὐτῆς. ὁ μὲν γὰρ ἐκ τῶν ἀναμνήσεων λόγος ἔδειξεν
ὅτι προϋπάρχει ἡ ψυχὴ τοῦ σώματος πάντως, οὐ μὴν ὅτι καὶ ἀεί ἐστιν· οὗτος
δὲ δείκνυσιν ἐκ τῆς ὁμοιότητος ⟨ὅτι⟩ μεθυπάρχει ὡς μᾶλλον ἀδιάλυτος οὖσα   5
καὶ ἐπιδιαμένει ὡς πολυχρονιωτέρα, οὐ μὴν ὅτι καὶ ἀθάνατος. ὁ δὲ φιλόσοφος
Ἰάμβλιχος καὶ τοῦτον τὸν λόγον βούλεται τελείαν ἀποδεικνύναι τὴν ἀθανασίαν τῆς
ψυχῆς. ὅσον μὲν γὰρ ἐκ τῆς ὁμοιότητος πολυχρονιωτέραν ἀπέδειξεν, ἐκ δὲ
τῶν κειμένων ἐν τῇ λέξει λημμάτων ἡ ἀθανασία τῆς ψυχῆς συνάγεται. ἀσύνθετον
γὰρ αὐτὴν εἶπεν [78c1–9] καὶ δεσπόζειν τοῦ σώματος [79e8–80a6]· κάλλιστα   10
δὲ τῷ Πλωτίνῳ [IV 7, 2–11?] ἤρεσεν πᾶν φθειρόμενον δι' ἕνα τῶν δύο τρόπων
τούτων φθείρεσθαι, ἢ ὡς σύνθετον ἢ ὡς ἐν ὑποκειμένῳ ὄν· τὰ μὲν γὰρ ἀσώματα
διὰ τὸ ἐν ὑποκειμένῳ εἶναι φθείρεται, τὰ δὲ σώματα ὡς σύνθετα. εἰ οὖν ἡ ψυχὴ
οὐδὲ σύνθετός ἐστιν (ὥς φησιν ὁ Ἰάμβλιχος, καὶ τοῦτο καὶ ἡ λέξις ἐδήλωσεν,
οὐδαμοῦ γὰρ 'ἀόρατον' αὐτὴν εἶπεν ἀλλὰ 'ἀσύνθετον', ὡς ἂν ταὐτοῦ ὄντος   15
ἀοράτου καὶ ἀσυνθέτου), ἀλλὰ μὴν οὐδὲ ἐν ὑποκειμένῳ ἐστίν, εἴ γε δεσπόζει
τοῦ σώματος, ζωοποιοῦσα αὐτὸ καὶ αὐτοκίνητος οὖσα, κατ' οὐδένα ἄρα τρόπον
φθαρήσεται, οὐδὲ ὡς σύνθετος οὐδὲ | ὡς ἐν ὑποκειμένῳ.   (79)
   Ζητεῖ δὲ ὁ Πρόκλος περὶ ποίων ἄρα εἰδῶν τῷ Πλάτωνι ὁ λόγος, ἆρα περὶ   5
τῶν ἁπλῶς τῶν ἐν τῷ δημιουργῷ ἢ περὶ τῶν ψυχικῶν. ἔστιν γὰρ ἑκατέρῳ
συνηγορῆσαι, τῷ μὲν πρώτῳ διότι δόξει περὶ τῶν ἐν τῷ δημιουργῷ εἶναι ὁ
λόγος εἰδῶν, εἴ γε 'αὐτοῖσον' φησὶν καὶ 'αὐτοκαλόν' [78d3], τὰ δὲ προσρήματα
ταῦτα ἐκείνοις τοῖς εἴδεσιν ἁρμόττει· καὶ ὅτι λέγει ἐοικέναι τὴν ψυχὴν ἐκείνοις   5
[79b4–17], εἰ δὲ περὶ τῶν ψυχικῶν ἦν αὐτῷ ὁ λόγος, οὐκ ἐκείνοις ὁμοία ἦν,
ἀλλ' αὐτὰ ἐκεῖνα ἦν. ἔστι δὲ καὶ τῷ ἀντικειμένῳ συνηγορῆσαι· δόξει γὰρ περὶ
τῶν ψυχικῶν εἰδῶν εἶναι ὁ λόγος διότι φησὶν ἐν τῇ λέξει 'περὶ ὧν θαμὰ θρυλοῦμεν
καὶ ἔχομεν λόγον διδόναι' [78d1–2], τὸ δὲ λέγειν καὶ κατ' ἐπιστήμην εἰδέναι ταῦτα
τοῖς ψυχικοῖς εἴδεσιν ἁρμόττει, ἐκεῖνα γὰρ νοεραῖς ἐπιβολαῖς γινώσκεται.   10
καὶ ἐπικρίνει ὁ Πρόκλος ὅτι περὶ ἀμφοῖν ἐστιν αὐτῷ ὁ λόγος· ἐπειδὴ γὰρ καὶ
παραδείγματα τὰ νοερὰ εἴδη τῶν ψυχικῶν καὶ εἰκόνες ταῦτα ἐκείνων, πρός
τι δὲ τὸ παράδειγμα καὶ ἡ εἰκών, τὰ δὲ πρός τι δίχα ἀλλήλων οὐ γινώσκεται,
ἀνάγκη περὶ τῶν παραδειγμάτων διαλεγόμενον καὶ περὶ εἰκόνων διαλέγεσθαι.

---

§ 4. 5 ⟨ὅτι⟩ μεθυπάρχει Fh: μεθυπάρχειν M — 15 ἀσύνθετον M^c: σύνθετον M^1
§ 5. 5 τὴν ψυχὴν Fh: τὰ ψυχικὰ εἴδη M — 6 ψυχικῶν M^c: ψυχῶν M^1 | ὁμοία Fh:
ὅμοια M — 7 post γὰρ] ÷÷ in ras. M^c — 8 θρυλλοῦμεν M^1 — 9 διδόναι] διδό- in ras. M^c

---

ἰδέαι, theol. III 19), in the universal Demiurge the fully developed world of εἴδη
(theol. V 12; in partial conformity with Plot.'s doctrine that the intelligibles are
in the intelligence), εἴδη or λόγοι in the soul, λόγοι in nature, finally ἔνυλα εἴδη.
   5. τὴν ψυχήν: Finckh's correction for τὰ ψυχικὰ εἴδη is necessary to make sense,
though as in several of these cases the mistake must have already been made in
the autograph.
   13. Ar., met. Γ 2, 1004a9–10 μιᾶς (scil. ἐπιστήμης) τἀντικείμενα θεωρῆσαι. Applied
to correlatives top. VI 4, 142a22–31.

6. An objection is made: 'How can the soul be said to be more indissoluble on the ground of its resemblance to the indissoluble? On this showing, since a dog is more like a wolf than a horse is, the dog will *be* a wolf.' But those who say this have not grasped the tenor of the argument: the soul was proved to be indissoluble because it resembles the indissoluble *more than the body does*, the implication being that the body too is indissoluble, whereas the dog without being a wolf is more like a wolf than a horse is; in the other case, however, both possessed the quality of being indissoluble.

Another objection is: 'On this line of reasoning, since form is more like the indissoluble than matter is, form will be more indissoluble; then how to explain that, while matter is indestructible, form should perish?' The solution is that form does not resemble indissoluble realities in every respect: in so far as it is limit and boundary and actuality it resembles them, but in so far as it can only exist in a substrate, it does not.

Others, again, object that as far as this proof goes, nature also ought to be indissoluble because it resembles indissoluble reality more than the body does, for it holds the body together and informs it. The answer: nature is not indissoluble for the same reason, that it depends on the body as a substrate for its existence. Thus far the survey.

7. **'Well then,' said Socrates, 'the kind of question ...'** [78b4]: i.e. 'We must next examine, young men, whether the soul continues to exist after death'; its previous existence has already been proved by the argument from recollection.

8. **What kind of thing is subject to this process of dispersal** [78b5–6]: Socrates seems to say the same thing three times; he says: 'What kind of thing is subject to this process of dispersal?' then 'For what kind of thing must we fear that this may occur?' then again 'And to whom can it happen?' However, each of these does not have the same meaning. The first refers to things themselves, 'What part is subject to dispersal', that is to say, the animal life of the body, not the soul; 'for what kind of thing we must fear' means 'to what being should we deem it possible that this may happen'; finally the question 'who has reason to be afraid that this should happen to him' is expressed in the words 'to whom'. The first relates to things, the other to judgment, the last to persons.

9. **Is not anything that has been compounded and is composite** [78c1]: This is a tenet of Plato, that the composite as such is dissolved. We

---

§ 6. On the remote possibility that the objections may come from Strato see Introduction pp. 7–8.

1–6. **Dam.** I § 336; II § 41. Ol. follows Pr., omitting the solution of Dam. (II § 41.3–4).

2–3. Pl., *Soph.* 231a4–6 Ἀλλὰ μὴν προσέοικέ γε τοιούτῳ τινὶ τὰ νῦν λεγόμενα. –

Ἀλλὰ ἀποροῦσιν ὅτι 'διὰ τί ἡ ψυχὴ μᾶλλον ἀδιάλυτος λέγεται διὰ τὸ ἐοικέναι 6
τῷ ἀδιαλύτῳ; ὅσον γὰρ ἐπὶ τούτῳ, ἐπειδὴ μᾶλλον ἔοικε κύων λύκῳ ἤπερ ἵππος,
καὶ λύκος ἔσται ὁ κύων'. ἢ οἱ ταῦτα λέγοντες οὐκ ἐνόησαν τὴν ἀγωγὴν τοῦ
λόγου· ἐδείχθη γὰρ ἡ ψυχὴ ἀδιάλυτος ὡς μᾶλλον τοῦ σώματος ἐοικυῖα τῷ
ἀδιαλύτῳ, ὡς ἂν καὶ τοῦ σώματος ἀδιαλύτου ὄντος, ὁ δὲ κύων οὐ λύκος ὢν 5
μᾶλλον τοῦ ἵππου ἔοικε τῷ λύκῳ· ἐκεῖ δὲ ἀμφοτέροις ὑπῆρχε τὸ ἀδιάλυτον.

Πάλιν φασὶν ὅτι 'ὅσον ἐπὶ τούτῳ, ἐπειδὴ καὶ τὸ εἶδος μᾶλλον τῆς | ὕλης (80)
ἔοικε τῷ ἀδιαλύτῳ, ἔσται μᾶλλον τοῦτο ἀδιάλυτον· καὶ πῶς τῆς ὕλης ἀφθάρτου
οὔσης αὐτὸ φθείρεται;' ἢ τὸ εἶδος οὐ κατὰ πάντα ἔοικε τοῖς ἀδιαλύτοις· κατὰ
μὲν γὰρ τὸ πέρας εἶναι καὶ ὅρος καὶ ἐνέργεια ἔοικε, κατὰ δὲ τὸ ἐν ὑποκειμένῳ 10
εἶναι οὐκ ἔοικεν.

Πάλιν φασίν· 'ὅσον ἐπὶ τούτῳ καὶ τὴν φύσιν ἔδει ἀδιάλυτον εἶναι, ὅτι μᾶλλον
ἔοικε τοῦ σώματος τοῖς ἀδιαλύτοις ὡς συνέχουσα τὸ σῶμα καὶ εἰδοποιοῦσα
αὐτό'. ἢ καὶ αὕτη οὐκ ἔστιν ἀδιάλυτος, διότι ἐν ὑποκειμένῳ ἐστὶν τῷ σώματι.
ταῦτα ἔχει ἡ θεωρία. 15

Οὐκοῦν τοιόνδε τι, ἦ δὲ ὅς ὁ Σωκράτης [78b4]: 'δεῖ', φησίν, 'ἐπι- 7
ζητῆσαι, ὦ νεανίαι, εἰ ἐπιδιαμένει ἡ ψυχὴ μετὰ τὸν θάνατον'· τὴν γὰρ προΰπαρξιν
αὐτῆς ὁ ἐκ τῶν ἀναμνήσεων λόγος ἔδειξεν.

Τῷ ποίῳ τινὶ ἄρα προσήκει τοῦτο τὸ πάθος πάσχειν, τὸ διασκε- 8
δάννυσθαι [78b5–6]: φαίνεται ὁ Σωκράτης τρίτον τὸ αὐτὸ λέγων· φησὶ γὰρ
'τῷ ποίῳ τινὶ προσήκει τὸ πάθος τοῦτο πάσχειν' καὶ 'ὑπὲρ ποίου τινὸς δεδιέναι
μὴ πάθη αὐτό' καὶ 'τῷ ποίῳ τινί'. ἢ οὐ τὸ αὐτὸ σημαίνει ἕκαστον τούτων.
τὸ μὲν γὰρ περὶ τῶν πραγμάτων αὐτῶν λέγεται, ὅτι 'ποίῳ μέρει προσήκει 5
τὸ διασκεδάννυσθαι', οἷον ὅτι τῇ ἐμψυχίᾳ, οὐ μὴν τῇ ψυχῇ· καὶ 'ὑπὲρ τοῦ ποίου
τινὸς δεδιέναι' τουτέστι 'περὶ τίνος δεῖ ἡμᾶς κρίσιν ἔχειν ὡς τοῦτο πεισομένου'·
καὶ 'τίνας δεῖ δεδιέναι ὡς τοῦτο πάσχοντας', διό φησιν 'τῷ ποίῳ τινί'. τὸ μὲν οὖν
λέγεται περὶ τῶν πραγμάτων, τὸ δὲ περὶ τῆς κρίσεως, τὸ δὲ περὶ τῶν προσώπων.

---

§ 6. 2 ἤπερ] ἤ- in ras. Mᶜ
§ 8. 1 τὸ²] τοῦ Pl. B — 3; 7; 8 δεδειέναι Mᶜ — 6 οὐ μὴν] in spat. vac. Mᶜ — 7 post
τοῦτο] ÷ in ras. Mᶜ | πεισομένου Mᶜ: πεισόμενο≡ M¹ — 8 τῷ Fh: τὸ M

Καὶ γὰρ κυνὶ λύκος, ἀγριώτατον ἡμερωτάτῳ.
7–11. Dam. I § 337; II § 42. Again Dam.'s solution (I § 337.3–4; II § 42.3–4)
is ignored.
12–15. Dam. I § 338; II § 43. Instead of φύσις, Pr. as reported by Dam. has
ἡ ἐν ὑποκειμένῳ ζωή (I) and ἡ μερικὴ ζωή (II).

have already raised the question of the celestial bodies and answered it
[§ 2]. 'Has been compounded' denotes the parts, which are actually
joined together; 'is composite' the whole, which is the thing made by
composition.

10. **This essence of which we give an account [78d1]:** From this, as
we said already [§ 5], it can be argued that Socrates is referring to forms
in the soul; for of the others no account can be given because they transcend
rational knowledge.

11. **The equal itself, the beautiful itself [78d3]:** This phrase makes
it clear that he is discussing ideal forms. Proclus's solution has already
been mentioned [§ 5].

12. **These you can touch and see and perceive with the other senses
[79a1–2]:** How can Socrates mention this as characteristic of ideal forms,
that they cannot be perceived with the senses? Surely this applies to
rational forms also? Still, the case is not the same for both: rational forms
can be apprehended through sense-perception (e.g. the signs observed
in the face give us a clue to a man's life, but also as to whether he
understands us or not, i.e. to his knowledge); ideal forms, on the contrary,
can in no way be apprehended through sense-perception.

13. **Be touched by anything else [79a3]:** Touch is a light contact;
Socrates does not say that we grasp it, but that, at best, we touch it.

14. **Could we say it resembles form more and is more akin to it [79b4–5]:**
The addition 'and is more akin to' serves to underline the strong likeness
and relationship.

15. **Not to men, at any rate, Socrates [79b8]:** it seems as if Cebes,
in this case, comes nearer the truth than Socrates does: Socrates has
asked 'Is the soul visible?' Cebes answers 'Not to men', whereupon Socrates
rejoins 'What is invisible to men is visible to no one else'. This seems
to be untrue, as there are other animals with particularly keen sight.
To answer this, we should observe that seeing can take place in several
ways: (1) by the usual process, by which we all can see; (2) by a natural
peculiarity, such as enabled Lynceus to see things at a distance; (3) by
artificial means, as Varus for example shows us how to get a changed
view of those present with the help of certain kinds of eye-salve; (4) by
mental vision in a state of ecstasy, for there is also an ecstasy of sight,
as in the story how Apollonius, while being in Rome, beheld what was

---

§ 9. 1–3. *Supra* § 2.32–40.
§ 10. *Supra* § 5.7–10.
§ 11. 1–2. *Supra* § 5.2–5.

Ἄρα οὖν τῷ μὲν συντεθέντι τε καὶ συνθέτῳ ὄντι [78c1]: ἰδοὺ 9 (81)
δόγμα Πλατωνικόν, ὅτι τὸ σύνθετον ὡς σύνθετον διαλύεται. καὶ ἠπόρηται
περὶ τῶν οὐρανίων καὶ λέλυται [§ 2]. 'συντεθέντι' δέ, ἵνα εἴπῃ περὶ τῶν μερῶν,
ταῦτα γὰρ συντίθεται· 'συνθέτῳ' δέ, ἵνα εἴπῃ τὸ ὅλον, τοῦτο γάρ ἐστι τὸ σύνθετον.

Αὕτη ἡ οὐσία ἧς λόγον δίδομεν [78d1]: ἰδοὺ ἐντεῦθέν ἐστιν συνη- 10
γορῆσαι ὅτι περὶ τῶν ψυχικῶν εἰδῶν διαλέγεται· περὶ γὰρ ἐκείνων οὐκ ἔστιν
λόγον διδόναι ὑπὲρ ἐπιστήμην ὄντων.

Αὐτὸ τὸ ἴσον, αὐτὸ τὸ καλόν [78d3]: διὰ τούτου δῆλός ἐστι περὶ τῶν 11
παραδειγματικῶν εἰδῶν διαλεγόμενος. καὶ εἴρηται ἤδη ἡ Προκλεία ἐπίκρισις [§ 5].

Οὐκοῦν τούτων μὲν κἂν ἅψαιο κἂν ἴδοις κἂν ταῖς ἄλλαις αἰσθή- 12
σεσιν αἴσθοιο [79a1–2]: πῶς ὡς ἐξαίρετον τοῦτο λέγει ὁ Σωκράτης τῶν
παραδειγματικῶν εἰδῶν, τὸ μὴ εἶναι αὐτὰ αἰσθητά; τοῦτο γὰρ καὶ τοῖς δια-
νοηματικοῖς εἴδεσιν ὑπάρχει. ἢ οὐχ ὅμοιον· τὰ μὲν γὰρ διανοηματικὰ εἴδη
δυνατὸν ἀπὸ τῆς αἰσθήσεως συννοῆσαι (ἀπὸ γοῦν τῶν ἐν τῷ προσώπῳ σημείων 5
τεκμαιρόμεθα τὸ εἶδος τῆς ζωῆς, οὐ μὴν ἀλλὰ καὶ εἰ νοεῖ ἢ μή, τουτέστι τὸ
εἶδος τῆς γνώσεως), τὰ δὲ παραδειγματικὰ κατ' οὐδένα τρόπον δυνατὸν αἰσθήσει
καταλαβεῖν.

Ὅτῳ ποτὲ ἄλλῳ ἐπιλάβοιο [79a3]: τὸ 'ἐπιλαβέσθαι' τὸ μετρίως 13
ἐφάψασθαι· οὐκ εἶπεν οὖν ὅτι δραττόμεθα ἐκείνων, ἀλλ' εἰ ἄρα, ἐπιλαμβανόμεθα.

Ὁμοιότερον τῷ εἴδει φαῖμεν ἂν εἶναι καὶ συγγενέστερον [79b4–5]:14(82)
ἵνα τὴν πολλὴν ὁμοιότητα δηλώσῃ καὶ οἰκειότητα, ἐπήγαγε τὸ 'καὶ συγγενέστερον'.

Οὐχ ὑπ' ἀνθρώπων γε, ὦ Σώκρατες, ἔφη [79b8]: δοκεῖ ὁ Κέβης 15
τελειότερον τοῦ Σωκράτους ἐνταῦθα ἀποφαίνεσθαι· ἐρωτήσαντος γὰρ ὅτι
'ἡ ψυχὴ ὁρατόν;' φησὶν ὅτι 'οὐχ ὑπ' ἀνθρώπων', καὶ ἐπήγαγεν ὁ Σωκράτης
ὅτι 'τὸ μὴ ἀνθρώποις ὁρατὸν οὐδενί ἐστιν ὁρατόν'. καὶ δοκεῖ ψεῦδος εἶναι τὸ
λεγόμενον διὰ τὸ εἶναι ἄλλα ζῷα μάλιστα ἠκριβωμένα περὶ τὸ ὁρᾶν. 5
α' ἢ πολλαχῶς τὸ ὁρᾶν ἐστιν· ἢ γὰρ τὸ συνεγνωσμένον τοῦτο, καθ' ὃ πάντες
β' ὁρῶμεν· ἢ κατὰ φυσικήν τινα ἰδιότητα, καθ' ὃ ὁ Λυγκεὺς ἑώρα τὰ πόρρω·

---

§ 9. 1 συντεθέντι] συνθέντι Μ¹, ξυντεθέντι Μ°, Pl. | συνθέτῳ] ξ supra σ- Μ°
§ 10. 1 αὕτη] αὐτὴ Pl.
§ 11. 1 τούτου Μ°: τοῦτο Μ¹ — 2 παραδειγματικῶν] -ρα- ins. Μ°
§ 12. 5 δυνατὸν Fh: ἀδύνατον Μ
§ 13. 1 post ποτὲ] ἂν ins. Μ° (Pl.)
§ 14. 1 φαῖμεν] φαμὲν Pl. TY | συγγενέστερον] ξ supra σ- Μ°
§ 15. 2 ἐρωτήσαντος Fh: -σας Μ — 3 ὁρατόν] -ν ex corr. Μ°

---

2. Supra § 5.11–14.
§ 15. Dam. I § 333; II § 38. Ol. follows Pr.; criticism by Dam. II § 38.5–7.
§ 15. 6 συνεγνωσμένον: Neoplatonic usage.

happening in Egypt. What is not visible to man in any of these ways is visible to nobody.

16. Now isn't this another thing we said a while ago [79c2]: the second argument that the soul is more like things indissoluble than the body is, the one pertaining to knowledge [§ 3].

17. To things that are never constant [79c6-7]: The activity of the soul is twofold: either it is natural, when the soul is not dragged along by the body, but is its master, or it is abnormal, when the soul follows the conditions of the body.

18. It wanders and is confused and dizzy as if drunk [79c7-8]: The word 'wandering' applies to the vital force and knowledge together, 'it is confused' to the vital force alone, 'it is dizzy' to knowledge alone. The word 'dizzy' is well-chosen: just as those who suffer from this, because of the spinning inside themselves think the outside world is in a similar motion, so the soul by looking at sensible things only believes that everything is in a state of flux and change.

19. And is not this affect of the soul called insight? [79d6-7]: In what sense does he call insight an 'affect' of the soul? In the sense in which all virtues are affects, for it is a Platonic doctrine that whatever participates is 'affected by' (i.e. is passively aware of) the participated. The participating, indeed, is passive in relation to the participated; hence Plato says that even real-existence 'undergoes' unity [*Soph.* 245b7-8], because it participates in the One. Since the soul, then, participates in the absolute insight that is in Intelligence, Socrates calls insight an 'affect' of it in this respect. Or the explanation may be that since the soul in its entirety is self-moved, and is active qua mover, passive qua moved, insight is also a passive process.

20. Look at it in this way, too [79e8]: The third argument, pertaining to the life of the soul [§ 3]: the soul rules the body (because the user rules the instrument), it animates the body, and it is self-moved. For the lower levels of soul are forms of bodily life, but they do not bestow life on bodies.

8-9. Pr., *Rep.* II 117.2-7 καὶ τοῖς ὀφθαλμοῖς τινες χυλὸν ἐνιέντες στρύχνου καὶ ποῶν ἄλλων εἴδωλα ἄττα δαιμόνων ἐν ἀέρι καθορῶσιν, καί τινες ἄνευ τῆς ἐπιτεχνήσεως ταύτης πάσχουσιν ταυτόν· καὶ προορατικοὶ γίγνονται τοῦ μέλλοντός τινες ἐκ τῶν καλουμένων ἀπογεύσεων, ἄλλων φύσει τὴν δύναμιν ταύτην ἐχόντων. 186.12-19 ἐπεὶ καὶ τοῦτό τινες ἔχοντες τὸ σῶμα διά τινων ἐγχρισμάτων αὐτοπτοῦσιν καὶ δαιμόνων σώματα ἀόρατα πρότερον ὄντα καὶ ἄλλων κοσμικῶν δυνάμεων· καὶ οὐ διὰ ζωῆς κάθαρσιν τούτων τυγχάνουσιν, ἀλλὰ δύναμιν [[ἢ]] φυσικὴν ἐντεθεῖσαν ἐκκαθαίρουσαν τὸ ὀπτικὸν φῶς ἀπὸ τῆς παχείας ὑγρότητος τῆς ἀναμεμιγμένης καὶ τῶν ἐκ τοῦ ἐγκεφάλου περιττωμάτων, καὶ ἐκεῖνο

γ′ ἢ τέχνη τινί, οἷαν Οὖαρος διδάσκει διά τινων ἐγχρισμάτων τοὺς συνόντας ἀλλοίους
δ′ ὁρᾶν· ἢ κατὰ ἐνθουσιασμὸν καὶ θεωρητικῶς, ἐνθουσιᾷ γάρ ποτε καὶ ἡ ὄψις,
ὥσπερ περὶ Ἀπολλωνίου λέγεται ὅτι ἐν Ῥώμῃ ὢν ἑώρα τὰ ἐν Αἰγύπτῳ ἐπιτε- 10
λούμενα. τὸ οὖν μὴ ἀνθρώπῳ καθ' ἕνα τῶν τρόπων τούτων ὁρατὸν οὐδενί ἐστιν
ὁρατόν.

Οὐκοῦν καὶ τόδε πάλαι ἐλέγομεν [79c2]: τὸ δεύτερον ἐπιχείρημα 16
ὅτι μᾶλλον ἔοικεν ἡ ψυχὴ τοῦ σώματος τοῖς ἀδιαλύτοις, τὸ ἐκ τῆς γνώσεως [§ 3].

Εἰς τὰ οὐδέποτε κατὰ τὰ αὐτὰ ἔχοντα [79c6–7]: διττὴ γὰρ ἡ ἐνέργεια 17
τῆς ψυχῆς, ἢ κατὰ φύσιν, ἡνίκα οὐχ ἕλκεται ὑπὸ τοῦ σώματος, ἀλλὰ δεσπόζει
αὐτοῦ, ἢ παρὰ φύσιν, ὡς ἐν ταῖς συμπαθείαις ταῖς πρὸς τὸ σῶμα.

Πλανᾶται καὶ ταράττεται καὶ εἰλιγγιᾷ ὥσπερ μεθύουσα [79c7–8]: 18(83)
τὸ μὲν τῆς 'πλάνης' ὄνομα κοινῶς καὶ ἐπὶ ζωῆς καὶ γνώσεως φέρεται, τὸ δὲ
'ταράττεται' ἐπὶ ζωῆς μόνης, τὸ δὲ 'εἰλιγγιᾷ' ἐπὶ γνώσεως μόνης. καλῶς δὲ
τὸ 'εἰλιγγιᾷ'· ὥσπερ γὰρ οἱ τοιοῦτοι διὰ τὴν ἔνδοθεν αὐτοῖς δίνην καὶ τὰ ἔξω
τοιαῦτα νομίζουσιν, οὕτως καὶ ἡ ψυχὴ διὰ τὸ μόνα τὰ αἰσθητὰ ὁρᾶν πάντα 5
νομίζει ῥευστὰ καὶ ἐν κινήσει εἶναι.

Καὶ τοῦτο αὐτῆς τὸ πάθημα φρόνησις κέκληται [79d6–7]: πῶς 19
'πάθημα' τῆς ψυχῆς φρόνησιν κέκληκεν; ἢ πᾶσαι αἱ ἀρεταὶ παθήματά εἰσιν·
δόγμα γὰρ Πλατωνικὸν τὰ μετέχοντα 'πάσχειν' (ἀντὶ τοῦ διὰ πάθους αἰσθάνε-
σθαι) τὰ μετεχόμενα. ὡς γὰρ πρὸς τὰ μετεχόμενα πάσχει τὰ μετέχοντα· διὸ
καὶ τὸ ὂν 'πεπονθέναι' λέγει τὸ ἓν [Soph. 245b7–8] ὡς μετέχον τοῦ ἑνός. ἐπειδὴ 5
οὖν τῆς αὐτοφρονήσεως τῆς ἐν τῷ νῷ μετέχει ἡ ψυχή, ταύτῃ 'πάθημα' αὐτῆς
ἐκάλεσε τὴν φρόνησιν. ἢ ἐπειδὴ ὅλη δι' ὅλης αὐτοκίνητός ἐστι καὶ ὡς μὲν
κινοῦσα ποιεῖ, ὡς δὲ κινουμένη πάσχει, διὰ τοῦτο καὶ πάθημα ἡ φρόνησις.

Ὅρα δὲ καὶ τῇδε [79e8]: τὸ τρίτον ἐπιχείρημα, τὸ ἐκ τῆς ζωῆς [§ 3], 20
ὅτι ἡ ψυχὴ δεσπόζει τοῦ σώματος (τὸ γὰρ χρώμενον τοῦ ὀργάνου δεσπόζει),
καὶ ὅτι ζωοποιεῖ αὐτό, καὶ ὡς αὐτοκίνητος. αἱ γὰρ ἄλλαι ψυχαὶ ζωαί εἰσι τῶν
σωμάτων, οὐ ζωοῦσιν αὐτά.

---

8 τέχνηι τινί, οἷαν ∼ οὖαρος Mᶜ: τέχνη (spat. vac. 12 litt.) ρος M¹
§ 20. 1 δὲ M¹, Pl. W: δὴ Mᶜ, Pl. BTY

πυκνοῦσαν καὶ διὰ τῆς πυκνώσεως ῥωννῦσαν. See E. R. Dodds, *Theurgy and its
Relationship to Neoplatonism*, Journ. of Roman Stud. 37, 1947, 55–69 (66), who
cites also texts from Psellus and magical papyri. Varus is otherwise unknown.
  10–11. Philostr., vit. *Ap.* 5,30; 8,26; Dio Cass. 67,18.
  § 19. Dam. I § 334; II § 39.
  3–4. Cf. Pr., *Tim.* II 304.19–22 καὶ γὰρ τὸ μετέχειν Πλάτων διὰ τοῦ πεπονθέναι
δηλοῖ πολλάκις, ὡς ἐν Σοφιστῇ μεμαθήκαμεν, ὅπου λέγει τὸ ὅλον πεπονθὸς εἶναι τὸ ἕν,
ἀλλ' οὐκ αὐτοέν, ὡς μετέχον τοῦ ἑνός. Dam., *Parm.* 43.9–11.

MARGINALIA

1 § 1.1. Ὀλυμπιοδώρου φιλοσόφου σχόλια εἰς τὸν Πλάτωνος Φαίδωνα. λείπει δὲ τούτοις τὰ ἐξ ἀρχῆς φύλλα ἕξ.

1 § 2.3. ὅτι οὐ δεῖ τοῦ σώματος ἐξάγειν ἑαυτοὺς ἀποδείξεις.

1 § 2.3–8 (inf.).

δυνάμεις πρῶται	δυνάμεις δεύτεραι	
θεός	προνοητικαί	ἀναγωγοί
φιλόσοφος	γενεσιουργοί	καθαρτικαί

1 § 2.6. ὁμοίωσις θεῷ ἡ φιλοσοφία Mˢ.

1 § 3.3. ἐπιχείρημα μυθικόν.

1 § 5.1–8 (inf.).

βασιλεῖς	βασιλεῖαι	ἀρεταί
Οὐρανός	Οὐρανία	θεωρητικαί
Κρόνος	Κρονία	καθαρτικαί
Ζεύς	Δίιος	πολιτικαί
Διόνυσος	Διονυσιακή	ἠθικαὶ καὶ φυσικαί

1 § 5.3; 4; 7. πόθεν εἴρηται Οὐρανός - πόθεν Κρόνος - πόθεν Ζεύς Mˢ.

1 § 6.8. παροιμία ἐπὶ τῶν τὰ μὴ προσήκοντα τοῖς ὑποκειμένοις λεγόντων εἰρημένη.

1 § 7.1. ἐπιχείρημα διαλεκτικόν.

1 § 8.1. εἰς τὸ ἐναντίον ἀποδείξεις, ὅτι δεῖ ἐξάγειν ἑαυτούς.

1 § 8.19–39 (inf.).

συμποσίου ἐξαγωγαί	βίου ἐξαγωγαί
α′ παρουσία φίλου	σφαγὴ ὑπὲρ ἀρετῆς
β′ αἰσχρορρημοσύνη	τυραννίς
γ′ μέθη	λῆρος
δ′ νοσερὰ βρώματα	νόσος ἀνίατος
ε′ ἔνδεια τῶν παρακειμένων	πενία

1 § 8.29. περὶ τῆς Πυθαγορίας γυναικὸς τῆς βιασθείσης ὑπὸ τυράννου φαγεῖν κυάμους.

1 § 8.38. ση. ὅτι πενομένοις ἡμῖν οὐ δεῖ τὰ πρὸς τὴν χρεί<αν> ἀπὸ φαύλων λαμβάνειν ἀνδρῶν.

1 § 9.1; 2. ἀπορία - λύσις.

1 § 13.5. περὶ Φιλολάου τοῦ Πυθαγορίου καὶ τῶν παραγγελμάτων αὐτοῦ.

1 § 13.6–13 (inf.).

δηλοῦντα	δηλούμενα
β′ ἀπιόντι εἰς ἱερὸν μὴ ἐπιστρέφεσθαι	μὴ διάκοπτε τὴν καθαρτικὴν ζωήν
α′ ἐν ὁδῷ μὴ σχίζειν ξύλα	μὴ σχίζε καὶ τέμνε τὸν βίον
γ′ μὴ ἀποτιθέναι ἀλλὰ συνεπιτιθέναι τὰ βάρη	συμπράττειν τῇ ζωῇ, οὐκ ἀντιπράττειν

1 § 13.15. περὶ τῶν Πυθαγορίων ὡς ἐπαίδευον, καὶ ὡς ὑπὸ πυρκαϊᾶς ἀπώλοντο Γύλωνος ὑφάψαντος αὐτήν.

1 § 17.1. ση. ὅτι νόμος ἦν Ἀθηναίοις μηδένα ἐν ἡμέρᾳ φονεύειν καὶ Πυθαγορίοις τὸ μηδένα ἐν μεσημβρίᾳ καθεύδειν.

1 § 20.3. ση. τὴν 'ἵττω' λέξιν Βοιωτίαν οὖσαν.

1 § 20.6. πόθεν εἴρηται Ζεύς Mˢ.

2 § 4.7; 9. ἀπορία - λύσις.

2 § 5.1; 2. ἀπορία - λύσις.

2 § 6.1; 3; 7. ἀπορία - λύσις - λύσις ἀληθ(ινή).

2 § 8.1. ση. ὅτι τὸν φάρμακον πιόντα οὐ χρὴ διαλέγεσθαι, ἵνα μὴ πεφθείη.

2 § 8.3 (sup.). κώνιον] κώνιον φυτόν τι καυλοὺς ἔχον γονατώδεις, φύλλα ὡς ἐλαίας στενότερα βαρύοσμα, ἄνθος ὑπόλευκον, σπέρμα ὡς ἀννήσου λευκότερον, ῥίζα κοίλη οὐ βαθεῖα· οὗ τῆς κόμης ὁ χυλὸς πωθεὶς ἀναιρεῖ, καθὰ τὸ ἀκόνιτον καὶ ὁ λευκὸς ἐλλέβορος διὰ κενώσεως καὶ μανδραγόρας ὁ ἄρρην κατὰ καρηβαρίαν, καὶ τοῦτο δὴ τὸ κώνιον κατὰ ψύξιν [cf. Dioscor. 4,78].

184

2 § 8.5–8 (inf.).

Σωκράτης	νοερὰ καὶ καθαρτικὴ ζωή
Κρίτων	δευτερουργὸς καὶ ἐξημμένη τῆς προτ(έρας)
φάρμακον τρίβων	φθοροποιὸς καὶ ὑλικὴ αἰτία καὶ στερήσεως ἔφορος

2 § 8.11. ση.

3 § 1.6–9 (inf.)

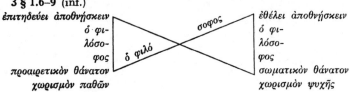

ἐπιτηδεύει ἀποθνήσκειν
ὁ φιλόσοφος
προαιρετικὸν θάνατον
χωρισμὸν παθῶν

ἐθέλει ἀποθνήσκειν
ὁ φιλόσοφος
σωματικὸν θάνατον
χωρισμὸν ψυχῆς

3 § 2.3. οὐκ ἀνίλλεται] οὐκ ἀπαξιοῖ.

3 § 2.6; § 3.1. ἀπορία - λύσις.

3 § 3.13. ὁρισμὸς θανάτου.

3 § 4.3. ση. περὶ τῶν ἐν τοῖς τάφοις σκιοειδῶν φαντασμάτων.

3 § 4.8. ὅτι ἡ τῶν ἀλόγων ψυχὴ οὐ χωρίζεται, ἀλλὰ συναποσβέννυται τῷ σώματι.

3 § 4.9. ση.

3 § 5.3–11 (inf.).

ἐνέρ-	φυσικαὶ καὶ ἀναγκαῖαι	τροφὴ ὕπνος	χρειώδη μετρίως
γει-	φυσικαὶ οὐκ ἀναγκαῖαι	ἀφροδίσια	ἄχρηστα
αι	οὔτε φυσικαὶ οὔτε ἀναγκαῖαι	καλλωπισμός	ἄχρηστον

3 § 5.9. ση. τί φησὶ περὶ ὀνειρώξεως.

3 § 10.2 (sup.). Βοιωτία ὗς· παροιμία⟦ι⟧ ἐπὶ τῶν ἀνοήτων καὶ ἀπαιδεύτων λεγομένη, ἐς τοῦτο γὰρ ἐσκώπτοντο οἱ Βοιωτοί· αἱ δὲ Θῆβαι πόλις τῆς Βοιωτίας, ἐξ ἧς ὁ Σιμμίας.

3 § 10.2. τὸ τοῦ Ἀλκιβιάδου· 'αὐλείτωσαν Θηβαίων παῖδες, διαλέγεσθαι γὰρ οὐκ ἴσασιν' [Ol., Alc. 69.4–5].

3 § 11.3. θανάτου ἐπιθυμοῦσιν.

3 § 13.2. ση. ὅτι χωρισμὸς ψυχῆς ἀπὸ σώματος προαιρετικὸς θάνατός ἐστιν, τὸ δὲ ἀνάπαλιν φυσικός.

4 § 2.1–4 (sup.).

ἐνέρ-	πρὸς τὰ δεύτερα ἐπιστροφή	αἰσθητῶν γνῶσις
γειαι	πρὸς ἑαυτὴν ἐπιστροφή	δι' ἑαυτῆς τῶν ὄντων γνῶσις
ψυχῆς	πρὸς τὸ νοητὸν ἀνάτασις	ἰδεῶν γνῶσις

4 § 2.4–7 (inf.).

γινώσκοντες	γινωσκόμενα
πολιτικός	αἰσθητά
καθαρτικός	ψυχικοὶ λόγοι
θεωρητικός	ἰδέαι

4 § 3.1–6 (sup.).

πολιτικός	ἀναγωγὴ ἐπὶ τὸ ἀγαθόν	λόγος	θυμός	ἐπιθυμία
αἰσθητὰ ἢ	παιδεία	φύλακες	στρατιῶται	θῆτες
πολῖται				

4 § 3.7–10 (inf.).

ἀνάγοντα	θεωρητικός	ἐν νοητόν	θεὸς ἓν ἁπλήθυντον	
ἀναγόμενα	αἰσθητά	πλῆθος	πλῆθος νοητὸν καὶ ἓν νοητόν	

4 § 3.11–16 (inf.).

πολιτικός	σώματος φροντίζει ὡς ὀργάνου	τέλος τούτου μετριοπάθεια
καθαρτικὸς	σώματος φροντίζει ὡς φλυάρου	τέλος τούτων ἀπάθεια
καὶ θεωρητικὸς	γείτονος	

4 § 4.6; 7. ἀπορία - λύσις.

4 § 4.7–11 (sup.).

καθαρτικός	διακεκριμένα εἴδη	ἐν ψυχῇ
θεωρητικός	ἀδιάκριτα εἴδη	ἐν τῷ νοητῷ

4 § 4.10. ση. δι' ἣν αἰτίαν ἀδιάκριτά ἐστι τὰ ἐν τῷ νοητῷ εἴδη, καὶ ὅτι τῷ δι' ἀλλήλων ταῦτα ἰέναι.

4 § 6.1. ἀπορία α'.

4 § 6.5. ἀπορία γ'.

4 § 6.6. λύσις γ'.

4 § 6.7. ση^{αι} M^r.

4 § 6.9. ἐξ ὀνύχων] παροιμία ἐπὶ τῶν ἀπὸ μέρους τὸ ὅλον γινωσκόντων.

4 § 7.1. ἀπορία β'.

ib. ση^{αι} M^r.

4 § 7.5. λύσις τῆς α'.

4 § 7.9. ση.

4 § 8.1. λύσις τῆς β'.

4 § 9.1. ὅτι κατὰ Πρόκλον ὄψεως καὶ ἀκοῆς μόνων μετέχει τὰ οὐράνια.

4 § 10.1. ὅτι κατὰ Δαμάσκιον πασῶν μετέχει.

4 § 11.1; 4. ἀπορία - λύσις.

4 § 13.3. ση. τὸ τοῦ 'Επιχάρμου λόγιον.

5 § 1.14. τίς ἡ διαφορὰ ψυχῆς καὶ αἰσθήσεως.

5 § 1.14–17 (sup.).

| ψυχή | ἐπιστρέφει πρὸς ἑαυτήν | οἶδεν ὅτι οἶδεν |
| αἴσθησις | οὐκ ἐπιστρέφει πρὸς ἑαυτήν | οὐκ οἶδεν ὅτι οἶδεν |

5 § 2 (inf.).

α' ἀγαθόν	δημιουργία	α' μέγεθος	πλῆθος ἡνωμένον
β' δίκαιον	ἰδιοπραγία	β' ὑγίεια	συμμετρία πρὸς ἄλληλα
γ' καλόν	κοινωνία	γ' ἰσχύς	κράτος κατὰ χειρόνων

5 § 2.1. ση^{αι} ὅλον M^r.

5 § 3 (sup.).

ἐφετόν	κάλλος
τέλειον	αὔταρκες
ἱκανόν	γόνιμον

5 § 3.1. ἐν Φιλήβῳ M^r.

5 § 4.8. ση. τὸ Πυθαγόριον παράγγελμα.

5 § 5.2. ση^{αι} πῶς (?) λέγει (?) M^r.

5 § 6.3. ἐν τῷ Διὶ αἱ ἰδέαι ὡς ἐν δημιουργῷ M^r.

5 § 7.2. ση. φασὶ Πλάτωνα τὰς ἰδέας ἐν τῷ παραδειγματικῷ αἰτίῳ εὑρόντα, οὐκ ἐν τῷ ποιητικῷ καὶ δευτέρῳ ἐκείνου, καθὼς οἱ πρὸ αὐτοῦ, ἑωρακέναι ἑαυτὸν τρίτον ἔχοντα ὀφθαλμόν [Proleg. 5.36–42].

5 § 8 (inf.).

πάντη ταὐτὸν τῷ γινωσκομένῳ	νοῦς
πρότερον μὲν ἕτερον, ὕστερον δὲ ταὐτόν	ψυχή
πάντη ἕτερον τοῦ γινωσκομένου	αἴσθησις

5 § 15.1; 3. ἀπορία - λύσις.

6 § 1.8–12 (inf.).

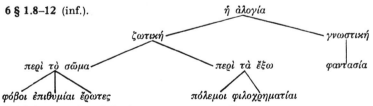

6 § 2.1. ση. τίνα τὰ δυσέκνιπτα τῆς ψυχῆς πάθη.

6 § 2.10. ὅτι παύεται ὁ ἐνθουσιασμὸς φαντασίας ἐπιγινομένης.

6 § 2.12. ἴδε τὸ 'Επικτήτου παράγγελμα περὶ φαντασίας ὁποῖον.

6 § 2.15; 16. ἀπορία - λύσις.

6 § 3.1. ση^{αι} ὅλον M^r.

186

6 § 3.14. *ση. ὅτι αὕτη ἡ ἄγνοι‹α› διπλῆ οὖσα ἐπιστήμης κρείττων ἐστίν.*

6 § 5.2. *ὁρισμὸς ἔρωτος.*

6 § 6.1. *ση. ὅτι ὁ φόβος ἐν τῇ τριμερείᾳ τῆς ψυχῆς θεωρεῖται.*

6 § 10.2 (inf.). *διλήμματον] διλήμματόν ἐστι παρὰ τοῖς ῥήτορσι σχῆμα λόγου καθ' δ δύο ἐρωτήσεις ἐρωτῶντες τὸν ἀντίδικον πρὸς ἑκατέραν ἐσμὲν εἰς λύσιν παρεσκευασμένοι· δεῖ δὲ τὰς ἐρωτήσεις ἐναντίας ἀλλήλαις εἶναι, ὡς πάντως ἢ ταύτην ἢ ἐκείνην ἀποκρινουμένου τοῦ ἀντιδίκου* [Hermog., *inv.* 4,6, 192.5–11 R.].

6 § 12.5. *ση. περὶ τοῦ ἐν τῷ πτάρνυσθαι 'ζῆθι' προσρήματος, δι' ἣν αἰτίαν λέγεται.*

7 § 2.8; 9. *ἀπορία - λύσις.*

7 § 2.14. *ση. ὅτι αἱ φιλοσώματοι ψυχαὶ διὰ τὸ μὴ καθαρθῆναι περὶ τοὺς τάφους εἰλοῦνται.*

7 § 3.10. *ὁρισμὸς γελοίου.*

7 § 3.14. *ση. διὰ τίνα ἡ ψυχὴ τὸν θάνατον φοβεῖται.*

7 § 4.6. *ση. τίνα λέγει αἰτίαν τοῦ ἐπί τινων ἀνθρώπων τὰ ἐπιτηδεύματα μὴ ταῖς φύσεσιν αὐτῶν συμφωνεῖν.*

7 § 4.9. *αἵρεσις· φύσις.*
        προβολή· ἐπιτήδευμα.

7 § 5.1; 2; 4. *ἀπορία - λύσις Πρόκλου - λύσις Ἀμμωνίου.*

7 § 5.9. *ση. δι' ἃς αἰτίας Ζήνων ὁ ἀμφοτερόγλωσσος ἐκ τῶν μαθητῶν μισθοὺς εἰσεπράττετο.*

7 § 6.2. *λόγιον (?) Χαλδαϊκόν (?)* M^r.

7 § 6.4. *περὶ ἐλπίδος καὶ τίς αὕτη, καὶ ὅτι τὰ λογικὰ μόνα ἐλπίζει.*

7 § 6.6. *ὅτι (?) δόξ(α) κατὰ Πλάτωνα* M^r.

7 § 6.9. *κατὰ Ἀριστοτέλη* M^r.

7 § 6.10–16. *ση^αι* M^r.

7 § 6.14–15 (inf.).   *ἀκίνητον   νοῦς*
                       αὐτοκίνητον ψυχή
                       ἑτεροκίνητον σῶμα

7 § 9.2 (sup.).   *νοῦς   θεωρητικὴ ζωή*
                     διάνοια καθαρτικὴ ζωή

7 § 10.16–18 (inf.).   *χωρίζοντα   χωριζόμενα*
                       ὕπνος   αἴσθησις
                       θάνατος φαντασία

7 § 11.3–4. *ση. τίνα τὰ τῶν ἐπιτηδευμάτων συστατικά.*

7 § 13.3. *ση. ὅτι τὸ 'διαβέβληται' δοτικῇ συντάσσεται.*

8 § 2.2. *περὶ ἀρετῶν.*
ib. *ση.* M^r.
8 § 2–3 (inf.).

ἀρεταί	ἀφ' ὧν ἐπιγίνονται	γινώσκοντα	γινωσκόμενα
φυσικαί	κρᾶσις	ἄλογα ζῷα	ἐγκόσμια σώματα
ἠθικαί	ἦθος	λογικὰ καὶ τὰ διδακ(τά)	εἱμαρμένη
πολιτικαί	τριμέρεια ψυχῆς	πολιτικός	ἐγκόσμια ἁπλῶς
καθαρτικαί	φυγὴ παθῶν	καθαρτικός	ὑπερκό‹σ›μια
θεωρητικαί	ἀπάθεια	θεωρητικός	νοερά
παραδειγματικαί	ἰδέαι	νοερός	νοητά

8 § 2.19. *ση. τί τὸ ἐν ἡμῖν ἔργον φιλοσοφίας καὶ τί τὸ τῆς θεουργίας.*

8 § 3.8–10 (inf.).   *ἕξεις   ἀρεταί*
                     σωφροσύνη ἠθικαί
                     δικαιοσύνη πολιτικαί
                     ἀνδρεία καθαρτικαί
                     φρόνησις θεωρητικαί

8 § 4.1; 3. *ἀπορία - λύσις.*

8 § 4.5. *διὰ τί αἱ φυσικαὶ ἀρεταὶ ἀνδραποδώδεις παρὰ Πλάτωνι, αἱ δὲ ἠθικαὶ σκιαγραφίαι καλοῦνται.*

8 § 4.8; 10. ἀπορία - λύσις.
8 § 4.8. ση. ὅλον Mr.
8 § 5.3. ση. τίνες τῶν ἀρετῶν καὶ πῶς λέγονται πάθη παθῶν ἀνταλλάττεσθαι.
8 § 6 (inf.).

ἀρεταί   ἴδια τούτων
φυσικαὶ καὶ ἠθικαί   αὐτῷ τῷ εἶναι ποιοῦσιν
ψευδώνυμοι   ἐπίπλαστοι μετὰ βουλῆς ὑποκρίνονται δ μή εἰσιν
πολιτικαί   σκοπὸν ἔχουσι τἀγαθόν, τριμερείᾳ χρῶνται ψυχῆς, τῷ ὄντι
                           εἰσὶν καὶ εἰσὶν ἀληθεῖς
καθαρτικαὶ καὶ θεωρητικαί τῷ ὄντι ἀληθεῖς· τελεστικαί

8 § 6.1. διάκρισις τῶν φυσικῶν καὶ ἠθικῶν ἀρετῶν ἀπὸ τῶν ψευδωνύμων.
8 § 6.4. διάκρισις τῶν ψευδωνύμων ἀπὸ τῶν πολιτικῶν.
8 § 6.6. διάκρισις τῶν πολιτικῶν ἀπὸ τῶν καθαρτικῶν καὶ θεωρητικῶν.
8 § 6.11. σηαι Mr.
8 § 9.1; 3; 6. ἀπορία - λύσις - λύσις.
8 § 10.2; 5. ἀπορία - λύσις.

9 § 1.1. ἀρχὴ τοῦ δευτέρου τμήματος.
9 § 2.2. ση. τοῦτο (?) Mr.
ib. ὅτι κατὰ Πλάτωνα διττὰ τὰ ἐναντία, ἢ αἱ ποιότητες ἢ τὰ δεδεγμένα ταύτας.
9 § 2.8. ὁ Πρόκλος ἤτοι ὁ Συριανός· διδάσκαλος ὁ Συριανὸς τοῦ Πρόκλου Ms.
9 § 3.1; 2. ἀπορία - λύσις.
9 § 3.4; 6. ἀπορία - λύσις.
9 § 4.1; 8; 10. ἀπορία α' - ἀπορία β' - ἀπορία γ'.
9 § 4.2. σηαι Mr.
9 § 5.1; 7; 10. λύσις τῆς α' - λύσις τῆς β' - λύσις τῆς γ'.
9 § 5.1. Πρόκλος ἤγουν Συριανός Mr.
9 § 6.9. ση. ὅτι καὶ ἡ ἄλογος ψυχὴ κατὰ τοῦτον μετὰ τὸν χωρισμὸν ἐπιδιαμένει τοῦ σώματος.
9 § 6.11. ση. τὴν ἀνασκευὴν τοῦ περὶ τῆς μετεμψυχώσεως δόγματος.
9 § 9.4. ση. τί φησιν Εὔπολις περὶ Σωκράτους ὁ ποιητής.
9 § 9.10. ση. ὅτι ψυχαὶ τῶν θεραπειῶν οἱ καιροὶ καὶ ὅτι καιρός ἐστι χρόνος προσλαβὼν τὸ εὖ.

10 § 1.1. σηαι Mr.
10 § 1.6. ἐπιτωθάζειν] ἐπιλοιδορεῖσθαι ἢ ἐπεμβαίνειν ἢ καυχᾶσθαι ἢ χλευάζειν [Suda s.v.; schol. Pl. A, Axioch. 364c].
10 § 3.19. ση. Mr.
10 § 4.10. Ἐνδυμίωνα] Ἐνδυμίωνος ὕπνος· παροιμία ἐπὶ τῶν πολὺ κοιμωμένων λεγομένη, παρ' ὅσον οὗτος τὰς νύκτας πόνῳ τε καὶ ἀγρυπνίαις τὸν τῆς σελήνης δρόμον ἐξεύρισκεν, μεθ' ἡμέραν δὲ πολλὰ ἐκάθευδεν. ἄλλοι φασὶν ὅτι ἔν τινι πόλει τῆς Καρίας ὁ Ὕπνος παιδὸς ἐρασθεὶς Ἐνδυμίωνος καλουμένου ἔτι καὶ νῦν κατέχειν αὐτὸν λέγεται κοιμώμενον.
10 § 4.13. περὶ Πτολεμαίου τοῦ μαθηματικοῦ ἱστορία.
10 § 5.1; 3. ἀπορία - λύσις.
10 § 5.4. ση. ὅτι Πλάτων τὴν ἄλογον ψυχὴν μετεμψυχοῦσθαί φησιν, εἶτα μετὰ πολλὰ φθείρεσθαι.
10 § 5.5. ὀστρέϊνα σώματα Mr.
10 § 5.7; 9. ἀπορία - λύσις.
10 § 7.8. Ἰάμβλιχος Mr.
10 § 7.9. Ἀμμώνιος Mr.
10 § 8.1. ση. ὅτι βούλεται ὁ Πλάτων τὸ μεῖζον καὶ ἔλαττον ἐναντία εἶναι.
10 § 8.4; 5. ἀπορία - λύσις.
10 § 8.11; 16. ἀπορία - λύσις.
10 § 9.4; 6. ἀπορία - λύσις.
10 § 10.4. ση. ὅτι πάντα τὰ ἐναντία ἔμμεσα εἶναι βούλεται Πλάτων.

188

10 § 12 (inf.).

ὁδοί	τέλη	ὁδοί	τέλη
ἐγείρεσθαι	ἐγρηγορέναι	ἀναβιώσκεσθαι	ζωή
καταδαρθάνειν	καθεύδειν	ψυχορραγεῖν	θάνατος

10 § 12.6. τί τὸ καταδαρθάνειν λέγεται.

10 § 14.3. ση. ὅτι οὐ βούλεται ὁ Πλάτων αἰωνίαν τὴν κόλασιν εἶναι.

ib. ση. Μʳ.

10 § 16.2. ση. ὅτι τοῖς ἀγαθοῖς κρεῖττόν ἐστι τὸ τεθνάναι τοῦ ζῆν, τοῖς δὲ κακοῖς ἀνάπαλιν.

11 § 3.3. τί ἐστιν ἀνάμνησις.

11 § 3.4. τί μνήμη· τί λήθη.

11 § 3.7–9 (inf.).

ὄν	ἀεί
ζωή	ἀθανασία
γνῶσις	μνήμη

11 § 4.5–9 (inf.).

πρώτη γνώσεως ἐπιβολή	μάθησις
δευτέρα λήθης μεταξὺ γινομένης	ἀνάμνησις
γνῶσις μὴ διαδραμούσης λήθης	μνήμη

11 § 4.10. ση. Μʳ.

11 § 5.1. ση. τίνα δεῖ καὶ πόσα συνελθεῖν εἰς τὸ γενέσθαι ἀνάμνησιν.

ib. ση. Μʳ.

11 § 5.16. ὁρισμὸς ἀκριβὴς ἀναμνήσεως.

11 § 6.1; 7; 12. ἀπορία - ἀπορία - λύσις.

11 § 7.9. ση. Μʳ.

11 § 9.4. ση.

11 § 12.2. βωμολόχως] ἡ λέξις μετεσχημάτισται ἀπὸ τοῦ ʿβωμολόχοςʾ ὀνόματος, ὅπερ ἐτοιμολογεῖται ἀπὸ τοῦ περὶ τοὺς βωμοὺς λοχεῖν, ὑπὲρ τοῦ τι λαβεῖν ἀπὸ τῶν θυόντων. μεταφορικῶς δὲ καὶ ὁ παραπλησίως τούτῳ ὠφελείας ἕνεκα τινὰς κολακεύων· καὶ ʿβωμακεύματαʾ καὶ ʿβωμολοχεύματαʾ. σημαίνει δὲ καὶ τὸν εὐτράπελον καὶ γελωτοποιόν, ἢ τὸν μετά τινος εὐτραπελίας κόλακα· καὶ τὸν πανοῦργον δὲ καὶ συκοφάντην [cf. Et. Magn., Suda s.v. βωμολόχοι, schol. Pl. A, Rep. 606c].

11 § 16.2. ση. ὅτι κατὰ τρεῖς τρόπους γίνεται λήθη.

12 § 1.1. ση. περὶ ἰδεῶν ἢ περὶ εἰδῶν τῶν ἐν τῇ ψυχῇ Μʳ.

12 § 1.7. ἀποδείξεις ὅτι εἰσὶν ἰδέαι.

12 § 2.1. ὅτι αἱ μαθήσεις ἀναμνήσεις ἀποδείξεις.

(inf. f. 237ʳ) εἰ ὑπὲρ συλλογισμόν ἐστι τὸ θεῖον, ψεύδεται ὁ συλλογισμὸς εἰς τὸ θεῖον Μʳ (non pert. ad textum).

13 § 1.1. λείπει φύλλα εʹ.

13 § 1.3. ση. ὅλον Μʳ.

13 § 1.7. τίνα τὰ ἴδια τῆς οὐσίας.

13 § 1.9. τίνα τὰ τῆς γενέσεως.

13 § 1.7–11 (inf.).

ἴδια οὐσίας	ἴδια γενέσεως
θεῖον	σωματοειδές
ἀθάνατον	θνητόν
νοητόν	ἀνόητον
ἀδιάλυτον	διαλυτόν
μονοειδές	πολυειδές
ἀεὶ κατὰ τὰ αὐτὰ καὶ ὡς αὕτως ἔχειν ἑαυτῷ	μηδέποτε κατὰ τὰ αὐτὰ καὶ ὡς αὕτως ἔχειν ἑαυτῷ

13 § 2.2. τί τὸ θεῖον λέγεται.

13 § 2.4. τί τὸ ἀθάνατον.

13 § 2.13. τί τὸ νοητόν.

ib. ση. τοῦτο Μʳ.

13 § 2.25. τί τὸ ἀδιάλυτον.

13 § 2.31. δόγμα Πλατωνικόν, ὅτι πᾶν σύνθετον διαλύεται.

13 § 2.32–40. ση. Μʳ.

13 § 2.36. δόγμα Πλατωνικόν.

13 § 2.41. τί τὸ μονοειδές.

13 § 2.47. τί τὸ ἀεὶ ὡς αὕτως καὶ κατὰ τὰ αὐτὰ ἔχειν ἑαυτῷ.

13 § 3.3–10 (sup.).   ἀόρατον   οὐσία
                      διανοητικόν   γνῶσις
                      δεσπόζον τοῦ σώματος   ζωή

13 § 3.10–11. ση. ὅτι ἡ λογικὴ ψυχὴ ζωοποιεῖ τὸ σῶμα, αἱ δὲ παρὰ ταύτην ψυχαὶ ζωαὶ αὐτοῦ εἰσιν.

13 § 3.10–12 (inf.).
ψ   λογική   εἰδοποιὸς ἢ ζωοποιὸς τοῦ σώματος
υ   ἄλογος   ζωὴ τοῦ πνευματικοῦ
χαί φυτική   ζωὴ τοῦ ὀστρεΐνου
13 § 3.11–12. ἄλογος   πνευματικοῦ
              φυτική   ὀστρεΐνου Μʳ.

13 § 4.2. ση. Μʳ.

13 § 4.7. Ἰάμβλιχος Μʳ.

13 § 4.11. ση. ὅτι πᾶν φθειρόμενον ἢ ὡς σύνθετον φθείρεται ἢ ὡς ἐν ὑποκειμένῳ ὄν.
ib. ση. Μʳ.

13 § 5.1; 11. ἀπορία - λύσις.

13 § 5.1. ση. Μʳ.

13 § 6.1; 3. ἀπορία - λύσις.

13 § 6.7; 9. ἀπορία - λύσις.

13 § 6.12; 14. ἀπορία - λύσις.

13 § 15.6. ὅτι πολλαχῶς τὸ ὁρᾶν λέγεται.

13 § 15.10. ση. περὶ Ἀπολλωνίου τοῦ Τυανέως παράδοξον.

13 § 18.2–3 (inf.).   πλανᾶται   ζωὴ καὶ γνῶσις
                      ταράττεται ζωὴ μόνη
                      εἰλιγγιᾷ   γνῶσις μόνη

13 § 19.2. ση. ὅτι αἱ ἀρεταὶ παθήματά εἰσιν.

13 § 19.5. ση. Μʳ.

13 § 20.4 (inf.). ὅδε λείπει, καὶ οἶμαι καὶ πολλά, ἐὰν ὅλως ὁ Φαίδων σχόλαια εἶχεν, ὅτι τὸ πλεότερον τοῦ διαλόγου λείπει, ὡς ἀπὸ β′ ἢ β′ ϛ″ τὸ α′ ϛ″ Μʳ.

INDEX I: REFERENCES

62a2–3: 1 19[1]. – 62a8–9: 1 20[1]. –
62b1–2: 1 21[1]. – 62b2–4: 8 7[11]. –
62b2–3: 10 3[13]. – 62b3–4: 1 4[2]. –
62b5–6: 1 22[1]. – 62b6–7: 1 18[3]. –
62b7: 1 23[1]. – 62c7–8: 1 8[8]. – 62c9–
63e8: 2 1[1]. – 62d6–7: 2 9[1]. – 62e1–2:
2 10[1]. – 62e8–63a1: 2 11[1]. – 63a1:
2 12[1]. – 63b1: 2 13[1]. – 63b2: 2 14[1]. –
63b4: 2 15[1]. – 63b4–5: 2 16[1]. –
63b9–c4: 8 17[3]. – 63e8–65a8: 3 1[1]. –
63e9–10: 3 6[1]. – 64a4–66a10: 7 3[4]. –
64a4–5: 3 7[1]. – 64a5: 3 8[1]. – 64a10–b1:
3 9[1]. – 64b3–4: 3 10[1]. – 64b8–9: 3 11[1].
– 64c2: 3 12[1]. – 64c4–8: 7 2[8]. –
64c5–6: 3 13[1]. – 64d1–4: 7 5[3]. –
64d1–2: 3 14[1]. – 65a2: 3 15[1]. –
65a9–d3: 4 1[1]. – 65a9: 4 11[1] 8 1[2]. –
65b1–2: 4 12[1]. – 65b2: 5 7[1]. – 65b3–4:
11 7[11]. – 65b3: 4 13[1]. – 65c2: 4 14[1]. –
65c8–9: 4 15[1]. – 65d4–66b7: 5 1[1]. –
65d4–5: 5 5[1]. – 65d6: 5 6[1]. – 65d9:
5 7[1]. – 65e1–2: 5 8[1]. – 65e4: 5 4[1]. –
65e8–66a1: 5 9[1]. – 66a3: 5 10[1]. –
66a3–4: 5 11[1]. – 66a4: 5 7[2]. – 66a9:
5 12[1]. – 66b1–2: 5 13[1]. – 66b3–4: 5 14[1].
– 66b4: 5 4[5]. – 66b5–6: 5 15[1]. – 66b6:
5 16[1]. – 66b7–67b6: 6 1[1]. – 66b7–c1:
6 1[7]. – 66b7–8: 6 4[1]. – 66c1–2: 6 1[7]. –
66c2: 6 5[1]. – 66c2–5: 6 1[9]. – 66c2–3:
6 6[1]. – 66c3–4: 6 7[1]. – 66c5–d2: 6 1[10]. –
66c7–8: 6 8[1]. – 66d3–7: 6 1[12]. –
66e1: 6 9[1]. – 66e6: 6 10[1]. – 67a3:
6 11[1]. – 67a3–4: 6 12[1]. – 67a6: 6 13[1]. –
67a7–8: 6 14[1]. – 67b7–68c4: 7 1[1]. –
67b7–c4: 7 1[3]. – 67b8: 7 1[9] 6[1] 7[1]. –
67c2: 7 8[1]. – 67c2–3: 7 9[1]. – 67c5–d6:
7 2[7]. – 67c8–9: 7 10[1]. – 67d7–8: 7 11[1].
– 67d12: 7 3[9]. – 67d12–e1: 7 12[1]. –
67e6–7: 7 13[1]. – 68a3–b4: 7 4[2]. –
68a3–4: 7 14[1]. – 68b5–c4: 7 4[13]. –
68b7–c3: 7 5[1]. – 68c5–69e5: 8 1[1]. –
68c5: 8 8[1]. – 68c11–12: 8 9[1]. – 68d5–6:
8 10[1]. – 69a6: 8 11[1]. – 69a9–10: 8 12[1]. –
69b1–2: 8 13[1]. – 69b2: 8 6[8]. – 69b3:
8 6[9] 14[1]. – 69b4–5: 8 6[7]. – 69b8–c1:
8 15[1]. – 69b8: 8 6[10]. – 69c3–d2: 8 6[15].
– 69c3–4: 8 16[1]. – 69c8–d1: 7 10[11]
10 3[14]. – 69d5–6: 2 6[10] 10 15[3]. – 69d5:
8 17[1]. – 69e3–4: 8 18[1]. – 69e6–70c5:
9 1[1]. – 70b3–4: 9 7[1]. – 70b6: 9 8[1]
10 3[2]. – 70b10–c1: 9 9[1]. – 70c5–72e2:
10 1[1]. – 70c5–6: 10 6[1]. – 70d7–71a11:
10 4[3]. – 70d7: 10 7[1]. – 70e3–4: 10 8[1]. –
71a3: 10 9[1]. – 71a12–72a10: 10 4[6]. –

71a12–13: 10 10[1]. – 71b9–10: 10 11[1].
– 71c9: 10 12[1]. – 71e9: 10 13[1]. –
72a11–d5: 10 4[17]. – 72b1–3: 10 14[1]. –
72d7: 10 15[1]. – 72e1–2: 10 16[1]. –
72e3–74a9: 11 1[1]. – 72e3–5: 11 9[1]. –
73a2–3: 11 2[14] 10[1]. – 73a5–6: 11 11[1].
– 73a8: 11 12[1]. – 73b1: 11 13[1]. –
73b6–7: 12 3[6]. – 73c1–2: 11 5[4]. – 73c2:
11 14[1]. – 73c4–d11: 11 5[9]. – 73c6:
11 15[1]. – 73e1–3: 11 5[11]. – 73e1:
11 16[1]. – 73e5–74a4: 11 5[15]. – 73e5:
11 17[1]. – 74a5–8: 11 5[16]. – 74a5: 11 18[1].
– 74a9–**: 12 1[1]. – 74a9–b7: 12 1[9]. –
74a12–b1: 12 3[1]. – 74b7–c6: 12 1[13].
– 74b7: 12 4[1]. – 78b4–**: 13 1[1]. –
78b4: 13 7[1]. – 78b5–6: 13 8[1]. – 78c1–9:
13 4[10]. – 78c1–2: 13 2[32]. – 78c1: 13 9[1].
– 78d1: 13 10[1]. – 78d1–2: 13 5[9]. –
78d3: 13 5[4] 11[1]. – 79a1–2: 13 12[1]. –
79a3: 13 13[1]. – 79b4–17: 13 5[6]. –
79b4–5: 13 14[1]. – 79b8: 13 15[1]. –
79c2: 13 16[1]. – 79c6–7: 13 17[1]. –
79c7–8: 13 18[1]. – 79d6–7: 13 19[1]. –
79e8–80a6: 13 4[10]. – 79e8: 13 20[1]. –
81d1: 3 4[4]. – 85e3–86d4: 10 2[3]. –
87b2–88b8: 9 6[6]. – 103a11–c2: 9 2[3].
Phaedr. 245c5–246a2: 3 3[9]. – 245c5–
d6: 13 2[36]. – 248d2–e3: 6 3[6].
Phil. 20d1–11: 3 3[11] 5 3[1]. – 32b9–c2:
7 6[3]. – 49c4–5: 7 3[10].
Rep. II 379b1–11: 5 2[7]. – III 407d4–
e2: 1 8[11]. – IV 427c6–444a3: 4 3[3]. –
X 618e4–619a1: 6 14[3] 8 17[8].
Soph. 245b7–8: 13 19[5].
Theaet. 144b5: 2 7[6]. – 173c6–174a2:
1 2[15] 6 3[14]. – 173e1–174a2: 4 15[3]. –
176b1–2: 1 2[6]. – 186c7–9: 4 6[6].
Tim. 27d6–28a1: 13 1[4]. – 29e1–2: 5 2[6].
– 30b1: 4 14[5]. – 42d4–5: 7 4[5]. –
47b1: 4 7[2] 8[7].
doctrines attributed to him: 8 4[1]
10 5[5] 10[5] 14[3].
apud Athen. XI 507D: 6 2[2].

Plotinus I 2,7.2–6: 8 2[12]. – I 6,8.21:
1 13[10] 16[4] 7 2[4]. – I 9: 1 8[17]. –
IV 7,2–11 (?): 13 4[11].
apud Iambl.: cf. 10 7[8]. – 13 4[11].
Plutarch, *Alcib.* 2: 3 10[2].
Proclus:
commentary on *Ph.* 65b1–8 (?): 4 9[1].
– 68b7–c3: 7 5[2]. – 68c11–12: 8 9[3]. –
69a6–9: 8 5[3]. – 78c10–79a11: 13 5[1,11].
cf. 11[2]. – Includes treatise by Syrianus

on 70c5–72e2: 9 2⁸ 5¹ 10 3¹⁹.
hymns, frg. I: 1 5¹⁵.
proverbs:
Diogenianus 3,46: 3 10². – 5,15: 4 6⁹.
Zenobius 5,40: 1 6⁸.
Ptolemy, *Stone Tablets of Canobus:* 10 4¹⁴.
Pythagoreans: 5 6² 10 2⁴.
'symbols': 1 13⁵⁻¹³ 5 4⁸ 11 13³.

Stoa: *SVF* II 1028–1048: 6 2¹⁴. –
III 643–644: 1 8³⁴. – III 660: 1 8³⁸. –
III 712 (p. 179.14–20): 1 8³⁴. – III
768: 1 8¹⁹.
Syrianus: treatise on 70c5–72e2 em-
bodied in Proclus' commentary: 9 2⁸.
– (= Dam. I § 185): 10 3¹⁹. – (= Dam.

I § 195): 9 5¹ 10 5¹². – (= Dam. I
§ 196): 9 5¹¹.

Thucydides II 49,8: 12 2¹⁰.

Varus (on eye salves) 13 15⁸.

Unspecified:
questions and objections: (on *Ph.*
69d5) 8 17⁵. – (70c5–72e2) 9 4¹. –
(71a3) 10 9⁴. – (80b2) 13 6¹˙⁷˙¹².
διὸ καί τις ἔφη 'Φαντασίη τανύπεπλε':
6 2⁸.
πολλοὶ Πλάτωνες τὴν γῆν σκάπτουσιν,
ὥς ἔφη τις: 7 4¹⁰.

INDEX II: VOCABULARY AND PROPER NAMES

Βοιωτία ὗς 3 10².
Βοιωτὶς διάλεκτος 1 20³.
βουλή: μετὰ βουλῆς 'deliberately' 8 6³.
βοῦς 8 2⁶.
βωμολόχως 11 12².

γείτων (φλύαρος) 4 3¹⁵ 6 3¹¹.
γελοῖον (τὸ) 7 3¹⁰.
γενεσιουργῶς 1 2⁷.
γένεσις 1 5¹³,¹⁴ 6¹,² 3 6⁷ 6 2⁴ 10 4³ 14⁹
    13 1⁴,⁶,⁹.
γενητός 3 13⁵ 13 2³³⁻³⁵.
γέρανος 8 2⁷.
γευστικός 1 8³².
γεωμετρικός 11 13¹.
γλῶττα (ἐγχωρία) 1 20⁴.
γινώσκειν 5 8²⁻⁴,⁶.
γνῶσις 4 2⁸ 5³ 6⁴,⁵ 7⁷,⁹,¹¹,¹⁶ 6 10⁴ 11²
    10 3²,⁴ 11 4⁴,⁵ 5²⁻³,⁵,⁷,¹⁷ 6³,⁶ 7⁵ 8²,³ 15²
    12 2²,⁵; (opp. ζωή) 4 1⁴ 6 2¹,⁵
    11 3⁶,⁷,⁹ 4³ 13 3⁵,⁹ 12⁷ 16² 18²,³.
γνωστικός (opp. ζωτικός) 6 1¹¹ 7 6¹⁰
    8 4²,⁴ 9 7².
γνωστόν 11 5⁵,⁶,⁸,¹⁷ 6²,³,⁶ 7⁶ 15².
γόνιμος 5 3².
Γοργίας (dial.) 1 21².
γραμμικός 'geometrical' 11 9⁵.
Γύλων 1 13¹⁸.

Δαμάσκιος 4 10¹ 8 9⁹.
δεκτικός 10 7⁷.
δεόντως 2 2⁵.
δεσμός 1 2¹⁷ 3¹¹ 7⁶.
δεσπόζειν 13 3⁹,¹⁰,¹⁵ 4¹⁰,¹⁶ 17² 20².
δεύτερος: τὰ δ. 1 2⁴,⁷ 5⁷,²⁰ 4 2² 8² 5 1²,⁵
    8 1⁸,⁹.
δευτερουργός 2 8⁶.
δευτέρως 11 4¹¹.
Δημήτηρ 1 5¹⁵ 7 10⁹.
δημιουργεῖν 13 2³⁰.
δημιουργός 1 5⁷ 4 14⁵ 5 2⁵ 6⁴ 13 5²,³.
διαβάλλειν 7 13¹.
διαβεβαιοῦσθαι 2 6¹.
διάθεσις 1 14².
διαιρετός 10 10⁷.
διακεκριμένως 4 14².
διακόπτειν 11 4² 8².
διακρίνειν 4 11⁵ 12 1¹⁵,¹⁹; (pass., opp.
    συγκρίνεσθαι) 9 3²,⁴ 10 5⁴. – διακεκρι-
    μένος 4 4⁸,¹⁰; cf. διακεκριμένως.
διάκρισις 9 2¹¹ 3²,⁶ 10 3²⁰ 4¹⁵.
διαλεκτικός 1 1⁶ 7¹ 8³².
διάλογος 1 13²² 2 8¹¹ 3 6⁵ 11 9⁴.
διαλύειν (pass.) 13 2²⁵,²⁶ 3²⁴ 9².

διαλυτός 13 1¹⁰ 2³⁴.
διανοεῖσθαι 13 3⁸.
διανοηματικός (εἴδη) 13 12³,⁴.
διανοητικός 5 4³ 11 7⁶ 13 3⁴.
διάνοια 4 4² 5 13² 7 9².
διαρθροῦν: τὸ διηρθρωμένον
    (opp. τὸ ὁλοσχερές) 12 1¹¹.
διασκορπίζειν 10 1¹⁸.
διατρέχειν: λήθης διαδραμούσης etc.
    11 4⁴,⁹,¹³ 5⁹,¹⁰ 8⁶ 12 2⁶.
διδακτικὴ φαντασία 8 2⁹.
διδασκαλεῖον 1 13¹⁵,¹⁹.
διδασκαλικὴ πειθώ 2 16³,⁴ 8 18³.
διέναι: δι' ἀλλήλων 4 4¹¹; διῆλθε διὰ
    πάντων 5 2⁵,¹¹.
δίκαιον 5 2¹.
δικαιοσύνη 5 2⁸ 3⁴ 8 1⁴ 3⁸ 9²,³,⁵,⁸.
διλήμματον 6 10².
δίνη 13 18⁴.
Διομήδης 4 13⁵.
Διονυσιακός 1 3¹² 6⁸.
Διόνυσος 1 3⁶ 5⁸,¹³,¹⁵ 6¹,⁵,⁸ 6 13¹ 7 10⁶,¹⁵
    8 7⁹,¹².
διορίζειν 5 2⁹; τὸ διωρισμένον (math.)
    4 14⁴.
διότι (τὸ) 8 4⁷.
διστάζειν 8 17².
δόγμα 8 4¹ 10 4¹⁵ 11 9⁸ 12 3⁵
    13 2³¹,³⁶ 9² 19³.
δόξα 4 6¹⁰,¹² 5 13²,³; 'opinion'
    10 2²,⁶,¹⁰,¹¹,¹⁴; (as a function) 4 6¹⁰,¹²
    7 6⁴; ζωτική, γνωστική 7 6⁶,⁹; διττή
    5 13²,³.
δοξαστικός 7 10⁵.
δοτική 7 13³.
δύναμις 'faculty' 1 2³,⁴ 5 10² 12 1¹⁸;
    'potency' 13 2³⁹.
δυσέκνιπτος 6 2¹.
δυσφόρως 7 12².

ἐγκατασπείρειν (corr.) 7 4⁵.
ἐγκόσμια σώματα 8 3¹.
ἐγκύκλιοι ἐξηγήσεις 1 11⁶ 4 8³.
ἐγρήγορσις 9 4⁷.
ἔγχρισμα 13 15⁸.
ἐγχρόνως 7 6¹¹.
ἐγχώριος 1 20⁴.
ἐγώ (opp. τὸ ἐμόν, τὰ τοῦ ἐμοῦ) 6 8¹⁰.
εἰδοποιεῖν 9 6³ 13 3¹¹ 6¹⁵.
εἶδος: τὸ καθόλου 1 5¹³ 4 4⁶; τὰ ἁπλῶς τὰ
    ἐν τῷ δημιουργῷ 13 5¹,⁵; νοερά
    13 2¹³ 5¹²; παραδειγματικά 13 1⁶ 11² 12³;
    νοητά (= ἰδέαι) 12 1⁷,⁹, cf. 1¹³; ἐν τῇ
    ψυχῇ, ψυχικά 4 4⁸,⁹ 11 6¹⁵

Ἰλιάς 1 5¹⁹.
Ἵππαρχος (Pythagorean) 1 13²⁰.
ἵστασθαι μέχρι 11 4¹⁸ 8⁶ 12 1²³ 2⁶.
ἰσχύς 5 2²,¹⁵.
Ἰταλία 1 13¹⁵.

καθαρμός 8 6¹⁶.
κάθαρσις 1 2¹⁰,²⁰ 2 14² 7 2⁷,¹²,¹³ 11².
καθαρτικός: διάλογος 3 6⁴; ζωή 1 13¹¹ 2 8⁶
    7 9² 8 1²,⁴,⁸ 15² 18⁵; ἀρεταί 1 4¹¹ 7 2⁵
    8 2¹¹ 3⁶,⁹ 6⁶,⁸,⁹,¹³⁻¹⁵ 15³; ὁ κ.   3 3⁴
    4 2⁶,⁷ 3⁶,¹²,¹⁴ 4⁵⁻⁷ 11²,³,⁶ 15² 5 16²
    6 3¹⁰,¹² 7 10¹⁴ 8 1⁶ 7⁶ 14².
καθαρτικῶς 1 2⁸,⁹ 5³ 13¹⁰ 5 4⁶ 6 3²,⁶,⁹ 12².
καθολικός (comp.) 1 12¹⁵ 7 2⁹,¹².
καθόλου 1 5¹² 2 2⁵ 3²,³ 16⁶ 4 4²,⁶ 6¹² 8⁵
    6 2¹⁶ 7 1²,⁴ 8².
καιρός (defin.) 9 9¹⁰,¹¹.
κάλλος 5 2¹⁰,¹¹.
καλόν 5 2¹.
Καλυψώ 6 2⁷.
Κάνωβος 10 4¹⁴.
καπνός 9 3⁸,⁹ 10 2⁵.
κατά: καθ' αὑτά 10 5⁹ 8⁸. – καθ' ἕκαστα
    4 4⁴. – καθ' ἡμᾶς 6 3⁴.
καταγίνεσθαι περί 4 3¹³ 4³,⁶,⁷,¹⁰ 11⁴ 5 2³
    6 13⁵ 8 3⁴.
καταλαμβάνειν 'perceive' 13 12⁸.
καταπίνειν 1 5⁵.
κατασκευάζειν (log.) 1 8³ 3 3⁷ 5² 4 1⁴
    7 4¹ 9 8³ 10 3⁸,¹⁹ 7⁵,¹⁰ 13 3²,¹².
κατασκευαστικός 11 2¹² 12 1¹⁴.
καταταρταροῦν 1 3⁵.
καταφρονητικῶς 2 8¹¹.
κατηγορεῖν (log.) 3 3⁹,¹⁰.
κατηγορικὸς συλλογισμός 3 3⁷.
κατιέναι εἰς γένεσιν 6 2³ 10 14⁹.
Κέβης 1 11² 12⁵,⁷,⁸,¹² 13¹³
    2 1⁵ 2³⁻⁵ 3²,⁵ 7⁴ 12¹,² 9 1⁶ 3⁷ 10 1¹⁶ 2¹⁰
    11 4⁸ 5⁶,⁹,¹⁴ 9²,⁷ 13 15¹.
κενοτάφιον 1 13¹⁷.
κεραυνοῦν 1 3⁸ 6⁸.
κεφάλαιον 2 7⁷.
κῆρυξ 4 8⁶.
κίνησις 1 5¹⁸ 7 6¹³,¹⁴,¹⁶ 10 10⁷ 13 2⁵⁰ 18⁶.
Κίρκη 6 2⁹.
κοινός 1 13¹⁶ 3 15³; (comp.) 1 12¹⁵.
κοινωνία 5 2¹⁰.
κόλασις 10 14³,⁵.
Κόρη 7 10⁸.
κορόνους 1 5⁴.
κορυφαῖος 1 2¹⁵ 6 3¹³.
κοσμεῖν 5 1³.
κόσμος (νοητός, αἰσθητός) 1 4⁶,⁷.

κρᾶσις 8 2³⁻⁵ 9³,⁴.
Κρατύλος (dial.) 1 20⁶.
κρείττων: τὰ κρείττω 5 1⁴,⁸.
Κριός (astron.) 13 2⁸,⁹.
κρίσις 8 4⁴ 13 8⁷,⁹; (medic.) 2 15³.
κριτικός 12 1¹⁸.
Κρίτων 2 8¹,¹⁰.
Κρόνιος 1 5⁴.
Κρόνος 1 3⁴,⁵ 5⁴.
κύαμος 1 8³⁰.
κυρίως 3 6⁵ 4 3¹⁰ 7⁶ 10 8¹²,¹³,¹⁶
    11 2¹³,¹⁵ 13² 13 2⁴,⁶.
κωμικός 1 6⁷ 6 13⁴.
κωμῳδία 1 6⁶.
κωμῳδοποιός 9 9²,³.
κώνειον 2 8³.

λέξις 'word' 7 10²,³; 'text under dis-
    cussion' 1 1⁵ 2¹ 3¹,¹⁰ 8³ 3 2¹ 4 5¹ 6¹
    6 8⁶ 8 4⁸ 10 1¹⁵ 3²,⁹ 4² 11 2⁹,¹⁴ 12 1²
    13 4⁹,¹⁴ 5⁸.
λεπτομερής 10 2⁵.
λεύκανσις 10 4⁴.
λευκότης 9 2⁵.
λέων 8 2⁴.
λεωφόρος 5 4⁵,⁷,⁸ 11 13³.
λήθαργος 11 16⁴.
λήθη 11 3²⁻⁵ 4²,⁴,⁷,⁹,¹³,¹⁶ 5⁹,¹⁸ 8²,⁶,⁸ 16²,⁵
    12 2⁶.
λήμη 11 3⁴,⁵.
λῆμμα 2 7¹ 11 6¹,⁷,¹²,¹⁵ 8¹ 14¹ 16² 17¹
    13 4⁹.
λῆξις 2 7²,⁵ 9 1⁴ 10 15⁴.
λῆρος 1 8³⁴.
λογίζεσθαι 4 14²,³,⁵,⁶.
λογικός 3 10⁵ 7 6⁴; (ψυχή) 3 4⁸ 5 1¹³,¹⁶
    8 3⁴ 6¹² 9 3⁵ 6⁶,¹²,¹³ 11 4¹⁸.
λόγιον (Chaldean) 7 1¹¹ 10 14⁹.
λογογραφικός 2 7⁷.
λόγος: 'argument, discussion' 1 9¹ 14³
    and passim; οἱ περὶ ἀθανασίας πέντε λ.
    2 7⁶, cf. 8 7¹³ 9 1⁸ 10 1¹³; ὁ ἐκ τῶν ἐναν-
    τίων λ. 10 5¹⁴ 16⁸; ὁ ἐκ τῶν ἀναμνήσεων λ.
    11 title 13 4³ 7³; ὁ ἐκ τῆς ὁμοιότητος
    λόγος 13 1³; ὁ ἐκ τῆς οὐσίας τῆς ψυχῆς
    11 2¹³ 13 4²; 'reason, account' 1 21¹
    13 10³; 'essential definition' 10 10⁷
    13 2⁹,³³; κατὰ πρῶτον λ. 9 5²; 'reason-
    principle' 4 2⁴,⁷ 3² 11 7²,³ 9⁷ 12 1¹⁴,¹⁷
    13 2²⁷,²⁹; 'faculty of reason' 4 3³
    6 2⁶,⁷ 6³ 8 2⁹.
Λυγκεύς 13 15⁷.
Λύσις (Pythagorean) 1 13²¹; (dial.)
    1 13²².

μάθησις 11 4⁷ 5⁴ 9³,⁶ 11² 12 1³,⁴ 2¹.
μακαριστός 8 11³.
μᾶλλον: ἀπὸ τοῦ μ. 2 5³.
μαντεία 6 13³.
μαντικός 1 6⁴; (comp.) 8 7⁸.
μάσησις 1 5¹⁰.
μεγαλόνοια: ἡ μ. Πλάτωνος 2 6⁷ 3 6⁴.
μεγαλουργός 7 4⁸.
μέγεθος 5 2²,¹¹,¹⁴.
μέθεξις 10 8¹⁷.
μέθοδος 10 3⁵.
μεθυπάρχειν 11 1⁴,⁷ 2¹¹ 13 4⁵.
μείζων: see πρότασις.
μελετᾶν θάνατον 1 13⁸.
Μενοικεύς 1 8²⁷.
Μένων (dial. and char.) 11 9⁴.
μερικός 1 5¹² 2 16⁴,⁶ 4 2⁹ 4²,⁴ 10 14⁶;
    (comp.) 1 12¹⁷ 7 1⁵ 2⁹.
μερισμός 1 5¹⁰,¹¹ 8 7⁷.
μεριστός 13 2³⁴.
μεριστῶς 5 1¹² 7 6¹¹.
μέρος: τὰ μ. τοῦ χρόνου 13 2⁷; τὰ κατὰ μ.
    7 8¹ 12 1⁸.
μέσος: τὰ μ. 4 3⁶,⁷ 10 10⁶,⁸; μ. ὅρος 3 3¹⁰.
μεταβαίνειν (of thought) 11 4¹² 12 1²⁰,²¹.
μετάβασις: (in composition) 2 7⁶;
    (in thought) 11 4¹⁴ 5⁵,⁷,¹¹,¹⁸ 6³,⁵,⁶,⁸
    7⁵,⁷,⁸ 8³,⁴ 15¹.
μεταβολή 9 2⁶,¹³,¹⁴ 10 9² 13² 13 2⁵⁰.
μεταδιδόναι 1 15³; (metaphys.) 5 3³,⁵
    11 4¹⁶.
μετάδοσις 11 4¹⁷.
μεταλαμβάνειν 1 15³.
μεταμπίσχεσθαι 9 6⁴.
μεταφορά (gramm.) 8 13¹.
μετεμψυχοῦσθαι 9 6¹¹ 10 5³,⁵.
μετεμψύχωσις 9 6²,³,⁵,¹³ 10 1²,⁴,⁹.
μετενσωμάτωσις 9 6²,⁵ 10 1².
μετέχειν 1 2¹²,¹⁴ 4 5³ 5 2¹³ 8 8² 10 8⁷,¹⁰
    13 19³⁻⁶.
μετριάζειν 2 6⁸.
μετριοπάθεια 4 3¹⁴ 11⁸.
μήλη (medic.) 4 7⁸.
μνήμη 11 3¹⁻⁴,⁶,⁷,⁹ 4⁹,¹⁰,¹³,¹⁵,¹⁷ 5²,¹¹.
μολύνειν 1 8³⁹.
μονάς: μ. Τιτάνων ὁ Διόνυσος 1 5¹³;
    μ. ἀγαθότητος ὁ θεός 2 5⁷; θεὸς μ.
    ἀπλήθυντος 4 3¹¹.
μονόβιβλος 8 17⁷.
μονοειδής 13 1⁸ 2⁴¹,⁴⁴.
μόριον (τῆς ψυχῆς) 2 14².
μύειν 1 22³.
μυθικός 1 1⁶ 3³ 7¹ 16² 18² 3 1⁴.
μυθολογία 9 8²,⁵.

μῦθος 1 4¹⁻³ 18² 9 8¹ 10 1⁸ 3²,⁴,⁶.
μυθώδης 8 16².
μῶλυ 6 2⁶.

ναρθηκοφόρος 7 10¹²,¹³ 8 7⁴,⁵.
νοεῖν 4 7¹¹ 11 4¹¹ 13 2¹³,¹⁴,¹⁹⁻²²,²⁴ 31⁴ 12⁶.
νοερός 2 8⁶ 5 4⁴ 8 3⁶ 10 3⁴ 13 2¹³,¹⁹ 5¹⁰,¹².
νόημα 4 10⁶.
νόησις 6 1¹² 2¹⁰,¹⁶ 3¹².
νοητός 1 4⁴⁻⁶ 4 2⁴ 3⁸,⁹ 4¹⁰,¹¹,¹³ 7¹⁰,¹¹
    5 2¹² 8⁴ 10¹ 12² 6 10³,⁶ 7 3²,⁷ 8 2²⁰ 3⁷
    10 14⁹ 12 1⁹ 13 1⁸ 2²,¹³,¹⁴,¹⁶,²⁰,²³.
Νόμοι (dial.) 1 8¹⁴.
νοῦς 4 7⁹ 14³ 5 8⁴ 7 1¹⁰ 6¹² 9² 8 1⁷ 2¹⁷,¹⁹
    11 3⁴,⁶ 4¹⁰ 13 2¹⁵,¹⁸,⁴⁸ 19⁶.
νύττειν 11 6¹⁴.

Ξανθίππη 8 1¹⁰.
ξέσις 9 5⁵.

ὁδός 'transition' 10 4⁴ 10²,³,⁹ 11³ 12⁴,⁸.
'Οδυσσεύς 6 2⁶,⁹.
ὁλικός 2 16⁵; 5 1¹³ (cod.).
ὁλίσθημα 11 12².
ὁλκή 5 9¹.
ὁλοσχερής 5 5³ 12 1¹⁰.
ὁμακόϊον 1 13¹⁴.
"Ομηρος 1 6⁴.
ὄμμα: νοῦ σύβολον 13 2¹⁸.
ὁμοειδής 4 6¹¹.
ὁμοιότης 13 1³ 4⁵,⁸.
ὁμοίως θεῷ 1 2⁶.
ὁμωνυμία 1 13²² 3 11⁴.
ὁμώνυμος 2 8¹¹.
ὀνειρώττειν 3 5¹⁰.
ὁρατός 13 3⁷.
ὄργανον 1 8³² 4 3¹³ 4³ 5 16³ 13 20².
ὀρεκτικός 6 10⁵.
ὄρεξις 6 10⁶.
ὁρίζειν (med.) 'define' 3 3¹³ 13²
    7 2⁷,⁸,¹⁰,¹² 11 3²; (pass.) 'be definite'
    10 8⁹.
ὁρισμός 3 3⁸,¹¹.
ὁρμᾶσθαι 3 15³.
ὅρος 'term' 2 4⁹ 3 3¹⁰ 10 3³; 'limit'
    12 1¹⁶ 13 6¹⁰.
'Ορφεύς 1 3³ 4⁸ 7 10¹⁰ 10 3⁹,¹³ 13 2¹⁵.
'Ορφικός 1 1⁶ 3 1⁵ 7 10⁵ 8 7¹ 10 6¹.
ὀστρέϊνος 10 5⁵ 13 3¹².
ὅτι (τό) 8 4⁶.
Οὔαρος 13 15⁸.
οὐράνια (τά) 4 9² 13 2³² 9¹.
Οὐρανός 1 3⁴ 5²,³.
οὐσία 4 6⁶,⁸,¹⁰,¹³ 9 8⁴ 11 2¹³ 13 4²;

τανύπεπλος 6 2⁸.
ταριχεύειν 13 3²².
ταυτολογεῖν 7 1⁴.
ταὐτότης 4 7¹⁰.
τεκμαίρεσθαι 13 12⁶.
τεκμήριον 12 2¹⁷.
τέλειον: see ἐφετόν.
τελεστικός 8 6¹⁴,¹⁵.
τελετή 8 6¹⁶ 7².
τέλος 3 2⁷,⁹ 3² 4 3¹⁴,¹⁶ 11⁷,⁸ 6 11²
   10 4⁵ 10⁴ 11³ 12³,⁸; ἐν τέλει εἶναι 3 2⁷,⁹.
τῇδε 'in this world' 1 5¹¹ 4 10²
   5 5²,³,⁵ 15⁴ 6 6⁴,⁵ 11 7⁴,⁶ 12 1¹⁵ 2³.
Τίμαιος (dial.) 4 7³ 8⁷ 14⁵ 7 4⁵ 13 1⁴.
Τιτᾶνες 1 3⁷,¹³ 5¹⁰,¹²,¹³ 6 13² 7 10⁶ 8 7⁶.
Τιτανικός 7 10⁸.
τμῆμα (of dialogue) 8 7¹² 9 1¹ mg.
τοπικός 7 6¹⁶.
τόπος 7 6¹³ 12³; νοητός, αἰσθητός 1 4⁴.
τραγικός 1 6⁷ 6 13⁵.
τραγῳδία 1 6⁵.
τριάς 5 2¹,² 3¹.
τριμέρεια τῆς ψυχῆς 6 6² 8 2⁹ 6⁷.
τριόφθαλμος 5 7².
τρίτως 11 4¹².
τρόποι (of hypothetical syllogism)
   2 4³,¹⁰,¹³.
Τρῶες 3 10⁴.
Τρωϊκός 6 8³.
τύχη 2 15².

ὑγίεια 5 2²,¹⁴,¹⁵.
ὕλη 1 3⁹ 15² 2 8⁷ 7 3¹² 8 3¹⁰ 7⁶ 10 9⁵⁻⁷
   13 2²⁸,³⁰,⁴³ 6⁷,⁸.
ὕπαρξις 13 2¹¹.
ὑπερβολή 4 7¹³.
ὑπερκόσμιος 2 4⁷ 8 3⁶.
ὑπερφυῶς (=ὑπὲρ φύσιν) 5 12¹.
ὕπνος 7 10¹⁶ 9 4⁷.
ὑποθετικὸς συλλογισμός 2 4³,¹⁰,¹³ 3 2¹.
ὑποθετικῶς 2 4³.
ὑποκείμενον: 'log. subject' 3 3⁸;
   'subject-matter' 2 16⁶ 8 3² 18⁵;
   'substratum' 13 4¹²,¹³,¹⁶,¹⁸ 6¹⁰,¹⁴.
ὑπόμνημα 9 2⁹.
ὑπόστασις 5 2⁸ 13 3⁵.
ὑποτίθεσθαι 9 5¹³ 10 9⁴.

Φαῖδρος (dial.) 3 3⁹ 6 3⁶.
φαντάζεσθαι 6 2¹¹ 12⁵.
φαντασία 6 1¹¹ 2¹,⁵,⁷,¹⁰,¹²⁻¹⁴,¹⁷ 12⁴,⁷ 7 10¹⁸
   8 2⁸ 11 5⁷,⁸.
Φαντασίη 6 2⁸.
φάντασμα 3 4³.

φθαρτός 13 2³⁴,³⁵,³⁷.
φθοροποιός 2 8⁷.
φίλαρχος 6 2³.
Φίληβος (dial.) 3 3¹¹ 5 3¹ 7 6⁷.
φιλήδονος 7 5¹,²,⁴,⁷.
Φιλόλαος 1 13²,⁵,¹³,¹⁹ 2 1⁷.
φιλόσοφος: ὁ φ. (=Olympiodorus)
   11 2⁹ 6¹³; ὁ φ. ὁ καθ' ἡμᾶς 6 3⁴.
φιλοσώματος 3 4¹ 7 2¹⁴ 4¹⁷.
φιλοτιμία 6 2¹,³,⁵ 8¹⁵ 7 5¹¹,¹².
φιλότιμος 6 2⁴ 7 4¹⁷ 5⁸.
φιλοχρηματία 6 1¹⁰.
φιλοχρήματος 7 4¹⁷ 5⁸.
φλυαρία 6 7¹.
φλύαρος γείτων 4 3¹⁵ 6 3¹¹.
φρόνησις 4 11²,³,⁵ 8 1²,³,⁶,⁷ 3¹⁰ 4²,³
   13 19²,⁷,⁸.
φρουρά 1 4².
φύλακες 4 3³,⁵.
φυσικός 1 2¹⁸ 8³⁴ 20⁴ 3 5³⁻⁶,⁸ 13 15⁷;
   ἀρεταί 1 5⁸ 8 2²,⁴ 3¹ 4⁵,¹¹ 6¹ 11⁴. –
   See θάνατος.
φυσικῶς 12 1¹⁹.
φυσιολογεῖν 13 2³⁸.
φύσις 6 10⁵ 8 6² 9 5²,⁶,⁸ 10 4⁶ 5¹⁰ 10⁶;
   (τῇ) φύσει 3 9² 10 8¹⁰; κατὰ, παρὰ φύσιν
   4 6³ 6 1⁶,⁷ 4² 13 17²,³.
φυτικὴ ψυχή 9 3¹,⁴ 10 5²,³ 7⁵ 13 3¹².
φυτόν 9 3² 10 7⁴,¹³.
φῶς 8 2¹⁵.

χιτὼν τῆς ψυχῆς 6 2².
χοαί 1 13²⁰.
χορηγεῖν 10 7⁹.
χορηγός 10 7⁶.
χορός: ὁ φιλόσοφος χ. ὁ τῶν Στωϊκῶν
   6 2¹⁴.
χρῆσθαι: τὸ χρωμένον (opp. ὄργανον)
   13 20².
χρονικός 13 2⁶,¹⁰.
χρόνος 11 4¹⁴ 13 2⁸,³³,⁵⁰.
χωλεύειν 10 4⁶.
χωρίζειν 1 2⁸,¹³ 3 3⁵ 4¹,⁹ 11⁶ 13²,³ 15²,³
   4 1⁶,⁷ 5⁴ 7 3² 12 2¹².
χωρίον 'passage' 8 17⁷ 10 7¹⁰.
χωρὶς εἶναι 3 4⁹.
χωρισμός 3 1⁸ 3¹⁴ 4⁷,⁹ 4 1⁸ 6 9² 7 2¹⁰
   9 6¹⁰,¹² 10 1¹²,¹⁹ 9⁷ 11 1⁴ 13 3²¹,²³.
χωριστῶς 5 9² 11³ 16³.

ψαμμιαῖος 5 5⁴ 11 7¹⁰ 12 1¹².
ψευδώνυμος: see ἀρεταί.
ψῦξις 10 7⁷.
ψυχή 1 4⁶ 2 6⁵,⁶ 7²,⁵ 14³

3 $3^{10,14}$ $4^{1,2,5,7}$ $13^{3,4}$ 4 4^9 5 1^2 8^5 6 8^{10}
7 6^{10} 8 2^{17} 9 1^5 10 2^2 $7^{2,6}$ $9^{3,4}$ $14^{4,8}$ 16^4
11 2^{13} $4^{3,11,13}$ 6^{14} 7^2 12 $1^{3,13-15,19}$ 2^2
13 2^{37} $3^{3,11}$ $4^{1,2}$ 6^4 8^6 17^2 20^3. −
See *λογικός, ἄλογος, φυτική*. − *ψυχαὶ*
τῶν θεραπειῶν οἱ καιροί 9 9^{10}.

ψυχικός 13 3^5. − See *εἶδος*.
ψυχορραγεῖν 10 12^9.

ᾠόν 4 4^{11}.
ὡσαύτως: τὸ ἀεὶ κατὰ τὰ αὐτὰ καὶ ὡ.
  ἔχειν ἑαυτῷ 13 $1^{9,11}$ 2^{47}.

The Prometheus Trust Catalogue

Platonic Texts and Translations Series

I Iamblichi Chalcidensis in Platonis Dialogos Commentariorum Fragmenta
John M Dillon   978-1-898910-4519

II The Greek Commentaries on Plato's Phaedo (I – Olympiodorus)
L G Westerink   978-1-898910-46-6

III The Greek Commentaries on Plato's Phaedo (II – Damascius)
L G Westerink   978-1-898910-47-3

IV Damascius, Lectures on the Philebus *L G Westerink* 978-1-898910-48-0

V The Anonymous Prolegomena to Platonic Philosophy
L G Westerink   978-1-898910-51-0

VI Proclus Commentary on the First Alcibiades
Text - L G Westerink, translation – W O'Neill   978-1-898910-49-7

VII The Fragments of Numenius R Petty   978-1-898910-52-7

VIII The Chaldean Oracles R Majercik   978-1-898910-53-4

The Thomas Taylor Series

1 Proclus' Elements of Theology
Proclus' Elements of Theology - 211 propositions which frame the metaphysics of the Late Athenian Academy. 978-1-898910-00-8

2 Select Works of Porphyry
Abstinence from Animal Food; Auxiliaries to the Perception of Intelligibles; Concerning Homer's Cave of the Nymphs; Taylor on the Wanderings of Ulysses. 978-1-898910-01-5

3 Collected Writings of Plotinus
Twenty-seven treatises being all the writings of Plotinus translated by Taylor. 978-1-898910-02-2

4 Collected Writings on the Gods & the World
Sallust On the Gods & the World; Sentences of Demophilus; Ocellus on the Nature of the Universe; Taurus and Proclus on the Eternity of the World; Maternus on the Thema Mundi; The Emperor Julian's Orations to the Mother of Gods and to the Sovereign Sun; Synesius on Providence; Taylor's essays on the Mythology and the Theology of the Greeks. 978-1-898910-03-9

5 Hymns and Initiations
The Hymns of Orpheus together with all the published hymns translated or written by Taylor; Taylor's 1824 essay on Orpheus (together with the 1787 version). 978-1-898910-04-6

6 Dissertations of Maximus Tyrius
Forty-one treatises from the middle Platonist, and an essay from Taylor, The Triumph of the Wise Man over Fortune. 978-1-898910-05-3

7 Oracles and Mysteries
A Collection of Chaldean Oracles; Essays on the Eleusinian and Bacchic Mysteries; The History of the Restoration of the Platonic Theology; On the Immortality of the Soul. 978-1-898910-06-0

Other titles available from the Prometheus Trust